THE PRACTICE OF
CULTURAL ANALYSIS

Cultural Memory
in
the
Present

Mieke Bal and Hent de Vries, Editors

THE PRACTICE OF CULTURAL ANALYSIS

Exposing Interdisciplinary Interpretation

Edited by Mieke Bal
with the assistance of Bryan Gonzales

STANFORD UNIVERSITY PRESS

STANFORD, CALIFORNIA 1999

Stanford University Press
Stanford, California
© 1999 by the Board of Trustees of the
Leland Stanford Junior University

Printed in the United States of America

CIP data appear at the end of the book

Contents

Illustrations

CULTURE AND CRITIQUE

Contributors

ERNST VAN ALPHEN is Director of Communication and Education at the Boijmans van Beuningen Museum in Rotterdam. Until 1997, he was Associate Professor of Comparative Literature at the University of Leiden. He is the author of *Francis Bacon and the Loss of Self* (1992) and *Caught by History: Holocaust Effects in Contemporary Art, Literature and Theory* (1997). He is a member of the Amsterdam School for Cultural Analysis (ASCA).

FRANK R. ANKERSMIT is Professor of Intellectual History and Historical Theory at the University of Groningen. His most recent English-language publications are *History and Tropology* (1994) and *Aesthetic Politics: Political Philosophy Beyond Fact and Value* (1997). He is on the editorial board of *History and Theory* and is a member of the Dutch Academy of Sciences and ASCA.

MIEKE BAL is Professor of Theory of Literature and a Founding Director of the Amsterdam School for Cultural Analysis at the University of Amsterdam. She is the author, most recently, of *The Mottled Screen: Reading Proust Visually* and *Double Exposures: The Subject of Cultural Analysis*. Among her areas of interest are literary theory, semiotics, visual art, cultural studies, postcolonial theory, French, the Hebrew Bible, the seventeenth century, and contemporary culture.

STEPHEN BANN is Professor of Modern Cultural Studies and Chair of the Department of History and Theory of Art at the University of Kent at Canterbury. He has published widely in the fields of art and cultural theory. His collaborations with landscape artist and printmaker Bob Chaplin began in the early 1980s and have led to, among other things, the copublication of the artist's *Eminent Views* (1995). Bann's most recent book is *Paul Delaroche: History Painted* (1997). He is a member of the International Advisory Board of ASCA.

JON COOK is Director of the Centre for Creative and Performing Arts and Senior Lecturer in English at the University of East Anglia. His publications include *Romanticism and Ideology* (coauthored with D. Aers and D. Punter, 1981), *William Hazlitt: Selected Writings* (1991), and numerous essays, articles, and reviews on Romantic writing, cultural analysis, and critical theory. He has taught at universities in the United States, Europe, and India, and is currently writing a book titled *Poetry and Modernity*. He is a member of the International Advisory Board of ASCA.

JONATHAN CULLER is Class of 1916 Professor of English and Comparative Literature at Cornell University, Chair of the English Department, and former Director of the Cornell humanities center, the Society for the Humanities. Among his publications are *Structuralist Poetics: Structuralism, Linguistics and the Study of Literature* (1975), *On Deconstruction: Theory and Criticism After Structuralism* (1983), and *Literary Theory: A Very Short Introduction* (1997). He is Editor of *Diacritics* and a member of the International Advisory Board of ASCA.

THEO DE BOER is Emeritus Professor of Systematic Philosophy at the Free University of Amsterdam. From 1968 to 1992, he was Professor of Philosophical Anthropology at the University of Amsterdam. His most recent publication is *The Rationality of Transcendence: Studies in the Philosophy of Emmanuel Levinas* (1997). He is a member of ASCA.

LOUIS DUPRÉ has been T. L. Riggs Professor of Philosophy of Religion and Philosophy of Culture at Yale University since 1972. Among his most recent publications are *Passage to Modernity* (1991, 1993) and *Metaphysics of Culture* (1994). He is currently writing a study on the Enlightenment. He is a member of the American Academy of Arts and Science, the Royal Belgian Academy, and the International Advisory Board of ASCA.

THOMAS ELSAESSER is Professor of Film and Television Studies at the University of Amsterdam. Since 1992, he has held a Visiting Professorship in the Department of Media Studies at the University of Bergen, Norway. His writings on film theory, national cinema, and film history have appeared in over eighty collections and anthologies. His most recent books include *Early Cinema: Space Frame Narrative* (1990), *Writing for the*

Medium: Television in Transition (1994), *A Second Life: German Cinema's First Decades* (1996), and *Fassbinder's Germany* (1996). He is a member of the Board of Directors of ASCA.

J. CHERYL EXUM is Professor of Biblical Studies at the University of Sheffield. She is the author of numerous studies in biblical literary and feminist criticism, including *Tragedy and Biblical Narrative: Arrows of the Almighty* (1992), *Fragmented Women: Feminist (Sub)versions of Biblical Narratives* (1993), and *Plotted, Shot, and Painted: Cultural Representations of Biblical Women* (1996). She is Executive Editor of *Biblical Interpretation: A Journal of Contemporary Approaches*, Editor of *Gender, Culture, Theory*, and a member of the International Advisory Board of ASCA.

JOHANNES FABIAN is Professor of Cultural Anthropology at the University of Amsterdam. In his theoretical and critical work, he has addressed questions of epistemology and the history of anthropology, especially in his *Time and the Other: How Anthropology Makes Its Object* (1983). His most recent publications include *History from Below* (1990), *Power and Performance* (1990), *Language and Colonial Power* (1986, 1991), *Time and the Work of Anthropology* (1991), and *Remembering the Present: Painting and Popular History in Zaire* (1996). He is a member of ASCA.

WILLIAM P. GERMANO is Vice President and Publishing Director at Routledge publishers in New York. He earned a Ph.D. in English literature, and has worked in scholarly publishing for twenty years. He speaks frequently on issues of concern to publishers and scholars. Among recent titles he has launched are *Cultural Studies* (ed. Grossberg, Nelson, and Treichler), *The Gay and Lesbian Studies Reader* (ed. Abelove, Barale, Halperin), and volumes by Donna Haraway and Gayatri Chakravorty Spivak.

HELGA GEYER-RYAN is Associate Professor in the Department of Comparative Literature of the University of Amsterdam and Life Member of Clare Hall and Queens' College, Cambridge. Her publications include *Fables of Desire: Studies in the Ethics of Art and Gender* (1994) and numerous articles. She is currently working on *Who Do You Think You Are: Ingredients of Identity, Venice: The Violence of Location,* and an edition of essays by leading scholars on Walter Benjamin entitled *Perception and Experience in Modernity.* She is a member of ASCA.

ISABEL HOVING teaches Comparative Literature at the University of Antwerp. She publishes regularly in the field of cultural analysis on intercultural and postcolonial theory, and has a specific interest in Caribbean literature. She is coeditor of the journal *Thamyris: Mythmaking from Past and Present.* Her dissertation, *The Castration of Livingstone and Other Stories: Reading African and Caribbean Migrant Women's Writing,* was published in 1995 by the University of Amsterdam. She is a member of ASCA.

EDWIN JANSSEN is a Dutch artist living in Rotterdam. He has exhibited widely, at institutions such as the Wiener Secession in Vienna, the Fridericianum in Kassel, the Boijmans van Beuningen Museum in Rotterdam, and the Museo Nacional de Bellas Artes in Buenos Aires. His latest book, *Do You Know Mr. Chauvin?* (1996), was published on the occasion of his exhibition in Buenos Aires. Recently, he began a series of collaborations with the Scottish artist Tracy Mackenna. They are currently working on the project "Ed and Ellis in Tokyo" for the "P3 Art and Environment" cultural manifestation and the City of Tokyo.

EVELYN FOX KELLER is Professor of History and Philosophy of Science in the Program in Science, Technology and Society at the Massachusetts Institute of Technology. She is the author of *A Feeling for the Organism: The Life and Work of Barbara McClintock* (1983), *Reflections on Gender and Science* (1985), *Secrets of Life, Secrets of Death: Essays on Language, Gender and Science* (1992), and, most recently, *Refiguring Life: Metaphors of Twentieth-Century Biology* (1995). Her current research is on the history and philosophy of developmental biology. She is a member of the International Advisory Board of ASCA.

JANNEKE LAM combines a career as an art photographer with academic research. She is currently a doctoral candidate at ASCA and is focusing on Comparative Literature and Visual Analysis. Her interests include childhood, the interaction of the visual and the verbal within discursivity, trauma, and affective semiotics. Among her photographic series are *Playing with Identity, My First Picture Book,* and *Learning to Read.* She is currently completing a project entitled *Discursive Boundaries: Representations of a Traumatic Childhood.*

JOHN NEUBAUER is Professor of Comparative Literature at the University of Amsterdam. He has also taught at various universities in the United States. His most recent publications include *The Fin-de-Siècle Culture of Adolescence* (1992), various contributions to the Hanser (Munich) edition of Goethe's works, an edition of Freud's correspondence with Hans Blueher (1996), and "Bakhtin vs Lukács: Inscriptions of Homelessness in Theories of the Novel," in *Poetics Today* (1996). He is a member of ASCA.

GRISELDA POLLOCK is Professor of Social and Critical Histories of Art and Director of the Centre for Cultural Studies at the University of Leeds. Her publications cover social histories of art and major debates in feminism and the visual arts and have recently focused on the relations between femininity and alterity within the framework of Jewish history, philosophy, and art. Her most recent publications include *Generations and Geographies in the Visual Arts: Feminist Readings* (1996) and *Avant-Gardes and Partisans Reviewed* (1996). Forthcoming are *Differencing the Canon: Feminist Desire and the Writing of Art's Histories* (1998) and a monograph on Mary Cassatt (1998). She is a member of the International Advisory Board of ASCA.

NANETTE SALOMON is Associate Professor of the History of Art at the College of Staten Island of the City University of New York. She has published on a wide range of subjects, varying from seventeenth-century Dutch genre painting to feminist methodology in the history of art. Her publications include "The Art-Historical Canon: Sins of Omission," first published in *(En)gendering Knowledge: Feminists in Academe* (1991), and, most recently, *Jacob Duck and the Gentrification of Dutch Genre Painting* (1998). She is currently working on a book on Vermeer.

CAROL ZEMEL is Professor of Art History at the State University of New York–Buffalo. Her most recent publication is *Van Gogh's Progress: Modernity and Utopia in Late Nineteenth-Century Art* (1997). Her current project, " 'Graven Images': Modern Visual Culture and Eastern European Jews," centers on Ashkenazic Jewish life between the two World Wars.

SIEGFRIED ZIELINSKI holds the chair for Media Archaeology and Theory at the Academy of Media Arts in Cologne, and is the founding director of this new art school. He has published numerous books on art, philosophy, history, and the theory of radio, film, television, and video. He is a member of the International Advisory Board of ASCA.

THE PRACTICE OF
CULTURAL ANALYSIS

Introduction

Mieke Bal

Cultural analysis as a critical practice is different from what is commonly understood as "history." It is based on a keen awareness of the critic's situatedness in the present, the social and cultural present from which we look, and look back, at the objects that are always already of the past, objects that we take to define our present culture. Thus, it can be summarized by the phrase "cultural memory in the present." As such, it is immediately obvious that cultural analysis entertains an ambivalent relation to history as it is or has been traditionally practiced in our faculties. Far from being indifferent to history, cultural analysis problematizes history's silent assumptions in order to come to an understanding of the past that is different. This understanding is not based on an attempt to isolate and enshrine the past in an objectivist "reconstruction," nor on an effort to project it on an evolutionist line not altogether left behind in current historical practice. Nor is it committed to a deceptive synchronism. Instead, cultural analysis seeks to understand the past as *part of* the present, as what we have around us, and without which no culture would be able to exist.

The papers gathered here represent the current state of a field of inquiry, and at the same time, they present to the larger academic scene what a particular group of scholars thinks about what cultural analysis can and should do, or be, as an interdisciplinary practice. The challenge for

FIGURE I. *Briefje*, graffito, photographed by Mieke Bal.

this volume is to counter the common assumption that interdisciplinarity makes the object of inquiry vague and the methodology muddled. I would like to devote a few pages to suggesting how this assumption is mistaken, and how cultural analysis does have an object that is specific enough, as well as precise methodological starting points. What, then, is its object?

This graffito (Fig. I), for example, has come to characterize the goals of the Amsterdam School for Cultural Analysis (ASCA), whose inaugurating, programmatic conference was the first step that led to the present volume.[1] In the most literal translation the text means:

> *Note*
> *I hold you dear*
> *I have not*
> *thought you up*

This piece of wall writing fulfills that function because it makes a good case for the kind of objects at which cultural analysis would look, and—more importantly—how it can go about doing so. The graffito represents a letter, or *brief* in Dutch, both visually and linguistically. The visual form of the text is an icon for the form of letters, with an address, "Dear so-

and-so," followed by the "body" of the letter. The word that has the visual shape of the address is linguistically self-referential. The word *briefje* means "note," short letter. But it rhymes with *Liefje*, a more usual address, meaning "Dearest" or "Sweety." This is the word that comes to mind in the afterimage of the visual shape of the self-referential word.

This implied other word fits in with the beginning of the rest of the text that says something like "I love you." Thus, the first line of the body of the letter drags along the absent term of endearment. The discourse of the love letter is now firmly in place, but as soon as that is so, it shifts to epistemic philosophy by continuing with: "I did not invent you" or "I did not make you up." The past tense, the action negated, the first-person speaking, all initiate the discourse of narrative only to make a point about what's real and what is not. If the statement is about ontology and epistemology, the narrative mode of the exemplum coincides with what it "illustrates." But this statement of nonfiction is inherently contradicted by the address that changes a real person, the anonymous writer's beloved, into a self-referential description of the note: a referential *liefje* becomes a self-referential *briefje*. This turns the note into fiction, and the addressee into a made-up "you," after all. Yet, by the same token, this inscription of literariness recasts the set of characters, for the identity of the "you" has by now come loose from the implied term of endearment that personalized him or her. So, the passerby looks again, tripping over this word that says "you!," as if in an Althusserian interpellation. Addressed as beloved and not as a guilty citizen, the city dweller gets a chance to reshape her or his identity, gleaming in the light of this anonymous affection. But is it real?

This tension between the epistemic affirmation and the literary suspension of ontology questions the very distinction between fiction and reality, which the note/graffito thematizes. It also inscribes academic reflection at the heart of an expression of contemporary, "popular" culture. This transculturation, which some people might think of as an upward movement and others as depressing heaviness, continues. The body of the text is identical to the ending of a poem, "Je bent" ("You are"), by Dutch poet Ellen Warmond, one of the early feminist Dutch writers active in the 1950s and 1960s. Thus, the interdiscursive complexity of the text, connecting it to academic inquiry as well as—through this reference—to "high literature," doubles up with intertextual citation, specifically to women's literature of a generation or two ago. For the knowledgeable Dutch reader, this reference resonates with the characterization of these writers as caught by "the Great Melancholy," thus turning the self-referential address of the note into a desperate anonymity: the beloved cannot be found; she or he is irretrievably lost, and the graffito mourns that absence.

But what if the poem's ending has found a place where the beloved can be located, because, no longer hidden in the recesses of psychic mourning, she or he is now spoken to in the public domain? The handwriting on the wall is accessible to everyone, visible and insistently visual in its bright yellow lettering on the red bricks of the city wall. For years and years it launched its cheerful yet melancholic alternative to the threats of ideological state apparatuses into the spokes of Dutch cyclists on their way to work.

Literature is allographic; painting is autographic. This common and handy distinction falls through here. The graffito is an autographic poem. Moreover, it is publicly accessible, semantically dense, pragmatically intriguing, visually appealing and insistent, and philosophically profound. Just like poetry. Yet it stubbornly remains a transient thing that can disappear at any moment. Thus, this accidentally found "text-image" has come to stand for the program of cultural analysis in more ways than one. Its unofficial, uncanonical, even slightly transgressive status, its transience and the concomitant insistent presentness, and its visual work on the verbal words are among the aspects that made it so fitting for its current use as the emblem of ASCA, and for the book series this volume inaugurates. But for me, perhaps the most important feature of the graffito is that it was there, on a city wall, for all members of our present, multicultural society to see, to see and hence to read, to read the handwriting on the wall. It is an exhibit; it is on show; and it shows itself, shows its hand, its presence. And in its capacity as visible exhibit, it exposes itself and what it has to say. This aspect of the graffito represents my vision of cultural analysis, and just like the authors of the contributions to this volume, I want to expose that vision, for such methodological explicitness is one feature of cultural analysis.

"Exposition" has been on my mind since I started the book-length study *Double Exposures*, which for me became programmatic for cultural analysis. In that book, from which the following thoughts are partly taken, I tried to connect three meanings of the verb "to expose": exposition, exposé, and exposure. These are the three issues which this "close reading" of the graffito brings together. The Greek verb *apo-deik-numai*, in the middle voice so dear to Roland Barthes, and in his wake to Hayden White, connects these aspects. The verb refers to "making a public presentation" or to "publicly demonstrating"; it can be combined with a noun meaning opinions or judgments and refer to the public presentation of someone's views; and it can refer to the performing of those deeds that deserve to be made public.[2]

Some aspect or version of each of these meanings is central in the issues that I would like to propose as the agenda for cultural analysis "beyond"—after, as well as in continuation of—disciplinary humanities, but also cultural studies as it is now commonly conceived in the United States and England. To make the point right away: the triple meaning of the verb "to expose" in this sense constitutes the field of cultural analysis because it defines cultural behavior if not "culture" as such. The graffito embodies such a concept of "culture."

An exposition makes something public, and that event of showing involves articulating in the public domain the most deeply held views and beliefs of a subject. "Briefje" has some things to say about love and its public discourse, and it argues against oppositions such as public versus private, romantic belief in unique individuality versus the masses, truth versus fiction, and high versus low culture. In this sense, an exposition is always also an argument. Therefore, in publicizing these views, the subject of exposing objectifies, exposes himself as much as the object; this makes the exposition an exposure of the self. The anonymous writer of "Briefje" exposes him- or herself as a transgressive philosopher and a daring poet using the strategy of appropriation art and doing all that is an act of producing meaning, a performance. Here performance has the double meaning compounded from the association of the performing arts and analytic philosophy or speech-act theory.

This view extends the meaning of "to expose" from the specific, literalized definition of it in, for example, the context of museum exhibitions to a broader, partly metaphorical use of the idea of "museum" as a mise-en-abyme of culture's present, a present that carries the past within itself. The present is a museum in which we walk as if it were a city, for exposing is a particular form of discursive behavior, the posture or gesture of which does the three things implied in the Greek verb. In *Double Exposures*, I examined the ambiguities involved in gestures of exposing; in gestures that point to things and seem to say: "Look!," often implying, "That's how it is." This ambiguity sketches the position and agency of practitioners of research and teaching in the humanities today. The "Look!" aspect involves the visual availability of the exposed object, which is thereby potentially objectified as the text, image, performance, film, or ritual that one sets out to study in order to understand "culture" in any of its well-known appearances. The "Look!" aspect is embodied by the "you" to whom the graffito appeals. The "That's how it is" aspect involves the authority of the person who knows. This epistemic authority is what scholars have, and what students labor to achieve, as do museum curators and anyone making an argument in the public domain. Graffiti writers do not have it, but perhaps they mock the arbitrariness of that discrepancy and thereby achieve some measure of it. Adopting the graffito here is an acknowledgment of that subversive claim. From now on, this graffito does have epistemic authority, at least for me; I will heed what it has to say. The gesture of exposing shifts between these two aspects. The possible discrepancy between the object that is present and the statement about it creates the ambiguities that I propose as the crucial element of "culture." This makes cultural analysis inherently self-reflexive. The graffito represents this ambiguity in its multiple contradictions and paradoxes, of which the specificity-in-multiplicity of the identity of the "you" is only the most blatant case. By this ambiguity it can be read as raising the question of identity politics and can begin to address its problems outside of the regression which has gratefully exploited these problems.

Cultural studies has evolved out of a polemic against the arbitrariness of disciplinary boundaries, the often exclusionary assumptions involved in the aesthetics on which much work by humanists is based, and the separations, first between aesthetics and ethics and then between art and social issues, which were relegated to the social sciences. These three self-critical notes might explain why it was, in particular, the museum which has become an attractive object of study, and why it can thus be a useful metaphor for the endeavor of cultural analysis. Whereas self-criticism is perceived by some as dis-integrative, the museum requires integration. It needs interdisciplinary analysis; it has the debate on aesthetics on its agenda; and it is essentially a social institution. As an object, it requires interdisciplinarity. As well as social institutions, museums are to a certain extent ritual institutions, calling for an analysis that draws upon cultural anthropology and theology for an understanding of their lay ritualizing of art and culture. They require reflection on aesthetics, which makes philosophy an important partner. Within the humanistic disciplines, they brutally confront scholars with the need to overcome disciplinary hangups that essentialize media, for museums insist on the visuality of their treasures, which not only are presented by the museums with the help of language but also constitute, through their presentation, an "intermedial discourse." And this intermedial, semi-anonymous discourse speaks to everyone from city walls as much as from museum walls. Museum analysis requires the integrative collaboration of linguistic and literary, of visual and philosophical, and of anthropological and social studies. This makes museums as good an example as any of the kind of cultural object on which cultural analysis can set to work. Instead of speaking of an abstract and utopian interdisciplinarity, then, cultural analysis is truly an interdiscipline, with a specific object and a specific set of collaborating disciplines.

True to the Greek verb, expository discourse is *apo-deictic*: affirmative, demonstrative, and authoritative on the one hand, and opining, often opinionated, on the other. But "discourse" does not mean here yet another invasion by language of fields that ought to be protected from it and kept "pure" in their visual or aural aspects; on the contrary, using such a term for the analysis of museums necessitates a "multimedialization" of the concept of discourse itself. Discourse implies a set of semiotic and epistemological habits that enables and prescribes ways of communicating and thinking that others who participate in the discourse can also use. A discourse provides a basis for intersubjectivity and understanding. It entails epistemological attitudes. It also includes unexamined assumptions about meaning and about the world. Language can be a part of the media used in a discourse, not the other way around.

My searchlight for the analysis of this discourse called "culture" is the notion that gestures of showing can be considered discursive acts, best considered as (or analogous to) specific speech acts. Those acts are not necessarily linguistic in terms of the medium used to perform them, but are based on the communicative possibilities that language offers. "Exposing" considered as a speech act thus becomes the object of cultural analysis that I would like to consider exemplary of the endeavor which this book presents, and our graffito nicely embodies that object. If anything, it "shows" a speech act in its purest form: direct address, to you and me in the present but loaded with "pastness," carrying along the long tradition of apostrophe in poetry.[3] The fictional "note" really addressing us and the real graffito thus becomes an ideal of a self-reflective museum.

But let me explain how this speech-act theory of exposition is not a case of linguistic imperialism. Here is how I see exposing as a "speech act," implying an utterance like "Look!" An agent, or subject, puts "things" on display, which creates a subject/object dichotomy. This dichotomy enables the subject to make a statement about the object. The object is there to substantiate the statement. It is put there within a frame that enables the statement to come across. There is an addressee for the statement, the visitor, viewer, or reader. The discourse surrounding the exposition, or, more precisely, the discourse that *is* the exposition, consists in "constative" discourse. Constative speech acts are informative and affirmative. They have truth value: the proposition they convey is either true or false. They are *apo-deictic* in that sense of affirmation. As in all discourse mainly consisting in such speech acts, in expositions a "first person," the exposer or curator, tells a "second person," the visitor, about a "third person," the object on display, who does not participate in the conversation. But in expositions, unlike many other constative speech acts, the object, although mute, is present. This presentness matters. It is one of the defining features of cultural analysis to focus on this present quality of cultural objects, including those that came to us from the past.

The inevitable implication of a "first person" who "speaks" or does the showing makes the expositional statement *apo-deictic* in the second sense: opining, opinionated. In terms of the distribution of roles, the situation of exposition has, typically, the following form: The "first person" remains invisible. The "second person," implicitly, has a potential "first person" position as a respondent; his or her response *to* the exposing is the primary and decisive condition *for* the exposing to happen at all. The "third person," silenced by the discursive situation, is at the same time the most important element, the only one *visible*, in the discourse. This visibility, this presence, paradoxically makes it possible to make statements about the object that do not apply to it; the discrepancy between "thing" and "sign" is precisely what makes signs necessary and useful. But the discrepancy in the case of exposition is blatant and emphatic, because the presence of a "thing" that recedes before the statement about it brings the discrepancy to the fore. The thing on display comes to stand for something else, the statement about it. It comes to *mean*. The *thing* recedes into invisibility as its *sign* status takes precedence to make the statement. A sign stands for a thing (or idea) in some capacity, for someone. This is a definition of a sign. And "sign" is perhaps the best synonym for performance in the other sense of the word, as it indicates the performing arts. The thing, then, becomes an actor, or singer.

In the space between thing and statement, narrative is one of the discourses that tends to creep in. Narrative is the discourse of affirmation and myth, of storytelling and fiction, of seduction and willing suspension of disbelief. The very fact of exposing the object—presenting it while informing about it—impels the subject to connect the "present" of the objects to the "past" of their making, functioning, and meaning. This is one way in which the expository speech act is narrative. Narrative also occurs in the necessarily sequential nature of the visit. The "walking tour" links the elements of the exposition for the "second person" and thus constructs a narrative. Walking through a museum or a city is like reading a book or watching a movie. The two narratives overlap but are not identical.

If the narrativity of display is, thus, a major topic in cultural analysis, providing narratology an object outside of the traditional domain of the novel, then the stark visuality of present culture is equally central to the program. One place where visuality as such can be analyzed self-reflexively is in the use of visual illustrations in writings *about* visual objects. This use is typical in art history, where the writing claims to be subservient to the image; in fact, more often than not, the image is printed merely to "illustrate" the text about it. One can imagine Plato objecting to this usage of images on the grounds that the image recedes yet further from the "real" thing it once was. But one does not need to be a Platonist to realize that, in such cases, the image is about the text rather than the other way around.

It seems to be impossible to conduct an analysis of exposition without clarifying to what extent and under which conditions and modalities writing is irremediably bound up with what it attempts to explore and exploit. This inevitable duplicity within, and involvement of, the field out of which the project of cultural analysis grew makes rhetorical analysis a third partner in the methodology debate. In the case at hand, rhetoric helps to "read" not just the artifacts in a museum but the museum and its exhibitions themselves, and likewise, not just the graffito but the wall on which it was painted. The narratological perspective provides meaning to the otherwise loose elements of such a reading. Most importantly, the analysis aims to yield, on the one hand, an integrated account of the discursive strategies put into effect by the expository agent, and, on the other hand, the effective process of meaning-making that these strategies suggest to the visitor or viewer. The reading itself, then, becomes part of the meaning it yields. In semiotic terms, display is based on indexicality: it points to what is actually present.

Furthermore, only authoritative subjects have the material access to the objects of display required for the gesture to be truly indexical. Only those who are invested with cultural authority can be expository agents. For only such subjects are able to routinely address an audience that is numerous and anonymous to the agent, an audience which tends to go along with the assumed general meaning of the gesture of exposing: to believe, to appreciate, and to enjoy. Incidentally, this is another place where the social sciences are indispensable allies in this endeavor.

Expository agency ought not, however, to be equated with individual intention. Here, again, our graffito helps us to see the issue with clarity. Its expository agent is both the anonymous writer and the city that provided its wall; the city, moreover, that decided not to remove the graffito for such a long time implicitly colluded in this exhibition, as did all those passersby who did not overwrite it or otherwise damage it. The success or failure of expository activity is a measure not of what one person "wants to say," but of what a community and its subjects think, feel, or experience to be the consequence of the exposition. In this sense, exposition is here considered as an arch-cultural practice, if not a keystone of how a culture functions. Meaning is slippery and variable, both smaller and endlessly greater than what the speaking subject would like to convey. An anonymous graffito whose author is long gone but which keeps insistently tugging at passersby struck by its beauty and enigmatic meaning—what better embodiment of this dissociation of intention and meaning can be found?

The project of cultural analysis, then, begins for me by making the positions of first, second, and third persons in the discursive sense shift around so as to destabilize the rigid relation of authority and mastery among expository agent, viewer/reader, and exposed object. Whereas I have focused on that aspect in *Double Exposures*, I am intrigued by the possibility that this avenue provides also a theoretical link between linguistic, visual, and aural domains that blend so consistently in contemporary culture but remain so insistently separated as fields of study in the academy. Tentatively, then, I would like to outline a possible theorization that helps cultural analysis challenge yet another rigid boundary without getting "muddled."

The concept through which to do this is space/place. Beyond the distinction between linguistic and visual or aural artifacts, I would like to make a more important place for the spatial coordinates that define culture not as a collection of things but as a process. One example may clarify this. In a brilliant discussion of psychoanalytic views of the formation of subjectivity and the place of the body therein, Kaja Silverman argues, "[O]ne's apprehension of self is keyed both to a visual image or constellation of visual images, and to certain bodily feelings, whose determinant is less physiological than social" (1996: 14). This statement explains how the relation between the individual subject and the culturally normative images is bodily without being "innate" or anatomically determined. In its insistent interrogation of the indexical relationship between image and viewer on the basis of a cultural myth, Caravaggio's famous *Medusa* is a good example of such bodily interaction "from within" subjectivity with the outside culture. In Silverman's statement quoted above, the issue is feeling: how the subject feels his or her position in space. What we call "feeling" is the threshold between body and subjectivity *and* between body and outside world. The external images are "attached" to the subject's existence experienced as bodily, locked together; the subject is "locked up" in the external world; and also, in the musical sense of the word "key," they are adapted, harmonized together: the one is "set into" the tonality of the other. But the word to key to can also be understood through the notion of code, the key to understanding, comprehending, communicating between individual subjects and a culture, a communication in which "abstract space" is practiced.[4]

The productivity of this "carrying along" or connotative use of a key concept from semiotics becomes obvious when Silverman writes shortly after the above quotation, still discussing the bodily basis of the ego, about proprioceptivity—the sensation of the self from within the body—that it is the "egoic component to which concepts like 'here,' 'there,' and 'my' are keyed" (16). She reuses the well-known linguistic concept of deixis, given currency by Emile Benveniste. Strictly speaking, by placing deixis "within" or "on" or "at" the body, she extends the meaning and importance of

Benveniste's thought that deixis, and not reference, is the "essence" of language.

Not only is language unthinkable, then, without bodily involvement, but, one can further argue, so is the idea that words can cause pain or harm, and arouse sexual and other excitement, and thus it is an integral part of linguistics, an insight this discipline cannot weasel out of. Conversely, this proprioceptive basis for deixis comprehends more than words alone. It comprises the muscular system as well as the space around the body, the space within which it "fits," as within a skin. Abstract space thus becomes concrete place within which the subject, delimited by its skin, is keyed in, into the space he or she perceives and is irrevocably a part of. Silverman indicates this place of the "keyed" subject with the felicitous term "postural function." The shadow can be taken as an allegory of this postural function's outward movement.

Deixis can become a key term for an interdisciplinary analysis of the visual domain as well as the literary, *without the reductive detour via language*. No longer confined to the domain of language, deixis is a form of indexicality, but then, one that is locked onto (keyed to) the subject. This bodily-spatial form of deixis gives a more specific insight into those forms of indexicality where the postural function of the subject—its shaping "from within"—sends back, so to speak, the images that enter the subject from without, but provides it with "commentary." [5] This, with a wink to the subject who wrote the graffito on the city wall, gives another turn to the "dialogic" relation to space.

Cultural analysis stands for an approach, for an interdisciplinarity that is neither nondisciplinary, nor methodologically eclectic, nor indifferent; this approach is primarily analytical. Often, the analysis involves "saying no to what you inhabit" (Spivak 1993: 281), thus impelling the analyst to reflect both on the "no" and on the habitat; the self and the present. The varied acts of reading that this book presents have in common a cohabitation of theoretical reflection and reading in which the "object" from subject matter becomes subject, participating in the construction of theoretical views. They also share a contemporaneity. This is not an indifference to history but a foregrounding of the active presence of the object, or text, in the same historical space as is inhabited by the subject, "me." The detailed readings of objects that the chapters offer do not propose an archaeology of meaning but an interaction with and through meaning that constitutes cultural practice. As an emblem of that project, the volume opens with a short presentation of two artists' engagement with the visual culture of the present.

This brief opening excerpt from a visual dialogue makes the comment that that dialogue, too, is a form of cultural analysis, but as such, it is also a cultural expression, an object of cultural analysis. For, in addition to being an intellectual engagement with the art of the past, it is also on show. When the artists, Edwin Janssen and Janneke Lam, presented the complete dialogue from which the "quote" is taken, a fundamental feature of the object, the "thing-event," was there for everyone to see, was there to be on show. As much as I would have liked to include the full dialogue in this volume, considerations of various kinds have made this too difficult. But because the brief presentation makes a statement about so many of the issues that define cultural analysis as we conceive it, it belongs here at least in the shape of a prelude.

After this short preface, the book offers three parts of five or six essays each, and closes with a kind of dual postface. With varying emphases, the three parts present the issues at the core of cultural analysis: the standpoint in the present and the subsequent relationship to history, close reading, and methodological (self-)reflection. In the first part, the emphasis is on the relationship between the present and the past; the essays embody the idea of cultural memory in the present. These essays focus those reflections on manifestations of visuality in a variety of manners. The second part is organized around the notion of close reading as a critical practice. Whereas the relationship between the present and the past is also an ongoing concern in these essays, their programmatic thrust is exemplified in their detailed engagement with a cultural object. And whereas Part I is thematically oriented toward visual culture, Part II is more text-oriented. This is not a return of the repressed of disciplinarity, but a relatively coincidental result of tradition: it has been primarily in textual analysis that close reading has been practiced. Hence, that is where the skills have been maintained as well as where the difference between traditional close reading and cultural analysis can be demonstrated most clearly. In other words, this coincidence is a case of cultural memory in the present in itself. If Stephen Bann's title, "The Veils of Time," can serve as the metaphoric accent of traditional close reading, then "transatlantic" is the spatial axis recurrent in cultural analysis.

Methodological and philosophical reflection, finally, become the major focus in Part III, which makes explicit what the other two sections have amply demonstrated: that method matters. The third part as a whole can be construed as the self-reflective moment of the group of scholars who wrote the essays in this book. The authors of Part III give their views of what they think cultural analysis ought to practice, and hence, they appear more explicitly programmatic. The essays here would probably tend to show up in the first section of a more orthodox academic book. But it seemed right to organize this book differently from that tradition. The decision was to start the book with actual *practices* of cultural analysis, so that the more self-reflexive essays fall on well-prepared ground. Moreover, the essays in the third part are thus deprived of their expository status, their epistemic authority as statements on what the rest of the book would do. As even a cursory glance at the table of contents affirms, many of these essays expose views on perhaps the hottest issue in cultural analysis: the tension between the need to account for difference and specificity, and the desire to construct, as Isabel Hoving phrases it in her essay, global comparative frames. Instead of resolving this tension, this book claims the importance of keeping this tension going as a productive dynamic.

For similar reasons of nonclosure, the double postface connects the book back to the actual state of things in the academy. The idea here is to get our feet back on the ground and set out, after reading what a certain group of people feels to be the best route for the cultural disciplines in the twenty-first century, to do the business of cultural analysis in the present, for the present.

Prelude

DIA-LOGIC: A DIALOGUE IN IMAGES BETWEEN
EDWIN JANSSEN AND JANNEKE LAM

Janneke Lam

Dia-logic is a picture book in two voices, a work of visual art, a shameless act of copying, and a slide-show version of cultural analysis. Here is how this dia-logic came into being.

Edwin Janssen and I, both artists working in the field of vision, were given the opportunity to present a visual experiment during the ASCA conference on the practice of cultural analysis: a dialogue by means of images instead of words. That is, we showed a communication which came into being through the interchange of all kinds of pictures, ranging from reproduction of artworks to illustrations, snapshots, postcards, and advertisements.

When we met, we realized that we shared a semiotic awareness and were both interested in the action of the collective repertoire of images stored in culture and activated in intersubjective processes. We immediately decided to design an interactive visual event. Thus, the idea of a visual dialogue came about: we were going to communicate through images only, without making any spoken or written comments during the process. We also made the decision to base our visual interaction on association, and not on thematic coherence.

Edwin started by sending me a reproduction of Brueghel's *Parable of the Blind*, thereby referring to the aggrandized heads from this painting that he used for his installation which hung in the stairwell during the conference. I was supposed to respond with a different image, with Edwin then taking his turn, and so on and so forth. To make the process of alternating replies visible for others, we made color slides that were projected onto two screens next to each other: the first slide was projected onto the one screen, and after fifteen seconds the second, the answer, was projected next to it. Then after another fifteen seconds, the first slide was replaced by the third, being the answer to the second. Thus, each image was in view for thirty seconds, successively accompanied by two other images.

The slide show was part of a debate on cultural analysis, but it was not meant to be a visual analysis in itself. I would rather describe it as the visualization of a process of looking, which incites the viewers to engage in visual analysis. That is to say, it is not a logically constructed argument. Instead, the slide show can best be characterized as an experiment.

JANNEKE:

Raymond Depardon, *A Patient in a Psychiatric Hospital in Turin*. Italy, 1980. Used with permission of Magnum Photos, Inc.

It was literally a trying out of a new idea: Edwin and I had never before conducted a visual dialogue, nor had we ever seen one. Moreover, when we started our project, we did not know where it would end. The result of this experiment makes it clear that the acts of looking concerned here are very complex and that the visual analysis of these acts is an important phase of the project: its moment of *dia-logic*.

Visuality is addressed at various moments and in distinct ways. First, visual material, that is, the product of other people's acts of looking and interpreting, is our starting point and, with a few minor exceptions, our sole means of expression: our only "language." Second, with respect to our own looking position, the individual processes of looking as well as the interchange of looking actors, is at issue. Third, by soliciting the attention of viewers for our looking we inevitably engage their looking and interpreting, and this, finally, can lead to the analysis of and reflection on all these processes of looking.

Our visual dialogue can also be characterized as a recycling of images

EDWIN:

Edwin Janssen, Untitled.

present in our culture, or rather, as working with "pictures" — *plaatjes* in Dutch — as in a "picture book." In this dialogue our own "hand" and originality, our personal creation, are of secondary importance. In contrast, we are more interested in the given elements of our cultural environment and the part which this shared collection of images can play in our production of meaning. Our creativity consists of the way we use images, of a mode of ordering. By reusing extant images in the new frame of an intersubjective process of communication, we give them a new life and new meaning.

Because the works of art used in this context do not fold back on the original maker anymore, the reference to her or him loses its relevance. The postmodern term "appropriation art" is coined for these processes. This art form should not be conceived in the pejorative sense of exploita-

JANNEKE:

w i m

A Dutch boy's name.

Janneke Lam, from *Het Leesplankje/Learning to Read* (1990).

tion but in the positive sense of its revivifying quality. To give you an idea of how we have appropriated and recycled images, we offer in this essay a small quotation from our dialogue in images.

Let me now summarize our experiences as conversation partners: Owing to our agreement not to communicate our view of the other's choice in writing or talk, we were forced to concentrate entirely on the visual "data" we gave each other. The importance of that starting point became clear only at the moment when Edwin broke the rule and told me that one of the persons in an amateur snapshot, which he had brought in, was his father. This remark changed the meaning of the photograph completely and kept me away from scrutinizing the rest of the visual information. The incident also indicated that, on the one hand, our personal

EDWIN:

Blood Is Thicker Than Water

Edwin Janssen, *Blood Is Thicker Than Water*.

history could not be excluded, but that, on the other hand, it could not be easily made visible.

The process of making became for us a materialization, that is, an embodiment and illustration of a post-structuralist conception of semiosis: the act of giving meaning consists of moments of arrest in a continuous stream of signifiers. This also emphasized that new images and new meanings do not emerge from a void but always tread in the steps of other, previous images. Our dialogue demonstrates this almost too emphatically.

We also became acutely aware of the fact that our production of meaning is equally based on formal and semantic elements. This was the case as early as during the first step: the almost unconscious, almost primary process of association pushed into movement by the visual text itself. It was also the case during the more conscious second step: the moment of definitive choice of a new image in response to the previous one. These primary and secondary reactions were not always easy to distinguish.

JANNEKE:

Moeder

Janneke Lam, from *Mijn Eerste Prentenboek/My First Picture Book* (1988).

Consequently, it has become clear to us that the intercourse with visual images cannot be reduced to visuality in any "pure" sense. Word and image cannot be so easily separated. The rebus principle of Freud's *Interpretation of Dreams* also applied to our dialogue. Incidentally, word and image explicitly interact in the pictures reproduced in this book, because the title plays an important part in three of them.

During our creative process we perceived two, more or less opposed movements: on the one hand, the material we used together was leveled, because all kinds of images were excised from their contexts and put in a general melting pot, a sort of reservoir of images; but, on the other hand, this leveling was never able to entirely ban a personal preference or familiarity with a specific visual discourse, because in each case we were dealing with the visual reservoir personally composed by each one of us. We both worked inevitably from our own gendered perspective, cultural situation, and personal preferences.

EDWIN:

Edwin Janssen, Untitled postcard.

This subjective element was strengthened by the choice of association and interaction as the guiding principles for our series. Hence, in this dialogue our personal development and history, our different personalities, are unavoidably present. This becomes particularly visible in the input of certain themes and the way that these are introduced.

The latter draws attention to the performative aspect of our communication, being by definition a relational process and inevitably emotionally charged. We were surprised by the great differentiation of "speech acts"—or should I call them "look acts"?—with which we could label our visual reactions to one another. To give you a few examples: continuing, spinning off, contrasting, reversing, changing subjects, going into detail, focusing or expanding, underlining, confronting, reverting to, simplifying, problematizing, and finally, humorously relativizing.

Our conclusion is that visual communication was in fact more effective and efficient than a person-to-person, oral communication. We got to know each other artistically in much more depth than a few personal encounters could have effectuated. For both of us, this was a suspenseful, surprising, revealing, intensive, intimate, delicate, fun, and instructive way of getting to know each other's relationship to images.

PART I

DON'T LOOK NOW

Visual Memory in the Present

THE PRIMARY ISSUE that cultural analysis needs to address in order to shape its identity and advance its program is the relation of this academic practice to history. Ever since the term "new historicism" achieved academic currency, the turn away from history that had tended to become popular in the early days of post-structuralist innovation has been checked. The call for history, as Jonathan Culler put it in *Framing the Sign*, has been loud and clear. To be sure, a certain naïveté about the possibility to reconstruct the past can no longer be assumed to characterize historicism, new or even "old." Few scholars still believe that the past can be bracketed and isolated from the vantage point of the historian living and working today. Yet how the situation of the historian in the present affects not only the knowledge of and insight into the past but also the presence of that "contaminated" past in the self-definition of scholars *in the present* may still deserve a closer look. Whereas many contributions to the historicism debate have been immensely valuable in their effect, they also kept at bay a most substantial issue that this section elaborates: the presence of the past in the present, as a rigorously synchronic element without which no present can even be conceived.

The six essays in this section each explore, in a detailed case study, the tricky consequences of the uncertainties regarding history that this presentness of the past entails. They do this around the theoretical theme of visuality, of looking. This theme lends itself particularly well to the kind of questioning that cultural analysis and history address to each other, not only because history has been so predominantly text-based, but more importantly, because "looking" as an act has been central to a philosophy of science that put observation at the core of its procedures of evaluation. Thus, looking became the protected element that only a committedly self-reflexive methodology is really able to critically engage. As Chapter 1 strongly suggests, the look as an instrument of the scientific or scholarly endeavor—as in biology, or art history, or astronomy, or film studies—is often entangled with the look as object of analysis.

Philosopher of science Evelyn Fox Keller, whose work of feminist critique of scientific theories, practices, and discourses has informed to an important degree the by-now important feminist intervention in the sciences, opens with a reflection on the nature and effect of the scientific look and its history. The question seems simple: what does it mean to look? Her argument leads to the troubling double awareness that observation involves intervention—a point new historicism would recognize—but also that it does not leave the subject of looking untouched. The importance of this paper as the opening essay of our volume lies in the connection between the meticulous study of the act of looking and the history it offers on the one hand, and its allegorical significance for the project of cultural analysis on the other.

Indeed, the practice of ethnography has amply demonstrated the uprooting, even destructive quality of mere observation. Keller shows this effect in the scientific practice of biology, and this for me serves as a useful metaphor for the critical examination of past culture in and from the vantage point of the present and for the denaturalizing practice of cultural analysis. Keller opposes the likening of the biological gaze to innocent "star gazing," which has so often been the case. Moreover, she argues how the microscope itself changed the meaning of "seeing." The difficulty of seeing the properties of the object apart from those of the instrument makes the microscope a useful metaphor for the practice of close reading as advocated in this volume. The microscope is the analog of the difficulty of seeing "it" in texts and images and sounds that constitute cultural practices and challenge the naturalized assumption on which an earlier tradition of close reading was based. It is the site of self-reflection as a necessary mediation between "instrument" and "object." In other words, the subject of cultural analysis is right in there. And when Keller concludes that the secret of life, the ultimate goal and accomplishment of biology, is already and necessarily transformed by the very technology of the gaze, the lesson offered also engages the history of cultural analysis. What we offer here, then, is not a pristine point of origin of some radically new approach, but an intervention, resulting from a good look at the history of the humanities.

It is indispensable to keep Keller's essay in mind, if not in our mind's eye, when reading the subsequent essays and the objects they address. Nanette Salomon, a leading Vermeer specialist as much as a reputed feminist art historian, offers a radically innovative vision of the work and career of this artist, a vision developed through her "microscope," and a detailed look at one painting in relation to the absence of others at the Vermeer exhibition(s) in Washington and The Hague, in 1995–96. This question whether the exhibition was one or two—already broaching the issue of "transatlantic transference"—firmly positions Salomon's historical inquiry in the present.

As I argued for Keller, the case that Salomon makes for a revision of Vermeer around the issue of sexuality and, or versus, civility stands out as a metaphor for more than the important art-historical issue alone. Focusing on a single painting, the chapter offers a close reading, the tenets of which are further and more explicitly developed in Part II. But the situationist discussion of the painting as it was—and as its relatives were not—present at the exhibition(s) is the microscope as instrument-affecting-the-object of this reading. Salomon demonstrates that the presence of the subject of inquiry, in the determination and articulations of questions that can be asked, and also in the frames within which interpretation becomes possible, does not in any way damage the historical validity of her claim. On the contrary, hers is a case for the increase of historical relevance of such positioning in the present.

Whereas Salomon brings the insights offered by Keller to the center of the canon of "high culture," Thomas Elsaesser, an influential film historian and theorist, speaks to these issues in his assessment of the—nonpristine—"origins" of what was to become the most popular cultural medium: film. He develops explicitly what Salomon had been so boldly suggesting: the idea that the question of "what is the history" of a cultural domain, such as art or film, is a question for and of cultural analysis. He demonstrates that the definition of "what film is," and hence of what one wants to write the history of, is itself a cultural decision, implying a vantage point and a speaking position from which alone a history becomes possible. The essay analyzes film history's "stereoscope" through a sketch of that instrument's object, the films made by the Lumière brothers, which allegedly initiated the art as well as the medium of cinema.

No pristine origin here, either. Elsaesser argues through a productive reluctance to endorse any of the extant definitions of film as the exclusive set of defining features—reproduction of movement, luminous traces on sensitive surfaces, in other words, iconic and indexical representation—definitions which are upheld at the cost of an alternative definition in terms of social practices. This enables him not only to suggest what kind of history such a definition would entail, but simultaneously to demonstrate a cultural analysis *of* history. Such an analysis shows the difficulty of both causal explanation and a view that has no explanatory power or determining force. It also demonstrates the dilemma of choosing between master narratives and a common denominator that gives up on specification. The latter dilemma calls for the practice of close reading as Part II exemplifies it. But Elsaesser's conclusion, that cultural analysis is both necessary and, in turn, in need of awkward, resistant historical objects, gives an additional turn to Salomon's view of "Vermeer in the 1990s" as a historical claim.

It also prepares the ground for the definite "awkwardization" of the object of the next chapter, an odd mix of "high art" and "popular culture." Griselda Pollock, whose reputation in feminist art history doubles with her importance in cultural studies, fields she has blended by creating a graduate program at the University of Leeds in both, probably speaks to a great many readers in her wish to carry out a joint, integrated analysis of these two domains that refuse to integrate in any scholarly account: Jackson Pollock, the hero of abstract expressionism, and Marilyn Monroe, the heroine of Hollywood film in all the definitions Elsaesser discusses.

The relation to history is clearly awkward as much as essential in this essay. "Doing" cultural history as a practice of cultural analysis focuses on its own "microscope" in the choice of moments where "high art" can be hinged to practices in the popular domain. The "hinge" here is femininity, and this involves Pollock herself, too. The confrontation of the art symbol and the sex symbol helps her to rearrange and traverse the historical thickets of the 1950s in the United States. Pollock makes the art that is so insistently present in major museums today look different by a chain of displacements that the multiple puns of her title's dyad exemplify. Displacing the progressive forms of the verbs "to die" and "to kill" grammatically and semantically, from active to passive and back again, she examines how the art symbol looks—pun intended—and what the sex symbol does—idem—so that the unfixing of gender positions becomes an unfixing of cultural domains as well.

Implicit in Pollock's essay is the issue of nationality, so crucially important in Eisenhower's America and the wars in Southeast Asia. Carol Zemel, also an art historian, trains her microscope on that issue as well in an essay that foregrounds the "autohistorical" perspective. Projecting Homi Bhabha's pair "nation and narration" on photographs of vanished worlds of Jewishness, Zemel starts out by stating her own position towards this historical material, a position that constitutes an uneasy mix of reluctance and commitment, distance and recognition. Thus her autohistorical position becomes in turn emblematic of the relation to history that Part I explores.

"Nation and narration" in this essay becomes a visual articulation of ambivalence. Zemel takes issue with the tendency of such recycling of visual material as the nostalgic framing of photographs of nationhood, a framing that inevitably produces stereotypes through the mode of the picturesque, hinges between myth and modernity, and brings class into the issue of nationalisms. The aura of doom that surrounds photographs like Roman Vishniac's *Vanished World* can only be applied retrospectively. But this post-holocaust nostalgia that affixes to the past all the conflicts of the multicultural present comes to stand for the position of the cultural analyst/historian who cannot look *now*, who cannot face the present and therefore turns away, turns to look back and sees there, looming large, the present as holder of the past.

For Stephen Bann, cultural analysis is a logical position, in that he has been founding director of a program in modern cultural studies at the University of Kent at Canterbury for a long time. A scholar of art, literature, history, and, more emphatically, of the links among these domains, Bann has consistently focused on the problem of historical inquiry neatly summarized by his title, "The Veils of Time." Here he takes stock of the contributions of important forerunners of today's developments in cultural analysis, in order to position himself more clearly. This enables him to exemplify, in yet another allegorical move, the very relationship to the past that is the object of cultural analysis, but clearly also its subject.

Bann discusses Marshall McLuhan's discourse of culture as self-degenerative and Umberto Eco's "preferential code" as both implicated in cultural analysis and historicized over time. The resulting historical entropy inexorably makes the critic also an object of historical hermeneutics. The obvious by-product of this view, self-reflection, is staged by Barthes in his famous theorizing of connotation through the visual claims of an extended French nationalism. In Barthes's essay, Bann argues, the critic becomes a kind of *flâneur* in historical mass culture.

The alternative Bann develops is based, not coincidentally, on his own work as curator of museum exhibitions. The historical recuperation he advocates is situated in a dialectic of loss and retrieval, which answers some of the points raised by Zemel while also announcing the difference, in the essays of Part II, from traditional close reading. If, as Bann argues, veiling and unveiling are hard to distinguish, glimpsing history in the extreme moments of its own metamorphosis is the best one can do. The key term here, "metamorphosis," will be central in Frank Ankersmit's essay, whereas the hovering between veiling and unveiling offers yet another image of the microscope of cultural analysis: one that inscribes time itself as nonlinear, hovering, perhaps even circular, but at any rate not "true."

—M.B.

The Finishing Touch

Evelyn Fox Keller

The film version of *The Race to the Double Helix* shows Rosalind Franklin gazing down, admiring the evidence of her latest experiment, and murmuring beatifically, "I just want to look, I don't want to touch." This is a twist on the association of vision with distance and aggression, and touching with erotic engagement that is so familiar to feminist scholars. Franklin reverses these. Yet, by appealing to a different association, most familiar to scientists, she is saved the feminine subject position. In scientific discourse, looking is associated with innocence, with the desire to understand, while touching implies intervention, manipulation, and control.

But what in fact does it mean to look without touching? Doesn't looking always imply some effect, some impact? Even looking at the stars touches something—if not the stars, then surely us. Looking always touches us, at least metaphorically. But I am more interested in the ways in which looking touches the object, the material entity at which we seem to be looking. Thus, I will not talk about star gazing, about telescopes and the technologies of looking at large and distant objects that we cannot even hope to touch, but rather about the forms of looking that scientists have developed in order to peer at, and into, the very small. Also, I am less concerned here with the gaze as metaphoric rape than as itself a form of literal, material transgression. Or, if not as itself transgressive, then as preparatory to the act of transgressing (or penetrating)—much in the sense in which Freud described the function of looking as "preparatory to the normal sexual aim" (1962: 23).

Especially, I am interested in the technologies developed in biology for peering into the secrets of life, into the fundamental processes of generation—a domain in which we can and do aspire (indeed may have always aspired) to intervene. In short, I take this occasion as a chance to meditate on the particular character of the biological gaze, once, but no longer, possible to think of as the natural counterpart of star gazing.

As Scott Gilbert reminds us (1994), the tradition of invoking the heavenly gaze as a metaphor for the study of embryology extends back to ancient times, and continues into the twentieth century. In 1939, for example, the American embryologist E. E. Just wrote:

The egg cell also is a universe. . . . The lone watcher of the sky who in some distant tower saw a new planet floating before his lens could not have been more enthralled than the first student who saw the spermatozoon preceded by a streaming bubble moving toward the egg-centre. And as every novitiate in astronomy must thrill at his first glance into the world of the stars, so does the student today who first beholds this microcosm, the egg-cell. (1939: 369)

It would seem that these scientists, like Franklin, also just wanted to look, not to touch. But I suggest that stargazing has always been a somewhat disingenuous metaphor for biology; certainly, it has no place in the biology of today.

This essay, then, is a meditation, an attempt to explore—tentatively and even a bit quixotically—the history of the biological gaze, focusing in particular on the different ways in which that gaze has become increasingly and seemingly inevitably enmeshed in actual touching, in taking the object into hand, in trespassing on and transforming the very thing we look at.

Let me return to Rosalind Franklin. Rosalind Franklin is a scientist of the grand tradition of innocent inquiry. She is a pure scientist. Like Barbara McClintock, she has no interest whatsoever in the use value of the objects she studies. She is not after control, only understanding. But what exactly is she looking at as she utters this seraphic line (Fig. 1)?

Despite the crucial (and somewhat infamous) role that this photograph turned out to play in Watson and Crick's race to the double helix, in leading them to their discovery of the secret of life, it is not, in fact, an image of a cell or of any other living object. It is an X-ray photograph of a

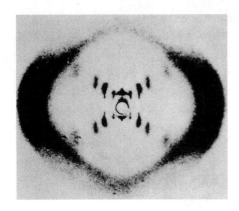

FIGURE I. An X-ray photograph of DNA in the B form, taken by Rosalind Franklin late in 1952. *Source*: Watson 1968: 116.

crystalline structure composed from cell extracts—that is, from extensive preparations and purifications (manipulations) of the homogenized contents of a vast number of cells. No living object could possibly survive these preparations. Indeed, no living object could even survive the process of imaging. To obtain this image, one needs to bombard the object at issue with a barrage of X rays that would quickly destroy the vital functions of any living thing. X-ray crystallography is thus too transgressive to enable us to see an animate entity in its living state.

But perhaps this is a bad example. If X rays are too powerful—and too intrusive—for an innocent gaze, perhaps I should be considering ordinary light rays, the more conventional vehicle for a nonintrusive act of looking. Indeed, I am prompted by the spirit of Rosalind Franklin's remark to turn back time as well, to the Edenic days before the study of vital phenomena became an experimental science, to a time when natural historians pursued their investigations by simply observing with the naked eye (or perhaps with a magnifying glass) the wonders around them. Surely, if there ever was a nonintrusive, nontransgressive biology, that was it. Innocence may be too much to claim, for we know that even the unaided eye does not see innocently. Observation always requires experience, skill, at least some kind of theory or organized expectation—but presumably, not yet intervention. Or is this wrong? Does not the naturalist in fact have to cut or otherwise uproot his or her specimens from the field, and preserve them for future study in the cabinet or museum? And are not his or her excursions into the field forays that alter that field, often mapping it for future, more massive incursions? So, even natural history intrudes—not actually by the act of looking, but in all the peripheral activities contiguous with that act. Therefore, it is perhaps better to say that the methods of natural history were relatively noninterventionist, certainly less intrusive upon the organism per se than the work of early anatomists, or, in our own time, of Rosalind Franklin's crystallograph. But then we must also note that natural history was at the same time relatively ineffective for seeing into the secrets of life. The naked eye, with the relatively gentle ways of touching that went with the scientific study of the biological form, left the mysteries of vital phenomena unexplored. Above all, it left the mysteries of embryogenesis—of reproduction and development—intact.

There was of course the microscope, one of the great developments of the seventeenth century. Long before biologists came to agree about the need for an experimental science, an instrument had appeared that promised to do for the living form what the telescope was already doing for the cosmic form, namely, to vastly enhance the power of the naked eye to peer at, and even into, the secrets of life. But even from the start, there was a crucial difference. The preparation of an object required for microscopic examination was necessarily more intrusive than that required by the naturalist. Before looking at an animate being, it was necessary to first cut and fix it, in a word, to deanimate it. As a tool for probing the inner processes of life, the microscope thus had obvious limitations. The gaze itself may have been innocent enough, requiring only the eye and not the hand, but immediately antecedent to the work of looking lay the work of the cutting. Consider, for example, the classic image of early microscopy from Buffon's *Natural History* (Fig. 2). Note the spatial distance here between the act of touching and the act of seeing—to be sure, closer than that for the natural historian—both acts are in the same frame, but still kept clearly apart. The hands of the microscopist are at his side.

And there were also other, yet more serious problems with the new microscope. Along with its promise to make at least the once-animate subvisible visible, it raised new problems for the very meaning of "seeing." What does it mean to see through a microscope? What in fact can one see? For most of us, even with a modern-day microscope, the answer is precious little—apart, that is, from one's own eyeball. Only with a great deal of practice, fiddling with the focusing knob, does one learn to see anything at all through a microscope. And once one does, the question arises, is it a real thing one sees? Is it an object on the slide, or a spot on the lens?

FIGURE 2. *Biological Research*, from Comte de Buffon, *Histoire naturelle* (1749–1804), 2: 1. Wellcome Institute Library, London.

And if on the slide, is it a shadow or a ridge? Robert Hooke, founding member of the Royal Society and often regarded as the founder of modern microscopy, himself admitted how it is often "exceedingly difficult" to distinguish between the real properties of an object and the artifacts of microscopic viewing. The solitary microscopist was left to make such distinctions and to painstakingly transcribe his impressions into a freely drawn hand sketch. And the public at large—the community of virtual witnesses—saw, of course, only prints from the engraving that ensued.

Not surprisingly, these engravings evoked tremendous curiosity. But perhaps more so among the general public than among working scientists, whose interest in the new instruments, although initially quite strong, had already subsided by the end of the seventeenth century. While useful for creating the impression of evidence, the early microscope produced results that proved to be extraordinarily unstable. In Bachelard's view, it "was an instrument for dreamers, an instrument whose optical shortcomings produced more artifacts" than facts (quoted in Luthy 1994: 2). As often as not, it made visible the invisible rather than the subvisible (see, e.g., Fig. 3, Hartsoeker's drawing of human sperm, 1694).

The problem for scientists was obviously a serious one. Of course they understood that the images they drew were also artifacts, or, as we

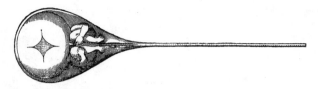

FIGURE 3. Nicolaas Hartsoeker, woodcut illustration of spermatozoon (1694), from his *Essay de dioptrique* (Paris: J. Anisson, 1949). Wellcome Institute Library, London.

now might say, constructions. But then as now, their job qua scientists was to ensure that these artifacts corresponded, in some sense at least, to the real. To quote Elaine Scarry, they needed not only to "make up" but also to "make real" (Scarry 1992). How was one to do this? How could one be certain that the image one saw was not an illusion? Indeed, how do we know that looking through a microscope actually gives rise to seeing at all?

Today, this problem—the question of whether or not microscopic objects are real—has long ceased to trouble scientists, but it does continue to trouble philosophers. We believe in the reality of the things we see with the naked eye, philosophers argue, because we can walk up to them and touch them. And with things of microscopic size, we cannot do that. Perhaps then they are merely theoretical entities, not real at all. Gustav Bergman, for example, wrote in the 1940s: "Microscopic objects are not physical things in a literal sense, but merely by courtesy of language and a pictorial imagination. . . . When I look through a microscope, all I see is a patch of color which creeps through the field like a shadow over a wall" (quoted in Hacking 1983: 187–88). Indeed, to this very day, some philosophers of science claim that we do not actually see anything at all through a microscope. Of course, practicing scientists merely laugh at such quibbles—maybe philosophers can't see through a microscope, but they have no problem at all.

The reason that this problem troubles only philosophers and no longer scientists is simple. Philosophers do not understand the nature of the activity of modern microscopic observation. The fact is that scientists have found a way to walk up to the object and touch it; no longer do they peer through the microscope with their hands behind their backs. This, in fact, was the great contribution to the rise of an experimental ethos brought to nineteenth-century biology: the desire—and increasingly, the skill—to reach in and touch the object under the microscope, and thereby to "make it real." In other words, once the microscope was joined with the manual manipulations of an experimental biology—marking, cutting, and dissecting under the scope—and the interdependency of hand and eye previously reserved for the naked eye was extended into the microscopic realm, the microscope became a reliable tool for veridical knowledge. By the close of the nineteenth century, hand and eye had begun to converge. In turn, and because of this rapprochement, the microscope provided an incalculable boon to the further advancement of experimental biology—perhaps especially, to experimental embryology.

At first with relatively crude instruments—perhaps a glass rod drawn very finely, or with a baby's eyelash—and later, in the twentieth century, with the carefully machined microtomes and micromanipulators, researchers could not only represent but actually intervene in the choreography of the minute primal stages of life. They could isolate the fertilized egg, watch it divide, gently mark one of the cells with a dab of dye and follow it as it continued to divide and ultimately became incorporated into the larger whole as a particular body part, or they could carefully separate the cells after the first or second division to see if the two halves of the young embryo could independently form whole bodies (Fig. 4).

Still later, after the arrival of micromanipulators, researchers learned to get inside the cell—much as their predecessors had gotten inside the organism—and manipulate the microstructure of the cell itself. By the 1950s and 1960s, for example, they learned how to exchange nuclei—or parts of the cytoplasm—between cells. Ian Hacking is one of the few philosophers of science to understand the indispensable role the hand has come to play in modern biological microscopy. He writes:

You learn to see through a microscope by doing, not just by looking. . . . The conviction that a particular part of a cell is there as imaged is, to say the least, reinforced when, using straightforward physical means, you microinject a fluid into just that part of the cell. We see the tiny glass needle—a tool that we have ourselves hand crafted under the microscope—jerk through the cell wall. We see the lipid oozing out of the end of the needle as we gently turn the micrometer screw on a large, thoroughly macroscopic, plunger. (Hacking 1983: 189–90)

So, now we know that the cell is real. And not only real, but also alive.

Indeed, after the great microscopical investigations of Theodor Schwann and Matthias Schleiden, the cell—a word Hooke had earlier

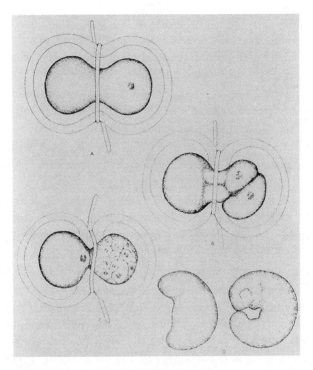

FIGURE 4. Summary of Hans Spemann's constriction experiment on newt eggs, from Spemann, *Embryonic Development and Induction*, originally published 1938. *Source*: Bruce M. Carlson, *Patten's Foundations of Embryology* (New York: McGraw-Hill, 1981). Used with permission of the McGraw-Hill Companies.

used to describe the cavities he observed in dead cork—came to be thought of as the atomic unit of vitality, displacing the organism from its prior position as the most basic unit of life. As François Jacob has aptly written: "For the eye armed with a microscope, every living organism was finally resolved into a collection of juxtaposed units" (Jacob 1976: 117).

But there is a lot more going on here than simply "making real" through touching. Already, even in Jacob's statement, we can read another agenda in the experimental attitude—an agenda I might describe as "making real" through causal efficacy, or making things real by using them to effect change in other things that we know are real. Here, by this reasoning, we know something is really real not simply by touching it, but, after touching it, by grasping it and hurling it at something else. As Hacking says of electrons, "if I can spray them, they're real" (see Hacking 1983). In this context, Jacob's choice of words is revealing, for an arm is indeed more than a hand. An "eye armed with a microscope" is an eye equipped not merely with fingers but with arms, that is, with the potential for projectile force.

For a microscope to acquire this potential for projectile force, it must be employed not simply to describe, but to search out and identify the units which presumably will, in the right hands, maximize causal efficacy. Thus, for the experimental biologist, the function of the microscope is not simply to enhance looking, or even to validate the tangibility of that which we are gazing at, but to employ that gaze as a probe in anticipation of action. A unit is fundamental if and only if it is a unit to which one can attribute primary cause. Once identified as the locus of primary cause, it becomes the fulcrum through or with which one may hope to leverage maximal effect. This is the meaning in Jacob's remark of the word "resolved," implying, as it does, a resolution of the organism into the "fundamental units" of life, entities which can hopefully be harnessed to bring about effective change—that is, can serve as agents of control.

Indeed the major arguments for experimental biology given in the nineteenth century were explicit on this point. Without experiment, it was argued, one could never find the underlying causes of a phenomenon, and without cause, one could not hope to effect change. One of the most articulate advocates for an experimental biology, Claude Bernard, had this to say regarding the need for an experimental approach to medicine:

Men have actually maintained that life is indivisible and that we should limit ourselves to observing the phenomena presented to us as a whole by living organisms. . . . But if we admit that we must so limit ourselves, and if we posit as a principle that medicine is only a passive science of observation, then physicians should no more touch the human body than astronomers touch the planets. . . . Medicine so conceived can lead only to prognosis and to hygienic prescriptions of doubtful utility; it is the negation of active medicine, i.e., of real and scientific therapeutics. (Bernard 1947: 19)

It was through experiment that we found the real, underlying causes of natural phenomena, in living bodies as well as in inorganic bodies, and hence the means to alter—to induce a change in—the course of natural phenomena.

In the early part of the twentieth century, the great experimental embryologist Hans Spemann thought that he (together with his student Hilde Mangold) had found the fundamental locus of causal agency for the developing embryo. He called it the "organizer." The "organizer" was not a single cell, but a group of cells, found in the dorsal lip of the frog embryo, and deriving from a particular region of the fertilized egg. When excised from one frog embryo and inserted into another, in a different location, it induced the formation of a second developmental axis — initiating the growth of something like a Siamese twin. Here Spemann thought he had found the head of the growing embryo — that which organized and commanded the growth of the subsidiary cells. He wrote: "The designation 'organizer' . . . is supposed to express the idea that the effect emanating from these preferential regions is not only determinative in a definite restrictive direction, but that it possesses all those enigmatic peculiarities which are known to us only from living organisms" (Spemann 1938: 182–83).

The discovery of the "organizer" in 1924 marked the high point of what is now referred to as classical embryology; it provided the cornerstone of a research tradition that flourished, and in fact dominated experimental embryology, at least until the late 1930s. By the 1940s, most biologists had lost interest in the organizer. Why? The usual answer given is that interest faded because it had been shown that any number of things — for example, a piece of dead tissue, even certain ordinary, off-the-shelf chemicals — could induce the formation of a second axis. This meant that the specific motive force was not in the organizer itself, but at least partially in the surrounding tissue. As Spemann himself wrote, "A 'dead organizer' is a contradiction in itself" (369).

Clearly, if biologists were to find the units which carried the motive force, or primary cause, behind embryonic development, that is, if they were to find the agents truly responsible for the secret of life, they would have to look elsewhere. Some biologists thought they already knew where to look. H. J. Muller, for example, a classical geneticist from the laboratory of T. H. Morgan, was convinced that the right place to look was at the gene. To Muller, it was the gene, not the cell, and certainly not the organism, that was the biologist's atom. Analogizing the problem of mutation of the gene to that of transmutation of the elements, he argued, as early as 1916, that just as control of transmutation "would render possible any achievement with inanimate things," so too would the control of mutation. It could "place the process of evolution in our hands." "Mutation and Transmutation," he wrote, are "the two keystones of our rainbow bridges to power." And just a few years later, in an essay entitled, "The Gene as the Basis of Life," he rhapsodized:

The secret of [the gene] may perhaps be reached first by an upward thrust of pure physical chemistry, or perhaps by biologists reaching down with physicochemical tools. . . .

We cannot leave forever inviolate in their recondite recesses those invisibly small yet fundamental particles, the genes, for from these genes, . . . there radiate continually those forces, far-reaching, orderly, but elusive, that make and unmake our living worlds. (quoted in Keller 1992: 99–100)

The gene was elusive indeed. A great deal of progress had been made in mapping out the microscopic substructure of the cell—the microtome appeared in 1870, permitting the cutting of exceedingly fine slices of tissue; new stains appeared every few years. By Muller's time, one could see the nucleus, one could even see the colored bodies called chromosomes, on (or in) which the genes would presumably be found. But one could not see genes. And despite Muller's success with X rays, one could certainly not (at least not yet) reach down into their "recondite recesses" and grab hold of them. It is sometimes even argued as a virtue of genetics (relative to, e.g., experimental embryology) that it is nonintrusive: it does not require cutting into the organism and manually manipulating its parts. Experiment, for geneticists, is rooted in the practice of genetic crosses—that is, controlled mating of organisms with particular properties—followed by close observation of the resulting progeny. Apart from the intrusion required in mutagenesis, what is manipulated is the environment in which the organism finds itself, not the organism per se. For Muller, as for all other classical geneticists, the existence of genes had to be inferred from the gross phenotypical properties for which they were presumed responsible. Indeed, because of its abstractness, many wondered whether the gene was real at all; perhaps it was just a hypothetical construct.

Furthermore, not everyone was convinced, even in principle, of the possibility of ever achieving Muller's goal of complete control of living processes—of extending the eye or hand so far that one could actually lay claim to the secret of life. Contrary to Muller, Niels Bohr argued that the science of animate matter is not, after all, just like that of inanimate matter. If we have learned anything from physics at all, it is that even in the physical domain, looking without touching is impossible: the very light we shine disturbs the object at which we gaze. Intuiting here a principle of profound epistemological importance, perhaps even more so for biology than for physics, in 1932 Bohr suggested a generalization of his principle of complementarity for the biological sciences. He wrote:

The conditions in biological and physical research are not directly comparable, since the necessity of keeping the object of investigation alive imposes a restriction on the former which finds no counterpart in the latter. Thus, we should doubtless kill an animal if we tried to carry the investigation of its organs so far that we could tell the part played by the single atoms in vital functions. In every experiment on living organisms there must remain some uncertainty . . . and the idea suggests itself that the minimal freedom we must allow the organism will be just large enough to permit it, so to say, to hide its ultimate secrets from us. (Bohr 1987a: 9)

But as we know, the story does not end here. The motive force of scientific inquiry was too strong, the desire to extend the biological gaze too great. And with the resounding success of atomic physics at the end of World War II, an entire generation of biologists (or physicists turned biologists) were ready to take up Muller's call to prove Bohr wrong, which they did.

In 1953, with the help of the X-ray crystallograph I showed at the beginning of this chapter, Watson and Crick found the structure of DNA, and in that structure they saw the secret of life: a Rosetta stone written in the alphabet of nucleic acid bases. This, as you know, was an event of immense importance to the history of biology, abruptly and dramatically transforming the pace, and also the course, of biological science. Even Bohr was obliged to recant, sort of. In his eminently cryptic fashion, he wrote in 1962, "Life will always be a wonder, but what changes is the balance between the feeling of wonder and the courage to try to understand" (1987b). Presumably, Watson and Crick had displayed a most remarkable courage. Of course, a DNA crystal is not itself a living thing, but the logic of its molecular structure left no doubt in most minds about its role in living cells. It provided an answer to at least one of what Spemann called "the enigmatic peculiarities which are known to us only from living organisms": it revealed a mechanism for replication, a way in which like could be produced from like. Never mind that it told us virtually nothing about how genes might orchestrate the development of actual organisms, the differential specification of body parts, their formation, the design of their structure, or their actual functioning. What we were now able to do, despite these shortcomings, was to give real content to the notion of "gene action"—a notion that classical genetics, as if anticipating the dramatic successes of molecular biology, had earlier made so popular: DNA makes RNA, RNA makes protein, and proteins make us.

But what, you may ask, do the successes of either genetics or molecular biology have to do with the connection I have been trying to map between looking and touching? Muller's vision did not in fact depend on the possibility of literally seeing genes; and insofar as one might speak of a gaze specific to genetics, it has to be said that the gaze—at least as far as classical genetics was concerned—intruded on the organism no more than did the gaze of the natural historian. Muller's vision depended on training the mind's eye, not the visceral eye, on these entities so deeply ensconced in innermost parts of the cell. Nor was any literal hand (certainly not any human hand) involved in the upward thrust, or downward reach, which he advocated; to make even the crudest contact with the gene, Muller had to settle for an unfocused barrage of X rays. Of course, other (more focused) techniques—both for looking and for touching—did soon become available.

The electron microscope, for example, made it possible to see something one could call a gene, but even so, it was hardly a gene in action. Electron microscopes incur even more damage to the object in view than do X rays. If one were to see genes through an electron microscope, one would first need to isolate and freeze them. Like the DNA in Rosalind Franklin's X-ray crystallograph, they would have to be completely extracted from their cellular environment and inactivated—as if visibility and activity obeyed a kind of complementarity principle.

Indeed, one of the great strengths of molecular biology in its early days was its disavowal of the very term "life," and its choice of a model system that resided midway between an inert molecule and a living organism, namely the bacteriophage, or virus. Viruses are little more than naked DNA; they cannot be seen through a light microscope, and, as I've already said, by some standards they are not even alive, but they proved their worth as a simple tool for effecting genetic changes in their more conventionally living hosts. The hosts for bacteriophages were independently growing and reproducing bacteria. These more bona fide organisms could, in turn, be cultivated and studied in the laboratory with astonishing ease, and with a complete lack of skill. Anyone could do it, even newcomers from physics or chemistry who had never studied biology. Generations of molecular biologists made their careers trafficking back and forth between bacteriophages and bacteria and the truly naked DNA they could extract from these rudimentary creatures.

However, during this period of roughly two decades, some biologists (those who were more conventionally trained and more organismically minded) complained bitterly that the enthusiasm for molecular biology was excessive if not actually misguided; at the very least, its claims were overblown. The very essence of life as they knew it was its complexity. Surely, it was too simplistic to claim that single-celled bacteria, or even worse, bacteriophages, could speak to the wonders of the living forms we see around us, let alone to the miracle of our own vitality. Little did any-one in those days realize — not even molecular biologists themselves — that the virus, itself only a quasi-vital entity, was already being fashioned into a vehicle for extending both eye and hand into the deepest recesses of the cell. There is even a technical term for the virus that serves this function: it is called a vector.

The breakthrough came in the 1970s with the development of tech-niques for isolating a particular genetic fragment from one organism, and attaching this fragment to a viral or plasmid "vector." We can inject this mixture into the cell nucleus of another organism with a micropipette, and the viral vector will do the rest of our work, inserting the fragment directly into the host genome. Such techniques not only led to the pro-duction of transgenic organisms, they also enabled the introduction of specific probes which could visually "report" on the activity of particu-lar genes. For example, the gene for luciferin could be isolated from the firefly and attached to a gene normally found in the host, and, by way of the viral or plasmid vector, the composite construct incorporated into its normal position in the host genome. Now, whenever the host gene is acti-vated, the firefly gene will also be activated, and its location in the cell will literally "light up." Here, a visual signaling device, able to reveal a level (and kind) of detail which the microscope never could achieve, has been introduced into the interior of the cell nucleus. In much the same way, other combinations of genes can also be constructed, introducing different visual markers; alternatively, tagged constructs can be introduced to bind to specific pieces of messenger RNA, which, once bound, can be "lit up" by the addition of appropriate antibodies. Or, antibodies can be used to directly target the proteins themselves. By such techniques, it has become possible to visually identify and to track—*in situ*—many of the particular RNA or protein molecules required to activate or deactivate (turn on or off) those genes involved in the developmental process. Needless to say, such techniques have revolutionized the study of embryology. They have made it possible—in ways that would have been utterly unimaginable to the great embryologists of even the recent past—to directly observe the generation of life, as it were, *in flagrante delicto*.

What does this say about looking and touching? Let me recapitulate. Once, it might have been possible to think of the eye as a purely passive instrument for the study of pristine nature, entirely separate from any intrusive act of touching, but, as I have tried to show, "armed with the microscope," the eye becomes ever more intricately interconnected with the hand. Here, in the most current life sciences, is a technology which merges looking and touching into an undifferentiable and unified act. What we see in these slides are the fingerprints left by the genes or gene fragments which, with the aid of viral vectors acting as prosthetic fingers, we have manually inserted into the cell's nucleus. Thus, what we see as we gaze at the secret of life is life already, and necessarily, transformed by the very technology of our gaze. And conversely, and simultaneously, that gaze provides the means of further transformation. Muller was right—by "reaching down with physico-chemical tools" into the "recondite recesses" of those "small yet fundamental particles," we do secure a handle on the "forces . . . that make and unmake our living worlds." But Bohr was also right: there is a principle of complementarity operating here. The "secret of life" to which we have so ingeniously gained access is no pristine point of origin, but already a construct at least partially of our own making.

Vermeer's Women

SHIFTING PARADIGMS IN MIDCAREER

Nanette Salomon

Even the most casual study of seventeenth-century Dutch genre paintings reveals a change in tone which occurs sometime just after mid-century. Over the course of time art historians have framed this change in a variety of ways, and the changing terms of their discussions may be taken as a measure of the changing terms of value in the field of historical inquiry in its own right. Before the iconographic revolution initiated in Utrecht in the late 1960s, this change was seen as an issue of quality. As such it was touted as evidence of the greater genius manifested in Dutch genre painting after 1650, especially in the so-called Delft school, with Vermeer as its most outstanding example. Iconographic considerations, with their emphasis on disguised symbolism as a primary pictorial mode and the didactic explication of good and evil as the primary pictorial message, gave genre paintings from the first half of the century a new validity and new terms of appreciation. As a corollary, many have characterized the change after 1650 as the advent or popularization of the home as the site of the new subject in Dutch genre painting.[1] The positive associations of this site are easily made coincident with the interpretive systems of Christian morality distinguishing the images along the binary divide of virtue and vice.[2] In the recent past, there has even been some discussion as to whether this change itself is evidence of a diminishing or erosion of meaning per se (Philadelphia 1984).

My interests in this paper are to sketch a new frame for understanding the change in genre after midcentury and to track this change in the early works of Vermeer by focusing on the subject of woman as a culturally produced sign. The recent exhibition(s) of Vermeer's painting in the National Gallery in Washington, D.C., and in The Hague has recently provided new occasion to discuss and understand his art (Washington 1995–96). While it may be argued that the two venues of the exhibition of Vermeer's paintings, The National Gallery in Washington and the Mauritshuis in The Hague (Washington 1995–96) constitute, in fact, one exhibition, yet from the perspective of cultural analysis the differences in the manner and place of the paintings' exhibition become more significant than their shared catalogue and curatorial intentions. These opportunities have produced a catalogue, symposia, and seminars. They have also allowed for, if not urged, the barrage of historical information embodied in Vermeer's work to be unfixed from its usual order and resifted and resorted through the grille of a modern perspective. Submitted to my art-historical eye,[3] feminist politics, and idiosyncratic curiosity, this historical information is regrouped. It is fashioned into whole new categories the contents of which cohere to one another in new alliances with newly found similarities. The analogy of poker comes to mind, where a winning hand may be had by cards of the same suit or by cards of consecutive numbers or value. Here a winning hand (that is, plausible claims to historical truths) can be had by renewed and diverse mixing and matching, although the possible combinations are enormous, and, alas, such clear markers as suits and numbers are not so easily seen.

Nevertheless, new plausible historical sense can be made from the work through these new groupings. With this paper I hope to broaden our definition of historical meaning and to relocate Vermeer's early work into what I am here suggesting was a mainstream of Dutch artistic practice that, because of its contemporary relevance, can only now be seen.

Vermeer's depiction of women as a central creative concern has often been remarked upon, most recently by Albert Blankert (Washington 1995–96: 34). Rather than reflecting any real woman (or women), these figures may be seen as formulations of evolving ideological constructs in early modern Dutch society. One of this paper's projects is to locate a change in the terms of these constructs that can be found in Vermeer's early work just after *The Procuress* in the Staatliche Kunstsammlungen in Dresden, *A Maid Asleep* in the Metropolitan Museum in New York, and

Officer and Laughing Girl in the Frick Collection in New York, all three sorely missed in the current exhibition(s). In examining the shift in priorities just after these early genre works, we can see how this all-important, culturally produced sign changes paradigms in the slightly later *The Girl with the Wine Glass* in Braunschweig. Within the changing constellations of Northern Netherlandish burgher culture, some issues at stake include, among others, native definitions of femininity and masculinity, as well as the related concepts of artistic mastery and aesthetics.

The three early paintings by Vermeer to figure male/female relationships belong, in my view, to a popular early category of Netherlandish genre paintings the subjects of which represent illicit trysts. The later paintings, signaled by *The Girl with the Wine Glass* in Braunschweig, belong to a new, modern pictorial category that represents what we may call for the moment civil trysts. Although not completely analogous, the seventeenth-century terms to delineate the change in women in Vermeer's paintings can be understood as a change from *minne* to *liefde* (that is, from eros to agape). The former is a highly developed subject in the burgeoning secular art of the Netherlands throughout the sixteenth and early seventeenth centuries (Renger 1970). *Minne* is defined there through a variety of tropes of so-called mercenary love — that is, representations of bordello scenes, so-called unequal lovers, the ruin of the Prodigal Son and others — which found ample expression in both paintings and prints. A consideration of these, if only a very brief one, is necessary here for a clearer understanding of the tradition to which I believe Vermeer was heir. The insightful work of Konrad Renger in his groundbreaking book *Lockere Geselschaft* (Loose company), published in 1970, allowed us to see the iconographic diversity and complexity of the sixteenth-century paintings and prints representing mercenary love. They had, theretofore, more often than not, been lumped together as simply illustrations of the biblical parable of the Prodigal Son. However, if we acknowledge that the story of the Prodigal Son is but one of several sexual narratives developed in the sixteenth century, this group of images can be opened up to an entirely different kind of analysis: one which allows it to be seen as a broader, even endemic, culturally produced ideological paradigm.

It is of no small consequence that the narratives of these formative secular works are dedicated to the economic exchange of sexual relations. Michel Foucault's work on this period's legal and literary history recognized that: "since the sixteenth century, the 'putting into discourse of sex,' far from undergoing a process of restriction (as moralist interpretations would have us believe), on the contrary, has been subjected to a mechanism of increasing incitement; that the techniques of power exercised over sex have not obeyed a principle of rigorous selection, but rather one of dissemination" (Foucault 1980: 12). Indeed, Foucault in speaking of this period describes what is for him a "veritable discursive explosion" (17). Rather than seeing this explosion as merely about sex, Foucault goes on to ask the crucial questions, "What were the effects of power generated by what was said (represented)?" and "What are the *links* between these discourses, these effects of power, and the pleasures that were invested by them?" (10).

One of the most consistent criticisms of Foucault's work in this area points to his failure to consider feminist issues as fundamental to understanding the power equations created through the discourses of sexuality (Diamond and Quinby 1988).[4] The compelling drive to develop visually the terms of gender difference, together with the persistent "upper hand" given to women in these images, prevents us from making Foucault's mistake.[5]

Despite the clichéd notion that prostitution as a social practice exploits women and that, by extension, a consideration of visual "images of women" as prostitutes would also yield an analysis of that exploitation, a close viewing of the visual language of these paintings produces a salutary caution against such easy "interpretations" of images. A careful scrutiny of these paintings reminds us that our categorized and delineated notions of historical realities are not the only ones that are possible, and, perhaps even more significantly, that "realism" in art can never be a simple, passive "mirror of reality" but is always rather a dynamic, organic, that is, interactive participant in the formation of realities. The realities shaped by visual culture are part of a discursive web, continually catching and disposing meaning on a myriad of social levels. John Tagg's discussion of nineteenth-century photographic realism is useful here. In articulating the characteristic components of realism as an artistic phenomenon he writes: "The dominant form of signification in bourgeois society is the *realist* mode. Realism is a social practice of representation, an overall form of discursive production, a normality which allows a strictly delimited range of variations. It works by the controlled and limited recall of a reservoir of similar 'texts,' by a constant repetition, a constant cross-echoing" (Tagg 1988: 99). It is precisely the realist rhetoric of these images that historically enabled them to perform so persuasively and productively in establishing the links Foucault saw, with other formations of power hierarchies in early modern relationships. The apparent realism of the *bordeeltje* (the seventeenth-century Dutch name for bordello scenes) is achieved by combining early Netherlandish realistic formal advances, such as replicating the "look" of the material and tactile world through the nuanced modulation of light and shade made possible by oil paint, with anecdotal modern subjects presented in contemporary settings, costumes, and hairstyles. Modern form and subject were activated throughout by a lively sense of narrative. The sense is conveyed of a "caught moment" spontaneously enacted yet replete with consequences.

These pictures' "effect of reality," to creatively twist the term coined by Roland Barthes, is still successfully influencing current art-historical interpretations that treat the images positivistically, as descriptions of actual bordello conditions. In fact, unlike actual bordello conditions in the Netherlands—which, as the work of Lotte van de Pol has shown, occurred across a tremendously varied spectrum of social conditions and locations—the image of the bordello in Netherlandish art quickly adhered to a series of discernible visual conventions. The fact that the repertoire of social types as class of locale in sixteenth-century imagery is so unvarying should itself attest to its contrived nature (van de Pol 1990). The impulse to read the images realistically is often linked, quite illogically, with the desire to read them as moralizing texts warning their viewers against lust, greed, and various other canonical sins. Although this is not the place, much can and should be said about the way contemporary interpreters "naturalize" the coupling of these two incompatible ideas.[6] And while these subjects do, in fact, bear some relation to Christian notions of female vice, the positive tone of most of these paintings and prints urges us to find more resonant ways of understanding them.[7]

It has long been observed that some of Vermeer's paintings had a certain relationship with this prestigious, early Netherlandish genre tradition. The combined affect of the so-called *Procuress* in Dresden and the presence of Dirck van Baburen's earlier image, *The Procuress* in the Boston Museum of Fine Arts, in no less than two of Vermeer's works, *The Concert* in the Isabella Stewart Gardner Museum in Boston and *The Girl Seated at the Vir-*

FIGURE I. Johannes Vermeer, *The Procuress*. Staatliche Kunstsamlungen, Dresden.

ginal in the National Gallery in London, ensured the consideration of this subject on various levels. However, more often than not, contemporary discussions turn on Vermeer's keen interest in Utrecht Caravaggism as a formal rather than iconographic choice. I would like to redirect our attention here by securing, not just the Dresden painting, but all of Vermeer's earliest genre paintings with men and women in them, within the various sexual narrative structures of the early Netherlandish genre tradition.

The first and most overt of these is, of course, the painting in Dresden dated 1656 (Fig. 1). Often called *The Procuress* despite the minor role

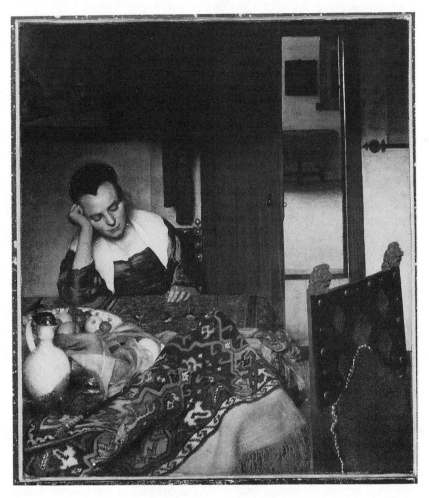

FIGURE 2. Johannes Vermeer, *A Maid Asleep*. The Metropolitan Museum of Art, bequest of Benjamin Altman, 1913 (14.40.611).

played by that figure, the painting has always been recognized as an image of mercenary love. The central couple engage in an exchange of money and physical favors within an ambience of bright colors and a rosy atmosphere. Unlike Baburen, for example, who gives the prominent foreground position to the old bawd in his Boston painting, Vermeer instead gives that position of prominence to a male figure often identified with the artist himself, an identification that rests on a comparison between this figure and the figure of the painter in Vermeer's later work *The Art of Painting* in the Kunsthistorisches Museum in Vienna.

His prominence in the Dresden *Procuress*, as in the Vienna painting, warrants a serious reconsideration of the statement made by the group. The idea that this toasting man is the artist is not at all alien to Dutch culture; examples of artistic self-portraits in bordellos have a long-standing, one might say legendary, history in Northern European paintings of the sixteenth and seventeenth centuries (Renger 1970: 132; Raupp 1984: 311–28; and Chapman 1990: 118). The often-cited examples in relationship to Vermeer's painting are Rembrandt's self-portrait with Saskia of circa 1635 and Gabriel Metsu's self-portrait with his wife of 1661, both considered self-portraits as the biblical Prodigal Son and all, remarkably, in the same museum in Dresden. There are, however, many other examples from the sixteenth and seventeenth centuries which show the Netherlandish artist as a rake. Among those from Vermeer's century may be counted Adriaen Brouwer's *Carousers* in the Metropolitan Museum of Art in New York, Frans van Mieris's *Bordello Scene* in the Mauritshuis in The Hague, and innumerable paintings by Jan Steen. Whether we see Vermeer's figure as indeed a bona fide portrait or, as is more likely, a generalized representation of the artist, it certainly must be figured among the seventeenth-century's most telling accounts of the Northern artist's early identification with an illicit lifestyle and its representation.[8]

Vermeer's *A Maid Asleep* in the Metropolitan Museum of Art in New York (Fig. 2) is the painting whose relationship to the mercenary-love tradition is the least obvious and requires the most explanation. On all accounts, it is a complex and experimental painting. It has been interpreted in a variety of ways. Most often, because of the sleeping condition of the woman, it is related to the sin of sloth. Its formative stages, revealed through X rays (Fig. 3) and more modern technologies, show a myriad of changes which range from superficial fine-tuning to fundamental alterations in the design and the concept of the subject. Among the latter, the presence of a man either leaving or entering the room, seen through the *doorkijkje* or view through the open doorway, and the dog in the interim space looking at him are the most consequential. By including them in the initial conception of this subject, Vermeer was participating in conventions well established within the bordello type. He draws on Netherlandish visual history, which developed the representation of contempo-

FIGURE 3. Composite X ray of *A Maid Asleep*. Sherman Fairchild Paintings Conservation Department, The Metropolitan Museum of Art, bequest of Benjamin Altman, 1913 (14.40.611).

rary interiors as meaningful and as having particularly sexual connotations for the women who inhabit them. I have elsewhere traced the early history wherein the pictorial space is structured as an enclosure that is, I propose, defined as both a woman's space and a woman's sexualized body.[9] Thus, Vermeer here turns to the subject as it was formulated in the sixteenth century and modernized in the seventeenth by another Utrecht painter, Jacob Duck, as in his *Bordello Scene* in the Museum of Fine Arts in Dijon.[10]

Thus, a figure represented in the open doorway of an interior space that houses a woman can be connected to the sixteenth-century visual convention wherein that space figures the woman's open, licentious body (Salomon forthcoming). The convention was often used in the sixteenth and seventeenth centuries, and it was eventually presented in an emblem of around 1630. The image shows a man entering a room where a young woman, with legs apart, warms herself before a roaring fire. The inscription, loosely translated, reads, "Why bother to knock when the door is always open?"[11]

Jacob Duck's painting *A Sleeping Courtesan* (Fig. 4), present location unknown, at once recalls the older tradition and introduces certain changes that announce the type's future. The visual comparison between Duck's *Sleeping Courtesan* and the initial version of Vermeer's *A Maid Asleep* makes a strong argument for the iconographic connection between the two. The coin being tendered in Duck's painting relates this work on some level to the Dresden *Procuress* as well. The man's hat, withdrawn position, and diminished importance clearly compare to Vermeer's male figure. It is, however, Duck's focus on a sleeping maid at a table, itself a natural extension of his own developed specialty of portraying sleep within the *bordeeltje* tradition, that connects the two paintings in a remarkably close way. The relationship between these two paintings clarifies the position of Vermeer's early concept within the Netherlandish *bordeeltje* tradition and links this work with its most immediate predecessor in his own oeuvre, the Dresden *Procuress*.

Even before the more radical transformation that took place when he omitted the man altogether, Vermeer's formulation worked to move the subject away from the realm of *minne* and towards that of *liefde*. The absence of a bed in Vermeer's work softened the licentious nature of the room, and thus defined the room in a more ambiguous way. Furthermore, Vermeer physically separated the sleeping woman and the man, for although he is seen through the doorway, he is in a distant secondary room, which, among other consequences, given her sleeping state, functioned as a more naturalistic narrative. Vermeer's figure is even more idealized than Duck's. She has white rather than black pearl earrings and a youthful blush in her cheeks. All in all Vermeer's painting softened the sexual nar-

FIGURE 4. Jacob Duck, *A Sleeping Courtesan*. Location unknown.

rative in its initial stage and moved the image along the spectrum from denotative towards its ultimate state as connotative.

Finally, there is Vermeer's painting in the Frick collection in New York, *Officer and Laughing Girl* (Fig. 5), which can also be located within the sexual project of early Dutch genre painting. While it can be related to the guardroom tradition popularized by the early seventeenth-century genre painters in Amsterdam, Pieter Codde and Willem Duyster, and the genre paintings of the Utrecht Caravaggisti, its iconographic roots are more complex. The introduction of the soldier into the female-dominated milieu of the bordello was a development which once again can be attributed to Jacob Duck. The small painting on copper of around 1630 in the museum in Cambridge is but one solution to the problem in Duck's work

FIGURE 5. Johannes Vermeer, *Officer and Laughing Girl.* Copyright The Frick Collection, New York.

in this decade. It is, in fact, Duck's only painting to develop figures in a close-up, half-length view, connecting it closely with his compatriots, the Utrecht Caravaggisti. Duck's *Soldier and Laughing Girl* brings together the heterogeneous couple in a spirited way, reminiscent of the open expression of happiness and well-being seen in other Utrecht *Procuress* paintings. Yet Duck's couple is unencumbered by moralizing details. The picture instead develops a broad treatment of the prurient relationship between the two. This is played out in the contrast of masculine sexuality signaled by the pipe held by the soldier and feminine sexuality figured by the glass of wine held by the maid.[12] In the cramped space of the composition their arms cross.

Once again, the animation and caricatured quality of Duck's figures are characteristic for him at this early date. The broad, humorous treatment of heterosexual *joie de vivre* in the Cambridge painting links it to another tradition of early Netherlandish secular images, one which stands somewhat to the side of mercenary love per se and is best represented by the art of Pieter Huys in his various versions of *The Bagpipe Player and His Wife*, which date between 1560 and 1570.[13] In this spirited half-length composition, bagpipes, rather than smoking pipes, figure the masculine member, and open tankards, rather than a glass of wine, represent the woman's sex.[14] In a later version, signed and dated 1571, in the Staatliche Museum in Berlin, Huys included the indications of an interior space with a window behind the bagpipe player. The sexual innuendos are made all the more explicit by the inscription he inserted, which loosely translates: "Ay, leave it alone / it's a lost cause / to grab my purse / you have emptied it / and my pipe is all piped out."[15]

Similar, although more subdued, half-length depictions of soldiers and their mates were to have enormous popularity among artists working in the generation after Duck's. Ter Borch painted the subject a number of times. However, especially relevant to this group is Vermeer's *Officer and Laughing Girl* in the Frick collection in New York.

Looking at the three paintings together, Huys's, Duck's and Vermeer's, gives coherence and meaning to all three. And in doing so, one gains more than simply the revelation of a new subtradition in the tropes of venal love traced by early Netherlandish secular history. What is gained is access to the process of refinement and naturalization of the heterosexual subject as a favored narrative which occurred over the one hundred years or so from Huys, through Duck to Vermeer. The process works through Huys's burlesque bawdiness with its broad, vulgar expression of libidinous desire, to the still farcical, sexual innuendo in Duck's work, to the sanitized and romantic theater of Vermeer's painting. The normalization process takes place on the level of relationships, attributes, and space. The stage in which these scenes are played out goes far in establishing the mind-set necessary to understand them.

In the course of the next few years, Vermeer's pictures of male/female relationships take on a specifically more ambiguous quality, one that allows them to be read less as salacious and more as civil—that is, within the terms of respectability and decorum.[16] Here, civility becomes an alternate to sexuality as both the defining characteristic of the feminine and that which is figured by the feminine. *The Girl with the Wine Glass* in Braunschweig (Fig. 6) offers the bridge. Its connection with the earlier paintings is partially established by the presence of a soldier behind the table, who seems to be a bored participant of the event. It is also partially established by the strong affect of the "girl's" expression, smiling broadly and, in her unmoderated exuberance, showing her teeth. Some have explained her clear breach of decorum by postulating that she is already drunk (Washington 1995–96: 114–19). Let me suggest that this open sign of uncontrolled gaiety and emotion ties the painting, as a type, backward to *Officer and Laughing Girl*. It is a sign best understood in the nexus of cultural, sociological, and anthropological concerns connected by the term "civilizing process," introduced by Norbert Elias and integral to the work of such English and Dutch scholars as Peter Burke, Keith Thomas, Jan Bremmer, and Herman Roodenberg and the American art historian David Smith.

As Castiglione and Erasmus tell us, in the history of manners, as in the history of art, smiling women showing teeth generally signified lower-class status or the precivilized, childlike exuberance expressed, for example, on the occasion of having mastered a certain skill.[17] A good comparison can be made with Giovanni Francesco Caroto's *Boy with Drawing* in the Museo del Castelvecchio in Verona.[18] In all ways the "girl's" demeanor conflicts with the sophistication and status communicated by her dress and environment, which is elevated by the still life, the respectable burgher portrait on the back wall, and the emblematic stained glass window. She certainly is no courtesan, and yet she is no lady; nor will tropes of vice and virtue help us here. Yet the stained-glass image is usually

FIGURE 6. Johannes Vermeer, *The Girl with the Wine Glass*. Herzog Anton Ulrich-Museum, Braunschweig.

identified as an emblem of moderation and control. Moderation is not, however, the exclusive domain of alcoholic intake.

In the face of prevalent interpretations which see the man here as a suitor, may I suggest that we see him as an instructor, allowing for the theatrical convention wherein instructors often turn into suitors. With this interpretation, the work would then be also forward looking, participating in the same category of painting type as those Dutch genre paintings representing music, drawing, or writing lessons.[19] Vermeer's *Girl Interrupted at Her Music* in the Frick Collection in New York shares the same male model. What is being taught in the Braunschweig painting could be precisely the kind of social graces—for example, the proper way to hold a glass, an item that Gerard de Lairesse would emphasize in his later treatise on art—that would bring the woman up to the level of her dress.[20] Vermeer's formulation of this man with his theatrical cape, moustache, and low-bowing gesture makes plausible his identification as a comic Monsieur, comparable to the comic doctors in Jan Steen's paintings. It is, however, not necessary for my argument, which rests, in any case, not on any particular narrative reading but on the shifting terms of that reading. In the paintings after 1660, the terms of the feminine have decidedly changed. The topic of woman as the representation of certain constructs of gender and class sidles from a world defined by the physical qua sexual to a world defined by the metaphysical qua civilized, from the world of *minne* to the world of *liefde*.

The practice of cultural analysis is like a game of volleyball, where information and knowledge move back and forth between the courts of "then" and "now." A well-hit ball hits its mark and returns to the other court without touching the ground and ending the game. If the inquiry of sexuality and civility is in our court now, how does this reading of Vermeer fit our own structures for the constituencies of our social life? Why is Vermeer so compelling as an artist and idea? Surely his focus on women as a subject belongs in large measure to the answer of this question. We are delighted to speak about women in paintings and especially in these two zones of discourse, as physical, material, and sensuous abandon and as metaphysical, abstract, and ordered control. As the heirs of early-modern ideologies and their communicative structures, we welcome the opportunity to permit his paintings and their exhibition to channel communication between and among us. His works allow us to tell each other about ourselves by giving color and form, both literally and figuratively, to our values and feelings. Here too, we can shift endlessly between the sensuousness of the paint and the women, their glistening eyes and moist lips, to the cool, controlled order of the rooms, light, and pictorial design which forever locks the figures in their environment. For us, in the "now" court, Vermeer constitutes us as either/and/both sexual and civilized beings. Who could ask for more from an artist?

"Le cinéma d'après Lumière"

REREADING THE "ORIGINS" OF THE FILMIC IMAGE

Thomas Elsaesser

The Space, Not the Place

As members of ASCA, we derive particular pleasure from being divided between a discipline with which we have grown up, or which we represent, and a field that we have chosen to call "cultural analysis" but which we are at pains to help become a discipline as well as to prevent it from becoming one—each in roughly equal measure. More specifically, this position at the cusp of pleasure and anxiety refigures—and perhaps sometimes even disfigures—our approach to an area that seems constantly to put pressure on the very concept of cultural analysis: namely how to mark its relation to history, or rather, how to mark the temporal and spatial speaking position from which cultural analysts need to define their own historicity. That this can be a source of additional anxiety is self-evident, while on the other hand, it also, conceivably, frees energies that are at once "performative" and "analytical."

In the following, I want to look at this double conjuncture around an object of study—the cinema—which has itself only recently been accorded the status of a discipline—film studies—and which, precisely because of its somewhat "performative" position in the academy compared to literary studies or philosophy, is constantly called upon to construct for itself a viable relation to history, at the same time knowing full well that such a history is itself something constructed, and thus the function of a process that in many ways has only just begun, depending as it does on the space allowed to "cinema" in the humanities. Its "place" in the academy is largely secured thanks to the movies' popularity among the university's primary "clients," the students, and film's perceived relevance to society and to the creation of jobs in what is known as "the media," but its "space" (cultural, aesthetic) is far from uncontested. Film studies, in other words, is rarely recognized as having a discursive field of its own, because in each case the space is already well occupied by sitting tenants who are unwilling to cede but are ready to annex films as convenient evidence in an argument or as raw material for an analysis focused elsewhere. In this situation, "history" becomes a sort of outhouse where the suspect is permitted to hibernate, or await his turn. As a colleague from another discipline memorably put it to me: "Film history—why not? Everything can have a history."

So what sort of "history" can the cinema have? As I shall try to show, a film history is itself a function of the very different discursive or analytical spaces that one may be able to invoke. On the other hand, the cinema's presence in culture, and thus its availability for cultural analysis, is such that it almost militates against the pertinence of history as a necessary dimension of its understanding. Just consider how often the cinema is associated with childhood and adolescence when its pleasures are being recalled, and with sex, violence, and death when its social impact is being assessed: in each case, with states of mind and body that mark the very margins and thresholds of the historical while designating central concerns for cultural analysis.

The problem I want to raise therefore is quite simply this: does the cinema have a part in history, and more specifically, in the history of the twentieth century, or is its cultural importance for this century precisely that it casts doubt on the very concept of history as we have come to conceive it? Strategically, I may be committed to the view that without taking the cinema into account, we shall never understand our century, but I do not have to open recent histories of the twentieth century, by such eminent historians as Eric Hobsbawm (1994) or Paul Kennedy (1993), to know that I shall look in vain for even a mention of Sergei Eisenstein's *October* or Leni Riefenstahl's *Triumph of the Will*, let alone the Hollywood musical or the films of the French *nouvelle vague*. Therefore, my claim that film is central to the twentieth century must habitually be hedged by defensiveness. When asked—as I often am here in the Netherlands—what I do, I reply: "I'm a film historian." And when—as is often the case—a look of bewildered embarrassment creates a pause that threatens to become terminal to the conversation, I sometimes add, only half in jest: "but only up to 1895."

For what is film history? Most of us associate the cinema with a collection of names, some vivid memories, and pieces of time spent in the company of D. W. Griffith and *Intolerance*, German Expressionism and *Dr. Caligari*, Charlie Chaplin and Buster Keaton, the Russian montage school and the Odessa Steps in *Battleship Potemkin*, Busby Berkeley and *The Wizard of Oz*, Humphrey Bogart looking Ingrid Bergman in the eye for one last time in *Casablanca*, and Clark Gable frankly my dear-ing Vivien Leigh in *Gone with the Wind*. We may even feel a special surge at the mention of Hitchcock and Hawks, Snow White and Bambi, Renoir and Rossellini, Jean-Luc Godard, *The Godfather*, and *Jaws*.

Taken together, they stand for very contradictory values and entities, from film and the arts to cinema and politics; childhood fantasies mingle with aching stories of high romance, film *auteurs* cross the Hollywood-Europe divide, and blockbuster movies signify geopolitical marketing triumphs. In other words, film history—where it does not constitute a footnote to economics or a case study for sociology—seems, in the field of the humanities, to be mostly a matter of cultural semiotics, a series of precariously historical fantasies that we can share and exchange, but which are nonetheless located in a realm that does not yield either an artistic geography or a textual corpus. For what conceivable discursive or chronological space could contain all of these tokens and icons: Marilyn Monroe and the history of luxury theaters, the demographics of gathering audiences to sell them soft drinks and popcorn, the urban anomie of a Monica Vitti in Antonioni's *L'Avventura*, the patent wars over sound technology and Technicolor, and Charlton Heston as Moses parting the waves of the Red Sea? What is a film: five reels of celluloid in tin cans or an experience we shall never forget, a night out with friends or the chance to buy some time which is neither supervised nor even shared?

Of course, there is no shortage of film histories, whether of great artists and masterpieces, of artistic movements and stylistic influences, or of cross-referenced motifs and genres, transformed and passed down from cycle to cycle. There are also film histories that move from country to country, with even Denmark and Poland, Italy and India achieving their moment of glory center stage as each in turn dominates a decade. And finally, there are the histories of the cinema's manifest destiny, that of greater and greater realism: at first silent and black and white, then learning how to talk, eventually adding color, with wide-screen and Dolby sound completing the march of progress. These are, however, not histories but historical fictions, narratives reinforced with anecdote, left circulating in the culture precisely to keep the question of history at bay and to disavow a heterogeneity that threatens to capsize the entire enterprise. On the other hand, one might venture that if film studies as an academic discipline needs a reason to exist, then it is to point out pedantically all of the errors of fact and assumption that are enshrined in these so-called histories of the cinema.

One of the most persistent assumptions—and perhaps the foundation narrative upon which all histories of the cinema have been constructed—is that of the inevitability of cinema. Like a baton relay, or the pieces of a jigsaw puzzle, from Plato's parable of the cave to Balinese shadow plays, from Leonardo's studies of water in motion to Alberti's perspective, from camera obscuras and mechanical drawing aids to magic lanterns, fog pictures, and phantasmagorias, from dioramas and phenakistoscopes to thaumatropes and chronophotography, historians have been at pains to line up, indifferently, philosophical speculations, scientific experiments, aids to observation, and optical toys, in order to give the appearance of logic and cogency to the cinema's creation myth: the moment when on March 21, 1895, the Lumière brothers projected their first film, *Workers Leaving the Factory*, to an assembly of savants and amateur scientists at the Société Pour l'Encouragement de l'Industrie Nationale in Paris.

The Pioneers: Inevitability of an Invention or Archaeology of an Imagined Future?

If this seems an unduly polemical way of commemorating the centenary of the cinema, then it is merely to focus on the simple fact that cinema is an invention without origin, because it is without a goal, function, or use. Or rather, defining what actually is cinema—the series of photographs which capture movement, images mechanically transported to give the impression of continuous motion, the projected image, the development of instant photography, the invention of the cellulose sheet upon which light-sensitive emulsion could be painted, the showing of projected images to a paying public—is an eminently cultural decision, implying a choice of vantage point, a speaking position or a declaration of interest, from which alone a history becomes possible and meaningful.

For as we know from our own contemporary historical moment, which is witnessing an unprecedented surge of new imaging devices and recording apparatuses, the introduction of a new technology never simply occurs by way of an additive process, that is, by merely improving or extending what is already there. Instead, it reconfigures in its entirety the environment upon which such a practice may have an impact. It changes the field, and even more so the idea that we have of that field, making apparent connections which had always been there but never seemed to matter, and thereby also redefining the histories that can be imagined as having brought about these very changes.

To take a relatively simple example, the telephone has been in existence and use longer than the cinema, but only video, the electronic image, and digitization have shown the complex filiations that have always existed between these apparently distinct technological systems—technically, economically, and in the ways their uses could be envisaged. But then, the purist would argue, the electronic image is no longer cinema, thus making yet another cultural-aesthetic-ontological judgment by insisting that the cinema is forever wedded to photography, that is, to that "pencil of nature" by which a real object leaves a luminous trace on a sensitive surface, producing a representation at once iconic and indexical. Yet, as I have suggested, if one were to see the cinema not primarily under its aspect of representation but in the light of the social spaces it creates (for courting couples, for instance, or for the power and control fantasies of adolescent males), then the material supports of sound and image (i.e., celluloid) become less important than the knowledge that an evening at the movies means an experience conforming to a certain horizon of expectation which a given (sub-)culture has taught its members to construct.

But the telephone could also lead us to a quite different point of entry to the cinema. For example, if what makes the cinema socially relevant and historically significant is the unconstrained but by no means unstructured time it buys, then its first cousins are other forms of popular narrative, considered as artifacts modeling time, yet when adding the fact of modeling time to the kinds of affective engagement a movie affords, then the telephone does once more come to mind, for its emphatic contact and interactivity gives its user the pleasure of ostentatiously "wasting time." The need to waste time, on the other hand, is itself a function of a modernity which, via the technologies of transport, has standardized and synchronized time to a point where leisure is almost synonymous with escaping such time constraints. By a curious irony, however, chrono-photography (or serial photography), the one definite contender for the role of the cinema's true ancestor by virtue of having made possible the analysis of movement, was devised precisely in order to break down lived time and analyze the laboring body so that it could be fitted around the standardized time of the factory production process and be synchronized with the motion of machines. Thus, underpinning the cinema is a technology whose social uses functioned as the causes of a cultural malaise for which the cinema appeared to be the cure.

In other words, the multiple entry-points and hermeneutic circles that I have here briefly sketched make the cinema an eminently suitable subject for cultural analysis, yet they also indicate why, for the very same reason, the cinema is not a phenomenon with which historians are particularly comfortable. The field that I have tried to lay out lacks a causal nexus, displaces agency into circular reasoning, has no explanatory power, establishes neither motivating drive nor determining force, and most damaging of all is hard pressed to identify what it might rule out as evidence and, therefore, how it could critically approach its sources. On the other hand, if these criteria were my priorities, then I would risk missing what makes the cinema so different from, for instance, all the technologies on which it depends, from all the capitalist risk investments and service industries it so tediously resembles, and from all the arts it so carelessly plagiarizes or vigorously vampirizes.

It is this impasse, this oscillation between two unsatisfactory alternatives (a menu of master narratives masquerading as history and a history which merely seizes the lowest common denominator and thereby denies its object any specificity), which I see cultural analysis potentially addressing. This is why I believe that the cinema needs cultural analysis, but cultural analysis as a self-critical and self-reflexive practice might do well to keep in mind the awkwardly historical object which is cinema. What I mean by this is that the cinema obliges me to have recourse to what historians sometimes qualify as counterfactual history and what a colleague of mine, in a slightly different context, has referred to as possibilist history. Such a possibilist history is not the opposite of "real" history, or "wie es eigentlich gewesen ist," but is one capable of thinking into history all those histories that might have been, or might still be, conjuring the ghosts that shadow the living, and not unlike the cinema, peopled as it is by all the undead: Greta Garbo forever young and James Dean's Porsche never hitting the delivery truck on the road outside San Luis Obispo.

In the possibilist vein, for instance, one might learn something about the cinema by looking at the apparent losers of the first hour—men such as William Paul and Louis Le Prince, Georges Demeny and Birt Acres, the Skladanowsky brothers and William Kennedy Dickson. Such a project would explore not so much the archaeology of the cinema but the archaeology of all the possible futures of the cinema, what it was envisaged to engender at the moment it was "born," which means all the pasts it was supposed to continue. For what did the cinema initially claim to be doing other than proclaiming itself as just these pasts' most logical continuation?

But the point that I want to single out for such a counterfactual account is actually a slightly different one, namely the curious fact that just about all the so-called pioneers—Etienne-Jules Marey, Eadweard Muybridge, Thomas Edison, and the Lumière brothers—seemed to think that the cinema was an invention without much of a future. Marey, the scientist and "father" of chronophotography, had nothing but haughty disdain for anyone interested in reconstituting movement rather than analyzing it; he actually sacked his assistant Demeny for trying to beat the Lumières to the first projection device. Louis Lumière would later dismissively say, "Of my many inventions, the cinematograph was the one that cost me the least effort," and by 1902 he had apparently lost all interest in either making films or copyrighting them. Edison of all people had actually neglected to register the patents on his kinetoscope in Europe, thus allowing the Lumières and countless others to buy his machines, take them apart, and—as we would now call it—reverse-engineer them. Edison also did not think at first that projection would catch on; he thought that it made no sense to show the same film to hundreds of people when you could extract five cents from each at individual kinetoscopes.

While triumphalist historians usually see in such judgments only the hollow irony of "if only they had known," the counterfactual historian might pause and ponder these gestures of hesitation, of doubt and disconcertedness, trying to extract meaning from the very force behind the act of withholding assent or withdrawing interest.

Let There Be Louis Lumière

This gesture of hesitation seems perhaps most pregnant and intriguing in the case of Louis Lumière, who not only was without a doubt the most accomplished film director for almost a decade, but who is also known for a body of work forever associated with documentary and the cinematograph's ability to give access to unmediated reality. Lumière's diffidence, on the other hand, obliges us to locate an energy of friction between the cinematograph developed as an improved "system of chronophotography" and the films Lumière took with it, or rather with the way these films came to be read and thus appropriated. Traditional wisdom has it that Lumière's films are "animated" views of the subjects before his camera, brought to life as if by magic. As the Parisian journal *La Poste* was to write after the December 1895 performance at the Salon Indien: "Picture a screen on which appears a photographic projection. So far, nothing new. But suddenly, the image starts to move and comes alive, the door of a factory opening to let out a flood of men and women workers, with bicycles, dogs running, carriages; all that is moving, swarming. It's life itself, it's movement taken from life." That the films may also be something completely different has taken us, I think, some time to appreciate, but the evidence now seems inescapable. And yet this evidence is problematic, because it is analysis, interpretation—interpretation, furthermore, of a kind that is self-consciously ahistorical: it comes from a generation of avant-garde filmmakers and critics from the 1970s, thanks to whose structuralist and formalist preoccupations our eyes were sharpened for what is so extraordinary about many of Lumière's films, especially the ones taken by Louis Lumière himself. Quite generally, it was critics schooled in the works of the American and Canadian avant-garde of the 1960s who rediscovered early cinema, albeit with polemical intent. Trying to establish a pedigree for their own nonnormative and nonnarrative practice, they saw how sharply early films deviated from the classical film image, thus freeing those who came after from the presumptions of judging the films of the pioneers as either primitive or spontaneous. Their willingness to think that the development of the cinema could have been otherwise, and their sheer anachronistic perversity in reading, for instance, the Lumière films such as *Workers Leaving the Factory, Demolition of a Wall, Arrival of a Train,* and *The Card Players* as if they had been made by Paul Sharits, Hollis Frampton, or Michael Snow, acted as a powerful defamiliarization device. I remember looking at *Boat Leaving the Harbor* after reading an essay by Dai Vaughn (1981) and seeing in it nothing but the heartbreaking drama of whether the boat might ever reach not the open sea but the frame edge. Here was a constructivist film of the purest kind, dedicated to the proposition that the frame edge equals space edge, thus ironically both foreclosing off-screen space and implying it by its negation.

It was convincingly argued (Deutelbaum 1979) that the Lumière single-shot, single-scene films shot with a static camera setup were not, as traditional film history has it, "plotless" or "the recording of unadjusted, unarranged, untampered reality" (29) but highly structured wholes "reflecting a number of carefully chosen decisions about sequential narrative" (30). By attending especially to the beginnings and the endings, Deutelbaum was able to show that most Lumière films record actions and events in which the end either rejoins or inversely mirrors the beginning (opening and closing the factory gates in *Workers Leaving the Factory*), thus providing a very effective narrative closure. *Demolition of a Wall,* for instance, was usually shown forward and backward, forming a visual palindrome, and often concluded the program. Alternatively, their films enact what have been called "operational processes" such as the breaking up of a slab of coke, the firing of a canon, the demolition of a wall: in each case, the film's temporal and spatial organization foregrounds the causal or functional logic of the event itself, making the beginning of the action coincide with and reinforce the beginning of the film.

Furthermore, one can say that scope and duration of the actions are signaled in the films themselves, providing a form of narrative suspense and anticipation which generates active spectatorial involvement. In films like *The Sack Race* or *The Arrival of the Delegates,* there is evidence of a very complex "structural use of space," through a doubling of protagonists, a repetition of action, movement within the frame, and an "arrangement in depth," which all indicate a sophisticated formal sense inflecting the apparently artless presentation of "simple content." Framing and camera placement are chosen to heighten closure, balance, and symmetry and thus to "impart a shape to the action depicted" (p. 37).

In a similar vein, Noel Burch (1981) pointed out, from the vantage point of an avant-garde filmmaker turned film theorist and as a film theorist turned film historian, how the Lumière films were experiments in what he called the illusion of haptic space, as in the exaggerated depth of field in *Arrival of a Train*, which eventually overwhelms us, or in *Workers Leaving the Factory*, where it is the people moving past the camera that greatly increase the sense of depth, of space not only expanding and existing past the frame (thus invoking the inverse "structural principle" from what I saw at work in *Boat Leaving the Harbor*). Because of the permanent movement into the off-frame, the spectator implied in the Lumière films becomes the spectator par excellence of the cinema, distinct from the "materially unrestricted time of contemplation" that is available to the spectator of painting or still photography. Additionally, the frame itself, and the function of camera placement in centering the eye and at the same time in containing movement, initiates a play of masking and doubling which makes the Lumière film its own mise-en-abyme, far removed from any "referential transparency" which traditionally is attributed to Lumière as the father of documentary. *Workers Leaving the Factory* is of course also a supreme example of a multiplication of internal frames: the double doors, one big, one small; the opening of the gates; the workers going out; and the closing of the gates after the last one has left. There is an intricate mirroring of process represented and the process of representation in the length of action, which is made to be congruent with the length of film and creates additional suspense by the knowledge of the formal constraints which the 50 seconds or 16-meter filmstrip imposes on the filmmaker. The two frames complement each other: the spatial one, pregiven by the fixed camera position, and the temporal one, given by the film length, forming together the set of constraints which already act as an aesthetic system (precisely that which makes Louis Lumière the first *cinéaste*).

And yet this system seems to be informed as well by an economic or institutional constraint. Right at the end of *Workers Leaving the Factory*, one worker is seen going in the opposite direction, as if to say there is no final closure: a formalist point of balance and asymmetry perhaps, but one which leads to the more specifically historical conclusion that the Lumière films were meant to be seen over and over again, that they were built as if to parody and at the same time better the loops of Edison's kinetoscope. This seems particularly evident in *The Card Players*. Utilizing a pictorial motif borrowed from Cézanne, the film, in its temporal articulation, is built like a perpetual mobile, whose source of infinitely renewable energy is the coin we see the player on the left first pocket and then put down once more on the table in the very last frames, thus signaling the commencement of a new round. The cycle represents as it were the spectator's position en abyme, for she or he, too, is caught in the cinema as a *dispositif* or institution based on repetition, a repetition activated by the coin placed at the box office.

What is of interest in such an analysis—which perhaps goes beyond the pleasures always derived from self-indulgently ingenious interpretations—is the realization that it pays to ask where the "structural features" noticed by the avant-garde critic might have found their historical rationale, and how these historical rationales might have found in Louis Lumière their ideal embodiment (this raises questions of reception, of the frames existing for the audience in the conditions of performance and presentation). But as I have said, it is evident that the success of the *cinematograph*—its technical superiority over the many similar machines—has to be thought of as different from, indeed distinct from, the films themselves, but that neither is conceivable without reflecting on the professional identity of the Lumières, namely as businessmen interested in promoting the use of their patented software: photographic plates (the famous *étiquette bleue*), which were increasingly used in the domestic environment of the amateur photographer and for which the Lumières were constantly developing new uses and applications.

It is therefore important to point out how strongly Louis Lumière's conception of cinematography was dictated by the practice of the photographic view, itself a tradition of thinking about images and a way of seeing deriving from at least a century of the picturesque but also implying an act of visual possession. The latter was enhanced by one of the view's most widespread variants, namely the stereoscope, which was popular as parlor entertainment and was also a publicly consumed show, having its heyday—with the machines developed by Charles Wheatstone and David Brewster—in the 1860s, and being revived in the 1890s with August Fuhrmann's Kaiser-Panoramas, circular carrousels where up to 24 people could sit and look in turn at a slowly revolving stereoscopic slide show. Without recalling just what the fascination of stereo images once was, it may be difficult to understand why Louis Lumière attached so much importance throughout his life to three-dimensional seeing. But the subtlety found in his film sequences staged in depth, his use of off-screen space, and the axis and angle of vision seem connected to a particular way of looking, which we need to understand in conjunction with stereoscopy. We should, however, avoid the danger of regarding his techniques as illusionism, and of claiming, as Noel Burch does, that three-dimensional seeing became irrelevant with the advent of the so-called "classical" cinema of continuity editing and mobile-point-of-view narration.

On the contrary, Lumière's practice, characterized at once by excessive symmetry (if looked at from the vantage point of illusionism) and the symmetry of excess (if seen as the careful and deliberate multiplication of planes of action, focal points of attention, and gradations in scale and distance), points in a quite opposite direction. For him the image is constructed not at all in conformity with the laws of perspective and the single vanishing point (the markers of the classical image), but according to logic that forces the eye out of the pictorially trained, monocular perspective. This logic splits the eye, pressing it to perceive the image as a bi-level or even tri-level representation, at once flat and in depth, at once unified and divided, at once anamorphic and hieroglyphic. In a remarkable way, the eye is enticed to scan the image, to seek out the deftly multiplied points of interest and attraction.

Apart from the already mentioned examples, such as *Workers Leaving the Factory* or *The Card Players*, one could cite the extraordinary *The Washerwomen*, with its frontal staging and triple picture-plane doubled by multiple action-spaces, or *The Fake Cripple*, with its left-right division, doubled by a foreground-background division, which allows the policeman to be visible to us—as the beggar's nemesis—for a veritable eternity before he eventually accosts the unfortunate faker, forcing him to run and the policeman to give chase. A similar anamorphosis—this time not in space but in time—can be observed in *Horse-Drawn Barrel*, in which a seemingly endless number of horses trot through the frame until we finally see what they are pulling: the enormous boiler drum of a steam engine or a locomotive—symbolizing, as one contemporary critic shrewdly remarked, the patient toil of the nineteenth century in ushering in the twentieth.

The fascination of the Lumière films, I would argue, comes in no small measure from something which—through avant-garde eyes—we can perceive as both a philosophical reflection and a formalist exploration of cinematic representation, a metacinema, if you like, before there was even cinema, yet a metacinema which, from another perspective, is merely the improved continuation of a history—that of stereoscopy—which we appear to have forgotten (Crary 1990). On the other hand, it is this avant-garde, always at the margins, always opposed to both realism of the documentary kind and illusionism of the Hollywood kind, and always insisting that "it could have been otherwise," which makes the link to a virtuality we can recognize as ours, and for which we could—quite anachronistically and yet with historical justification—claim Louis Lumière as godfather.

For one of the most salient features of the Lumière system, as I tried to show, is its excessive symmetry and its peculiar ability to create a mise-en-abyme of both space and time. Were I to venture into territory usually not open to a historian of a technological device such as the cinematograph, I would no doubt want to ask myself whether a life and a work lived with a brother had something to do with the inner logic of this system, since Louis was bound to his brother not only by blood ties but by the open secret of a pact "that formally acknowledged that [they would] collaborate in the most complete and absolute fashion" throughout their lives (Wakeman 1987: 700). Was this pact not itself a symmetry of excess, especially when we consider that "Louis was married to Rose, the sister of his brother's wife, and the two families lived in facing apartments in the same villa while the two brothers worked side by side in the same laboratory" (ibid.: 701).

Be that as it may, perhaps it would not be too counterfactual to conceive of the first moving pictures not so much as exercises in animating or bringing to life what had hitherto been static and frozen (the effects that a Georges Méliès so appreciated at the first Lumière showings, and from which he drew maximum effect in his own films), but as a kind of perversely improved version of the stereoscope. After all, moving pictures could generate more effectively and more efficiently the impression of a new kind of space, apparently three-dimensionally illusionist but actually structured so as to allow for entirely novel readings of the visual field and experiences of pictorial space. At the same time, moving pictures were committed neither to the aesthetics of perspectival realism nor to the effects of illusionism, both of which were to determine the history of cinema in direct proportion—so one might surmise—to Louis Lumière's disaffection with and lack of interest in the future uses of his own invention.

At this juncture, it is perhaps just as well to recall that the scientific point about stereoscopy, about three-dimensional vision, is precisely that it occurs not via the retina and in the eye, but as a computational process in the brain: it is a cognitive effect, in other words, rather than a perceptual fact. And when we recall that stereoscopy, far from having fizzled out as a nineteenth-century fad, is to this day crucial in space research and weather reports, and in the form of photogrammetry remains an essential tool for topographical measuring and surveying, then a none-too-distant line connects, after all, the cinematograph considered as an improved system of chronophotography with the first Lumière films considered as stereoscopic cognitivist exercises. The taking of successive images and the converting of their temporal distance into a spatial distance in order to reconstruct volume, mass, and contours also allows us to understand why Lumière might have been interested in sonar probes capable of measuring the topography of different terrains—an aural stereoscopy if you like. And what about Louis Lumière's interest in artificial limbs? The standard history of the stereoscope informs me that since Oliver Wendell Holmes applied stereoscopy to the design of the replacement limbs fitted to American Civil War veterans, doctors have continued to this day to use stereoscopy in order to calculate and thereby optimize the motor coordination of patients obliged to wear prostheses.

"Le cinéma d'après Lumière"

The victory of illusionism in the cinema is thus, in a sense, merely the trace of a positivist history behind which stand innumerable possibilist or counterfactual histories: those symbolized by Louis Lumière as the first master of the virtual. It is a mastery he achieved by seeing into and through the illusionism that his cinematograph could—but need not—give rise to, and by putting into his own films the detail and precision he would expect of a scientist and an engineer, while following an agenda as idiosyncratic and personal as it proved to be prescient—in and for another history: that of the filmic image. We might say that Lumière's disaffection with the cinema at the threshold of the twentieth century has preserved him for the twenty-first century—for the complexities and also the possibilities which the paradigm of the virtual is bound to bring in its train as the cinema becomes not so much a virtual medium as the first medium of virtuality, in more senses than one. And whether one regrets this virtuality or sees in it a new adventure of the human spirit, one can salute Louis Lumière as one of its ancestors and begetters. This may well be the only way that the discrepancy between "place" and "space," with which I opened, can be bridged, and the only way that the difference between the cinema's contemporary relevance and its right to a history of its own can be "sublated" and made productive in and for cultural analysis. We have cause for celebration, after all, with the cinema turning one hundred and ASCA turning one. And now when I am asked what I do, instead of saying "film history, but only until 1895," I can add, with a nod in the direction of counterfactual history, virtuality, and cultural analysis, "and possibly after 1995," but in any case, always "after Lumière."[1]

Killing Men and Dying Women

GESTURE AND SEXUAL DIFFERENCE

Griselda Pollock

This paper is an exploration of "doing cultural history" as a practice of cultural analysis. That involves bridging the divided domains into which culture is segregated. As an art historian, I focus on high art: what people designated as artists produce within a historical field. As Director of the Centre for Cultural Studies at Leeds, my remit is far wider: representation and its diverse apparatuses and institutions. My recent work, aiming to avoid the split personality involved in these two types of academic projects, considers moments of conjunction in which I can hinge high-cultural practices to those in the popular domain in order to track across a cultural moment the continuities and structurally determining discontinuities which alone might allow us both to grasp the wider ideological and cultural conditions in which "artists" make "art" and, at the same time, to undermine the false dividing walls that keep "popular culture" separate from high art.

The impetus, however, for this study derives from the necessities and problematics of feminist studies in cultural history and analysis. Never simply a matter of shifting existing methods and theories to other subjects: women, feminist cultural studies and histories disturb the very frameworks that have been established for cultural analysis. Sexual difference, what it means, how it is produced, lived, negotiated, how it shapes and

FIGURE 1. Sidney Waintrob, *Lee Krasner, 30 August 1956*, seated with her *Prophecy* on her right. Photograph © Sidney Waintrob, New York. Used with permission of Mr. Waintrob.

is shaped by representation and cultural practices, is, for me at this moment, the compelling perplexity for an academic adventure that demands realignments of both the forms and the contents of knowledge. I have taken this on at a critical moment of high modernism—abstract expressionism—and at a culturally significant moment in the histories of the postwar settlement—Eisenhower's America.

The art-historical problem goes like this: In 1956 the American painter Lee Krasner (Fig. 1), an abstract painter since the 1930s, was unnerved when she produced a semi-figurative painting called *Prophecy* (Robert Miller Gallery, New York). The shock of this painting lay in its radical deviation from the disciplined abstraction, the systematic surface-making, the dramatic play of color and form through collage that had characterized Lee Krasner's work as a major player in New York painting since 1940. Out of Picasso's *Demoiselles d'Avignon* (1907), in Willem de Kooning's *Woman I* (1952), large, fleshy, pink figures press against the picture frame that hardly contains the not-quite-human forms. In the upper right-hand corner, one large incised but sightless eye hovers in the curtain of black that borders the painting. "The image was there, and I had to let it out. I felt it at the time. *Prophecy* was fraught with foreboding. When I saw it, I was aware it was a frightening image" (Krasner, in Munro 1979: 116). On July 12, 1956, Lee Krasner departed for a trip to Europe and a break from the worsening relations between herself and her husband, the painter Jackson Pollock. He had shared her uneasiness about the painting, advising her to paint out the incised eye. She left *Prophecy*, however, on the easel, unchanged. Within a month she received a phone call informing her that Jackson Pollock had been killed in a car crash on August 11. She returned to the United States as the artist's executor and sole heir, responsible for the management of the estate of the "most famous living American painter." In the next eighteen months, Krasner's own work became the site of an important struggle for her own continuing artistic identity as Lee Krasner, for now, in her husband's permanent absence, she was perhaps more than ever captured and erased by her role as "Mrs. Jackson Pollock"—or rather, "the widow of Jackson Pollock" (Wagner 1989).

On her return to the United States, Lee Krasner had to deal with *Prophecy*: "I had to confront myself with this painting, again, and I went through a rough period in that confrontation" (Krasner, in Nemser 1975b). Out of this unexpected turn in her own work, Lee Krasner eventually produced a series of paintings, one of which, *Sun Woman I* (1957, New York, private collection), is the object of this analysis. How did Lee Krasner get to this painting? What are we seeing?

In feminist interventions in art's histories, we have to confront the problem of how to see what artists who are women produce. Their works come to us already framed by existing cultural discourses that define the meaning of the period and practices within which the artists worked. Such frames can make the work perfectly invisible, and worse, illegible except as something lacking in relation to what the dominant discourse produces as the canon. It is my contention that the artists who are women work across a doubled field. As ambitious painters shaped by the formation we call the avant-garde, they must negotiate the conditions of their own intervention just like any other. They must evolve their own gambits in the complex play of "reference, deference, and difference" (Pollock 1992). The resources from which they will inevitably draw to do so will include dimensions of social, cultural, psychic, and even corporeal experience that is unacknowledged by a phallocentric culture. Such experience is not gendered in essence, but our minds, memories, and bodily sensations are marked by the process that, in shaping our subjectivity, demands its submission to an always-already and yet constantly renegotiated organization of sexual difference. How can this be spoken of without letting an interest in the difference—call it femininity—radically undermine our concern with the making of art? Why should femininity negate the status of the art produced in dialogue with the psychic or corporeal specificity associated with the feminine?

This study offers a lengthy footnote to this major feminist problem, probing the necessary relations between a woman who is an artist, her cultural moment, and the discursive terms available for historical analysis and interpretation. In the 1950s, such a confrontation was framed through as rigid a sexual division and ideological polarization of gender as we have seen since the mid-nineteenth-century creation of the doctrine of separate spheres. The war against fascism and the postwar settlement under American hegemony, which produced the Cold War against so-called Red fascism, interrupted the historical struggle for a modernization of sexual difference that has been the major impetus of the early twentieth century: what we can call the generation of 1928. I use this date because it stands for the decade which politically and culturally represents a major moment not just of modernist culture but of the struggle for a "new woman." It thus becomes another moment in which we can establish profound historical and philosophical connections between femininity, representation, and modernity. It was not until the revolt of the generation of 1968 that a revitalized feminist movement repoliticized the question of gender. High modernist culture had disavowed gender in the name of socially transcendent universalism, censoring any reference to social and personal contingency within the purified domain of art. At the same time, within the dominant ideology that permeated popular culture, a rigid division of the sexes was reinstalled, asserting the absolute difference between masculinity and femininity that pop art would later ironize.

The profound and impossible antagonism between the terms *woman* and *artist*, still unchanged within modernism even if publicly disavowed in the name of transcendent truths, played their disfiguring games in the 1940s, and especially the 1950s, in the United States in ways which did not, however, prevent two generations of artists who were women from sharing in the ambitious enterprise that was American abstract and gestural painting in those decades.

To do so, they had to take a considerable risk. They had to stay near enough to the action to be part of it and grasp what was on offer. They had to make a space within which to make a difference, to make their own particular difference, which resulted from the whole complex of who each one of them was, while endlessly dodging the curatorial sniffing out of what would be deadly to their desires for recognition, the contaminating signs of a disqualifying "femininity." In this study, I want to take the reader on a journey through the ideological thickets of the avant-garde moment as it played out in the 1950s in order to be able to "see" one or two paintings by one artist, Lee Krasner. About these few paintings by Lee Krasner, I will not have much to say, for I hope they will start to look different, to become visible within a feminist vision, open to a different kind of debate. The idea is to create a different frame that acknowledges the play of difference so as to suggest how an artist like Lee Krasner dealt with the necessary, and inevitable, confrontation with the powerful artistic figures who dominated the field in which she also wanted to be an acknowledged artistic presence. Did she do it by "killing men"? Perhaps, for she certainly was not a "dying woman."

Some Word Play; or, Gentlemen Prefer Blondes, They Say

"Killing men" could imply that someone is killing men: men are the object of homicidal attack. On the other hand, "killing" could be an adjective, qualifying the character of men, making them the active subject of

FIGURE 2. *Marilyn Monroe in Korea*, performing songs from *Gentlemen Prefer Blondes* (1953) before U.S. troops, February 16–20, 1954. Copyright Corbis-Bettman/UPI.

violence: men who kill. Killing men are soldiers, for instance, warriors in a cold war perhaps. A similar undecidability nestles in the second phrase of the title: "dying women." When spoken, it is a little exemplar of what Derrida called *différance*. "Dying" could be heard to suggest that women are meeting their death. Women d-i-e. It could also suggest women changing the color of something. Women d-y-e. In the 1950s, what women dyed was their hair. And there was only one color that signified dyeing, because we all know that Gentlemen Prefer Blondes.

In her cultural critique and autobiographical reflection on "Blondes," Teresa Podlesney writes: "Gentlemen prefer Blondes, but only if their roots don't show. I am determined to make mine visible" (1991: 70).

A moment in American culture of the 1950s was paradigmatic of modern culture internationally. Dying women met killing men and dying men had to be killed—metaphorically, in paint. One of the key personae of this moment is Marilyn Monroe, made stellar by Twentieth Century Fox's release in July 1953 of the film of Anita Loos's novella and Broadway play, *Gentlemen Prefer Blondes*. In the role of "dumb blonde" gold digger Lorelei, Marilyn Monroe condensed a history of woman as image in the cinema within that decade's cinematic myth of femininity.[1] The other key character is the painter Jackson Pollock—himself almost a method actor and, as a result of some spectacular publicity and photography, the high-art version of the masculinity that Marlon Brando in his wildest role would project on screen.[2] Jackson Pollock was cast as a symbol of modern, American artistic masculinity.

They look so different: Marilyn and Jackson (Figs. 2 and 3). Crude as such a juxtaposition is, it underlines the fact that the 1950s was a decade of extreme gender polarization when the postwar American state attempted to put the genie back in the bottle by making all the Rosie the Riveters of the war years go home, bake brownies, and live the suburban dream that Betty Friedan would expose in 1963 as a nightmare, the problem with no name: the feminine mystique (1963). Yet, at another level, Marilyn and Jackson, icons of America in the 1950s, are disturbingly convergent. Both died unnecessary and tragic deaths: Jackson Pollock on August 11, 1956, at the age of 44, and Marilyn Monroe at the age of 36 on August 4, 1962. Both deaths created the absence of the subject in history that paradoxically made each of them an object of commercializing and academic myth. Both deaths have fueled a fascination with a mythic identity suddenly augmented by mortality.

Many artist-women survived the decade, its art politics and its gender politics. Neither dyed nor dying, Lee Krasner lived into creative old age; she was born in 1908 and died in 1984, aged 76. Helen Frankenthaler, born in 1928, is still alive and working, as is Grace Hartigan, born in 1922. Elaine de Kooning (1928–89), Joan Mitchell (1926–92), Louise Nevelson (1900–1988), and Alma Thomas (1891–1978) all lived into old age—but not really into history, canonization, or myth. While we celebrate with

FIGURE 3. "Jackson Pollock: Is he the greatest living painter in the United States?" *Life Magazine*, August 1949. Photograph of Jackson Pollock copyright Arnold Newman. Used with permission of Arnold Newman Studios, Inc.

unabashed adulation the modern masters such as Picasso or de Kooning, who enjoyed considerable longevity, there is no comparable discourse that accords venerated status to the long-lived artist who is a woman.

Did they make it by killing men rather than becoming dying women? Is creativity a necessarily sadistic, even murderous activity? I derive this idea not from a repertoire of feminist man-hating, but from the work of Georges Bataille and, later, Clement Greenberg. Both writers posed modernism as an act of extermination, seeing art as freeing itself from those legacies of association with other arts that impeded the discovery of what Mallarmé in 1875 called "steeping painting in its own cause" (Greenberg 1940: 303). For Greenberg, Manet was an artist who took on traditional subject matter and exterminated it on the canvas, while Bataille saw Manet creating a new form of meaning for painting that lies in the release of sadistic and erotic acts of "obliteration."

As part of this same logic, Bataille defined the role of surface in painting differently from what we are accustomed to see through formalist criticism. The surface of the painting can be imagined as a kind of lid, which conceals its deadly freight, as a tombstone in a graveyard covers up a corpse. Attracting us and yet obscuring the view, the lid could also lead down a thread of association to Pandora's box, the image in Greek myth that evokes a container with both a deadly content and a seductively beautiful surface, the box being both the woman Pandora and her invisible, but mortifying, sexuality. The myth of Pandora is a critical one for my text. The phallocentric version conjugates danger and death with any form of interiority, linking both to Woman's body while rendering women's curiosity about feminine sexual interiority a deadly mistake. *Box*, *tomb*, *sex*, these terms together with the painted surface create a chain of fantastic signifiers that circle around a feminine Other, sliding into death, with secrets that mortify, and an imaginary feminine body on the edge of both abjection and ecstasy (Fer 1995: 160).

In a recent paper that aims to interrupt the fetishistic and voyeuristic logic of the phallocentric culture encoded in the myth of Pandora's box, Laura Mulvey has reclaimed the image of the dangerous beauty of woman as both a treacherous surface and a deadly, death-dealing interior (1992). Displacing these equally negative images, she reformulates the tale to produce an aesthetics of feminine curiosity, a desire to know about the feminine interior or rather about the interiority, subjectivity, and sexuality of the feminine—as yet hardly knowable under the phallic regime of meanings which attribute to Woman only a negative dimension. She uses this feminist revision of the myth to imagine both a feminist pleasure in knowledge and the possibilities of enquiring feminist aesthetic practices.

The blonde cinema star Marilyn Monroe can stand as a modern incarnation of the masculine Pandoran fantasy—a glittering, artificial surface. Such a fabricated image functioned as a representational obstacle for women, who as artists might have needed to break through the excessive and fetishistically fabricated carapace called femininity to explore for themselves the kind of interiority—physical and psychic—that was imagined as the possibility of post-surrealist abstract painting, which was mythically represented only by the tragic hero—exclusively in the masculine—of a Promethean quest: Jackson Pollock.

But, I shall suggest, women as artists engaged, Pandorically, in a strategy of feminine curiosity, and located at the heart of the modernizing enterprise in painting, may have had to "kill"—in a Bataillean sense—to gain access to it.

Hot Lady in a Cold Zone

"It was in 1953–4 that Monroe became indistinguishable from her image—so much so that whatever she might do she would never seem out of character. Her bombshell performance in Niagara, and the back-to-back release of How to and Gentlemen made her the nation's number one box office attraction for 1953–4" (Hoberman 1994: 11). Consider the following conjunctions: the first issue of Playboy (Dec. 1953); the English translation of Simone de Beauvoir's Second Sex (1953); publication of the Kinsey Report Human Female Sexuality (1953); release of Gentlemen Prefer Blondes (1953) (Podlesney: 1991). Shortly after gracing the cover of the initial issue of Playboy, Marilyn Monroe was again in the headlines because of her marriage to the famous baseball star Joe DiMaggio. Amidst a blaze of publicity, they honeymooned in Japan. Monroe was invited to perform for the troops then guarding the frontiers of the Free World against the Red Peril in Korea, the first major military front opened up in the so-called Cold War. The war itself was over; a truce had been signed in the summer of 1953. To entertain the troops still guarding the border, Monroe agreed to put together a show based on her numbers from her 1953 box-office hits. She performed ten times in four days between February 16 and 20, 1954.

In freezing, sub-zero temperatures, scantily clad in a clinging lavender dress and shoes that barely deserve the name, she sang "Bye, Bye Baby" and "Diamonds Are a Girl's Best Friend" to a hooting, laughing, and applauding male audience that had in fact never seen the films from which the songs came. But Monroe was already the pinup of the American troops, extensively photographed, reproduced in magazines and calendars. A MASH team in Korea had voted her "the girl we would most like to examine." On the final show of the tour, the troops rioted. The Army launched an investigation into Monroe's activities in a Cold War zone, while a disaffected reporter for the *New York Times* referred to the concurrent hearings on the Army by leading Cold War zealot Senator Joe McCarthy. Bemoaning the exposure of such weakness of morale in the overexcited and "feminine" way the soldiers responded to Monroe, the reporter's comparison of them to bobby-soxers was fuel for this domestic investigation as well as for America's "enemies": "Their conduct must have delighted the Communists and all who hope for signs of degradation and decline in the United States" (quoted in Hoberman 1994: 11).

Marilyn Monroe was sent to galvanize the troops—with what? She was an American. But how she was "American" in that political climate was based on her vanilla-ice-cream whiteness, for as Richard Dyer has argued, "the ultimate embodiment of the desirable woman" is not simply the white woman "but the blonde, the most unambiguously white you can get. . . . Blondeness, especially platinum (peroxide) blondeness is the ultimate sign of whiteness" (1986: 42–43).

Monroe was on offer to the killing men as a sex symbol. She is not a symbol of her sex, and certainly not of her sexuality. As Luce Irigaray has argued, in patriarchal society there is only one sex of which anyone can be a symbol (1985). Reworked through codes of dress, hair, makeup, and, nowadays, body sculpting through exercise and dieting, woman's body as image, however, signifies masculine anxiety about sexual difference that is deferred through the psychic defense of fetishistic scopophilia: covering up the danger of feminine otherness so that, remade as image, "she" presents a perfect, seamless, and reassuring surface. The beautiful mask is, however, double-edged. While allaying the fear that difference inspires, it also marks its very spot. Fetishism merely veils what remains menacingly hidden: displacing and yet intensifying the threat of what is concealed beneath that glossy packaging. Pandora's box suggests the oscillating movement between surface and interior, between masculine subject and that which, as its Other, can never cease to provoke his anxiety and reworking.

The Most Famous Living American Artist

Why did they not think to send the most famous living American artist to Korea to galvanize the troops? In August 1949, *Life Magazine* ran an article on Jackson Pollock under the headline "Is he the greatest living painter in the United States?" and featuring a photograph by Arnold Newman of the artist in paint-splattered denims with a cigarette dangling from his lips, standing in front of *Summertime*. Willem de Kooning commented when he saw the article, "Look at him standing there, he looks like some guy who works at a service station pumping gas." Budd Hopkins is reported as having said:

He had everything. He was the great American painter. If you conceive of such a person, first of all, he had to be a real American, not a transplanted European. And he should have big Macho American virtues—he should be rough and tumble American—taciturn ideally—and if he is a cowboy so much the better. Certainly not an Easterner, not someone who went to Harvard. He shouldn't be influenced by the Europeans so much as he should be influenced by our own— the Mexicans, the American Indians and so on. He should come out of native soil—a man who comes up with his own thing. And he should be allowed the great American vice, the Hemingway vice, of being a drunk. It's no wonder that he had a popular Life magazine success, because he was so American and unique, and quirky and he had this great American face. Everything about him was right. (quoted in Naifeh and Smith 1989: 595)

Pollock also appeared in film and photography. Hans Namuth photographed Jackson Pollock at work during the summer of 1950 and then, in the fall, began two films with Paul Falkenberg, a past associate of German directors G. W. Pabst and Fritz Lang. The first film was in black and white and showed Jackson Pollock painting in his cold barn at the Springs, East Hampton, Long Island; the later one was in color and included some famous outdoor shots. Both Namuth films and photographs offer us a crucial kind of access to the problem of sexual difference and painting precisely in that failure to coincide with the prevailing representation of the modern artist.

As photo documentaries, Namuth's photographs locate Pollock's performance in a totally different space from that of Monroe's. It is the un-heated but interior space of the studio at the Springs, a seemingly private place where the artist worked alone with his materials. The artist in the studio had become a major trope of early-twentieth-century vanguardism (Duncan 1993). This iconography confirmed the artist as a symbol of art as surely as Monroe was made through cinema and pinup into a symbol of sex.

Hans Namuth's photographs of Jackson Pollock—who became, per-haps as a result of these images, the most famous sign of "body of the painter" of the modernist century—frame the space of the producing body and his activity not as the studio, a social space of encounter between culture—the artist and his work—and its resource—nature/woman/other —but as the canvas from which that other has been banished. The un-framed and uncut canvas lies on the floor receiving the flurry of his gestures, which mark and record the artist's presence to declare, however, a Dionysian rather than an Apollonian masculine creativity. The sexual hierarchy directly pictured in the prototypical modernist image of artist in studio with nude female model is not visualized directly in Namuth's images. But the legacy is surely there in the potency and activity of the masculine body now directly mastering the canvas, which has subsumed into its uncharted space the once-necessary feminine object, the sign of painting's referent, that from which art is made because art is other to it. The artist patterns the canvas's displacing and condensed surface with his signature, overlaying lid, screen, and mirror with his painted, or dripped, and even urinated inscriptions as he dances around its immense, inviting, but also threatening expanse.

I am not suggesting something so crude as that the canvas now equals Woman. Rather, I want to open up the possibility that the struc-tural relations between artist/world/art involved a mediating term for which the nude female model had stood in symbolic explorations of the act of making art in the early-modernist moment. This structure is both a product of, and the condition for, a historically particular ordering of sexual difference, articulated through the symbolic site of the studio.[3] Ab-stract painting such as Pollock's banishes that middle term, to leave us with both a practice, and a representation of that practice, that sets up a dyadic reflexivity between painter and painting. But I want to mark the point of disappearance of the body of Woman and suggest the lingering trace of that once necessary feminine Other projected now, as one of many dimensions and associations, onto the space of inscription — the canvas as both a mirror in which the artist will inscribe his mark and a screen which might veil the feminine term. Thus, instead of the painting registering the process of artistic transformation of something in the world, a referent of a different order, the canvas becomes the support for marks that immediately make it the other to that marking, involving it both formally and psychically in a dialectic with the painted trace. The canvas as the field of action, the support of paint, the surface for inscription as much as for the inevitable projection of fantasy, can thus play a variety of roles in this art of worldly renunciation. I merely want to introduce into its multiple registers traces of the Other (historically coded as feminine and figured through the female body) that had been structural to the self-conception of the virility of modernist art, and that, paradoxically, becomes all the less mastered by disappearing into the infinite otherness of the unrolled sheet/space of the unprimed canvas.

Between, therefore, these two incommensurate icons of the 1950s, Marilyn Monroe and Jackson Pollock, structural binaries were reified: high art and popular culture, painting and cinema, art and commodity, authenticity and artifice, masculinity and femininity. Between their opposition, which was also a structural complementarity, painting — as opposed to dying — women were caught in dilemmas and riddles posed by the gender polarities of that culture which were inevitably but the form of these many divisions. Part of the current feminist project is to dismantle the falsely dividing walls that segregate areas of social practice so that we can track what Foucault called the discursive regularities that constitute the formations of gender, class, and race between high and low, elite and mass, because they all end up meeting in *Life* — the magazine that is. I am looking for signs of the discourse and negotiated practices constitutive of a historical regime of sexual difference so that I can begin to answer the question: what would it be to be a woman painter caught in the inevitable web between these two representational scenes that produced such diametrically opposite and yet mutually confirming symbols: a symbol of art and a symbol of sex? Both served to symbolize each element as one, and that one was the masculine. For both were symbols within a single system: a white, phallocentric, and imperial culture that denied, however, any symbol or "representational support" to the identity of a creative femininity. It was clear that to aspire to be an artist meant the total negation, not of being a woman, but of being Woman, yet being a woman meant it was not likely that anyone could recognize you as an artist, however much or well you painted. It is this contradiction that I want to explore.

Looking for Difference

In our search to develop a feminist analysis of the relations between subjectivity, art, and sexual difference, in *Old Mistresses* (1995 [1981]), Rozsika Parker and I turned to the Hans Namuth photographs of Pollock painting in 1950. We juxtaposed a series of photographs by Ernst Haas of Helen Frankenthaler at work in 1969. We used the juxtaposition to ask some heretical, feminist questions: What is the difference that these images may allow us to see being inscribed? Does Pollock's slashing and throwing of paint, his gyrations around a supine canvas, enact a macho assault upon an imaginary feminine body? Are the traces of paint on canvas the residues of a psychic performance? Is this *écriture/peinture* masculine at its most vivid? How then could we read Helen Frankenthaler's pouring, pushing, smoothing gestures as she stood on the canvas, or knelt near its edge as a surface continuous with her space and her body's large spreading or delicate shaping movements. Is this a feminine modality inviting us to invent metaphors that might link female bodily experience to fluidity in order to account for the sensuousness and lusciousness of her effects?

To raise the specter of the feminine in talking of a painter who is a woman is to tangle with a complex historical legacy that she must disavow and we must theoretically question. It is a conundrum we cannot avoid as historians or as feminists. The term "feminine" marks the place of the recalcitrant issue of sexual difference and the riddles of how we, named women, live it and create within its unsettled and contradictory formations. Precisely because the Namuth and Haas photographs abandon the formal iconography of artistic portraiture for the mundane record of painting as activity/action, do these gestures of laboring, painting bodies register some profoundly different way of being in the body and of being a differentiated, psychically imagined corporality in that actual, as well as symbolic, or phantasmatic space — the canvas/studio — the products of which a viewer will, later, read according to prevailing cultural signs of gendered sexuality?

To go beyond modernist criticism is to defetishize and decommodify the gesture/signature/author complex by returning both to the laboring, producing body and to a subjectivity—in process and on trial—in history, a subjectivity whose psychic and social practice the gesture indexes as it works across and within the representational space of its aimless signification. Instead of using painting as a metaphor, a substitution for the artist, rendering "him" (as this logic demands) the symbol of art, we could explore the practice of painting, in social as well as symbolic space, as a metonymic trace, an index of a socially formed, psychically enacted subjectivity at work, both consciously and unconsciously, upon its own and its culture's materials. The key to this process in the painting practices under consideration is to think through the possible relations between the gesture (understood not as mere formal device or technique, and not just as a way of putting on paint, but as the overall semiotic process of a specific context), the surface (imagined not as flat support, but rather as a territory, a field, a mirror, a screen), and the subject (not the coherence retrospectively attributed by the name of the author/artist, but a process, divided, heterogeneous, negotiating difference and the radical instabilities of identity).

At this point, I would have taken the reader on a journey through a range of recent psychoanalytic theories of (a) the gesture and sexual difference (Irigaray questions the general applicability of Freud's famous observation of his grandson playing with a cotton reel, the so-called fort-da game, and suggests that girls negotiate the separation from the mother through playing, dancing, and rhythmic sound rather than through defensive mastery of symbolically invested objects) and (b) the relations between metonym and metaphor in the history of painting. (Rosolato suggests that painting always hovers between a realm of non-sense and the slow degrees by which meaning achieves full symbolic articulation as metaphor.[4] Abstract-expressionist painting worked at keeping closer, through metonymy, to archaic bodily traces, which meant every work had to be carefully assessed for its precarious achievement of enough sense to produce affect without becoming a symbolic substitute for the processes that generated its making.) In addition, I survey the discussion of which psychic mechanism best refers to art making—perversion, particularly fetishism, which links back to the fort-da relations of knowing and disavowing knowledge of lack and loss, or hysteria, which would involve the artist in hysterical identifications that disrupt and undo the culturally coded boundaries of sex and gender. The male artist as hysteric may identify through art with the maternal, hence painting as metonym. The material is also lost and disavowed through the fetishistic mechanisms of substitution, hence painting as metaphor. This discussion of the possibility of sexual difference and a moment of its unfixing allows a way to redefine the practice of Jackson Pollock as more than a mere symbol of artistic machismo, while also creating the means to explore the identifications and resistances to both maternal and paternal moments the artist as woman may be playing with through such a shifted artistic practice in which the coordinates are the gesture, surface, and subject-on-trial. With these brief thoughts in mind, it is possible to see how this argument leads back both to an image of the interior of Marilyn Monroe and to the "dancing space" of the gesture in the paintings Lee Krasner produced in 1957, after Pollock's death but in the presence of de Kooning's *Woman*, who is—who else?—Marilyn Monroe.

Representation, as canonical art history has institutionalized it, is a world orchestrated by psychic desires, traumas, and drives of the masculine subject. Made to the measure of masculine fantasy, it has gained hegemonic status. This then determines the very terms within which we are obliged to be creatively masculine or feminine. Not only have artist-women been placed in an asymmetrical relation to the art world / world in representation because of the current ordering of sexual difference and whatever specificity that might imply, but they are positioned dissymmetrically both to the popular figurations of femininity within the culture and to the figurations of artistic identity which hysterically appropriate both parental figures, maternal and paternal. The very theory that enables us to see this also allows us to break down the ideological fixing of a binary system of sexual identity—art history's hegemonic attachment and neutralizing universalization of masculinity—so that the masculine process in artistic practice looks less fetishistic and is conceived as hysterical, unstable in its relation to a gender position. This move creates a gap wherein we can glimpse how a subject in the feminine orchestrates her hysteria, her unstable and creatively destabilizing relations to both maternal femininity and paternal law, into creativity.

At the beginning of this essay, I proposed a very fixed, binary and fetishistic opposition of sex symbol and art symbol: Marilyn and Jackson, movie icon and artist. The suggestion that masculine art is a form of male hysteria, that it might contain a destabilizing of the fixity of masculine subjectivity in relation to the maternal in the same move as it inscribes once again the paternal law through avant-gardist rivalry, opens up the mobility of sexual identity so that we may consider the play around women's bodily and fantastic inscriptions in the texts of culture. We thus discover a way to theorize the practices of painting in their historical and stylistic diversity as a kind of staging of the drama of the subject. What is produced is not a style or an object but a moment of identity, which, in the male canon, has been achieved only through the encounter with and specific negotiation of sexual difference, that is, with the constituting symbols of sex in Western culture: the mother and the father. If we relate the canvas, the material resources like color, and the gesture to the framing psychic relations within which identity is shaped—the fantastic figures of the mother and the father—we can ask what is going on within a feminine subject-on-trial on this stage. By including Freud's work on art as hysterical within the larger psychoanalytical framework, it is possible to see the drama of art as the drama of sexual difference through which there will be several possible individual trajectories, indeed in the end, as many as there are artists. Thus, we can escape the perennial trap, when discussing the impact of sexual difference, of determining all artists as merely exemplars of its asymmetrically polar terms: Artist / Woman Artist. Being an artist "in the feminine," working in a practice that generates historical and aesthetic possibilities of "inscriptions in, of, and from the feminine," does not reduce Helen Frankenthaler or Lee Krasner to "being women." Their work is instead made legible, as it plays on this historical stage when the semiotics of artistic practice within modernist painting opened up the very questions of identity, pleasure, and difference in which the bodily and the psychic traces of the produced but always unraveling subject of sexual difference could reconfigure their relations in and through painting.

Thus, instead of leaving unchallenged and unreconstructed the dominant narratives of abstract expressionism in order to make a sideways move off the map of serious art history to consider "women artists," I hope to have sketched the central playing field differently. The binary opposition of sex symbol and art symbol is revealed as an ideological fixing of processes that, in the studios where abstract expressionist or American-type painting was being made, may have been far less stable—or at least differently orchestrated. This alone allows us to understand modernist women painters' investment in the protocols of modernist painting, and to grasp their embrace of that extraordinary practice of painting in which women like Helen Frankenthaler and Lee Krasner and so many others engaged, day in and day out, for a lifetime. These women of the 1950s were drawn to practices of painting that structurally exposed spaces for the exploration of what had not yet been inscribed through painting—an invitation existing in the synonymy of *énoncé* and *énonciation*, of what is said and the means of saying of it, representation as the process itself.

They practiced, however, in an art world that, shaped in the ideological polarities of the moment, was barefacedly misogynist. Curators, gallery owners, critics, and other artists created an ambiance that was not only masculinist, but virilist and sexist. Part of that culture was imaged through its popular icons, of whom the supreme sign and symbol was Marilyn Monroe. She was the fetish supreme, all perfected, shiny, glossy surface. We need to pierce that carapace to return her to her body and subjectivity, to get to Lee Krasner, who as a painter was closest to Pollock and was thus—artistically—in mortal danger, and, finally, to get to the maternal body buried in her art that *Prophecy* fearfully presaged and *Sun Woman I* allusively contacted.

Massacred Women Don't Make Me Laugh

In her essay "A New Type of Intellectual: The Dissident," first published in *Tel Quel* in 1977, Julia Kristeva identified several types of modern dissidence that stand in opposition to the assimilation of the intellectual to the modern establishment of power. The rebel attacks political power. The psychoanalyst holds a contest between death and discourse and finds his archetypal rival in religion. The writer (we might add artist) experiments at the limits of identity, shifting the relations of law and desire by stripping the latter down to its basic structure: Kristeva calls this rhythm, the conjunction of body and music. But from these three spaces of politics, analysis, and art/writing, Woman is absent because she represents a fourth kind of dissidence. Woman does not mean female people in the social sense. Woman is a sign within the ordering of sexual difference that manages the potentialities of humans as corporeal, psychosymbolic entities within historically shaped social and semiotic forms. Woman, that is, sexual difference, is a particular moment of historical dissidence, because it is as Woman that we who are named women encounter as writers, analysts, or political rebels the intransigence of a patriarchal ordering of sexual difference. Because of our specific potentialities in sexuality and through maternity, those defined and signified by the sign Woman are caught up, according to Kristeva, with what she calls divine law, death, and religion in opposition to human law, government, politics, ethics. This results from Woman's being in touch with death through her role in life: that is, through reproduction. From the point of view of human, patriarchal law, Woman is thus a kind of exile—who, when captured for its social forms, is either made into the demonic image of the witch (femme fatale, movie star, name her as you wish) or targeted for total assimilation to the existing order. We can either join in by trying to be the president or by singing, as did Marilyn Monroe, happy birthday to the president in a dress so tight she had to be sewn into it. This tension is a result of the lack of a language in which to speak of childbirth, of the specificity of those processes that both provide the structure of particular feminine experience and erase all subjectivity in an encounter with an other than is literally within. Thus, Kristeva concludes:

Under these conditions female "creation" [*la "création" féminine*] cannot be taken for granted. It can be said that artistic creation always feeds on an identification, or rivalry with what is presumed to be the mother's jouissance (which has nothing agreeable [*de plaisant*] about it). This is why one of the most accurate representations of creation, that is, of artistic practice, is a series of paintings by de Kooning entitled Women (sic): savage, explosive, funny [*drôle*], inaccessible creatures in spite of the fact they have been massacred by the artist. But what if they had been created by a woman? Obviously she would have had to deal with her own mother, and therefore with herself which is a lot less funny [*c'est beaucoup moins drôle*]. (Kristeva 1986: 297)

This comment has fascinated and yet also shocked me for years. It is useful because of the direct link between the kind of feminist theory I have been using elsewhere and the American painting of the 1950s. My reading of Frankenthaler's joyous and humorous paintings of the 1950s, I hope, belies the idea that women cannot deal with their mothers or themselves pleasurably. Indeed much of the purpose of this paper is to imagine a way to read for exactly that which Julia Kristeva finds unlikely: an alliance between *le rire féminin* and *la création féminine* that, according to Kristeva, may pass through a relation to maternity—not as an actuality, but as a relation between desire, loss, and identification. Kristeva concludes the paragraph from which the above is cited: "Maternity may thus well be called Penelope's tapestry or Leibniz's network, depending on whether it follows the logic of gestures or of thought, but it always succeeds in connecting up heterogeneous sites" (Kristeva 1986: 298).

It is the idea, however, of killing men, men killing—massacring—women in their art, being funny—the word she uses twice in the paragraph: once of the massacred painted women and once of those whom women might produce in painting—that I resolutely cannot handle. De Kooning's paintings stand at the opposite pole to that at which I would situate Pollock's dripped canvases. In the *Women* series there is less metonymy and more metaphor. The paintings yield a readable image: *Woman* (1953, Museum of Modern Art, New York). The paint, however, retains a powerful indexicality to the bodily intensity of the gestures and physical movements of the artist as he produced on canvas this monstrous form, with searing, toothy, blood-red smile and stark, staring, idol or cartoon-like eyes. The feminist art critic Cindy Nemser had a conversation with the painter Grace Hartigan about these paintings, expressing a straightforward feminist distaste for the violence perceived in de Kooning's interpretation of women. Grace Hartigan disagreed. Nemser then suggested that there might be unconscious impulses behind an artist's gestures, generating the effect of violence against which Nemser and others have reacted. But Grace would have none of it. "No one is going to convince me that Bill de Kooning does not love women." [5]

I think one could make a case with de Kooning's *Women* paintings either way. Like Picasso, de Kooning clearly loved "cutting up women," to borrow a phrase from the ever insightful and much lamented Angela Carter. At the same time, to get back to dying women and killing men, I could put forward an argument from de Kooning's paintings of Woman about men killing the fetish through the violence of their painting's assaults on the airbrushed, artificial, fetishized perfection of the living doll. Laura Mulvey has suggested that Hollywood cinema, at its height in the 1950s, condensed the fetishism of the commodity and the psychic economy of fetishism into the spectacle signified by the image of woman on screen (1995). Woman as spectacle is all surface, all appearance, but turn the psychic screw of fetishism and this image is all threat. Marilyn Monroe's exceptional appeal lay in the cosmetically and chemically achieved allaying of that menace by the combination of her intensively signified sexual display with an almost delectable goodness: like vanilla ice-cream, as Norman Mailer put it (1973). Some of the complexity of Marilyn Monroe's appeal lay in the conjugation of female laughter, a maternal trace, and femininity released from its role as signifier of castration anxiety, threads that Julia Kristeva tried to weave together. Monroe was, however, destined to become the screen version of the funny, inaccessible creature massacred by culture.

De Kooning's series of *Women* paintings, which includes one named *Marilyn Monroe* (1954), clearly brings together the legacy of Picasso's cut-up women and the iconic objectification of Woman in the blood-red lips that are the displaced and violated sign of her "wound." De Kooning uses Picasso to allow him to cut the female open so that out comes, not vanilla ice-cream, but ruby-red blood, her jewels. The ambiguity of these images lies precisely in their oscillation between metonymic and metaphoric figuration of female sexuality on the one hand and of fantasies of masculine castration on the other. In a sense the shock offered by de Kooning's paintings is that they are so little fetishized. They appear to expose the female body. They give it so frankly a sex—yet in so displaced and disavowed a fashion—rubies? blood? They bluntly imagine an interior. Yet they are made from a massively built-up density of paint. "The violence is in the paint," said Hartigan to Nemser. But the signature, the gesture in the paint, makes the revelation a violent disrobing. We cannot escape the aptness of Julia Kristeva's notion of a massacre / dying women. By contrast, we have to hypothesize a specifically feminine relation to the mutual imbrication of violence and creativity, to the deeply problematic necessity to deal with the mother within the differentiated psychic trajectories for men and women as artists using their art to stage this encounter.

Another Look at Surface and Depth

Bataille's idea of artistic progress through murder finally converged on women painters of the 1950s who knew that they wanted to be part of a project that included the painting of Pollock and de Kooning. These men would have to be dealt with. What they were doing was important, interesting, necessary for anyone who wanted to be part of this ambitious moment. Yet how would an artist who was a woman prevent them from overwhelming the resources from which a woman must create and separate? I suggest that a brief and final view of Lee Krasner's painting will reveal that she was a good Bataillist. She took on the others' work but killed it, right there, on her canvas—but with such radically different effects that it has awaited feminism to allow us to read that event as a differentiating realignment within that artistic moment and not a lack or a diversion from it. In an interview on film in 1976, Lee Krasner reported on how Bryan Robertson, preparing a retrospective of her painting for London's Whitechapel Art Gallery in 1965, had interviewed Clement Greenberg. The critic had confirmed that Lee Krasner's collage work of 1955–56—the work made just before *Prophecy* emerged—was a major breakthrough and a force in contemporary "new American painting." Greenberg never said so publicly, in print, at the time. Lee Krasner's biting comment, "That's nice. But it's ten years too late," touches the raw nerve of historical prejudice which effectively deprived Krasner of her place within the competitive avant-garde moment of New York painting. But it has been through a feminist interest that her painting has been readdressed since the 1970s. This has allowed the work to be read for a differentiating set of aesthetic maneuvers that can be grasped for a cultural politics of sexual difference.

Any survey of Krasner's work from the mid-1940s through the mid-1950s serves to underline the radical shock that the emergence in July 1956 of the image in the painting *Prophecy* represents. (The painting is visible on the right-hand side in Fig. 1.) The painting was a disaster. The artist was mortified. Amidst all the other factors bringing this work into being, a long-standing dialogue with de Kooning's work broke through all censorship, demanding its own price: life or death. De Kooning was not just the other big name on the current New York scene to be dealt with. He was the painter of Woman, one (all?) of whom was Marilyn Monroe. For an artist of Krasner's, namely his, generation, that dominance inscribed the violent if ambivalent mythemes of masculinity's tortured relation to femininity/maternity/creativity into the heart of modern American painting. As such, it could not be avoided. Even more so was it inevitable for a painter such as Lee Krasner to take de Kooning on in her canvas, in her painting, through her gesture.

Krasner's creative practice can be read according to Bataille's thesis on hybridity and decomposition in modernism. Bataille's interest in decomposition and destructive reworking affords a way to relate Krasner's knight's moves across the board of New York painting that could allow Pollock, de Kooning, Rothko, Motherwell, and the others their necessary contribution to what was interesting in making paintings at this moment while also creating the space for her own decisive reconfiguration of the project of painting. But *Prophecy* stands outside this model, at this point. Welling up into view are bodies, fleshy and plantlike with sightless eyes dislocatedly on the watch. A series of seventeen works created in the eighteen months after Pollock's sudden death in August 1956 were clearly about Pollock ("Pollocks" of the early 1940s perhaps) and about killing him again—reliving the very crux of their relationship as a mythic competition between the sexes, killing men and dying women. The dead man—the dead Father that a canonized Pollock would become for that generation—could not be killed openly. He must be included in the work and exterminated then and there on the canvas through the work of undoing—decomposing—painting.

But that deadly other with whom the painter-woman, Lee Krasner, had to struggle was also de Kooning, from whom the woman as artist must reclaim her body, the body he has used, the sexuality he has prostituted, the interior he has torn open and bloodied with his grandiose gesturing in paint. Sadism must be released and then creatively sublimated to avoid being just another dying woman—to reach what I elsewhere named "the creative woman's body."

Out of this struggle emerged *Sun Woman I* (1957). The explosive ebullience of the centrifugal composition, the lightness of the painted touch with its deep reds and yellows, the repeating circularity of gesture that tempts us to read a face or two, with open (singing?) mouths, a breast, a belly, seems a liberated universe away from the clogged surfaces and desultory colors of paintings, like *Birth* (1956), that followed *Prophecy*. Not massacred and funny creatures, these clearly gynomorphic forms belie Julia Kristeva's doubts about the possibility of "female creation" and female laughter. Kristeva argued that for a woman to paint pictures like de Kooning's that index the dissidence of Woman, of sexual difference, the woman as artist would have to deal with her own mother and thus herself as woman. At no point have I assumed that woman is, that is, that

FIGURE 4. Ernst Haas, *Lee Krasner at Work in her Studio* (1981). Copyright Ernst Haas. Used with permission of Magnum Photos, Inc.

Woman is on the plane of being, a given entity. I work with the difficult notion of the feminine being both inside and outside a designated social space and a semiotic sign, shaped by the complex configurations (of psyche, fantasy, and concept) that constitute both a Symbolic order and a regime that produces sexual difference. This regime is equally disrupted by the excess—femininity—that the very process of sexual ordering and differentiating generates. Yet I feel more and more compelled to allow that excess, as well as that ordering, to include a corporeal schema, an image or sensation we might tentatively call bodilyness.

Without falling right back into the trap of a founding anatomical basis to the difference of the sexes, I would want to embrace the possibility that our psychic and symbolizing experience of the corporeal—filtered through its psychic representatives and our symbolic signifying systems—will be always marked by bodily specificity. But a particular Symbolic order might preclude certain bodily specifities from representation, forcing them onto the plane of hallucination, the uncanny, and apparition. The pulsational rhythms of the masculine experience of sexuality mark a different possibility of what is never just the body's repertoire of sensations and meanings. Bodies are always my body, his body, her body; and even that is not simple, for hers may be a lesbian body, a black lesbian mother's body, a marked body, and so on. With *Sun Woman I*, I have not found the authentic moment of "women's art." I have worked towards a possibility of recognizing, in the space of this painter's actions, gestures, processes, meditations, responses, decisions, desires, ambitions, distress, a moment of what a phallically ordered culture does not allow us to see, let alone name, and finally enjoy: pleasures in the jubilant identification of a difference that the language of even sympathetic formal analysis will kill.

A modest proposal is on offer after a lengthy theoretical and historical journey to lay in the conditions of this painting's visibility—for me at least. What my working through prompts me to see is a joyous revelation of body schema on a canvas, a surface, incorporating the calligraphic signature encountered in the *Little Image* series from the 1940s. The painting leaves evident the traces of the circular movements of the arms that produce the possibility of an image that is a corporeal schema invented for projective identification—a moment of stabilization that structures the viewer's visual tourism within the elaborated surface. Then there is the measured play of absence and presence, of paint and canvas, of painting and not painting, of color and ground. These create what I must call, in gratitude to Luce Irigaray, a dancing space. This is not like the literal dance performed by Pollock around his canvas and mythicized in photo session and film by Hans Namuth. It is a created effect, a produced illusion, made through the play of color, the energy of line, the ebullient fullness of the central image on the canvas. The viewer perceives the canvas optically but experiences it empathetically as a dancing space, a play around presence and absence that is pleasurable because it does not index an obsessive repetition of mastery (Pollock) or the need for violence (de Kooning).

To end, I'll consider one more photograph: Lee Krasner at work in 1981, by Ernst Haas (Fig. 4). She has been painting, standing up at a large table. She is now thinking about what she has done. She is reading her own work—with her eyes but also with her hands. The gesture is captured in the photograph—but here, the gesture is nothing so literal as the action that made the painting. Her hands describe a kind of imaginary space, prompted as well as indexed by what she has done on the canvas. Those hands, circling above the canvas as an unconscious bodily response to what the painting is for her at that moment, provide a visual clue, a glimpse beyond the visible sign, beyond the object that is an index, to what this practice offers: much less dramatic than Pollock's elaborate choreography; more detached than Frankenthaler's pouring and stroking. The photograph holds in view the complex sense of gesture in painting—woman's body in the studio space creating, thinking, dancing with death.

Imagining the 'Shtetl'

VISUAL THEORIES OF NATIONHOOD

Carol Zemel

Pictures like these of eastern European Jews by Roman Vishniac and Alter Kacyzne have always scared me (Figs. 1 and 2). Or rather, they both fascinated and repelled me. First of all, they signified a place of origin, and so they embodied my family's flight from Russia to Canada in 1922. But these romantic fascinations also contained something more threatening; the pictures encompassed places and practices that enticed me and, at the same time, denied me place. Looking at them, I felt engulfed in a world far away and out of time, a world so filled with sentiment, but also so dark and strange, and even so repudiated, that I could scarcely tie it to the Jewish life I knew. To explore these images with any hope of personal connection seemed to muddle my identity as a Jewish woman and modern Canadian.

Impatient with these feelings, I began to look more closely at these photographs, and to think about them not only art historically, as images of a particular culture and history, but also as figures of my own ambivalence. Perhaps the mixed feelings and the confusion about self-as-subject that the pictures provoked were indices of more diffuse, less articulated concerns about assimilation, ethnicity, and modern national identity. And perhaps photographic images, as agents of visual culture, delivered these pleasures and uncertainties in significant ways.

To explore these questions, I turned to photograph collections produced in the 1920s and 1930s by Alter Kacyzne, Moshe Vorobeichic, and Roman Vishniac. The pictures were made for a variety of reasons: documenting social conditions for Jewish welfare agencies, celebrating forms of Jewish culture and society, perhaps rescuing a culture some thought about to disappear.[1] But as images of Jews by Jewish photographers for mainly Jewish audiences, they also constitute images of a people—self-images, in fact—and in doing so, I suggest, they set before us photographic formulations by Jews of Jewish identity.

Today, it is hard not to see these images through the lens of the Shoah, or Holocaust, and to a large extent, that catastrophic history has shaped their impact and meaning. Vishniac's work in particular—largely unpublished until after the war—has been presented and marketed that way. His best-known collection, published in 1968, is titled *A Vanished World* (Fig. 1); it shows a melancholic old man on the cover, contains a foreword by Nobel laureate and Holocaust spokesman Elie Wiesel, and like many of the images within, it is deeply shrouded in black. But the notion that these pictures show a doomed people "on the brink of extermination" (*Newsweek*, Mar. 22, 1993: 68), as reviews tend to describe them, is only one possible reading. To my mind, it narrows the pictures' history and obscures other, more vital dimensions of the tales they tell.

It is true that even in their own time, for many viewers, such photographs proclaimed an aura of distance and time past. Departure, absence, and memory, these qualities are keystones of the photographic, as Roland Barthes reminded us in *Camera Lucida*, his meditation on photography and grief. In these pictures, absence and memory trigger nostalgia and longing, but also relief and dismay, for they encode a people seemingly at odds with modernity. In part, this was the pictures' purpose: to reassure American viewers, for example, of their own modern identity and distance from that old-fashioned world. But this is only one context and audience. Although there is little record of contemporary response to the images, the conditions and context of their production evoke other possible readings: cultural pride and community, for example, as well as cultural anxiety and distance. With these broader possibilities in mind, I want to consider how these photographs represent a Jewish people, and how that representation might inscribe a national character and consciousness.

Perhaps no people has troubled the idea of nationhood more than the Jews. For centuries, Jews existed in the European imagination as meta-

FIGURE I. Roman
Vishniac, *A Vanished
World* (cover photo-
graph). Used with
permission of Mrs.
Mara Vishniac Kohn.

phors of exile, condemned for their refusal of Christianity to various ex-
pulsions and wandering homelessness. But if they were a people without
a land, Jews were not without a geography. Persistently the "other" population in the eastern European lands where they lived in great numbers
from the sixteenth to the twentieth centuries, Jews inhabited—actually
they were confined to—the so-called Pale of Settlement, a now-legendary
territory that stretched from the Baltic to the Black Sea. The Pale was
established by Russian laws of 1795 and 1835, but as borders fluctuated in
the course of the next century and a half, Jews of the region found themselves recurrently inhabitants—though not necessarily citizens—of Russia, Lithuania, Poland, and the Ukraine. Even within the shifting political
boundaries, the Pale was an unusual supranational space, a geography of
culture and consciousness that I would call a sort of living palimpsest.
Like the superimpositions of an ancient parchment in which one text
hovers over the partial erasure of another, national frontiers and conven-

tional centers within the territory were overlaid by less charted routes and landmarks, related to synagogues, yeshivas, study centers, and rabbinical courts. Within the Pale, Jews developed an extensive *shtetl* culture (*shtetl* is Yiddish for "small town" or "village"), by which is generally meant a Yiddish-speaking, provincial society, religious orthodoxy, and a traditional Jewish way of life; it is now best known through stereotypical images like the Sholem Aleichem / Marc Chagall amalgam, *Fiddler on the Roof.* [2]

The Pale, then, is the geographic setting for these photographs. Historically, these images coincide with a period of secularization, modernization, and large-scale emigration by Jews to western Europe and America. Major waves of emigration began in the 1880s, not only in response to anti-Semitic oppression and poverty, but also as a way to leave behind the culture of *shtetl* Orthodoxy. In fact, eastern-European Jewish history through the nineteenth century is riven with disputes between proponents of Orthodox tradition and the proponents of *haskalah* or modernization, which many feared would lead inevitably to assimilation and absorption within the gentile world.

FIGURE 2. Alter Kacyzne, *Market Day*. Used with permission of the Yivo Institute for Jewish Research.

Politically, it was also a period of nation building, and the efforts of Jews in the Pale to modernize were poised around this issue with special ambivalence. In describing their many (and often contentious) positions, inevitably, I must simplify.[3] Zionism—the effort to establish a territorial Jewish homeland and to forge a "New Jew"—was one (and the most conventional) national possibility. Assimilation to the host country's national identity, where possible, was another modernizing route. But a third—and more immediate—possibility was continuity as a distinct minority culture, for example, a modern affirmation and secular expansion of the Yiddish-speaking culture already flourishing in the Pale—what historian Simon Dubnow called "diaspora nationalism" (in his letters on old and new Jewry, published in St. Petersberg, 1897–99). By the early decades of the century, in cities like Minsk, Vilna (Vilnius), Warsaw, and Lvov, the Orthodox habits of the *shtetl* were augmented by a growing secular Judaism. A network of educational, social, and cultural institutions developed. The Jewish labor organization known as the Bund was founded in 1897; in 1908 the Czernowitz Conference proclaimed Yiddish a national language of the Jews; and in 1925, YIVO (Yidisher visnschaflekher institut [Yiddish Scientific Institute]) was established. An extensive print culture flourished. The classic texts of modern Yiddish literature by Mendele Mocher Sforim (Sholom Jacob Abramovitz), I. L. Peretz, and Sholem Aleichem were well known by the 1920s; Warsaw boasted more than a dozen Yiddish dailies in the same period; and a Jewish Press Photographer's Guild was established in that city in 1910. All of these drew *shtetl* culture and consciousness into a modern Jewish society and a potentially national frame.

One might argue that the Jewish population of the Pale, bound by language, religion, a shared history and social practice but without little political power or agency, constituted a people rather than a nation. But the distinction between a people and a nation is surely conditioned by circumstance, depending on who poses the question, and when. In a famous essay of 1882, French historian Ernest Renan, author of a five-volume study of the Jews, asked "What is a nation?," and framed what might be called a modern, liberal response: "A nation is . . . a large-scale solidarity, constituted by the feeling of the sacrifices that one has made in the past and of those that one is prepared to make in the future. It presupposes a past; it is summarized, however, in the present by a tangible fact, namely consent, the clearly expressed desire to continue a common life" (Renan 1990: 19).

Renan proposed that nationhood depended on shared memory—"the fact of having suffered, enjoyed and hoped together"—as well as on a willed sense of community, what he called the nation's "daily plebiscite" (1990: 19). Such a definition, which discards ideas of national "purity" and structures such as religion, blood, land, and even language as determinants of nationhood, would suit the melting-pot rhetoric of the United States, but it might apply to modern eastern-European states as well. Following World War I, under the terms of the Treaty of Versailles, the newly redrawn states of eastern Europe (Poland, Rumania, Hungary) were bound to protect the rights and privileges of their minority populations. Reluctantly or not, nations which had been the chief regions of the Pale became multiethnic states.[4] The Soviet Republics forged a Socialist Union of different peoples; modern Poland, established in 1919, also adopted a constitution guaranteeing the rights of its minorities. Certainly, Jews in these areas suffered hardship and oppression; virulent anti-Semitism was recent history there, and such campaigns intensified through the 1930s as right-wing ideologies gained force. Still, under the law in modern Poland, Jews had equal rights and cultural autonomy, and members of Jewish political parties—Zionist, Orthodox, and socialist—held seats in the Polish government. Jews, in fact, were the only minority whose interests did not include territorial claims and did not contest Poland's sovereignty or borders.[5]

It is in this context of hectic nation-building and national consciousness that, along with the Jewish social institutions and literary forms, these photographs of Jews deliver the notion of a people or define, in Benedict Anderson's phrase, an "imagined community" (1991). As visual formulations of a society, dispersed to varied Jewish audiences through an active print culture, the pictures, we might say, perform a cultural task, what Homi Bhabha labels, in a literary context, "narrating-a-nation" (1990). Like national epics or novels of panoramic social sweep—those of Balzac, Zola, Dickens, and Tolstoy, for example, or like the writings of Schlomo Ansky, Mendele Mocher Sforim, and Sholem Aleichem—these picture collections selectively present, celebrate, and critique aspects of ethnic identity and Jewish community life. They are, to be sure, somewhat eccentric as national discourse, for the people they represent are always embedded within other national and cultural territories, as a self-differentiating and parallel culture, neither opposed to nor even necessarily in conflict with their unpictured national hosts. In such circumstances, the ambivalence that Bhabha describes as an inevitable condition of both nation making and national discourse is especially relevant, complicating the idea of Renan's cheerful "daily plebiscite." "Ambivalence," Bhabha writes, "haunts the idea of the nation, the language of those who write of it and the lives of those who live it" (1990: 1). To accommodate this ambivalence, nation-narration is riven with polemic; it necessarily produces stereotypes, but its emphases—on religion, labor, material property, and study in these cases—can be signposts of tension and disjuncture, as well as strength. Seen as such cultural narration, as a sort of visual theorizing of nationhood, these photographs prompt me to ask not only, what configuration of a Jewish people do they narrate, but also, what conflicts and ambivalence do they inscribe? What features are emphasized or muted in order to articulate a people or national imagery? And how might that construction accommodate or affront the burgeoning nationalisms of their moment and environment?

The three photograph collections I have selected are similar in subject, but different in photographic style. None of the images is a casual souvenir, a private commission, or a personal memento. Rather, a sense of cultural purpose pervades the work, and as they appear in newspaper series, in institutional archives, or in published books and galleries, their status shifts between social ethnography, historical document, and work of art.

Alter Kacyzne's pictures offer the broadest repertory of scenes and types. A poet and playwright as well as photographer, Kacyzne (1885–1941) had an extensive portrait practice, photographing, among others, his colleagues in literary and theatrical circles. He was also a disciple of Schlomo Ansky, and as Ansky had done in prerevolutionary Russia, Kacyzne traveled through the Pale photographing scenes of Jewish life.[6]

His pictures appeared in several contexts: many were taken for Jewish welfare agencies like the Joint Distribution Committee (JDC) or the Hebrew Immigrant Aid Service (HIAS), and as such their mission was clear: to detail an impoverished people and their "rescue" by modern Jews.[7] Other pictures appeared regularly in the "Art Section" of the *Forward*, the leading Yiddish daily paper in New York, with a circulation of over 200,000.[8] Published there under topic headings like "The Principal Streets of Grodno, Poland" (December 30, 1923) or "Pictures of Jewish Life and Characters" (December 5, 1923), they rely on the potent "thereness," the apparently artless realism of the documentary camera, to create

FIGURE 3. Alter Kacyzne, *Shtetl Street.* Used with permission of the Yivo Institute for Jewish Research.

a seemingly unmediated ethnography of the *shtetl* and eastern-European Jewish sites.

The documentary qualities are evident in numerous exterior views, postcard-like images of synagogues, markets, and towns. Some are shown as landmarks, like the fortress synagogue of Husiatyn with its crenellated roof, crowning a hillside. Meaning in such images is produced by the capacity of the photograph both to generalize and to specify. To our eyes, such structures, towns, and markets suggest a generic cultural landscape. These could be almost any Jewish center in the Pale, large or small, swarming with carts and horses, and figures haggling for goods (Fig. 2).

But to immigrant readers of the *Forward*, this was also a known geography, studded with familiar structures and types. It was also a world abandoned, and as much as it triggered memory, it also reiterated the decision to leave, and more importantly, the decision to modernize. Whatever nostalgia viewers felt at the sight of village streams, busy markets, wooden houses and synagogues was matched by the discomforting sight of muddy streets and dilapidated houses, barefoot children in tattered clothing, bent

FIGURE 4. Alter Kacyzne, *Cobbler*. Used with permission of the Yivo Institute for Jewish Research.

old men. This is hardly a typical myth of national pride or of ownership. Synagogues are the only monuments; houses are picturesque shelters, not property; the broad vistas are about exchange and barter; there is little sense of land or landedness. As cultural reportage in the *Forward*'s special illustrated section, the pictures confirmed the space between the old country and the viewer's modern world. And by reminding viewers how different their lives were from the scenes before them, the images conveniently reinforced the national promise of America—the ability to succeed as modern citizen and as ethnic minority at the same time.

A closer look at this old-world ethnography shows us peddlers, laborers, mischievous boys, and traditionally dressed elders—an impoverished populace of disempowered men. As if at random, Kacyzne's camera takes in incidents of the street (Fig. 3): a uniformed schoolboy and father in one picture, a shoeless boy in the background, waiting carts and horses. The pictorial emphasis, however, is the older men wearing the long-coated costume of Orthodoxy, slow-footed on their canes, negotiating the mud.

Another street image takes a detached vantage point, looking down from a window at a listless gathering of street-corner idlers and unemployed men.

Moving indoors, other images show more traditional types: artisan figures like a romantically lit, bearded cobbler (Fig. 4), or an old man in synagogue, enclosed in prayer and solitude. Women and domestic sites also appear as social genre. Market women suggest hard work; elderly *bubbes* nurture children; bewigged religious women instruct young girls. As familiar figures of tradition and Orthodoxy, they also seem to fix *shtetl* society in that unmodern frame.

Even so, it is not a homogenous assembly of picturesque types. Underscoring the social concerns of Kacyzne's camera are images of a modern world: a youthful farmer, gymnasium teachers, striking factory workers, and members of the socialist Jewish Bund (Fig. 5). In contrast to the village scenes, these pictures frame special events, or they are camera-staged group portraits, and they lack the documentary social flux of the street and market scenes. They appeared less often in the pages of the *Forward*, but their presence in the collection signals the variety of Jewish

FIGURE 5. Alter Kacyzne, *Members of the Bund*. Used with permission of the Yivo Institute for Jewish Research.

FIGURE 6. Alter Kacyzne, *The Rabbi's Daughter*. Used with permission of the Yivo Institute for Jewish Research.

life in the region and its transformative possibilities. Taken together with the more picturesque imagery, the single artisan becomes the industrial workforce, the aged scholars become the teachers, the barefoot kids form gymnastic and athletic groups, the listless laborers become the mainstay of the Bund.

But there are also omissions in this emphatically proletarian frame. Bourgeois Jews and the world of culture typified by Kacyzne's studio practice are hardly present.[9] We glimpse it in photographs like the stereotype of dark Jewish beauty, labeled *The Rabbi's Daughter*, that would easily join the images of actresses and beauty queens featured in the *Forward*'s picture page (Fig. 6). But the image may also alert us to the problematic place of desire in this cultural repertoire.[10] Indeed, for the most part, these photographs are remarkably modest and proper; physical pleasure appears restricted to the ideals of clean living and good health, with occasional pictures of children's camps, sports teams, and clubs. The far more numerous images of rustic poverty and idle workers, the prominence of bearded elders and traditional types, the attention to religious structures and study—all of this suggests an accommodating, docile, and even de-eroticized populace.

In fact, the old-fashioned people in most of these pictures hardly seem candidates for modern nationhood; only the modern workforce hints at the vigor, the energy—the "manliness"—of nation. Indeed, the irony of these images as ethnographic salvage seems to be their fixing of *shtetl* culture in a powerless, nonthreatening picturesque. Herein lies their ambivalence, for if these images emblematize traditional sites and figures, then for readers of the *Forward*, this was memory to be acknowledged and cast off; the pictures effectively reframed the viewers' lingering guilt as nostalgia and relief. But even within the Pale, where *shtetl* landmarks, labor, learning, and prayer were a more immediate heritage, the ambivalent recognition and distance was a function of the photographer's and the viewers' modernity. Through Kacyzne's camera, the picturesque sites and that self-differentiating otherness become both historical documents and cultural metaphor, just as the photos hinted at new social formations and the vigor of modern citizenship. These terms are held in tension: how to modernize and how to reject, retain, or transform the past? Without closure on these questions, the images shape the mythos and ambivalence of a modern Jewish consciousness.

The ambivalent tug from myth to modernity is handled differently in Moshe Vorobeichic's collection, *The Ghetto Lane in Vilna*, published in 1931 in bilingual Hebrew-German and Hebrew-English editions. Vilna, of course, was never merely a *shtetl*. Commonly referred to as the "Lithuanian Jerusalem," in the 1920s it was a major center of modern Yiddish scholarship, exemplified by the founding in 1925 of YIVO, which was dedicated to the study and promotion of Jewish history and modern Yiddish culture.[11] Thus while the "ghetto lane" of Vorobeichic's title encloses the work within the *shtetl* picturesque, the collection of images by an artist who had studied at the Bauhaus (where he was known as "Moi-Ver") and the Paris Ecole de Beaux-Arts is clearly meant for a more modern and even internationalist avant-garde milieu.[12] This is signaled immediately by the dramatic photomontage technique and by captions in Hebrew, German, and English. An introduction by Yiddish novelist Salman Chnéour

FIGURE 7. Moshe Voro-
beichic, *The Old Shul*, from
The Ghetto Lane in Vilna
(Hentrich, 1928).

asserted the project's high-minded aims. "There is a difference between reading and seeing," Chnéour wrote, and he went on: "This Album is not meant to satisfy the tastes of only the aesthetic few, but also the taste of the masses, to bring them in touch with the Jewish street. It shows true Jewish life, and its ethnographic materials make it a handbook for everyone" (in Vorobeichic 1931: 7).

Chnéour's text makes ambitious claims for visual discourse. "Seeing," and photographic seeing in particular, delivered a verifiable immediacy, and so presumably eliminated class barriers to culture. Thus affirming the "truths" of both art and ethnography, Chnéour and Vorobeichic presented Jewish readers with a progressive guide to "true Jewish life." The book not only iconicized traditional sites and figures; it also linked both its readers and subjects to modern art and modernity.

The book opens and closes with a smiling laborer bonded to the elegant architecture of a great synagogue (Fig. 7). To maintain the reversibility of Hebrew and European texts, the same man, recaptioned *The Jewish Smile*, is the last image as well. In dramatically cropped and tilted pictures, the camera seems to zoom cinematically from point to point. Streets are cobbled corridors seen from odd or tilted angles, and the page layout emphasizes their narrow confines. Two pages show tiers of books from the Strashun Library in a patterned display; they emblematize Vilna's scholarly culture and Jewish identity as "the people of the book." Other pages rehearse the poverty and picturesque types. The repeating pattern of wooden shutters encloses a waiting market crone (Fig. 8); a cluster of

FIGURE 8. Moshe Vorobeichic, *Market Woman*, from *The Ghetto Lane in Vilna* (Hentrich, 1928).

hands evokes the stereotype of Jewish argument and bargaining; a pile of tin and shoes labeled *The Wealth of Israel* makes an ironic statement about Jews and money; an old man teeters along the street, his figure already a ghost in double exposure at his feet.

Vorobeichic's montaged imagery is an effective strategy that literally reframes a diaspora people and consciousness. The fusion of traditional content and radical style draws a poor, laboring, scholarly, and spiritual populace into modernist culture as pictorial fragments and artifacts. At the same time, the combinations and disruptions that drive the photomontages' formal success force home and concretize the subjects' identity. These fragmented figures, gestures, and objects become fetishized emblems of Jewish tradition, even as the fragment itself, seized by the camera from the social clutter, functions as a dynamic sign of modernity.[13] Thus, Vorobeichic harnessed traditional Jewish culture to a new and distinctly modern discursive space, installing it—with the imagery of Chagall, Lissitzky, or Leger—within the protectorate of international modernism, and at the same time pictorially voicing the cultural nationalism of his milieu.

As different as Vorobeichic's strategies are from Kacyzne's—one works through modernist high culture, the other through mass media—both, I think, try to open a vital Jewish cultural space. In Roman Vishniac's pictures, published in *A Vanished World* as cultural eulogy, the recurrent tropes and figures acquire a more elegiac mood and sinister meaning (Fig. 1). I have already pointed to the aura of doom that has shaped the pictures' postwar marketing and made them overshadowing signifiers of death. Their status as precious documents is also enhanced by Vishniac's elaborate tale of their making, most notably the claim that the images were taken clandestinely, with the camera and shutter release concealed in his clothing. Still, little about them seems furtive or awkward. Like Kacyzne, Vishniac was commissioned in the late 1930s by HIAS and the JDC to photograph the Jewish poor of eastern Europe. His own account designated the project a mission of photographic rescue.[14] The flyleaf of the 1983 edition continues the eerie elision of image and person as survivor: "Of the 16,000 photographs [Vishniac] managed to take—secretly and under difficult circumstances—only 2,000 survive." As in Kacyzne's photographs, the camera style promises the truths of documentary witness. But Vishniac's high-contrast prints, dramatic lighting, extreme close-ups, and frequently anecdotal, storytelling captions intensify the drama of body and soul.

FIGURE 9. Roman Vishniac, *Open Sewer, Lublin.* Used with permission of Mrs. Mara Vishniac Kohn.

Poverty and powerlessness are the center of Vishniac's "vanishing" world. It is true that by the late 1930s the situation for many Jews had become desperate. As an economic depression engulfed Europe, Jewish merchants and businesses were frequently boycotted, and the deprivations increased. Now in these pictures, streets are more miserable (Fig. 9); the children are pathetic ragamuffins, the women exhausted caretakers, the men down-and-out porters or pious rabbis. Occasionally, yeshiva students move through the streets of Warsaw in adolescent clusters, or Nalewski Street teems with life, but these are rare signs of social exuberance. More typical are pictures of caftaned and bearded rabbis, or stooped old men,

FIGURE 10. Roman Vishniac, *Nat Gutman, the Porter.* Used with permission of Mrs. Mara Vishniac Kohn.

whose exotic garb and inching steps emphasize strangeness and vulnerability. Repeated figures, several shown close up, make the misery more palpable. A dramatically lit, pensive woman, labeled *Nat Gutman's Wife,* is shown opposite a still life of her family's meager meal. A few pages later, pictorially separated from this domesticity, the porter Nat Gutman appears (Fig. 10), a quizzical half-smile etched into his features, as the camera highlights the tears of his ragged coat.

The poverty, vulnerability, and hopelessness of these Jews gives way entirely, however, in the scenes of religious life. As photographic partner to the miseries of the body, in Vishniac's text spirituality is the only coin of this realm. Interspersed between the public and domestic views,

such images function as pictorial interludes and reminders of what ultimately defines this populace. The book opens with an extreme close-up of
a religious-school leader, moves on to children crowded over holy books,
and further on to ecstatic figures rapt in prayer and ritual. The piety is
compelling, impassioned, exotic (Figs. 11, 12), especially as the camera
enters the study hall of the Mukachevo Rebbe packed with fur-hatted
men, the walls lined with tattered volumes and holy books.

As a space of learning, ritual, and prayer this is an entirely masculine
and patriarchal world—from little boys and teachers, to solitary scholars,
to the rabbi-sage. Fervent and intensely focused, it is also a space of homosocial community, where material lack and powerlessness in the secular
world is replenished through spiritual desire and ritual. In these images

FIGURE 11. Roman Vishniac, *Rabbi Rabinowicz and His Students, Mukachevo.*
Used with permission of Mrs. Mara Vishniac Kohn.

FIGURE 12. Roman Vishniac, *Choir Singer*. Used with permission of Mrs. Mara Vishniac Kohn.

of men draped in fur hats and prayer shawls, huddled together or rapt in prayer, a kind of eros appears, its energy, concentration, and release. It is only here—the least validated sites within the modern secular nation— that Vishniac pictures a community of effective men.

At the same time, images of narrow, arched passages, darkened chambers, outlandishly dressed figures poring over ancient Jewish texts— all this suggests enclosure and arcane mystery, a sort of Hasidic Gothicism, to borrow the phrase of film critic J. Hoberman (1991), with all the pleasures and terrors the Gothic implies.

Such photographs have become tokens of nostalgic sentiment, as well as texts of mourning and loss. But as a documentary narrative of nation or image of a people, they are troubling markers of difference. Cultural identity is standardized as spiritual magic or misery and reinforced as stereotype. Indeed, Vishniac's pictures so effectively represented the figure of the despised Jew that they were used—misused—by a Dutch-Nazi publication in 1942 as evidence of Jewish barbarism and inferiority.[15] Emphasizing exhaustion and defeat, the helpless and the strange, they present a costumed and pathetic people, without potency or agency, at ease only in study, prayer, and Orthodoxy.

In distinctive ways, then, these three representations of *shtetl* and traditional Jewish culture play against, but also with, core structures of the modern nation: its poverty, piety, and difference are the nation's sites of stability and oppression, its strength and weakness, the tests of its tolerance. The image of *shtetl* Orthodoxy is exotic and strange in the modern state—though perhaps a fitting partner to fervently Catholic Poland. Mired in poverty, these Jews are a colorful and distinct people. But for Kacyzne at least, and to some extent in Vorobeichic's modernist imagery, they are also the basis of a modern populace, their energy organized not through militant revolution or conquest, but as continuity through labor, learning, and community. Only in Vishniac's images is this narrowed to misery and piety, marked by its difference, and tacitly doomed.

The Pale of Settlement and *shtetl* culture are gone, and Yiddish culture struggles to survive without a fixed geography. Some might say these pictures forecast its disappearance, though, I think, that goes too far. Sixty years ago, the pictures offered Jewish viewers moments of nostalgia and reason to modernize. But they are also meaningful now amid the continuing nationalisms of the present, the conflicts of multicultural-isms, and renewed debates among Jews about Jewish identity. To viewers, then as now, they raise questions of modernization, ethnic assimilation, and the problematic condition of the "distinct society" within the modern nation-state. With less certainty than conventional nationalism and more complexity than nostalgia or relief, the pictures pose the ambivalence of Diaspora culture and minority nationhood.

The Veils of Time

ON THE HISTORICAL DIMENSION
IN CULTURAL ANALYSIS

Stephen Bann

It has been said that a little theory takes us away from history, but a bit more theory leads us back again. This would perhaps be a dispiriting thought if we did not take into account that the history we come across the second time is perhaps quite different from the one we said good-bye to originally. My intention in this paper is to look at the various implicit models of historical reference that we can observe in different types of contemporary cultural analysis. Then I shall pass to a model of my own, which has been particularly influenced by my recent work in the area of exhibitions. It will be up to the reader to judge how far, if at all, the mode of historical inquiry is revised by the different paradigms or models which I shall put to use.

I want first of all to make a rapid survey of a number of influential pieces of cultural criticism from the postwar period which introduce history in widely differing ways. These are Marshall McLuhan's *The Mechanical Bride* (a book published shortly after the end of the war and no doubt overshadowed by its author's later productions); Umberto Eco's analysis of the *Steve Canyon* cartoon strip, first published in *Apocalittici e integrati* (1965) but referring to a strip which appeared on January 11, 1947; and Roland Barthes's famous essay "Myth Today," first published in *My-*

thologies (1957) but referring to a cover of *Paris-Match* which had appeared two years before.[1]

To take McLuhan first of all, it is notable that history itself constitutes a kind of degenerative spiral in which the cultural critic is involved—and from which he must strive in some way to emancipate himself. In the preface to his book, McLuhan quotes from Edgar Allan Poe's story "Descent into the Maelstrom." Poe recounts the tale of a mariner who was drawn, with his hapless ship, into the force field of the maelstrom, and began to descend into the vortex of destruction. On observing the motion of the water, however, he came to the conclusion that smaller, cylindrical objects were proceeding down the vortex at a slower rate than large, irregular objects. Acting on this discovery, he lashed himself to a barrel and jumped overboard, thus preserving his own life while the ship proceeded ineluctably to its fate. For McLuhan, this is the brief of the cultural critic: to observe the laws of the degenerative discourses of the mass media, and so to obtain a perhaps provisional escape from the dynamic of its debasement.

Thus for McLuhan, the discourse of culture is in itself degenerative. The strip cartoon figure of Tarzan, for example, is a crude but identifiable transformation of the myth built around Lord Byron, the English aristocrat and poet "gone native" in his Mediterranean escapades. The critic should note this, but should be under no illusions that the degenerative vortex is not also dragging him down. As opposed to this existential involvement, the role of the cultural critic for Umberto Eco is decidedly cooler and more objective. History is by no means absent from the analysis of the *Steve Canyon* strip. But its presence can be detected *punctually*, that is to say, here and there, in the interstices of the semiotic analysis.

For example, Eco rightly emphasizes the role played in establishing Steve Canyon in the first frames of the strip by the codes of wartime camaraderie. Steve is a long-distance traveler—we know this from the start, even though we have not seen him face to face, and simply rely on the greetings of his various interlocutors. We cannot yet tell that he is a private detective, but the exchange with the blind (no doubt war wounded) "Sarge" informs us that the two of them have been involved in recent service together. Furthermore, the encounter with Steve's faithful secretary, puzzlingly arrayed with a rose tucked behind her ear, becomes entirely comprehensible if we refer it to the immediately postwar scene. To quote

Eco: "She too stands for a prototype that can be classified by a preferential code of the 40s. She represents a discreet mingling of Mediterranean and Oriental glamour, and this refers in turn to the two main theatres of war, from which the Americans subsequently imported their models for post-War eroticism" (1976: 24). It will be evident that this type of historical reference is wholly different in kind from that of McLuhan. The semiotic critic is also, inevitably, a historian: that is to say, the critic must be able to discern the operation of the "preferential code."

But this has an interesting consequence, as far as our own perspective is concerned. For Eco, the 1940s were, at the time of his writing, within the range of recent memory. From the late 1990s, however, their codes are so remote as to require a positive program of historical research. We might say that, while McLuhan's cultural critic experiences the degenerative dynamic of mass culture, the critic following Eco has to cope with the historical entropy of "preferential codes." Unless the critic is confined to the analysis of contemporary or nearly contemporary material, he is obliged to enlist the aid of the historian, or become a historian himself.

This issue of the necessarily historical component of semiotic analysis becomes especially acute as we look back on the great age of semiotic analysis in the 1960s and 1970s. How far shall we have to fill in—as time progresses—the unstated assumptions that are relative to particular, historically conditioned states of knowledge, which the critic took for granted? The obvious conclusion is that the critic also becomes the object of a historical hermeneutics, insofar as he is unable to stand outside and make explicit the totality of the codes in which and through which he operates.

This leads me to the third of my opening examples: Roland Barthes. One might indeed say that Barthes accurately foresaw the need for the cultural critic to accept his own immersion in the codes of his own times. Indeed he self-consciously stages his own access to mass culture—in many if not all of his writings—not as a scientist objectively analyzing the systems of sense, but as a *flâneur* witnessing in casual terms the sights and sounds of the surrounding world. This is certainly the case with his celebrated analysis of the "black soldier saluting the French flag," glimpsed on a magazine cover at the barbershop. When Barthes reconstructs the second-order signification of "France having an empire on which the sun never sets," he does no doubt faithfully disinter a "preferential code" of the mid-1950s, when the nation was painfully extricating itself from its colonial presence in Algeria. But it is less certain that he correctly interprets the *Paris-Match* cover to which his attention was originally drawn. In effect, Steve Baker has demonstrated conclusively that this cover of the magazine from June 1955, which Barthes of course never illustrates, can only with difficulty be accommodated to Barthes's inferences. A historical investigation of other photographic sources from the mass media of the time suggests that the codes in play were by no means as unequivocal as Barthes implies.[2]

I mean no criticism of Barthes in reaching this conclusion. On the contrary, I see it as part of his strategy that he does not, precisely, offer a definitive interpretation. He simply uses the chance experience of the glimpsed *Paris-Match* cover to draw attention to a coding of French nationalism which he, as a contemporary, could not fail to detect. This leaves us the task, with regard to any potential historical reconstruction, of taking into account all the rest of the remaining evidence, including Barthes's own testimony as a privileged, but not exclusive, register of meaning.

I have run rapidly through these three examples of cultural criticism, not in order to exhaust their rich and individual implications, but in order to extract a range of positions which the critic can take up in relation to history. In his existential involvement, McLuhan's critic rightly diagnoses that he is caught up in the same dynamic as the rest of society. But his ambition is simply to delay his own descent by the observation of the laws of the vortex. And who knows? The vortex may reverse itself, as Poe's maelstrom eventually did, and restore him to safety. This literally apocalyptic possibility is perhaps fulfilled, for the later McLuhan, by the Pentecostal prospect of a world whose distances and contradictions have been annihilated by the grace of the electronic age, ushering in the society of the "global village."

For Eco, no such prophetic fulfillment is envisaged. The cultural critic makes no explicit judgments of value on the relationship of contemporary codes to the prestigious iconography of the past. For example, "Steve is an iconographic element that can be studied iconologically, like the miniature of a saint with its canonical attributes and a fixed kind of beard or aureola" (1976: 24). The system of Christian iconography can be interpolated within an overall semiotics without any derogatory implications, and almost without irony. The only ironic factor, perhaps, lies in the potential disentanglement, over a period of time, of the function of semi-otic criticism and the historical culture which, in Eco's case, so powerfully and continuously underlies it. We have the luxury of an Eco who knows about the traditions of iconography, as well as how to apply them to the dissection of a cartoon strip. But what will happen if a later cultural critic is ignorant, not merely of iconography, but even of the codes of the im-mediate postwar period which Eco can so effectively and helpfully supply?

One answer lies in the example of Barthes, as I have described it. The cultural critic aspires to a condition of self-effacement: that is, he re-fuses to be anything but the casual observer of a feature of his times, from which he has drawn a meaning which we can ourselves discover to be no more than provisional. According to this reading, the cultural criticism in-evitably has to be resumed again and again, with all the evidence that can be brought to account. There is no way of short-circuiting or otherwise facilitating the task of historical reconstruction, which remains indispens-able. The most that can be credited to the cultural critic is that he may have constructed a viewpoint at which it suits us, for a short moment at any rate, to take up our stand.

To put forward my own model of cultural analysis in the context of these different approaches is not, by any means, to present it as an "Open Sesame" which will avoid the difficulty of accommodating criticism to a historical viewpoint. On the contrary, what interests me is precisely the possibility of modeling a cultural approach which takes into account the evolution of historical consciousness over the last two centuries. The main difference is that, whereas the historical model applied in all three pre-vious examples has been one of degenerative or entropic loss, my own inclination is to construct a model of historical recuperation, which is dia-lectical, contrasting the dynamic of loss with a desire for retrieval. This, perhaps, is one way of establishing a persona for the cultural critic which is intimately related to the revolution in historical consciousness which took place between the end of the eighteenth century and the beginning of the nineteenth.

For reasons which will no doubt become clear, my materials for this demonstration derive from my direct engagement with objects, all more or less cultural in their origin, that I have encountered in the course of re-cent work on exhibitions and other artistic projects. In particular, I draw upon my participation in the exhibition *Corps de la Mémoire* and at various exhibition sites in the city of Toulouse (March–June 1995), and upon my collaborative work with the artist Bob Chaplin on the artist's book, *Eminent Views*, privately published in 1995.

The primary reason for choosing this particular emphasis is to insist, perhaps hyperbolically, on the point that the cultural critic is not simply someone who analyzes and reorders textual material, even to the point of undermining it and exposing its hidden ideologies. Barthes wrote in 1970, in the second edition of *Mythologies*, that, in relation to the "essential enemy" which is "the bourgeois norm," there can be "no semiology which cannot, in the last analysis, be acknowledged as *semioclasm*" (1970a: 9).

This may be true. But no less important is the point that the cultural critic works on discourses which have already been fragmented, already destroyed, if we set them within the broader historical perspective. McLuhan's view of contemporary culture as a degenerative vortex into which the great myths of romanticism tumble like fragments of a shipwreck caught in the maelstrom may seem too overheated as a portrayal of the post-semiological critic's field of operation. But there still remains the necessity of defining the historical viewpoint in relation to the dialectic of loss and desire which romanticism set in place.

Prominent among the works of art which were my own contribution to the *Corps de la Mémoire* exhibition was a drawing by the Toulouse artist and architect Pascal Virebent, entitled *Les temps voilent l'Antiquité* (The times veil Antiquity) (Fig. 1). Virebent the architect was responsible for much of the eighteenth-century layout of the city of Toulouse, and his life span, from 1746 to 1831, covered the entire gamut from *ancien régime* through Revolution and Empire to Restoration. This drawing is clearly based on the engraving used as a frontispiece for the Comte de Caylus's *Receuil d'antiquités* (third volume, 1759). However, Virebent's dramatic light and shade create a very different atmosphere from the dry cross-hatching of the engraver, and a marginal gloss on the drawing suggests at the very least a new interpretation of the original. We learn that the figures of time are "making every effort to hide and obscure" the Egyptian sphinx, but simultaneously the putti are "raising parts of the veil in order to uncover this object of their curiosity."

A paradox is neatly presented by this drawing. First of all, there is the impossibility of clearly distinguishing in the static work of art between

FIGURE I. Paul Virebent, *Les temps voilent l'Antiquité*. Musée Paul Dupuy, Toulouse.

"veiling" and "unveiling." If we were told that this drawing bore the title *The Times Unveil Antiquity*, we would easily be able to interpret it in this way. This is not a trivial point because, in a sense, to veil is to unveil, provided that we leave a significant fragment which can serve as a focus for attention. Virebent may or may not have overinterpreted the original engraving by insisting that it showed both processes taking place at once. But he certainly did not misunderstand the psychological significance of a reading which would acknowledge the intensity of "curiosity" in the same measure that it lamented the fact of loss.

There is no conclusive way of dating this fascinating work. It is tempting to imagine, however, that it may have been produced around 1800, when Napoleon's Egyptian expedition had facilitated the study of hitherto legendary antiquities.

Indeed Virebent's drawing makes a piquant comparison with the print, dated 1811, which the English artist and antiquarian Thomas Stothard placed at the beginning of his great survey *Monumental Effigies*: its title is *The Monumental Effigies Rescued from Time*.

On one level, Stothard's image celebrates a movement exactly contrary to that of Virebent. "Time" is being trodden underfoot by a triumphant female figure who may be the Muse Clio, and the putti are aiding the escape of the effigies in their upward movement. But this resurrection only goes as far as rescuing the vestiges of the past as fragments. How will they come to life?

The answer can only be that there is a displacement, in the ensuing combination of texts and images, from the carefully visualized images of medieval knights recumbent on their tombs to the accompanying narrative, which essays the full-blooded history of their life and deeds. To be truly "rescued from Time," these fractured effigies need the articulations of romance: of a historical novel by Sir Walter Scott, perhaps, which would construct a scene for them.[3]

It is my contention that we can now quite fully understand the mechanisms which such a description of these two drawings calls to mind. Michel Foucault, in particular, has written eloquently on the recuperative strain in the romantic repossession of history, which he sees as a reaction to the overpowering sense of being "dispossessed" of history experienced at the threshold of the modern (i.e., post-eighteenth-century) world.[4] But what model shall we take to signify this further stage in the consciousness

FIGURE 2. The Waldershare Belvedere, Kent, England. Photograph by Bob Chaplin. Used with permission.

of the modern investment in the past? To evoke the main question posed by this paper: how can contemporary cultural criticism incorporate the dialectic of veiling/unveiling as a historical dimension governing the perception of the cultural field?

I take for my first model the configuration which is also the opening section of Chaplin's *Eminent Views*. Across a plowed field, we observe a partly ruined building, which is the Waldershare Belvedere (Fig. 2). Built in 1725–27 for Sir Robert Furnese and probably designed by the foremost English Palladian, the Earl of Burlington, this impressive building is a double cube, with a high window in the Venetian style, and a terrace (under restoration in the photograph) from which the desired view was to be obtained. I have never climbed to the top of the Belvedere to see the vista from the terrace, since the state of repair has made that impossible. I suppose, however, that the view from this Belvedere placed at the edge of the Waldershare estate, between Dover and Sandwich in East Kent, would have been historically significant in the highest degree for those who constructed it: nothing less than a vista of the coast of Kent, where the Romans first landed and built their Accessus Britanniae (the fort of Richborough), and, a few centuries later, St. Augustine came to bring Christianity to the court of King Ethelbert of Kent.

Frank Ankersmit has referred to the historical text as a Belvedere: that is to say, it is constructed so as to offer us a clear vista of the historical terrain. But what if the Belvedere is in ruins? What if the view it offers can only be imagined, or reconstructed, as something which once upon a time was available to viewers? We may indeed respect the intention of classic historiography as one of constructing the means of access to an unclouded view. But what happens when the conditions of viewing become problematic? The great German historian Friedrich Meinecke well understood that a change in such conditions had occurred when he asserted that, before the Renaissance, history "looked to be one simple flat level that could easily be surveyed," but after that period, "was seen to be a matter of perspective, and [possessed] infinite depths of background."[5] What Meinecke perhaps did not take into account was the likelihood that perspectival thought, in its turn, would reach a stage of self-consciousness and indeed crisis. The recipe for producing, and controlling, "infinity"—namely the unique vanishing point—would lose its validity.

My reference to the Belvedere, which I have never ascended, is a fragment found at the base of the building but certainly derived from its stone facing (Fig. 3). It resembles, in itself, the fragments of stone dating from the Stone Age—ax heads, arrowheads, and other implements—but could not be confused with one of these, since its parallel striations are the infallible signs of masonry in the classical and Palladian tradition. It therefore relates to a specific historical break—let us say, that between stone as an instrumental agent of primitive man's domination of his environment and postclassical man's attention to the ornamental dressing of sacred or public buildings.

I will not go any further in explaining the mode in which this fragment in my possession might be an emblem of access to history except by way of an illustration from Barthes. As we have argued, Barthes took the *Paris-Match* cover and used it to reconstruct a coded message which he, and the rest of the French public of 1955, were held to subscribe to: that of the French Empire transcending national divisions. But what if Barthes had been able to consider the press photograph, which originated the *Paris-Match* cover, as Steve Baker unearthed it? What if he had looked

FIGURE 3. Fragment of stone fallen from the facing of the Belvedere. Photograph by Bob Chaplin. Used with permission.

at it as a photograph with the specific tools of analysis that he had developed by the stage of his last book, *La chambre claire* (1980)? Barthes once referred to the status of the photograph as an "ephemeral monument."

He also drew attention to the "paradox" that "the same century invented History and Photography."[6] My piece of stone from the Belvedere perhaps counts also as an "ephemeral monument"; and just as my stone bears the traces of the imposing structure from which it came, so the press photograph—any photograph—stands in relation to an original historical scene in a state of fragmentariness and incompletion which remains, nonetheless, a guarantee of past propinquity.

I will take one further illustration to supplement the message of the stone. Also in the *Corps de la Mémoire* exhibition at Toulouse, I was permitted to include one of the major paintings of the city's collections, usually displayed in quite unpropitious circumstances, and place it in the medieval refectory of the Jacobins church, where the accompanying works included antique Roman busts and contemporary drawings by the American artist Cy Twombly. The painting was Ingres's *Tu Marcellus Eris* (Fig. 4), which for the period of the exhibition was therefore placed in a historical continuum involving "original" classical pieces as well as contemporary works invoking classical subject matter in very diverse ways. *Tu Marcellus Eris* is not a ruined Belvedere. But it is a work which concretizes, in an extraordinary way, the implication that the classical discourse has been interrupted—brought to an irrevocable conclusion—and yet remains the source for subsequent invocations whose character must be irreversibly changed by the recognition of that fact.

Ingres composed more than one version of this subject, somewhat diminishing its complexity by concentrating on a restricted composition as in *Augustus Listening to the Aeneid* (1812), which is in the Belgian

FIGURE 4. Jean-Auguste-Dominique Ingres, *Tu Marcellus Eris*. Musée des Augustins, Toulouse.

National Collection. However, the Toulouse version is larger and contains four main figures instead of three. One may suppose that the attraction of painting the simpler version lay precisely in the fact that the emperor receiving the message, in the company of his wife and sister, does not have to suffer the inconvenient presence of the poet. Yet it is precisely in the confrontation of the poet/enunciator and the emperor who cuts him short that the main interest of the subject resides.[7]

The scenario is a simple one. Virgil is reading the *Aeneid* in the presence of Emperor Augustus, his patron, and he has reached the point in his text where reference is made to the future heroes of the Roman state, shown to Aeneas in a vision by his old father Anchises. "Tu Marcellus eris" is the identification of one of these future warriors, the son of Augustus's sister, Octavia, who, by the time of Virgil's reading, has been put to death at the behest of the jealous wife of Augustus, Empress Livia. Ingres shows Augustus lifting his hand to arrest the embarrassing prophecy, while Livia gazes impassively and the distressed mother faints across her brother's lap. One may note that Ingres has constructed a scene clearly reminiscent of the Davidian neoclassicism of the contemporary French school, with a friezelike arrangement of personages and a stone surface, draped with a blue cloth, to bring the arresting profiles closer to the spectator. He has also, however, conceived this dramatic confrontation as a night scene, with a single torch offering dim illumination.

What is remarkable about this work in the neoclassical context is that Ingres foregrounds the enunciation of the poet. The words have been spoken. Augustus cannot unsay them, nor can he reverse the writing of the *Aeneid*, whose message has come down to us as it came down to Ingres and his patron, the General Miollis.

The prophecy which Virgil has just enunciated can be seen written on the scroll from which he reads. While it is unfulfilled on one level— Marcellus will not be a great soldier, since his career has been mercilessly cut short—it is vindicated on another. The prophecy, "Tu Marcellus eris"—"you will be Marcellus"—comes across to us, insofar as the written text, metonymically asserted by the title, points to the futurity which we ourselves occupy.

Another way of putting this would be to say that the painting stages before us the displacement of the word (the prophecy) from *énonciation* to *énoncé*. Virgil has fallen silent, arrested by the gesture of Augustus. Only

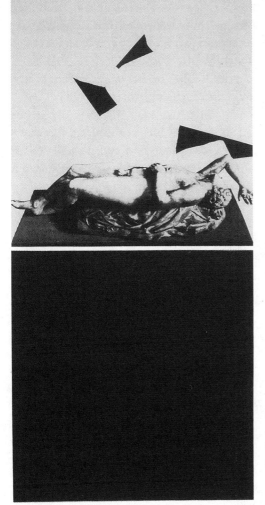

FIGURE 5. Giulio Paolini,
Niobide blessé (1982).
Courtesy of the collection
of Yvon Lambert, Paris.

the scroll retains the cursive trace of the message which has been so dramatically foreclosed. In our own period, artists still continue to refer to the classical tradition. But it is as if the suspension in discourse caused by the emperor's ban had been indefinitely perpetuated. The access to the classical world passes by way of the fragment. So the Italian artist Giulio Paolini, in his contribution to the Toulouse exhibition, stages the confrontation of two nineteenth-century classicizing figures, *Allégorie de la*

Tragédie and *Allégorie de la Comédie,* by F. M. Duret, and surrounds them with upturned pedestals and fragments of a sheet of paper, distributed at random on the ground. Or, in another work in the Yvon Lambert collection, *Niobide blessé* (1982) (Fig. 5), he places jagged black fragments over the collage photograph of a classical sculpture, fragments which do duty for the arrows of Minerva piercing the hapless children of Niobe.[8]

The access to the classical world also passes by way of the textual fragment. Cy Twombly's compositions invoke the classical precisely through their titles: titles on occasion lifted from earlier works of art, such as *Aristaeus Mourning the Loss of His Bees.* Scenography is reduced to a mere staining and smudging of the surface with pigment, crayon, and pencil. But the word persists. What has been a pretext in the history of the classical tradition for the creation of "history paintings" and sculptures withdraws into its own verbal status, but is recuperated by the cursive flow of Twombly's "straying signs."[9] History is glimpsed in the extreme moment of its own metamorphosis.

PART II

CLOSE-UPS AND MIRRORS

The Return of Close Reading,
with a Difference

CLOSE READING: what's new about it, and what's the big deal? In spite of all the gains in recent developments in the humanities, it seems fair to say that the major loss has been close reading. This seems paradoxical in light of at least one main development, that of the widespread practice of deconstruction. Indeed, deconstruction is crucial as the new version of close reading even for those who do not endorse its philosophical position. But that is precisely the point, because, paradoxical as it is, close reading as it used to be practiced quite generally—to the point of stultification—in literary departments is now mostly out of style in that general fashion and confined to a particular corner of the academy considered idiosyncratic by others in the academy.

Close reading, as it was advocated by New Criticism as a polemical position against genetic and deterministic historicism, claimed some sort of "purity" from the subject of analysis. Indeed, subjective criticism, under the combined guise of the intentional fallacy and the affective fallacy, became target number one in New Criticism's polemics. These fallacies have returned with a vengeance since identity became a widely recognized cultural element. But as tends to happen with such returns, the wholesale reendorsement "forgot" to eliminate from the intentionalist and affective positions what had made them so problematic in the eyes of the opponents in the first place. As a result, we got stuck with a dichotomy between objectivist and subjectivist positions that no amount of subtle reasoning was able to uproot.

One of the under-illuminated issues in this debate is the locus of value, in other words, the grounds for critical judgment. New Criticism, as is well known, argued for a valuation of literary density, complexity, and paradox, what later came to be imported from Russian Formalism as "literariness." De facto, the resulting position became a dogmatic separation between ethics and aesthetics. It is one of the merits of deconstruction to have reintroduced the problematic yet important connections between these two by way of a third domain, that of logic. The relentless critique of Western metaphysics has yielded as a by-product a renewed interest in values that brought support to feminists' and postcolonial critics' claims. But a remaining tension in this renewed reading practice has been the unbridgeable gap between the particularistic, microscopic view of close reading and the larger claims of those important critical perspectives. A bridge is needed, as are two firm banks to support it.

The close readings, which the following section offers, have in common a constant focus on that potential bridge and the real gap underneath it. They make loud and clear statements about their programmatic nature, while demonstrating that this loudness does not need to overrule the subtleties and nuances of the objects; indeed, "listening" to the object without the New Critical naïveté that claims that the text speaks for itself creates the kind of dialogical situation that is a major characteristic of cultural analysis. The text does not speak for itself, but it does speak back; the theory will not get away with overruling the object, nor with obscuring its own contributions, impositions, and control. Between the text and the theory, a mobile mirror shifts back and forth to clear the space required by vision, like the close-readerly version of Keller's ambivalent microscope.

Thematically, a recurrent focus on issues of space further binds the essays in this part together. Based in comparative literature and film studies, Helga Geyer-Ryan takes on a topos with a long history that exemplifies the spatial metaphor in cultural analysis that Hoving will address up front. In her attempt to deconstruct the discourses of stability, totality, completeness and presence as her version of "adopting" the past within the presence, Geyer focuses on novels and films in which "agents of masculinity" are trapped by the seductions of Venice. Venice is a topos in the full sense: a place, a rhetorical figure, and a site of questioning the existence of the subject. The wavering "ontology" that Geyer takes from Derrida's *Specters of Marx* makes Venice a place of unhinging and dislocation. She engages the notion of utopian thinking, which has barely survived the collapse of the Marxist states in eastern Europe and the dystopic reality that it revealed as having resulted from the utopic thought that inspired it.

As in a version of the spatial deictic that I briefly sketched in the introduction, Geyer connects the problem of utopia to Lacan's theorization of the dislocation of psychic space, which she then binds to nationalism and gender through her chosen topos. Venice comes to embody nationalism's imaginary suturing of social constructedness to biological offspring and sexual difference, along with the colonizer's claim to ownership. Motherhood and territory become blurred into each other. Through its opposition to the tensions in and between social cohesion and ethnic purity, the topos of Venice becomes the utopian other of such problematic hang-ups of present cultural imaginations.

Working in comparative literature and in art history, Ernst van Alphen is a specialist of contemporary culture. Whereas much of his work analyzes visual art and theories of history, the essay here is unambiguously literary. Or is it? Alphen develops his close reading of Djuna Barnes's classic *Nightwood*—perhaps the most famous work of the modernist as well as of the lesbian canon—as a self-reflexive case for self-reflection as a methodology. His concept of "affective reading" appears as a provocative challenge to New Criticism's rejection of such reading, but those who expect a plea for a mere subjectivism will be disappointed. In fact, the argument is philosphical as much as it is literary.

"Affective reading" positions the act of reading in the present, as self-reflexive, and as based on a "deictic" relation between reader and text. The thematic focus on self-loss in a reading experience with a novel that is "about" the loss of self enables the critic to read not "about" the loss but through the pain that loss produces. This leads to an analysis of reading as pain, and its difference from reading in terms of sensations like hearing and seeing, which are more object-oriented. The essay provides yet another version of the "methodology of deixis," which I briefly proposed in the introduction as a connecting view that binds domains that are normally separated.

Frank Ankersmit is a historian, or rather, a theorist of history and historiography. If he figures in this part and not in Part 1, it is because of his engagement with the historical texts that he read as "closely" as possible. Like the other contributions to this part, his essay patiently and brilliantly disentangles, from the complexity of his texts, a view of cultural analysis in its relation to history which is also a practice of history. He also focuses on identity and its instabilities, and to that effect, he confronts an ancient mythical and a modern historical text, along with some literary ones.

What Gibbon and Ovid have in common, Ankersmit argues, is a nontragic manner of narration in accounts of tragic events. But this crude rendering of his argument only offers a glimpse into the beginning of a complex analysis of the very notion of metamorphosis, which, already in Bann's essay, embodies the wavering of the veiling and unveiling of time. Metamorphosis stands for the change of identity and loses its tragic character if there is an "essence" that resists change. This view is embodied in Ankersmit's own procedure, which juxtaposes, or superposes, Ovid and Gibbon, and by extension, myth and history, as structurally similar over time.

As much as Ankersmit is a historian, this essay is a sample of literary reading in the best tradition of close reading. He analyzes both the narrative structure, or the mode of narration, and the philosophical underpinnings of the two major texts: Ovid's *Metamorphoses* and Gibbon's *Decline and Fall of the Roman Empire*. To announce just a few junctures: stoic ontology is adapted by both authors to their narrative purposes; Rome's fall is less interesting than its long subsisting; and history can only give the story of metamorphosis. The suspicion, which is hardly avoidable I hope, that Ankersmit's reasoning is yet another case of the doubleness of cultural analysis comes to be confirmed at the end. Reluctant as I am to give away his conclusion, I cannot resist suggesting that his essay should be read all along as self-reflexive.

Belief, in whatever form, is an important element in cultural dynamics. Mythical texts and their ideological effect are as present in contemporary culture as they were in more ancient times, in spite of postmodernity's attempt to disavow myth. This is one of the reasons why religious studies as a discipline has an invaluable contribution to make to cultural analysis. Interdisciplinary in itself, this academic field is represented here by a biblical scholar, J. Cheryl Exum, and a philosopher, Louis Dupré, whose essay figures in Part 3. In her essay here, Exum, who is a renowned scholar of the Hebrew Bible, boldly draws on her in-depth knowledge of biblical literature to address the cultural life of mythical texts that Roland Barthes called *doxa*. The shifting truths of the meaning of texts and images need to be left shifting, she contends. The question of her title, "Is This Naomi?," is to remain a question.

Her case is, logically, not the biblical text of the Book of Ruth, although "Ruth" is her case. Instead, she focuses her analysis on a nineteenth-century painting. Exum offers a reading of a visual reading. Thus, she reenacts Keller's point that there is no pristine origin. The rather blunt question of Exum's title is a most important one, for it asks who is who, and who is embracing whom, in a painting of romantic relationship that capitalizes on the déjà vu that underpins the *doxa*. The more general question underlying this particular one asks what the link is between fixing gender identity and the use of recognition as a powerful tool for misreading. Confronting the ancient text, the modern painting, and a 1960 film, the critic makes the biblical text gain from the destabilizing preoccupations of the present.

The methodological point Exum addresses, not only to biblical scholarship but to all historical inquiry, is a renewed version of the classical point of self-reflection as Habermas formulated it: that any choice between possibilities is interest-based. While she claims that misreading is not only inevitable but necessary, she argues that any appeal to "original meaning" and "authentic context" prevents us from noticing that important fact. The point is well taken, and ushers us into the next essay, which further broaches the problematic of particularism and generalization underlying this dilemma.

This problematic is perhaps the most important one in cultural analysis, and the most distinctive feature that sets this endeavor apart from many of its relatives with which it also shares so much, such as cultural studies, postcolonial theory, and feminism. Isabel Hoving, a specialist of Caribbean literature and culture, takes this issue up in a discussion of precisely the difference that cultural analysis can make for those areas. Taking up the spatial metaphor or topos that has been recurrent in the entire second part, her analysis of three literary texts by black women writers focuses on boundary crossing as the site of cultural analysis's special interest in space. In the face of the somewhat idealized and universalizing trope of global nomadism, as in Deleuzian thought, she boldly posits the need to particularize and situate as well as to critique the reality of global migration. This entanglement of literary or philosophical metaphor and social reality offers her the setup for an analysis of the construction of black female identity in the three texts she has selected. This construction is Hoving's "case," and its blending of local and specific issues and meanings, with the need to construct global comparative frames, is her springboard for the articulation of the specific contribution of cultural analysis to postcolonial theory. This intervention is greatly helped, of course, by the fact that she constructs her view through a close reading of literary texts that, written as they are by and about black women, constitute the partner in the very dialogue she attempts to conduct. Her own position thus reflects, and facilitates reflection on, the very dilemma she is discussing. This is yet another angle from which the essay demonstrates what it argues.

There is another kind of text haunting the cultural space. Siegfried Zielinski, founding director of the Kunsthochschule für Medienkünste in Cologne, scrutinizes the implications of the academic structure within which cultural analysis functions, in the face of art in the new media, through the double meaning of the word "power" as energy and cultural authority. "Power" will also be prominent, albeit it in altogether different meanings, in Johannes Fabian's contribution in Part 3. Zielinski raises a number of burning issues through detailed commentary on three paradoxes: the organized regulation of expression as it collides with subject matter that resists such structuring; the loss of self in a culture of self-affirmation; and heterogeneity pushed to the limit. This last paradox is explored through an artistic practice that exemplifies the kind of art produced in Zielinski's institution.

Demonstrating what they argue: the six essays in this section all do this, each in its own way, and together they offer a great variety of methodological reflections articulated, performed, and deictically connected to their objects of study.

—M.B.

Venice and the Violence of Location

Helga Geyer-Ryan

Death in Venice, the title of Thomas Mann's famous novel, is the dominant signification attributed to the image of Venice in twentieth-century cultural productions. Because this text was written in 1911 and published in 1913, its meaning, in hindsight, has disclosed an uncanny programmatic character for the political experiences of the last hundred years of our millennium. But why should Venice be allocated such symbolic significance at all? Why should it figure as the symbolic space in which our accumulated knowledge of history can be acted out in fantasies? Isn't Venice, after all, just another cultural artifact in Italy, whose main function is to offer the Western imagination a mirror of its own grandeur? The mirror is one of Venice's faces and perhaps the one most central to the city's reception in the nineteenth century. But with *Death in Venice*, there emerges another side to the imaging of the lagoon city, a destructive one for the victims of its sudden morbid appeal, and a deconstructive one for the discourses and formations which support or simulate stability, totality, presence, and completeness.

Most of us probably know of the downfall of Gustav von Aschenbach, the celebrated author who had written a vita of Frederick the Great and whose polished prose had become so admired during his own lifetime that he was knighted and his texts were printed in schoolbooks. But to become the poet laureate, von Aschenbach had to repress the other in himself, the dimensions of the emotional, the sexual, and the ethical. In his encounter with Venice, the repressed returns, but it returns with a horrible vengeance. The insistence of his unconscious erupts into his everyday reality and carries him far beyond the pleasure principle and the symbolic order into an impossible *jouissance* under the sway of the death instinct. The surfacing of the perverse, inseparably bound to the ethical dimension in the human psyche, as explained by Lacan in *The Ethics of Psychoanalysis*, has been connected with Venice by several authors since *Death in Venice*. I am thinking in particular of Daphne du Maurier's *Don't Look Now*, Ian McEwan's *The Comfort of Strangers*, the Esther episode of Edgar Reitz's *Die zweite Heimat*, and Michael Dibdin's *Dead Lagoon*. All of these novels or films derive their power from the encounter between agents of masculinity and the seductive trap of Venice.

The catastrophic collapse of the phallic masquerade, so succinctly staged by Thomas Mann, is accomplished by the entropic imperatives of a place which in reality is a nonplace, a true outopia, not in the sense that it is a place that does not exist, but in the sense that it is not a place at all. Venice is neither land nor water, just as its water is neither river nor sea. Nevertheless, it has a heroic past, a past of imperial politics, extreme wealth, and unprecedented artistry. It is precisely the city's geographical ambiguity, combined with the unrivaled abundance and sedimentation of its symbolic order, which captivates the Western imagination and makes Venice the most sublime place in our cultural fantasy. Indeed, Venice has been so relentlessly symbolized, rhetoricized, and allegorized that its normal reality as an Italian community has practically vanished behind its sublimated image.

In twentieth-century culture, Venice has become, above all its other significations, the arche-topos of the uncanny. The fascination that Venice exerts on us has to do with the phenomenon of transference. In the formation of the city, we confront and read the topology of our own psychic reality. There is the symbolic order that is built in stone, painted on canvas and walls, and written down on paper. It is reflected, distorted, and supported in the imaginary mirror of the water. Both are structured around the frightening emptiness and unfathomable depth of space beneath the surface of the water, with all the horrors of the abject ready to emerge unexpectedly, preferably at night. The psychological urgency of its geotopical formation gives Venice its unhinging aura of desire, deconstruction, and destruction. Just as von Aschenbach's phallic fetish, the pen, falls out of his hand (the famous writer's block), his unifying, isolating body armor disintegrates. When his desire flares up, it is for an object, which forces him to transgress every law that has been decisive in the formation of his social and cultural identity. In the figure of Tadzio, von Aschenbach, the celebrated figure of public integrity, deciphers his repressed desire for the ethnic other, the sexual other, and the incestuous other. In the expectation of the gratification of his desire he goes beyond the law of the signifier by willfully risking infection with cholera and the putrefaction of his diseased body.

Cholera, just like the plague which struck Venice several times in its history, is a disease of the abject. The decomposition of the unified body provokes abjection, the fascinated mixture of horror and *jouissance*. Abjection signals the virulence of the real, the field marked by the retreat of the signifier, the law, back into the body of the archaic mother where the subject/object structure vanishes and the individual dissolves. According to Lacan, the resurfacing of the real entails for the desiring subject the fatal experience of entering the field between two deaths. It is a state of being and nonbeing at the same time. One death is the physical death of the body, the other is the ratification of this death by the symbolic order, which gives even the dead flesh meaning in the form of a name, a place, and a rite, thus transforming a corpse into a dead body. Being between two deaths can take two forms: in the first, an individual, normally accorded its symbolic rights, is reduced effectively to nothing and knows that his physical death will immediately follow; in the second, an individual is already physically dead, but there is no proper sublimation into the symbolic memory. This second form provides the background for narratives where ghosts return to settle accounts, as Lacan says, so that they can rest in peace. Hamlet would be an obvious example of this, along with all the other narratives of popular culture where revenants want their proper death recognized by the community.

In the cultural construction of Venice, however, we witness chiefly the first phenomenon. It is not the apparition of the protagonist who seeks, as a revenant, his final rest. Instead, what returns as a specter from the outside is the subject's repressed alterity, which rips apart the symbolic order that support the self's existence as a named individual. In this respect, Venice appears as a purveyor of truth, but it is a truth which is fatal in the end for a subject imprisoned in the narcissistic mirages of its ego and deceived by the supposed stability of its social bonds. It is in this catastrophic sense that Venice is a eu-topia, a place of well-being, as well as a nonplace, an ou-topia, and hence an a-topia, an area of strangeness, eccentricity, and otherness. Of course, those who cannot come to terms with the alien and fluid aspect of all existential phenomena will find in Venice their true dys-topia.

If we perceive Venice as a topos, a place, and a rhetorical figure, whose construction has such a decisive impact on the existence of the subject, then we can truly speak of an ontopology in the sense that Derrida has given to his neologism in *Specters of Marx*. For the moment, I will quote only part of the passage from this work that I will cite in its entirety later. Derrida says: "By ontopology we mean an axiomatics linking indissociably the ontological value of present-being (on) to its situation, to the stable and presentable determination of locality, the topos of territory, native soil, city, body in general" (1994: 82). The ontopology of Venice is an axiomatics of dislocation, of unhinging, of disjoining. Units fall apart in Venice. It is the true place of de-construction.

In film and literature of the twentieth century, it is mainly the bonds of sex and gender which are shown being severed by Venice. Nevertheless, we can also see that sexuality and gender are categories constitutionally linked with the ethnic and national ties in which people find themselves entangled. Tadzio, in Thomas Mann's novel, is Polish, and thus a slave, the traditional racial other of Germany. The same is true of Edgar Reitz's Esther, a Jewish heroine. Both figures of desire bring about the downfall of the central male character, who is of German nationality. In *Don't Look Now*, *The Comforts of Strangers*, Harold Pinter's *Betrayal*, and Anita Brookner's *A Friend from England*, it is always the otherness of the Venetian Italian against which Englishness is outlined and simultaneously questioned.

Because men, for reasons such as the threat of castration and the identification with the father and the paternal order, are more bound to the law than women, and therefore more prone to the forbidden *jouissance* of transgressing the law, the victims of Venice are mostly male. This connection between sexual, ethnic, and national politics has, of course, been thrown into sharpest relief by Shakespeare in his two so-called Venetian plays, *Othello* and *The Merchant of Venice*.[1] Here, Venice herself, as an economically and politically flourishing Renaissance city-state, exerts a self-destructive influence on her children. In the figures of Othello and Shylock, Shakespeare shows us that power, as a totalization of activity, is riven and suicidal by definition. The sea and the lagoon, the very factors that guarantee Venice its power, are also the passageways of its imperilment. The openness of Venice makes it vulnerable. Not only can the fleets of other military and economic powers force their way into the Venetian precincts, but so can the diseases that accompany soldiers and traders. *Death in Venice* illustrates that perfectly, for the cholera that kills von Aschenbach is imported by a greengrocer and a boatman. Venice must not forget Venice.

While sharing in Venice's power, Othello and Shylock have forgotten Venice's warning. They have been corrupted by an attitude of which they are also the victims. Money can no more complete the Jew Shylock than military success can seal off the Moor Othello. The discriminating meaning of their respective Jewishness and blackness must be read not only as demarcations of an imperial and racist ideology but also as indices of a lack at the core of the Venetian's existence, which has been wrongly translated by their ruling classes into the signifiers of racial power politics. When both seek their pound of flesh to plug that existential void, they both tragically fall victim to an illusion, in whose thrall they already languish.

Venice unsettles not only the bonds of love, of nation, and of race, but all delusions of security. It is no coincidence that Hegel speaks about the necessary connection between water and mobility precisely in his *Philosophy of Right*:

The principle of family life is dependent on the soil, on land, on terra firma. Similarly, the natural element for industry, animating its outward movement, is the sea. Since the passion for gain involves risk, industry, though bent on gain, yet lifts itself above it; instead of remaining rooted to the soil and the limited circle of civil life with its pleasures and desires, it embraces the element of flux, danger, and destruction. Further, the sea is the greatest means of communication, and trade by sea creates commercial connections between distant countries and so relations involving contractual rights. . . . Rivers are not natural boundaries of separation, which is what they have been accounted to be in modern times. On the contrary, it is truer to say that they, and the sea likewise, link men together. (Hegel 1942: 151)

I want now to come back to the title of my essay and the quotation from Derrida's *Specters of Marx*. In fact, I want to link the geotopical allegory of Venice to the tradition of utopian thinking. In modern times, the possibility of a utopian construction of society has mainly been pursued by political philosophies oriented in one way or another towards Marxism. Since the collapse of the Eastern bloc and the exposure of the truly dystopian character of its practical politics, the site of utopia has become empty. But the recognition of emptiness and the working through of its implications in the social, political, and cultural field could well be the manifestation of the utopian heritage at the end of this millennium. It was not just for any reason that I insisted, at the beginning of my text, on the term "millennium." The Millennium is an older form of utopia: it is the return of paradise to the earth. We are living at the end of a millennium, at the end of a thousand years of political experience, during which the concept of Utopia has been used so often to camouflage the vilest practices of a politics of power, the latest one having been the notorious "millennium of the thousand-year Reich." The disastrous ideology of the Third Reich had everything to do with the disavowal of emptiness and the nostalgia for fullness, presence, identity, totality, and social bonding. In short, it was a worldview in which otherness, the recognition that every form of knowledge is marked by an alienating existential lack, was repressed in its ultimate form. The catastrophic consequences of such an imaginary polarization of the ego and its other found their atrocious expression in the extinction of a whole population.

It is at this point I want to quote the whole passage defining the concept of ontopology from *Specters of Marx*:

Inter-ethnic wars (have there ever been another kind?) are proliferating, driven by an *archaic* phantasm and concept, by a *primitive conceptual phantasm* of community, the Nation-State, sovereignty, borders, native soil and blood. Archaism is not a bad thing in itself; it doubtless keeps some irreducible resource. But how can one deny that this conceptual phantasm is, so to speak, made more outdated than ever, in the very *ontopology* it supposes, by tele-technic dis-location? (By ontopology we mean an axiomatics linking indissociably the ontological value of present-being [on] to its *situation*, to the stable and presentable determination of locality, the *topos* of territory, native soil, city, body in general.) For having spread in an unheard-of-fashion, which is more and more differentiated and more and more accelerated (it is acceleration itself, beyond the norms of speed that have until now informed human culture), the process of dislocation is no less arch-originary, that is, just as "archaic" as the archaism that it has always dislodged. This process is, moreover, the positive condition of the stabilization that it constantly relaunches. All stability in a place being but a stabilization or a sedentarization, it will have to have been necessary that the local differance, the spacing of a displacement gives the movement its start. And gives place and gives rise (*donne lieu*). All national rootedness, for example, is rooted first of all in the memory or the anxiety of a displaced—or displaceable—population. It is not only time that is "out of joint," but space, space in time, spacing. (Derrida 1994: 82–83)

The "heritage of our time" or, to use a contraction of titles from books by Ernst Bloch, who also wrote *Geist der Utopie und Das Prinzip Hoffnung*, the utopian heritage of our time is the permanent awareness of our archaic dislocation. This dislocation which Derrida describes on the level of national, ethnic, or social rootedness is what I called, in connection with the topos of Venice, an a-topia, a spacing, whose utopian moment consists of the disclosure of otherness or emptiness which marks every phenomenon in our world. This a-topia resonates powerfully in the dislocation of our psychic space, where, as Lacan says, the ego and the subject are never in the same place, but where the subject is always ectopic, out of place, or hetero-topic, at another place. If the personal is political and vice versa, then the "homelessness" they share is the utopian a-topia which Venice offers to experience. It is a warning.

The persistent attraction of the nation, the classical locus of utopian blueprints, bears witness to the fundamental and irreparable dislocation of psychic and social existence. The enchantment that the concept of nation exerts on so many people results from their urge to have that social wound healed, to be completed by being inserted in the totality of a "naturalized" and "organicized" society. This ideological repair-work is carried out at the expense of women. "Nation" originates from the Latin *nasci*, "to be born" and thus sutures the arbitrariness of the social construct by its reference to biological offspring and sexual difference. That the social imaginary invests the term "nation" with the supposed essence of Woman can be read from the fact that the actual presence of women and children marks a strong sense of ownership in the process of colonization (the settlements of the English in America, and of Israel in the Gaza strip and West Jordan). It is also apparent in the measures taken by various nations against the immigration of the families of their foreign male workforce. Nation is an imaginary space where motherhood and territory blur into each other. This fantasmatic construction not only imprisons real women within the narrow confines of biology but also burdens them with the impossible task of representing social cohesion and ethnic purity.

To both claustrophobic fantasies, Venice is anathema. Venice re-
leases from the illusion of bonding, and Venice adulterates the illusions of
purity. It is itself a mixture, a composite, a pastiche: of water and land, of
styles and periods, of streets and canals, of Occident and Orient. It is no
coincidence that male thinkers criticized Venice for its impure and vexing
character: the futurists, Georg Simmel, Jean-Paul Sartre, and, most recently, Regis Debray in his book *Contre Venise*. Venice herself, powerfully
exceeding the narrow confines of the Italian nation-state by her history
and her cultural importance for Western civilization, propels the imagination into the utopian space of the open society.

While I was preparing this paper, I reread by chance Karl Popper's
seminal work from 1945, *The Open Society and Its Enemies*, and I was
struck by its unexpected topicality with regard to the political problems
haunting the world today: xenophobia, neo-nationalisms, ethnic purification, interethnic wars. Therefore, let me finish with a quote from Popper,
where he says:

The principle of the nation-state, that is to say, the political demand that the territory of every state should coincide with the territory inhabited by one nation,
is by no means so self-evident as it seems to appear to many people today. Even
if anyone knew what he meant when he spoke of nationality, it would be not at
all clear why nationality should be accepted as a fundamental political category,
more important for instance than religion, or birth within a certain geographical
region, or loyalty to a dynasty, or a political creed like democracy (which forms
one might say, the uniting factor of multi-lingual Switzerland). But while religion,
territory or a political creed can be more or less clearly determined, nobody has
ever been able to explain what he means by nation, in a way that could be used
as a basis for practical politics. (Of course, if we say that a nation is a number
of people who live or have been born in a certain state, then everything is clear;
but this would mean giving up the principle of the national state which demands
that the state should be determined by the nation and not the other way round.)
None of the theories which maintain that a nation is united by a common origin,
or a common language, or a common history, is acceptable, or applicable in practice. The principle of the national state is not only inapplicable, but it has never
been clearly conceived. It is a myth. It is an irrational, a romantic and Utopian
dream, a dream of naturalism and of tribal collectivism. (Popper 1990: 2: 51)

Affective Reading

LOSS OF SELF IN DJUNA BARNES'S 'NIGHTWOOD'

Ernst van Alphen

> What would it mean to say that in sexuality, pleasure is somehow distinct from satisfaction, perhaps even identical to a kind of pain?
> —Leo Bersani, *The Freudian Body*

Reading as Loss of Self

Djuna Barnes's *Nightwood* has been my favorite book for a long time, and therefore it never occurred to me to write about it. Every reading of this novel had been an experience of total engagement, of being dragged along, but also *dragué* in the French sense. Perplexity about the level on which this novel touched me left me speechless: it was not even possible to formulate what the novel was about or what aspect of it hurt me so deeply, nor to distinguish its characters, nor to reconstruct the chronology of its plot, however cursorily.

The phrase that seems most appropriate to account for this incapacity to reflect upon the very aspects of works which touch me, that which in particular does the touching, is the idea of *loss of self*. I submit that this phrase can provide a productive orientation for that particular aspect of cultural analysis without which this endeavor would lose an indispensable element of its critical edge: self-reflection.

Moments of experiencing reading and looking as an intensive emotion are moments of loss of self which, precisely, preclude awareness of or reflection upon the state they entail. The capacity to reflect seems annihilated or temporarily narcotized at such moments. Rather than using this insight to plead innocent, and to refrain from further efforts to account for the how and the why of the strong affect that reading a novel like *Nightwood* produces on its readers, I rebel against such a verdict. This rebellion has pushed me before (in my book on Francis Bacon) to inquire more or less intellectually into the question of affective reading through an analysis of *Nightwood*. This was all the more urgent as the dominant theme of this novel turns out to be the loss of self. This novel, which causes me to lose myself while reading it, deals with the loss of self. The opportunity is too good, therefore, to miss; it cannot but contribute to the understanding of the affect of reading. And affect is a good place to think about analyzing culture from the vantage point of the present, and through an engagement with self-reflection.

The Desire for Identity

The novel "is about"—if such an attempt to summarize is bearable at all—Felix Volkbein, Nora Flood, and Jenny Petherbridge, who all suffer in one way or another from a lack of identity. They all traverse moments of illusion, erroneously thinking that their lack will be filled by the love they feel for Robin Vote. Robin, however, time and again eludes the person who thinks he or she has found his or her "self" in her. First, she runs away from Felix—after having borne him a son, Guido—then subsequently from Nora, and in the end from Jenny. Most of the novel consists of conversations that these three abandoned characters sustain with the oppressive and depressive figure of Doctor Matthew O'Connor. While in their despair, they are hardly able to listen, and the doctor holds prophetic monologues in which their despair is not softened but, on the contrary, mirrored and aggrandized in a theatrical way. His monologues to Nora, in the chapters "Watchman, What of the Night?" and "Go Down, Matthew" are among the most impressive segments of the novel.

Felix is the first character in the series of three who establishes his hope in Robin as a solution for the problem of the lack from which he suffers. His lack is the result of repressed self-hatred, which is clearly an inheritance from his father, Guido Volkbein, who was unable to accept the humiliations that his people, the Jews, had to undergo in order to survive.

In the fall he was often to be seen in the Viennese Prater with a yellow and black handkerchief in his clenched fists. The handkerchief was a witness to the decree promulgated in 1468 by Pietro Barbo which stipulated that the Jews were to walk around the Roman Corso with a rope around their necks, in order to amuse the Christian population: "This memory and the handkerchief that accompanied it had wrought in Guido (as certain flowers brought to a pitch of florid ecstasy no sooner attain their specific type than they fall into its decay) the sum total of what is the Jew" (1979: 13).[1] Guido has made his self-hatred bearable by imagining that he belongs to an age-old Austrian noble family. For nobility, just like Jewishness, although primarily a social class, can be reduced to a mythical, fairy-tale-like view of humanity, wherein identity runs in the blood. Guido adopted "the sign of the Cross" and alleged as evidence of his noble descent all kinds of proof, such as an emblem and a list of ancestors.

Felix follows the habits of his father, who was already deceased when he was born. Just as his father had done before him, he calls himself Baron Volkbein. Felix is the wandering Jew who "seems to be everywhere from nowhere" (20). The fact that Felix is of mixed descent (his father married a Hedvig of Viennese blood) intensifies his sense of a lack of identity. His passionate interest in "the Old Europe," in aristocracy, nobility, and royalty, becomes obsessive. As a result, he is highly excited when one of his acquaintances, Frau Mann, whose trade was the trapeze and who referred to herself as "Duchess of Broadback," introduces him to a count:

"Is he really a count?" he asked.

"*Herr Gott!*" said the Duchess. "Am I what I say? Are you? Is the doctor?" She put her hand on his knee. "Yes or no?" (43)

That he desires an heir suits Felix's obsession with nobility. The bond of blue blood has to be confirmed over and over again. He falls for Robin Vote, which she allows to happen, and they wed. After some time, she bears him a sickly child and shortly afterward departs, leaving the child with Felix. Years later in a restaurant in the Bois de Boulogne, he tells the doctor what had possessed him when he decided to marry Robin. He explicitly formulates his desire for fixation, the unchangeable, immortality. He manages to reverse his lack of identity into its opposite in terms of family ties, of descent: "My family is preserved because I have it only from the memory of one single woman, my aunt; therefore it is single, clear and unalterable. In this I am fortunate, through this I have a sense of immortality" (161). Yet this immortality needs to be reconfirmed—through marriage: "Our basic idea of eternity is a condition that *cannot vary*. It is the motivation of marriage. No man really wants his freedom. He gets a habit as quickly as possible—it is a form of immortality" (161; emphasis in text). The doctor expresses this even more emphatically by pointing out that anyone who assaults our self-image, the "image of our safety," will be rudely blamed. Robin, however, represented for Felix the ideal image of unchangeability, of permanence; hence, she was the ideal realization of his ideal: "This quality of one sole condition, which was so much part of the Baronin, was what drew me to her; a condition of being that she had not, at that time, even chosen, but a fluid sort of possession which gave me a feeling that I would not only be able to achieve immortality, but be free to choose my own kind" (162). Felix's relationship with Robin is not at all passionate. She seems to be only the indispensable link in his fervent obsession with his past, his hereditary descent, and his fragile identity, which seems based on quicksand. The women who subsequently engage in a relationship with Robin are radically different from Felix in this respect. Nora's love for Robin is a sickening passion. Yet this relationship, too, seems to grow out of a lack of "self."

Nora is an American who robbed herself for everyone (79). She is constantly used and abused by others, and "carrie[s] her betrayal money in her own pocket" (80). She seems to be without core, without self, without identity through which she would be able to relate to others. People like to confess to her, for she does not know baseness and therefore can listen without blaming or accusing the other. This capacity, or rather, this incapacity, is caused by her relationship to herself: "She recorded without reproach or accusation, being shorn of self-reproach or self-accusation. . . . The world and its history were to Nora like a ship in a bottle; she herself was outside and unidentified, endlessly embroiled in a preoccupation without a problem" (81, 82). Her encounter with Robin will radically change this situation. In this love relationship Robin ends up in the position that is invariably bestowed upon her: that of anonymity. After closing down her home in America and traveling for some time through Europe with Robin, Nora buys a house for Robin and herself in Paris, in the Rue du Cherche-Midi. The house is stuffed with tangible proof of their love: circus chairs, wooden horses, Venetian luster, Viennese putti, a spinet from England, and so forth. The house becomes the museum where their encounter is "exposed"—in the triple sense of that verb.[2]

It is precisely those pieces of evidence that become unbearable as soon as Robin is drawn toward Parisian nightlife, leaving Nora behind more and more often. She suffered "from the personality of the house, the punishment of those who collect their lives together" (85). The fixation of their love in a home has yielded an excess of personhood and has throttled love: "Love becomes the deposit of the heart, analogous in all degrees to the 'findings' in a tomb. . . . In Nora's heart lay the fossil of Robin, intaglio of her identity, and about it for its maintenance ran Nora's blood. Thus the body of Robin could never be unloved, corrupt or put away" (86). Over and over again Nora turns out to have lost a part of herself by losing Robin. The latter's nightly adventures become, while the night's hours draw on, "a physical removal, insupportable and irreparable" (89). Nora then walks into the night, "that she might be 'beside herself,' skirting the café in which she would catch a glimpse of Robin" (90). Much later, while still mourning Robin, she tells the doctor the following:

"I thought I loved her for her own sake, and I found it was for my own."

"I know," said the doctor, "there you were sitting up high and fine, with a rose-bush up your arse." . . .

. . . "Matthew," she said, "have you ever loved someone and it became yourself?" (214, 215)

The one moment when Nora's self is at stake is paradoxically the moment when her lack of self merges with Robin. Nora *is* this merging with the other. The loss of Robin is therefore experienced entirely according to this identity of hers: as loss of self.

Jenny's lack of self is revealed in yet another manner. The image we get of her is partly produced by the external narrator and partly by Matthew, the doctor. The aggression with which they represent Jenny seems to suggest that they hold her responsible for Nora's broken heart. Just like Nora, Jenny is an American. She is a middle-aged widow who has been married four times, and none of her husbands have survived her attempts to turn them into important persons. Without ever stealing, Jenny is the prototypical thief: "Her walls, her cupboards, her bureaux, were teeming with second-hand dealings with life. It takes a bold and authentic robber to get first-hand plunder. Someone else's marriage ring was on her finger" (99). Nothing is her own, everything is derived from others. The photograph of Robin which had been made for Nora adorns her table. The difference between person and character is opaque to her; she sends enormous baskets of camellias to actors out of admiration for the characters they represent. The end of the passage in which she is characterized is as damning as one can expect:

She defiled the very meaning of personality in her passion to be a person. . . .
. . . No one could intrude upon her, because there was no place for intrusion. This inadequacy made her insubordinate—she could not participate in a great love, she could only report it. Since her emotional reactions were without distinction, she had to fall back on the emotions of the past, great loves already lived and related, and over those she seemed to suffer and grow glad. (101, 102)

Nobody can reach her because she is nobody, she has no substance, no content. And because she does not have emotional reactions herself, she robs a love, stealing Robin from Nora.

The three characters I have so far presented all suffer from a lack of "self." Felix does so as a consequence of self-hatred, Nora because she is self-sacrifice incarnate, and Jenny because as "thief" she is convinced that she does not have what others have, and therefore must provide herself with it. The desires which their lacks set into motion all have Robin as their object. What kind of person is Robin? Which of her features make her into the desired love-object for all of these people who suffer, each in a different way, from an extreme lack of identity?

Robin is not the only character whose provenance is unclear: she does not have an explicit nationality, for example. She is called the born *somnambule*, the sleepwalker who lives in two worlds—a combination of a child and a desperado (52). Her attitude displays self-annihilation (57). I will return to this later. When she is pregnant, her reactions are the contrary of all the clichés about that experience. She was "strangely aware of some lost land in herself" (70). She takes to traveling, always alone and self-absorbed, as if searching for a part of her that has been lost. Immediately after the delivery, the sense of loss in all its acuteness hits her, not the loss of the child but of herself:

Shuddering in the double pains of birth and fury, cursing like a sailor, she rose up on her elbow in her bloody gown, looking about her in the bed as if she had lost something. "Oh for Christ's sake, for Christ's sake!" she kept crying like a child who has walked into the commencement of a horror.
A week out of bed she was lost, as if she had done something irreparable, as if this act had caught her attention for the first time. (74)

In contrast to the other characters who constantly experience the self as a lack, Robin experiences the loss of self as a unique event which is inflicted upon her. And in contrast to the others, she manages to undo her provisional loss of self. First, Felix sees her "standing in the center of the floor holding the child high in her hand as if she were about to dash it down" (74), and then she ends up running off, leaving the child with Felix.

And after that, she is "herself" again. Robin manages to recover her wholeness. She is, Lacan would say, in the imaginary stage; she knows no desire because she coincides with herself. The doctor describes the difference between her and the other characters thus: "You write and weep and think and plot, and all the time what is Robin doing? Chucking Jack Straws, or sitting on the floor playing soldiers; so don't cry to me, who have no one to write to, and only taking in a little light laundry known as the Wash of the World" (180). The fact that Robin knows no desires also shows in her sense of time. She does not look forward to what is to come, nor does she anticipate it: "And Robin? I know where your mind is! She, the eternal momentary—Robin who was always the second-person singular" (181). Robin is always the addressed—Benveniste's "you"—but she does not speak herself. The word "I" is of no use to her. The Lacanian perspective demonstrates the implications of this restraint. The entrance into the symbolic order, the law, language, generates desire. The experience of total identification characteristic of the imaginary yields to an experience mediated through language. Meaning and unity are lost forever; they can only be promised by language in an indirect way. The desire that this permanent mediation produces is ultimately a desire to return to the unity of the imaginary stage, as fantasized in retrospection. Robin, then, knows of no desire, for she stands outside the symbolic order. She has no desire, and precisely because of this, she is the suitable object of the desire of others. She represents, for the other characters, the once-experienced unity of the imaginary stage.[3]

Body Only

Felix, Nora, and Jenny, the three characters who undertake to redeem their lack of self through their love for Robin, experience, because of that very love, an even greater loss of self. How is that possible, and what does it mean to lose one's self? Elaine Scarry offers a theory of loss of self in her impressive study *The Body in Pain* (1985). The concept of loss of self is central to her analysis of the role of language and bodily pain in situations of torture. In Leo Bersani's analyses (Bersani and Dutoit 1985; Bersani 1987) of Freud's writings on sexuality, loss of self also receives a primary place as the basic experience in any form of sexuality. In the latter case, what is at stake is not the purely negative experience of pain as caused by torture, but rather the ecstatic experience of sexuality. Yet, what these experiences—pain and sexual pleasure, which seem opposed at first sight—have in common is that in both cases the core of the experience is the loss of self. Both are intense, bodily experiences wherein the aware-ness of self seems to be reduced to that of the body. I will briefly present Scarry's view, and then Bersani's, in order to mobilize both to understand (my reading of) *Nightwood*.

According to Scarry, pain differs from other feelings in that it has no referential object. Fear has something or someone as its object: one fears, feels ambivalent toward, loves, or hates someone. Pain, in contrast, is usually experienced in the absolute, without an object. Precisely because pain does not have an object it is not translatable into language; one can-not describe it. Scarry notices a series of consequences which pain, caused by torture or otherwise, may have for the subject experiencing it. One of the crucial consequences consists in the destruction of the boundaries between the self, the I, and the world. That destruction is experienced spatially: "It is the intense pain that destroys a person's self and world, a destruction experienced spatially as either the contraction of the universe down to the immediate vicinity of the body or as the body swelling to fill the entire universe" (1985: 35). Because the awareness of self is reduced to that of the body, the distinction, the boundary between body and world, is canceled. The experience of the body is so overwhelming and intense that either it occupies the entire universe or the universe gets reduced to the body, so that no universe other than the body exists. In an extreme man-ner, the boundaries between inside and outside, between self and other, between I and the world are suspended. The delimited ego dissolves into the experience of this intense bodily experience. For the self can only exist by virtue of a nonself, as distinct from what it is not. When the outside world disappears, so does the sense of self.

This negative reduction in pain of self to bodily experience can be opposed by language. Through a discussion of Sartre's *Le mur* and Shake-speare's tragedies, Scarry shows how the voice, talk, and just talking for the sake of talking can function as a means to prevent the reduction of self to body. In this light we can begin to understand both the monologic speeches of the doctor and the need of Felix, Nora, and Jenny to speak endlessly with the doctor, but also with each other, about their failed loves. It is talking, and in Nora's case also writing, not with a communicative goal but out of sheer self-preservation, in order to preserve the voice and thereby an experience of self other than that of the body only. That is why Robin has to be the second person, the addressed "you": as long as there is a you, the "I" exists as well.

For Scarry, the dissolution of the boundaries between self and world, and the loss of self it entails, is the consequence of physical pain. The doctor, however, seems to be describing in his monologues a similar phe-nomenon of loss of self and in the same terms, yet invariably as a conse-quence of altogether different situations. He summarizes his monologues himself as an answer to the questions the others keep asking him "of degra-dation and the night" (227). And the various cases of degradation which he surveys are invariably cases of degradation, fading of the I, hence, cases of self-loss. All of these situations of degradation are experienced so in-tensely, are so confusing for the self-awareness of the subject, that they become similar in structure to the destruction of the subject which is the consequence of physical pain. "There are only confusions" (39), says the doctor already in the beginning, before the three "lost" characters have as much as met Robin.

The moments of degradation which the doctor evokes and analyzes in utterly brilliant language are sleep, dream, love, death, and drink. They all are subsumed under the heading of the Night. The title of the novel is then an allusion to the wood of degradations which sleep, dream, love, death, and drink constitute together.[4] About the night, the doctor says that it is related to the day precisely because of what distinguishes it from the day. While the day is carefully divided beforehand, the night comes unannounced and unpremeditated. Nora draws the right conclusion: " 'I used to think,' Nora said, 'that people just went to sleep, or if they did not go to sleep, that they were themselves, but now,' she lit a cigarette and her hands trembled, 'now I see that the night does something to a person's identity, even when asleep' " (119). The doctor distinguishes between the attitudes of the French and the Americans towards the night. We should keep in mind in this respect that Nora, Jenny, and the doctor are Americans. The American keeps day and night carefully separated out of fear of losing his dignity (124). The French, in contrast, see day and night as a continuous whole. The Parisian nights (the nights during which Robin wanders around, is drunk, allows men to finger her, and commits adultery with women) are the nights which pass over into the days by means of the drunkenness caused by the wine drunk during the day. The American, in contrast, begins to drink only "when his soap has washed him too clean for identification" (131). The Americans lose their identity precisely through their forced, obsessive attempts to keep it, while the French are chaotic and derive from that feature a kind of continuous, firm self. Robin, with her French way of life in the Parisian nights, is opposed in this respect to her American lovers.

Sleep leads to a form of loss of self similar to this, according to the doctor: "Let a man lay himself down in the Great Bed and his 'identity' is no longer his own, his 'trust' is not with him, and his 'willingness' is turned over and is of another permission" (119). The sleeper gets so used to sleep that the dream forms itself with increasing ease over the years and "eats away its boundaries" (127). The doctor seems to suggest here that the dream can also penetrate into waking life so that the self gets lost within the dream. Robin has been called a somnambule, and is a sleepwalker day and night, living day and night in a world whose boundaries are not fixed.

The doctor quotes with approval the poet Donne, who once wondered if a man could sleep on his way from prison to the place of his execution. Yet he concluded: "Man sleeps all his life," and the doctor adds that therefore man is all the more a prisoner of sleep when "he is mounted on darkness" (140). "Sleep" thus becomes the metaphor for the total and continuous degradation, as the Night had been already before.[5]

All this talk about the night, sleep, dream, and drink must prepare Nora for what the doctor has to say about the "night of nights." Each of these expositions can be read as a metaphor for the loss of self to which Nora's love for Robin has led. The night of nights is the night in the beginning of the fall when Jenny met Robin for the first time in the Opéra, and fell in love with her. The doctor was present at this event:

I went into a lather of misery watching them, and thinking of you, and how in the end you'll all be locked together, like the poor beasts that get their antlers mixed and are found dead that way, their heads fattened with a knowledge of each other they never wanted, having had to contemplate each other, head-on and eye to eye, until death; well, that will be you and Jenny and Robin. (145)

The image of the three women entangled together is equivalent to the one the doctor uses to describe his own suffering. While in the former image the self is assaulted because it can no longer be distinguished from that of others, in the following image the self is presented as torn:

If you don't want to suffer you should tear yourself apart. Were not the several parts of Caroline of Hapsburg put in three utterly obvious piles?—her heart in the Augustiner church, her intestines in the St. Stefan's and what's left of the body in the vault of the Capucines? Saved by separation. But I'm all in one piece! (231)

Because his body is still whole, he experiences himself as torn to pieces. The loss of self which is usually seen as characteristic for the moment of death is here presented as the property of life.

Masochism: Fragmentation of the Self

The various forms of loss of self which the doctor distinguishes in his monologues generate in their mildest form confusion, and in their more extreme form intense suffering. Precisely because of this negative experience of the loss of self, it is possible to view sleep, dream, drunkenness, love, death, and the night as close to the negative, anguished experience of loss of self which Scarry describes in her analysis of pain in torture. Bersani, in his reinterpretation of Freud's writings on sexuality, arrives at a much more positive view of the loss of self. Bersani's revaluation of the loss of self seems relevant for the kind of sexual experience which is represented in *Nightwood* as a form of loss of self, and which I have so far left undiscussed: homosexuality, specifically, lesbian love.

Bersani demonstrates how Freud, in his *Three Essays on the Theory of Sexuality* (1905), mixes two views of sexuality which might appear to be incompatible. In the first place, Freud presents the teleological view in which infantile sexuality prepares the way for the goals of "adult," postoedipal, genital heterosexuality. This "adult" experience of sexuality would then be characterized by a hyperbolic experience of the self, a strengthening or aggrandizing of the ego. The sexual pleasure involved amounts to a discharge, a relaxation, a disappearance of sexual excitement, the latter being seen as confusing, painful, unbearable. The problem with this view of sexuality is, however, that it does not explain why the subject aims not only for relaxation, for a discharge of the undermining, fracturing effect of sexual tension, but also for an increase and repetition of that tension. Bersani then goes on to argue for a view of sexual experience as a movement, an oscillation between a hyperbolic experience of self and a loss of any awareness of self.

According to Bersani, the limited view of sex as self-hyperbole represses the experience of sex as self-loss or self-destruction. In his seminal essay "Is the Rectum a Grave?" Bersani suggests that such a repression is caused by the phallocentric order in which power is respected and powerlessness is a shameful taboo. By analogy to the male sexual organ, he calls the strong, tumescent, hyperbolic experience of the ego a "phallicizing of the ego." But this does not necessarily entail the privilege of this sexual experience as psychic tumescence for men:

If as these words suggest men are especially apt to "choose" this version of sexual pleasure, because their sexual equipment appears to invite by analogy, or at least to facilitate, the phallicizing of the ego, neither sex has exclusive rights to the practice of sex as self-hyperbole. For it is perhaps primarily the degeneration of the sexual into a relationship that condemns sexuality to becoming a struggle for power. As soon as persons are posited, the war begins. It is the self that swells with excitement at the idea of being on top, the self that makes of the inevitable play of thrusts and relinquishments in sex an argument for the natural authority of one sex over the other. (1987: 218, emphasis in text)

Bersani's gesture here is to disconnect the hyperbolic, phallic experience of sex in principle from the possession of a penis and the capacity for erections—the literal swelling of what is conceived of as, but need not be, the metaphor for the ego—and from the privileges which a phallocentric society bestows on that possession. But the fact that the struggle between the sexes is often fought through sex explains why the experience of sex as loss of self and destruction of self needs to be repressed. For Bersani, phallocentrism, therefore, should be defined not as the denial of power to women, although it is crystal clear that in practice that is invariably the form it has taken, but rather as the denial of the positive value of powerlessness and loss of self in both women and men (1987: 217).

According to Bersani such a view of sexual experience as loss of self and as self-destruction is not absent from Freud's work, although its presence is fragmented and incomplete. Time and again Freud reverts to a way of thinking about sexual experience in which the opposition between pleasure and pain is canceled. Sexual pleasure then becomes a "jouissance of exploded limits," an ecstatic suffering in which the human organism is temporarily suspended when "it is pressed beyond a certain threshold of endurance" (Bersani 1986: 39). But here masochism takes on not the traditional negative meaning of passivity and submission, but instead a positive valuation of powerlessness. How is that possible? Masochism is not, for Bersani, a perverse and exceptional deviation, but "an evolutionary conquest in the sense that it allows the infant to survive, indeed to find pleasure in, the painful and characteristically human period during which infants are shattered with stimuli for which they have not yet developed defensive or integrative ego structures" (1986: 39). The sexual experience of children is not, in this view, the first step on the road to adult, genital sex but the model and foundation for any form of sexual experience. The only way to survive the situation of powerlessness in which the infant lives the beginning of life is by drawing pleasure from it. Sexuality emerges in this perspective as a typically human phenomenon in the abyss between the number of stimuli to which the infant is exposed and the early development of ego structures which will be in charge of the task they do not yet master: to withstand those stimuli, to "bind" or "cathect" them, in Freudian terminology. Sexuality is then that which cannot be tolerated, bound, by the structured self. Sexuality emerges as a kind of psychic falling apart, as a threat to the stability and integrity of the self. Thanks to the masochistic nature of sexual pleasure, we are able to survive this threat.

If male heterosexuality is, for Bersani, the image par excellence of the phallocentric, proud, and swollen subjective experience of both men and women, he goes on to take male homosexuality as the image of an experience of the subject in terms of sacrifice and loss of self. Against the dramatic backdrop of the AIDS crisis, which gave this image a shocking literalness, Bersani regards the rectum as the grave in which the ideal of proud subjectivity is buried. The sacred value of the self is thus deconstructed in the rectum of the homosexual man:

Gay men's "obsession" with sex, far from being denied, should be celebrated—not because of its communal virtues, not because of its subversive potential for parodies of machismo, not because it offers a model of genuine pluralism to a society that at once celebrates and punishes pluralism, but rather because it never stops re-presenting the internalized phallic male as an infinitely loved object of sacrifice. Male homosexuality advertises the risk of the sexual itself as the risk of self-dismissal, of losing sight of the self, and in so doing it proposes and dangerously represents jouissance as a mode of ascesis. (1987: 222, emphasis in text)

In Djuna Barnes's *Nightwood*, homosexual love appears equally exemplarily as the image of the loss of self, which the novel describes in all forms of repetition and in all variations. With the exception of the marriage of Felix and Robin, all relationships are homosexual. The doctor, Matthew O'Connor, is also a homosexual. The gay characters experience their loss of self, caused by their love, more intensely and violently than Felix, who appears slightly naïve and little given to self-reflection. The exemplary meaning of homosexuality becomes obvious as soon as we realize in which terms this novel represents self, identity, and self-confirmation in a love-relationship. In contrast with Bersani, however, *Nightwood* proposes not male but female homosexuality as the experience par excellence of the subject in terms of the loss of self.

The doctor defines homosexuality in general when he explains to Nora why Robin had begun to feel confined by her relationship with Nora:

She saw in you that fearful eye that would make her a target forever. Have not girls done as much for the doll? — the doll — yes, target of things past and to come? That last doll, given to age, is the girl who should have been a boy, and the boy who should have been a girl! The love of that last doll was foreshadowed in that love of the first. The doll and the immature have something right about them, the doll, because it resembles, but does not contain life, and the third sex, because it contains life but resembles the doll. The blessed face! It should be seen only in profile, otherwise it is observed to be the conjunction of the identical cleaved halves of sexless misgiving! Their kingdom is without precedent. Why do you think I have spent near fifty years weeping over bars but because I am one of them! (209–10)

I have quoted this passage in full because it is highly programmatic in its suggestion that homosexuality emerges out of suspicion, a suspicion, precisely, concerning the coincidence of I and self cleaving the face. This split kills the I, which makes the I similar to the doll. The doctor specifies this same phenomenon in earlier passages for the case of homosexual women: "'And do I know my Sodomites?' the doctor said unhappily, 'and what the heart goes bang up against if it loves one of them, especially if it's a woman loving one of them. What do they find then, that this lover has committed the unpardonable error of not being able to exist—and they come down with a dummy in their arms'" (135–36). The dummy seems to suggest that the lesbian lover is a fiction, that she does not really exist. But there are other passages in the novel where the dummy or the doll reappears with an even more sinister meaning. There the motif of the doll connects lesbian love with death, as if to subscribe to the standard homophobic link between lesbianism, sterility, corruption, and death inherited from the nineteenth century. One example is the passage where Nora tells the doctor about the doll which she had seen on the bed at her visit to Jenny: "'We give death to a child when we give it a doll—it's the effigy and the shroud; when a woman gives it to a woman, it is the life they cannot have, it is their child, sacred and profane; so when I saw that other doll—' Nora could not go on. She began to cry. 'What part of monstrosity am I that I am always crying at its side!'" (201). According to this logic the doll could be seen as the symbol of lesbian love. Similarly, the two wooden horses which Nora and Robin have in their bedroom seem to have that meaning. When Nora, in her desire to avenge Robin's betrayal, takes a sailor to her home, the latter takes a run at the apparently revealing sight of the two horses: "Mon dieu, il y a deux chevaux de bois dans la chambre à coucher" (221), and off he goes.

Yet to suppose that the doll is the symbol of the child that lesbian love cannot produce seems too easy an answer to the question why lesbian love specifically should be experienced as death, as a total loss of self—an answer that ignores the novel's polemic against its intertexts. In one of his oracular phrases the doctor seems to say not that motherhood is regarded in lesbian love as an unwanted side effect but, quite to the contrary, that it is the very motivation for that love, its object: "Love of woman for woman, what insane passion for unmitigated anguish and motherhood brought that into the mind?" (112). Motherhood may seem comparable to lesbian love to the extent that it is an emotional bond of a woman with someone else who is maximally similar to her. That similarity can be symbolized by the same blood, as in the relationship between mother and child. But the similarity can also, or even more directly, be expressed by the same sex. The shared identity of mother and child, the same blood, thus becomes the image of the subjective experience in which the self is recognized in the other, is transferred onto the other, is the other. Motherhood is therefore the foundation of lesbian love in the doctor's view. That relation of identification is realized in lesbian love in a manner which maximally emphasizes the other—the child or the lesbian lover—as the same, own, shared identity: as cleaving. The part that is split off is the remaining self. Motherhood in this view is in the first place splitting, cleaving, cloning. Fatherhood, in contrast, cannot possibly be experienced in this way. There is no unmediated contiguity between father and child. Therefore, fatherhood can be established "only" on the basis of metaphoric similarity. In contrast with that fatherly metaphor, motherhood, grounded in existential contiguity between mother and child, is not only a metaphorical relationship (similarity) but also a metonymical one.[6] The child, a clone of its mother, is thereby the loss of self incarnate: the mother's identity is split up. That situation enables us to understand Robin's need to kill the child that Felix fathered, for she is the only character who does not suffer from a lack of self. That need to kill should, of course, be taken not literally—after all, she does not do it—but as an imaginative representation of the loss of self, which is also represented in parturition. The integrity of her self has been assaulted by giving birth to the child. Self constructed by other produces external wholeness and boundaries; from within, the self can only perceive itself as fragmented and slippery. The self that is assaulted by birth is not the former but the latter; the fragmented self has been ideally experienced during pregnancy, when the other within exemplified the nonwholeness of the self-aware subject. Birth is, precisely, a restoration of the whole subject, with the clone split off and the self seen as complete by the eye of the other.

Doctor Matthew O'Conner, the homosexual who often calls himself a woman and dresses as a woman, gives a paradoxical definition of lesbian love when he characterizes his relationship to his brother and his brother's children. He acutely formulates why lesbian love is in this novel the ideal representation of loss of self:

Is not a brother his brother also, the one blood cut up in lengths, one called Michael and the other Matthew? Except that people get befuddled seeing them walk in different directions? Who's to say that I'm not my brother's wife's husband and that his children were not fathered in my lap? Is it not to his honor that he strikes me as myself? And when she died, did my weeping make his weeping less? (226)

The love for his brother and the latter's children is imagined by the doctor in a description of nonsexual splitting.[7] Barnes seems to allude here to, and present a variation on, Plato's *Symposium*. In that text Aristophanes gives an account of the origin of the sexes. He distinguishes three sexes: male-male, female-female, and a third sex, the male-female called androgyne. The double people become too proud and try to chase the gods from Olympus. Zeus punishes them by splitting them in two halves. Subsequently the people try to retrieve their original state by embracing each other. The originally androgynous ones find satisfaction in that reunion, a satisfaction that entails the procreation of the species. The androgynous couple thus becomes the representative of a heterosexuality primarily destined to procreation. The male-male sex and the female-female sex do not find satisfaction in the embrace with the other sex; they continue to seek their former other half. Finding that other half leads to great friendship amid love which continues even into the realm of the dead. It is an everlasting bond which is not destined for procreation but for love only. Barnes uses Plato's story to cancel the distinction between love and procreation. She redefines love as procreation from the perspective which sees both as love of self.

The doctor's description also reminds us of the reproduction of worms. There, the other is not complementary but the result of parting, the mode of reproduction in which one being is split into two. The other is a clone of the self, not just someone in whom the subject recognizes herself metaphorically, but also someone in whom the subject has been lost, metonymically, as the mother relates metonymically to her child. From this perspective it is understandable that, according to the doctor, lesbian love consists of the mad desire for motherhood. The dummy is not, then, the child that one cannot get but the fixed self-image in the other, outside of the self; the dummy is a symbol of lesbian love and thereby the ideal of absolute loss of self.

When lesbian love in *Nightwood* becomes the representation of an experience of subjectivity and of sexuality as loss of self, then it is telling that the doctor is the one who defines lesbian love from his own experience. His fatherhood over the children of his brother is lesbian because the children are clones, split versions of himself. His fictional fatherhood is experienced as motherhood. He defines himself by means of what he is not. He is the boy who should have been a girl, and he shapes motherhood through the fatherhood that he was denied. By losing himself in men he is the woman that he is not. Loss of self is magnified in the impossible desires of the doctor. For him sexuality leads not to a swollen experiencing of his subjectivity but to becoming totally lost within the object of his desire. He degrades into a woman, a mother, and this degradation, this loss of self, turns him into a lesbian; and that is what he has formulated in the passage quoted above.

This figurative use of lesbianism is not likely to be welcomed by women who are lesbians. A quality which formerly turned them away to the margins of society is now taken away from them as soon as it can bestow honor upon them. Yet I submit that this widening of the concept of lesbianism could also have a positive reflection for those who know the reality of lesbianism. History has demonstrated that heterosexual men were effectively privileged by the fact that their sexuality has become the image of the swollen, phallic experience of self. It can only be fair if lesbians can now draw advantages from the same tension between literal and figurative language use: the image of lesbian love as the ideal of the subject in self-loss.[8]

Reading in Self-Loss

The preceding interpretation of *Nightwood* does not account for the loss of self which characterized my reading experiences of this novel until now. My analytical approach seems therefore to deny my introduction. The fact that the novel is about loss of self does not yet explain why it should produce loss of self in the reader. And I am not alone in this experience; the few articles about this novel tend to say similar things.[9] But as a model of a self-reflective and critical cultural analysis, this is just not a good enough answer. Self-reflection ought not to remain enclosed in a self-mirroring which cannot be but narcissistic. Instead, it owes it to its allegiance to intellectual work to overcome such a stifling pose and embark upon a more analytical, intellectual reflection that engages and involves the self as positioned within the collective endeavor of cultural analysis. In view of such a commitment the question needs addressing: Why was I speechless, why did words fail me, which feature of the novel produced loss of self?

Again, Scarry offers a perspective which helps me to formulate an answer to these nagging questions. Pain is exceptional on the scale of perceptions and feelings because it is experienced as having no referential object. Imagination, Scarry argues in the second part of her book, is the exact opposite of pain, equally exceptional. Imagination consists only of its object. It is impossible to imagine without imagining something (1985: 162). And imagination is only experienced in the images it produces (164). Therefore, Scarry opposes pain and imagination as complementary: "Physical pain, then, is an intentional state without an intentional object; imagining is an intentional object without an experienceable intentional state. Thus, it may be that in some peculiar way it is appropriate to think of pain as the imagination's intentional state, and to identify the imagination as pain's intentional object" (164). It is, however, problematic to view pain as an intentional state or situation, precisely because pain is not directed. One undergoes and suffers pain, but one does not aim or direct it. Therefore, it seems more exact to suppose that pain becomes an intentional state at the moment it is connected with the objectifying power of imagination. In that connection pain is transformed from a passive, helpless happening into a "self-modifying and, when most successful, self-eliminating one" (164). While intentionality in pain is rigorously made passive, intentionality in imagination is maximally made into self-objectification. Scarry clarifies these extremes with the example of a woman working on the land, who feels the wheat with her hands. She feels not only the wheat but also her hands feeling the wheat. The more a perception is experienced as the perception itself rather than its object, the closer the perception comes to pain. And the other way around: the more a perception is experienced solely as the object of perception, the closer it comes to the self-transformation of imagination. These relative differences enable us to distinguish the senses. Because hearing and seeing tend to be discussed exclusively in terms of their objects of perception, these senses tend to be chosen as images of imagination. Feeling, in contrast, is rather described in terms of its bodily localization. In traditional descriptions of the senses, feeling is therefore seen as closer to pain than seeing and hearing are.

Reading should be considered as an example of imagination rather than of pain. Because reading is by definition object-oriented—since we read a text—it comes close to the situation of imagination. Yet this is precisely what *Nightwood* seems to disturb. Reading this novel is closer to the situation of pain in the sense just discussed. The reader, now, is not in the situation of the woman feeling the kernels of wheat with her hands and experiencing thus the feeling of the object, wheat. The reader is rather in the situation of a woman whose finger is cut open by a thorn. She feels at that moment not the thorn but her body, which hurts. Initially I did not experience *Nightwood* as an object, not the plot, the characters, a thematics; I only experienced the effect of the object, the effect of the thematics of self-loss: pain. I did not read a plot in which characters lost their selves, but I read the pain that loss produced. I did not feel the thorn hurting her body, but I felt her body hurting her.

But in what sense can this view (or experience) of reading as pain be used in a self-reflexive practice of cultural analysis? This is an important question because one could argue that "affective reading" cancels the possibility of self-reflection. Yet I would like to distinguish affective reading from more object-oriented reading not as self-indulgent versus self-reflexive, but as a different way of relating to a cultural object. Instead of identifying the object, grasping it, pinning it down, or absorbing it in our understanding, affective reading establishes a relationship by touching the cultural object. This act constitutes a challenge to the inside-outside opposition which so often regulates epistemological questions. Touching takes place on the undecidable edge between inside and outside. And that, I contend, is precisely what makes such acts of reading a practice of cultural analysis. For, whereas a reader, at least in a literal and concrete sense, stands outside the book she reads, she stands inside the culture within which that book makes sense. Touching the object, then, is a way of taking part in that culture, in the strongest possible sense.

History and/as Cultural Analysis

GIBBON AND OVID

Frank R. Ankersmit

"Many experiments were made before I could hit the middle tone
between a dull chronicle and a rhetorical declamation: three times did I
compose the first chapter, and twice the second and the third, before I
was tolerably satisfied with their effect" (Gibbon 1923: 141). This is the
way Edward Gibbon describes, in his *Autobiography*, the agony of arriving at a satisfactory style for his *Decline and Fall of the Roman Empire*, the
book that would assure him his fame as a historian down to the present
day. Indeed, few historians have paid more attention to their style and the
"effect" that it might have on the reader than Gibbon did. He had the
habit of reciting his sentences aloud in order to test the rhythm of his language; he fully exploited all the possibilities of suggestion and persuasion
given by alliteration, and he saw to it that the majestic flow of his prose
would be experienced by the reader as a textual mimesis of the immeasur-
able grandeur of the course of the events that he chose to narrate. Like
many other eighteenth-century historians, Gibbon was fully aware that
style is not merely a matter of presentation but also determines the content of narrative (Gossman 1990: chaps. 7 and 8). "The style of an author
should be the image of his mind" (Gibbon 1923: 141), wrote Gibbon in a
way that may call to mind Buffon's well-known dictum; that is to say, style
expresses the personality of the historian, and the nature of his personality
will define his conception of the past and so the content of his story.

Not surprisingly, therefore, Gibbon's style has been much discussed by historiographers. One may distinguish between two approaches to Gibbon's style. The more customary approach is to focus on his irony. In fact, almost all studies devoted to *The Decline and Fall* consider the all-pervasive irony of Gibbon's writing to be an important clue to the secrets of his texts.[1]

In his influential *Metahistory*, Hayden White demonstrated that style, more specifically, the tropes favored by the historian, give expression to his most fundamental assumptions about the nature of historical reality. Elaborating this assumption for Gibbon, White likewise came to the conclusion that irony is Gibbon's master trope. And Gibbon's most recent biographer, David Womersley, added, "Gibbon is famous as an ironist; but it should by now be apparent that, even when one can discern no ironic *tone*, the prose of Volume I of *The Decline and Fall* tends to be ironic in its creation of a disingenuous relationship between writer and reader" (1988: 89). Here Gibbon is the eighteenth-century gentleman, expatiating on the crimes and follies in the history of mankind with the tongue-in-cheek irony in which only the Enlightenment historian could, and so much liked to, indulge.

However, there is another, less conventional approach to the historian's text that urges us to concentrate on the nature of narrative (its genre, focus, voice, etc.) rather than on matters of style. Leo Braudy, for example, has brilliantly shown that Gibbon, whose admiration for Fielding was as deep as it was sincere,[2] saw in the latter's novels a model worthy of imitation for the narrative organization of his own history. "Fielding's benevolent judge, and Fielding's whimsical but controlling novelist-historian" (1970: 214–15) fascinated Gibbon, and when writing *The Decline and Fall* he tried, insofar as his subject matter allowed him, to write from the same kind of perspective as that from which the narrator of *Tom Jones* told his story. Such is the essence of Braudy's argument.

Like Braudy, I shall not discuss Gibbon's tropology but concentrate on the narrative structure of *The Decline and Fall* and, more specifically, on the features that it shares with a classical author whom Gibbon admired just as deeply as Fielding. That is to say, I want to demonstrate in this essay the similarities between *The Decline and Fall* on the one hand and Ovid's *Metamorphoses* on the other. I hasten to add that I do not claim that Gibbon actually took the *Metamorphoses* as his literary model:

though Gibbon was no less eager a reader of the *Metamorphoses* than were so many of his contemporaries, there is no evidence that Gibbon ever seriously considered it an appropriate model for his own scholarly enterprise. My thesis is merely that a comparison of Gibbon and Ovid may illuminate some characteristics of Gibbon's text that will remain obscure as long as we are unaware of what these two authors have in common. Comparisons like these can be enlightening even when imitation was not deliberately intended by the author whose work we wish to understand, and since Roland Barthes, it has often been argued that stylistic similarities of different literary works can be discovered on the surface as well as on the deeper, structural levels of the texts in question.

I shall begin with a material similarity. No doubt the story of Narcissus, if only because of its role in contemporary psychoanalysis and, more generally, in our contemporary "culture of narcissism," is at present the best known of all the metamorphoses that are related by Ovid in his book. We all know the sad story of how the nymph Echo fell in love with the beautiful youth and how she was handicapped in her effort to reveal to Narcissus the true nature of her feelings. For, like the historian, Echo could only echo what had already been said, and, once again like the historian, being condemned to repetition and inaction, Echo found herself effectively prevented from a union with the object of her strong desire. Repetition and imitation (and we might add inaction to the list) are both the grandeur and the inevitable shortcoming of history; they are what we expect the historian to achieve, but precisely his success in being an echo of the past irrevocably puts the past beyond our reach. For the more the historian's story substitutes acceptably for the past, the less reason we have to value the past itself. Good substitutes, good "echoes," tend to make us oblivious of what they are substitutes for. Echo's unhappy fate is therefore a reflection on the historian's predicament in his relationship to the past. Moreover, this theme of the misfortunes of imitation and repetition is reiterated in the story of Narcissus's falling in love with his own image. From this perspective it surely is no coincidence that it was Echo who fell in love with Narcissus, and we may admire Ovid's wisdom when presenting Echo as Narcissus's adorer in this metamorphosis. For the misfortunes of both originated in the treacherous traps of imitation and representation: Echo was incapable of any initiative since she could only repeat (represent) the words of others, while Narcissus could attain no requitement of his desire since he desired himself via a "representation" of himself. And we may say that the historian always has to discover the right balance between merely echoing the past (like Echo) and the other extreme of becoming fascinated by his own image as it is reflected by the past (as was the case with Narcissus). The story of Narcissus is therefore, apart from its other meanings, an allegory of the problems occasioned by historical writing, and this may explain the interest of this metamorphosis when comparing the *Metamorphoses* to *The Decline and Fall of the Roman Empire*.

When Narcissus was born, his mother asked the seer Tiresias whether this boy would live to a ripe old age. Tiresias replied: "Yes, if he does not come to know himself" (Ovid 1955: 83). But, as we know, he did. Wishing to quench his thirst with the clear water of a spring, Narcissus fell in love with the reflection of his own face in the water, and at the same time, he realized the impossibility of satisfying this love:

My distress is all the greater, he sighed, because it is not a mighty ocean that separates us, nor yet highways or mountains, or city walls with close-barred gates. Only a little water keeps us apart. My love himself desires to be embraced: for when I lean forward to kiss the clear waters he lifts up his face to mine and strives to reach me. You would think he could be reached—it is such a small thing that hinders our love. Whoever you are, come out to me. Oh boy beyond compare, why do you elude me? (1955: 86)

Unable to bear this torture any longer, and incapable of living with this love doomed to eternal frustration, Narcissus gradually wasted away "as golden wax melts with the gentle heat, as morning frosts are thawed by the warmth of the sun" (1955: 87). So in this most peculiar manner Tiresias's prophecy was fulfilled. And it was precisely at the moment of Narcissus's death and metamorphosis into the flower bearing his name that Echo, who had closely and desperately watched all that happened, became unusually explicit: "Woe is me for the boy I loved in vain," she sighed, repeating Narcissus's last words and thereby for the first time properly expressing her own feelings. Hence, only at the moment that the object of her love becomes unattainable forever does she succeed in repeating Narcissus's lamentations from beginning to end. Similarly, the historian can only be articulate and adequate in his task when the object of his story is no more and when his "echoes" can therefore become more real than the past itself.

In fact this is a nearly perfect parable of Gibbon's account of the causes contributing to Rome's fall. Assessing the reign of Diocletian, Gibbon observes:

Like the modesty affected by Augustus, the state maintained by Diocletian was a theatrical representation; but it must be confessed, that of the two comedies, the former was of a much more liberal and manly character than the latter. It was the aim of the former to disguise, and the object of the other to display, the unbounded power which the emperors possessed over the Roman world. (Gibbon 1787–94: 2: 137)

This passage suggests what was, in Gibbon's opinion, the *vitium originis* of imperial Rome. Rome became a "theatrical representation," a reflection or a copy of its original self. It was Augustus who had been the first to transform Rome into a political construction carefully respecting all the outward appearances of republican Rome and who therefore initiated the process that would gradually transform Rome into a lifeless representation or imitation of its own former self. Augustus and his successors, more precisely the best and most perceptive among his successors, looked into the spring of republican Rome and fell in love with the self-image that they discovered on the surface of its waters. Like Narcissus, Rome, in the successive persons of its most constructive emperors, was fascinated by its own image, and it was Rome's love of itself that destined it to the same fate as Narcissus. For owing to this lust of imitation, all authenticity disappeared; "the fire of genius was extinguished and even military spirit evaporated" (Gibbon 1787–94: 1: 74). From then on, Rome was no longer inspired by the republican virtues; from then on, "men of their own accord, without threat of punishment, without laws, [no longer] maintained good faith and did what was right"—to borrow from Ovid's description of the Golden Age. Rome had become a mere construction with which the citizen could no longer identify himself. The citizen "sunk in the languid indifference of private life," and the pleasures of private life were now valued above the participation in public and political debate (Gibbon 1787–94: 1: 75). If republican Rome had almost naturally sprung from the "patriotism" inspiring its citizens, from Augustus onwards an elaborate administrative machinery was gradually developed—and had to be developed—in order to substitute for this evanescence of patriotism and republicanism. Like Narcissus, Rome became fascinated by its own image and wasted away in fruitless contemplation of it.

This infatuation of Rome with its own image, this desire to save Rome in its most difficult predicaments by the desperate attempt to breath life and energy into a mere "representation" of republican Rome, would reach its culmination in the reign of Julian the Apostate. No emperor was more intent upon restoring Rome to its former greatness, and no emperor was more serious in his attempt to resuscitate the traditional, "manly" virtues of pre-Augustan, republican Rome. Precisely this is why Gibbon finds it so hard to present his readers with a well-balanced final judgment of Julian's short career as emperor. For on the one hand Gibbon admires republican Rome no less than Julian did, but on the other hand he is well aware that no "theatrical representation" can actually replace what it represents. This becomes clear when we see how Gibbon applies the representation metaphor to Julian. Discussing Julian's plans to reform Rome, he writes: "But if these imaginary plans of reformation had been realized, the forced and imperfect copy would have been less beneficial to Paganism, than honourable to Christianity" (Gibbon 1787–94: 4: 73–74). Ironically, imitating republican Rome, far from resulting in a return to republican purity, would instead only benefit Christianity, that archenemy of "the Genius of the Empire." And the disasters in which Julian's short reign ended prove the soundness of this view. The paradox, therefore, is that Julian was the worst of the Romans precisely because he was the best of them, precisely because he had best understood the nature of republican Rome and because his love of these virtues was most sincere. Insofar as we can see the emperor as the incarnation of the empire, Julian's empire had, just like Narcissus, fallen in love with itself. Tiresias's prophecy that Narcissus would die of self-knowledge found its historiographical counterpart in Gibbon's view of the causes of Rome's fall. Narcissism was the cause of Rome's fall (and Rome is probably not the only civilization to suffer this fate). Narcissism, Narcissus's and Rome's infatuation with their respective self-images, effected in both cases a "Spaltung der Persönlichkeit und Verlust der Identität" ("personality split and loss of identity") (Eller 1982: 23) that eliminated the possibility of all meaningful and purposeful action.

So we may say that the cause of Rome's fall can be attributed to the propensity of some of the best Roman emperors to become, so to speak, the "historians" of republican Rome and to try to "reenact" in actual reality their historical appreciation of the ancient republic. In the attempt, a distance between Rome's original identity and its mimesis was inevitably created, and it may be argued that this distance is the source of Rome's (self-)destruction. Lionel Gossman, in his study *The Empire Unpossess'd*, gives us the following comment on Gibbon's conception of history:

History and civilization are in themselves a process of alienation and dispossession [hence the title of Gossman's book], by which an original, closed and self-contained being—a being that can never be found in history, however, since it is already divided by the very fact of being historical—extends outwards, multiplies, enters in contact with others, and is altered by this contact. (1980: 58)

In other words, according to Gossman, Gibbon sees in history a permanent propensity towards a narcissistic mimesis of a previous original world, where each mimesis (or signifier) is always an alienation and a corruption of the signified in which it has its origin; next, the arbitrary distance between signifier and signified allows room for all the abuses that may bring about the fall of a nation or civilization—as actually was the case with Rome. Hence, a theory of language and of the signifier's necessary inadequacy as a substitute for the signified is Gibbon's ultimate, "narcissistic" model for his explanation of the fall of Rome.

This raises, of course, the interesting question whether the historian, that is, not only the Roman emperor assuming the historian's role, is susceptible to the same kind of narcissistic delusions as these architects of Rome's downfall. If so, that would imply that Nietzschean conclusion that all writing of history is inevitably a corruption both of the historian (or the historical consciousness he exemplifies) and of the historical reality described. The historian is then invariably a kind of Narcissus who generates in culture this same kind of "Spaltung der Persönlichkeit und Verlust der Identität" that we observed a moment ago, which led to Narcissus's death and was the principal cause of Rome's destruction.

There is, however, one more interesting parallel between the *Metamorphoses* and *The Decline and Fall*. G. K. Galinsky draws our attention to the peculiarly "untragic" character of Ovid's *Metamorphoses*. If we take the Narcissus story as an example, it is true that Narcissus's life comes to a premature and sad end. Nevertheless, the story does not invite us to lament Narcissus's fate or to meditate on the tragedy of the human condition as exemplified by it. We are moved by the story, but sadness is not what it effects in our minds. Part of the explanation lies in the purpose of the book. Ovid wishes to inform his readers what transformations the things in our world have undergone "from the earliest beginnings of the world, down to my own times" (1955: 29). Hence, Ovid's aim is to teach rather than to evoke pity or even to impart a moral message to his audience. The result is a peculiarly "untragic manner of narration" (Galinsky 1975: 61). Indeed, Ovid's narrative is playful, ironic rather than tragic; the many stories related by him seem to take place in an idyllic and, on the whole, harmonious world that is singularly devoid of drama and pathos.

It is here that Ovid's emplotment interestingly differs from the best-known metamorphosis written in our own time: Kafka's *Verwandlung*. On the one hand, Gregor Samsa's tragic end seems to be foreordained right from the beginning of the story: the reader is immediately made aware of the unbridgeable gap that Gregor's metamorphosis into a beetle has created between himself and his world. A compromise between Gregor and his world is obviously unthinkable, and the reader realizes that Gregor's destruction will only be a matter of time. But on the other hand, there is also something peculiarly playful and untragic about the story: Gregor does not seem to be aware of this gap; his recognition of his metamorphosis does not rank any higher in his self-consciousness than his awareness of the weather on that fateful day of his metamorphosis, or of his failure to be on time for the train. And this is where Gregor's metamorphosis most significantly differs from those related by Ovid, despite their initial similarity. For if there is something "untragic" about the metamorphoses of Ovid's subjects, this is because their metamorphoses seem to be the logical and satisfactory fulfillment of their manifest destinies; Gregor Samsa's metamorphosis, however, is presented by Kafka as "untragic" since this metamorphosis (and all that follows from it) seems to have nothing whatsoever to do with the person he is, nor with his deepest feelings. Gregor's personality seems to lie in a quasi-autistic self that remains completely unaffected by his metamorphosis and thereby effectively robs it of the dimension of the tragic. Nothing was lost simply because there never was anything to lose; in Ovidian metamorphosis, however, nothing is lost since a potentiality (that had always been there) has now in fact been realized. Thus in both cases, though for entirely opposite reasons, all sense of tragedy can properly be said to be absent.

Obviously, metamorphosis typically involves identity. Even more obviously, the whole point of metamorphosis ordinarily is to preserve identity despite (often dramatic) change. An intriguing exception to this rule is Alison Lurie's "The Double Poet." The story is about the fight of Karo McKay, a highly esteemed poetess, with a double who tries to impersonate her. Finally, like a vampire, this double succeeds in taking over McKay's identity, and the original McKay is changed into Carrie Martin, an unemployed, anonymous elderly woman. The only property preserved through change is the poet's being the mother of "a sensible and wonderful grown daughter" (Lurie 1994: 182), which is therefore implicitly presented by the story as her only and true identity. This most ingenious story is further complicated by its carefully upholding the possibility that McKay suffers from a delusion. And it is interesting that, insofar as McKay would really be deluded, two possibilities present themselves: either there never was a double and the end of McKay's career was caused by her mere belief that there was such an impostor, or we are being told the story of this impostor who initially imagined herself to be McKay and finally discovered that she was merely the anonymous Carrie Martin and made her peace with that.

McKay's not being deluded about what happened to her is, of course, compatible with this second possibility, but then the end of the story makes clear that we have been reading it from the wrong perspective all the time. That is to say, the story is not about McKay but about Carrie Martin, and is written from the latter's perspective.

We encounter the same propensity for "untragic" narrative in Gibbon's *Decline and Fall*. Needless to say, there is enough tragedy in the more than one thousand years of history that is related by Gibbon, and if he had wished to convey to his audience the tragedy of the self-destruction of the political edifice that he himself admired so much, history could have provided him with ample material. But just like Ovid's "carmen perpetuum"[3] Gibbon's calmly flowing prose is free from the cataracts and whirlpools in which the dimension of the tragic could only manifest itself. His aversion to decisive and dramatic caesuras is illustrative; historical events are never presented by him as radical beginnings or endings in the "carmen perpetuum" of his narrative. The way he deals with the fall of the Western Empire in A.D. 476 is characteristic. As Gibbon's biographer, P. B. Craddock, observes, the event "is passed over almost parenthetically" (1989: 152) and certainly does not mark the end of the third volume, as one might have expected. For that volume ends with a sketch of the rise of the new kingdoms in the West, and in this way the tragedy of Rome's fall is effectively mitigated by the construction of new political entities. Histories overlap, and what is destruction from one point of view is construction from another. So nothing ends in A.D. 476 that had not yet ended already, and nothing began in that year that had not begun already—such is the message of Gibbon's narrative. Moreover, Gibbon's resistance to dramatic incisions induced him to give his narrative the form of a set of stories rather than the form of the unified story of one nation (i.e., Rome). For one of the most striking features of *The Decline and Fall* certainly is that it so successfully avoids the temptation to see the world only from the point of view of Rome. Just as Ovid's *Metamorphoses* most artfully weaves together some 250 separate stories, so Gibbon's history is, in fact, an intricate web of many individual stories that partly overlap, partly have their own autonomy, and are never forced into one scheme. Both Ovid's *Metamorphoses* and Gibbon's *Decline and Fall* are a "carmen perpetuum" rather than a "carmen unum."

Explaining the untragic character of the *Metamorphoses*, Galinsky points out that the fate of Ovid's protagonists is most often the realization of a potentiality that was already present in their personality or nature rather than a dramatic or tragic break with that potentiality. There is therefore something peculiarly reassuring about their fate that effectively precludes the dimension of tragedy. Thus the Narcissus flower expresses something that had always lain in Narcissus's personality, and his metamorphosis into a flower is therefore, in a way, only natural and elicits our agreement. Sometimes the relationships between the lives and characters of Ovid's protagonists and the metamorphoses they undergo are rather strained, as when Philemon and Baucis are transformed into two trees when death comes to them. But even here one might say that the two trees, standing next to each other, are a permanent testimony to the marital love of the old couple. Moreover, many metamorphoses, like this one, suggest the harmonious relationship between nature and the world of humanity. There is thus a peculiar logic in Ovid's metamorphoses in the sense that the subject of metamorphosis can be said to become what it has always been. And this is not a Goethean, evolutionary "werde wer du bist" (though Ovidian metamorphosis strongly influenced Goethe in his speculations on the origin of plants, their flowers, and their leaves [Eller 1982: 34–36]) but rather a revelation of the true nature of the subject of metamorphosis already manifest in the subject before his or her metamorphosis. Ovidian metamorphosis is quite unlike historical change or development. It is a return to an origin, or the revealing of an origin rather than a development of it.

This view of Ovidian metamorphosis is expressed by Galinsky as follows:

Most metamorphoses deal with the changing of a person into something else such as, for instance, a tree, a stone or an animal. Regardless of the way they are brought about such transformations often are not capricious but turn out to be very meaningful because they set in relief the true and everlasting character of the person involved. . . . The physical characteristics of the personages may change but their quintessential substance lives on. (1975: 45)

In other words, in the *Metamorphoses* we have to deal with change, sometimes even radical change—the metamorphosis of a beautiful youth into a flower surely is no trifle—but the substance of change always remains "quintessentially" the same substance. And it is this characteristic of Ovid's metamorphoses that keeps at bay the dimension of tragedy.

Expounding "the teachings of Pythagoras" in the fifteenth book, Ovid explains what we may consider to be his own view of change and of metamorphosis as follows:[4] "Nor does anything retain its own appearance permanently. Ever inventive nature continuously produces one shape from another. Nothing in the entire universe ever perishes, believe me, but things vary and adopt a new form" (1955: 341). Hence, the world as we currently know it is the result of an infinity of metamorphoses of an infinity of substances all functioning as the unchanging substrate of morphological change. Nothing is ever essentially (or substantially, to use the right word) new; we only encounter new forms (the new external envelopes of a substance) as the result of metamorphosis. It is quite characteristic that when discussing in the first book how the world came into being, Ovid makes it clear that no creation in the true sense of the word was involved but that creation was, instead, a process of separation. Initially there was a chaos in which "everything got in the way of everything else," but this strife was

finally resolved by a god, a natural force of a higher kind, who separated the earth from heaven, and the waters from the earth, and set the clear sky apart from the cloudy atmosphere. When he had freed these elements, sorting them out from the heap where they had lain, indistinguishable from one another, he bound them fast, each in its separate place, forming a harmonious union. (1955: 29)

There is no true genesis and no real change, in the sense that something develops out of something entirely different; all the "substances" out of which the world is built up have been present forever. It is only that they may present themselves in the guise of different "metamorphoses."

Change—and history—only affects the external, peripheral, and contingent features of the substance.

The same picture is suggested by Ovid's account of the four ages. It is illustrative to observe how Ovid uses negations when describing the Golden Age: in that age there were "no penalties to be afraid of," "no bronze tablets were erected," "no judges," "no helmets and no swords," and so on.[5] Obviously, the Golden Age can only be characterized by having recourse to the world as it currently is (that is, by negating it), and in that sense the present is already present in that remote past and vice versa. That Ovid's world is a world whose inventory is fixed once and forever is also clear from the fact that there is no real development through the four ages; it is as if a big wheel is turned before our eyes so that different parts of the eternal and unchanging properties of the wheel gradually become visible to us from our fixed perspective. But the wheel remains as it has always been. "All things change, but nothing dies" (1955: 339), as Ovid makes Pythagoras say; and where nothing dies, nothing is really born either. Ovid in all likelihood owed this undramatic conception of change to Posidonius, a Stoic who had quite a following in the Rome of Ovid's day. The part of Posidonius's teaching that is relevant in this context is his view that neither man's physical quality nor his soul constitute his real character but that his actual substance is an unchanging nature behind these more peripheral manifestations of a person's identity (Galinsky 1975: 47). Hence, Ovidian ontology presents us with a universe consisting of substances that eternally remain the same, despite the fact that their outward appearance may be subject to dramatic changes.

We encounter much the same picture in *The Decline and Fall*. As in Ovid's initial chaos, all the elements that will play a role in Gibbon's narrative are there right from the beginning. It is true that in the first three chapters of *The Decline and Fall*, Gibbon presents his readers with an account of the empire in its happy days under the Antonines—the Gibbonian equivalent of Ovid's Golden Age—rather than of the initial chaos with which the latter began his story. Rome in the second century A.D., writes Gibbon, "is marked by the rare advantage of furnishing few materials for history; which is, indeed, little more than the register of the crimes, follies and misfortunes of mankind" (Gibbon 1787–94: 1: 102). Ovid's negative characterization of the Golden Age repeats itself here in Gibbon's characterization of Rome under the Antonines in terms of the absence of the crimes, follies, and misfortunes that constitute the substance of human history.

But beneath this apparently harmonious surface lies a more complex account of the political reality of second-century Rome that announces itself already on the first page of the book. Gibbon confronts his readers with the provocative paradox that Rome's "peaceful inhabitants enjoyed and abused the advantages of wealth and luxury." In peace, harmony, and the cultivation of the arts and sciences there lay, where we would least expect them, the seeds of destruction—such is his suggestion. More than any other of Gibbon's modern commentators, J. G. A. Pocock has made us aware of the importance of the theme suggested by this paradox. In his *Machiavellian Moment in the Atlantic Tradition* (1975), Pocock analyzed eighteenth-century political discourse in terms of the opposition between "court" and "country." The republican "country" tradition required the transparency of the political domain; that is to say, the active participation of the citizen in matters of government was considered essential for preventing its corruption. The state must be transparent with regard to the will of the free and politically active citizen. Freedom is thus political, positive freedom—and this freedom is the pillar on which the state rests. In fact, the state can be said to be nothing but that "pillar": the state has, or ought to have, no existence outside the minds of the citizens, inspired by republican virtue. The "court" tradition, on the contrary, is prepared to accept the autonomy and the nontransparency of the political domain; it favors representative government and recognizes the State as an entity sui generis, which cannot be reduced completely to the free will of the individual citizens. Within this political matrix, the adherents of the "country" tradition (so named since it had its most active and characteristic supporters in the seventeenth-century gentry) saw in the "court" tradition the source of corruption, greed, and political dependence on debilitating luxury—in short, the source of all the evils that the good society ought to avoid.

There can be no doubt that Pocock is right when he places Gibbon firmly in the "country" tradition (Pocock 1977: passim). And, indeed, it is not hard to find statements in *The Decline and Fall* that confirm Pocock's view. Gibbon's adherence to the "country" tradition is illustrated by his assertion that "public virtue," called patriotism by the ancients, "is derived from a strong sense of our own interest in the preservation and prosperity of the free government of which we are members." And a loss of freedom is to be expected as soon as "war was gradually improved [Note Gibbon's irony!] into an art, and degraded into a trade" (Gibbon 1787–94: 1: 12, 13). And elsewhere he laments the dependency, the passion for self-enrichment, and the corruption that invariably is the consequence of the disappearance of civic, positive freedom:

Under the Roman Empire, the labour of an industrious and ingenious people was variously but incessantly employed, in the service of the rich. In their dress, their table, their houses, and their furniture, the favourites of fortune united every refinement of conveniency, of elegance and of splendour; whatever could soothe their pride or gratify their sensuality. Such refinements, under the odious name of luxury, have been severely arraigned by the moralists of every age; and it might perhaps be more conducive to the virtue, as well as the happiness of mankind, if all possessed the necessaries, and none the superfluities of life. (Gibbon 1787–94: 1: 70–71)

This is, in a nutshell, the political message of the "country" tradition that Gibbon explicitly embraced in this passage.

In other words—and this is the intellectual challenge that the "country" tradition had to face but was unable to answer—all that contributes to Roman civilization, as to any other civilization, is also what contributes to its decline and its corruption. Part of Rome's greatness lay in the achievements of Roman culture, its arts and sciences, but these achievements are the no less unmistakable signs of its decline. We may observe a similar paradox in Ovid when he carefully avoids the Augustan theme of the eternity of Rome, as we find it, for example, in Book I of the *Aeneid* when Virgil's Jupiter declares, "his ego nec metas rerum nec tempora pono;/imperium sine fine dedi" (To Romans I set no boundary in space or time/I have granted them dominion and it has no end) (lines 278–79). An equally indicative example of Ovid's reticence with regard to the Augustan Age is his rejection of the topos, common in his day, of equating that age with the Golden Age: "and what else could one conclude from this than that thus Ovid's discontent with his own age is expressed? Admittedly, sometimes Ovid praises his time, but on such occasions he praises its culture and material well-being, never its social, moral, or political conditions" (Gatz 1967: 72). So both Gibbon and Ovid (and here they are in agreement with several other classical historians) are aware of the dangers of culture and of the fact that the arts and sciences may fatally weaken a civilization.

Having finally arrived at this stage, we may begin to reap the fruits of our comparison of Ovid and Gibbon. Above all, we should realize that Gibbon did not write the *Bildungsroman* of Rome—the *Bildungsroman* of the past would be the model for the German historist historians of a later generation, who typically wanted to present their readers with the edifying picture of the gradual development and the gradual unfolding of a nation or culture. Gibbon's narrative is free from the kind of substantial change that was always at stake in historist historical writing: Gibbon presents us with the metamorphoses that Rome underwent in the course of more than one thousand years of history. That is to say, in contrast to historist historical writing, Gibbon's work presents the essence, or the substance, of the subject of his "carmen perpetuum" as invariably remaining the same in spite of all the dramatic changes that transformed Rome from the world's master into a Byzantine Empire that was to go through a protracted agony of some thousand years. We have every reason to be surprised by the suggestion that such a sad deterioration can take place without substantial change; but do we not have even more reason to wonder that the metamorphosis of human beings into stars, trees, rivers, and so on involves no substantial change?

Perhaps we may even discern here the unparalleled narrative potential of the metamorphosis as a literary form; and if at first sight we now consider Gibbon's narrative to be unconvincing, it is primarily because the triumph of historist, evolutionist narrative has made us forgetful of the powers of the literary convention that preceded it. More specifically, we can only dream now about the historical accounts that might be given of Western history if they were modeled on Ovidian and Gibbonian metamorphosis. "The return of the repressed" that is so much a feature of contemporary European history and that does not fit within historist, evolutionary models could be plausibly accounted for within the Gibbonian model. Historist models of historical change, by contrast, will not permit the idea of the persistence of an unchanging essence that remains untouched by even the most dramatic historical metamorphoses, and they will leave us empty-handed when we wish to account for them. Generally speaking, the literary model of the metamorphosis is ideally suited for rendering justice to both the synchronic and the diachronic aspects of the past. Here lies its decisive advantage over the kind of historical writing to which we have become accustomed. One might argue that it was precisely this fact that made the Burckhardt of *Die weltgeschichtliche Betrachtungen* see in the past a continuous metamorphosis in the relationship between state, church, and culture rather than the modernist metanarratives that are presupposed by historist historical writing. And if we would agree with Gossman that Burckhardt seems both to anticipate and to transcend the tensions between modernism and postmodernism by sidestepping the polarization between past and present presupposed by both positions (Gossman 1996), we have in our "post-postmodernist" age every reason to be interested in Ovidian metamorphosis as a model for historical change.

The structural similarities between Ovid's and Gibbon's narratives can be explained by their shared Stoicism. Though Ovid had no philosophical pretensions, and the philosophy that is implied by the *Metamorphoses* has correctly been described as "a mixed bag" (Myers 1990: 154), we can certainly agree with Galinsky's claim that Ovid's metamorphoses in several respects betray the Stoic influences of Posidonius. Stoic panlogism, with its conception of the *logoi spermatikoi*, as the unchanging rational principles that constitute the essence of the cosmos in its many manifestations, is undoubtedly the ontology suggested by the Metamorphoses. Next, with regard to Gibbon, we should recall that he, as an exponent of Enlightenment historical writing, accepted without reservations the *Weltanschauung* of natural-law philosophy. And, as has been pointed out by many historians since Dilthey, seventeenth- and eighteenth-century natural-law philosophy can well be seen as a continuation of Stoic ontology. The conception of a universe consisting of entities essentially remaining the same during change is the ontological intuition that is shared by Stoicism, the stories that Ovid tells us, and lastly, Gibbon's narrative of the history of Rome.

Moreover, there is a striking similarity between the ways that Ovid and Gibbon adapted Stoic ontology in order to make it fit their narrative purposes. In both cases external, peripheral causes effect a change in the substance so that its true nature can reveal itself. In Ovid the cause of the metamorphosis is typically merely accidental and could, in principle, be exchanged for another cause (a striking exception, as we have seen, is the encounter between Echo and Narcissus). Yet it is as if these accidental causes "trigger" an internal, substantial cause that determines the nature and the outcome of the metamorphosis. The same causal pattern is found in Gibbon's *Decline and Fall* (Ankersmit 1995: passim). Having come to the end of his work, Gibbon observes: "In the preceding volumes of this history, I have described the triumph of barbarism and religion" (Gibbon 1787–94: 12: 186). Undoubtedly barbarism and Christian religion are presented in his work as the causes of Rome's fall; yet we must note that these causes are external in the sense that they did not originate within Rome itself, but only affected it, so to speak, "from the outside." And this certainly is part of Gibbon's analysis—no one could plausibly disagree with this summary that Gibbon himself gave of his work. However, in the "General Observations" that conclude chapter 38, Gibbon reflects on the deeper causes of Rome's destruction as follows:

The rise of a city, which swelled into an Empire, may deserve, as a singular prodigy the reflection of a philosophic mind. But the decline of Rome was the natural and inevitable effect of immoderate greatness. Prosperity ripened the principle of decay; the causes of destruction multiplied with the extent of conquest; and as soon as time or accident had removed the artificial supports, the stupendous fabric yielded to the pressure of its own weight. The story of its ruin is simple, and obvious; and instead of inquiring why the Roman Empire was destroyed, we should rather be surprised that it subsisted so long. (Gibbon 1787–94: 8: 323)

After having been touched by a magic wand as it were—by barbarism and Christian religion—Rome underwent a metamorphosis that would reveal its true nature. Thus, in a certain sense the ultimate truth about Rome is its agony of more than a thousand years—including the history of the Byzantine Empire—and it is only befitting that Gibbon decided to tell us that history and not, for example, the history of the triumphant republic. No less to the point is Gibbon's statement that the question of why Rome fell is, in the end, less interesting than the question of how Rome could have subsisted so long. For the fact of Rome's metamorphosis is, in itself, sufficient explanation of its fate; and, as always with metamorphosis, the only enlightenment we may expect from the historian is simply the story that he can tell us of the metamorphosis. More one cannot do—and it is all we need.

But this can be elaborated. We need not be satisfied with the insight that prolonged agony is the final truth about Rome. Truth always effects a separation between truth itself and what it is a truth of; the true statement inevitably creates a gap between itself and what it is about. When discussing the similarities between Ovid's story of Narcissus and Gibbon's story of Rome, we found that for Gibbon this distance, this gap between the sign and the signified (in Gossman's terminology), between truth and what it is a truth of, is the gap in which republican virtue and Rome's greatness were lost. It was self-knowledge (as Tiresias had prophesied) that decided Narcissus's death; likewise, the search for truth about Rome (as best exemplified by Julian) occasioned an alienation from truth and what that truth is about, and it is in this alienation that all the evils originated that would lead to Rome's destruction. So, in the final analysis, historical truth is what this essay has been about all along, and in this "metamorphosis" of the topic of my exposition, we may situate the affinities between Ovid and Gibbon.

"Is This Naomi?"

MISREADING, GENDER BLURRING, AND
THE BIBLICAL STORY OF RUTH

J. Cheryl Exum

A painting by Philip Hermogenes Calderon (1833–98), in the Walker Art Gallery in Liverpool, is my point of departure for this essay (Fig. 1). When I first saw this painting, I knew only that its subject was the book of Ruth, and I must admit that it took me a moment to make the connection between the painting and the biblical story. Clearly the woman in white was Ruth. But whom was she embracing? The pose struck me as romantic, even erotic, and the figure clasped in Ruth's arms looks like Rudolph Valentino. Upon reflection, it seemed evident that the figure must be Naomi and that, if the painting is meant to represent some episode in the book of Ruth, it can only be Naomi's leave-taking of her daughters-in-law and Ruth's dramatic display of loyalty.

But is the identification so straightforward? "Is this Naomi?" (I take the question from the women of Bethlehem, who, in Ruth 1:19, have difficulty recognizing Naomi too.) I have shown this painting to friends, colleagues, students in class, and anyone I can persuade to look at it, giving them only the same initial information I had: the painting's subject is the book of Ruth. So far, opinion is fairly evenly divided between those who think that the figures embracing each other are Ruth and Naomi and those who identify them as Ruth and Boaz. In favor of the identification

FIGURE I. Philip Hermogenes Calderon, *Ruth and Naomi* (1886). Oil on canvas, 116.2 × 207.6 centimeters. Walker Art Gallery. Used with permission of the Board of Trustees of the National Museums & Galleries on Merseyside.

of the figure in black as Boaz are the facts that he is significantly taller than Ruth; his clothing, both the long-sleeved robe and the more elaborate headdress, is different from the women's; and—the strongest argument— the figures appear to be locked in a romantic embrace. Indeed, Ruth, who is dressed in white like a bride, has what could be called a look of rapture upon her face. Who, then, is the figure in blue to the side? A servant? She alone carries what appear to be provisions. Is *this* Naomi? "Naomi" was the answer I most often received from viewers who take the central figures to be Ruth and Boaz. Naomi, observing the match she has made, is now tangential, if not quite left out of the picture. This answer and its implications, I think, are suggestive, though if one looks at the original painting and not a reproduction, this woman looks too young to be the other's mother-in-law. Another possibility is that she is Boaz's wife—thus filling a gap already perceived by the rabbis and echoed in modern commentary. No wife is mentioned in the story, but is it likely that Boaz would be un-married? Is his wife dead? (According to one midrashic source, Boaz's wife died the day Ruth arrived in Bethlehem.) [1]

Those who see the figures as Ruth and Naomi argue that there is no other scene in the book of Ruth that fits this picture. In chapter one, Naomi urges her widowed daughters-in-law to return to their mothers' houses, with the hope that they might be able to marry again. In an emotional scene, where twice they burst into tears, she kisses them and bids them farewell. Orpah follows Naomi's advice and returns to her own people, but Ruth clings to her and makes her famous vow of loyalty, "Where you go I will go, where you lodge I will lodge, your people shall be my people and your god my god" (1:16). Only this scene can account for the young woman in blue in the painting: she is Orpah, preparing to return home, while Ruth clings to her mother-in-law. In the biblical ac-count, in contrast, Ruth never openly embraces Boaz. Her one intimate scene with Boaz is on the threshing floor at night, not in the desert in broad daylight—and not with someone watching.

What interests me about the conflicting identifications of this couple is not which is right and which is wrong, but the fact that opinion is so clearly and strongly divided, and the arguments each side brings forward in favor of its view. If viewers cannot agree on the sex of the person in black, then clearly there is something androgynous about this figure. I sus-pect that if the picture were cropped to show only the embracing couple (Fig. 2), and no clue as to who they might be were provided, most people would say they are a man and a woman.

Now one could argue that literary and artistic competence will settle the issue. Above, I used the terms "evident" and "it can only be" in identifying the scene painted by Calderon as Naomi's taking leave of her daughters-in-law. These terms invoke a certain kind of competence that is required to make this identification, specifically, sufficient knowledge of the painting's source text to identify the event represented in the painting with a particular event in the story. Familiarity with High Victorian paint-ing and its conventions, especially the classical revival of the 1860s, will also help (Calderon's painting was voted the best religious picture of the 1886 Royal Academy Exhibition). But as Mieke Bal demonstrates so forcefully in her study *Reading "Rembrandt,"* this kind of competence, while offering

FIGURE 2. Calderon, *Ruth and Naomi*, detail. Walker Art Gallery. Used with permission of the Board of Trustees of the National Museums & Galleries on Merseyside.

a powerful interpretive tool, also exercises a powerful control over interpretation. By providing a program of how to analyze a work of art, it encourages us to interpret within established parameters and thus can prevent us from noticing details that don't fit and from exploring alternative interpretations (Bal 1991: 177–79). Certainly the scene from the book of Ruth in which Ruth "clave unto" her mother-in-law, as the King James Version has it, is well enough known, and a competent reading will recognize it as Calderon's source. But such a competent reading is likely to ignore the mannish appearance of the figure in black and to suppress the erotic element in the painting. Thus a good case can be made for misreading.

Identifying the figure in black with Boaz opens new possibilities for interpretation. The question is one not just of competence but of the implicit sexual character of the scene and the sexually ambivalent nature of the figure in black. Unlike Ruth and Orpah, this figure is almost totally covered by clothing. We cannot see the arms or hands (though the part of one hand visible around Ruth's waist looks rather large for a woman — but then, so does Orpah's hand). The features, in profile, are not soft, but neither are they harsh. The person has no beard, which suggests she might be a woman, but this does not rule out the possibility that he is a man.

The dual identifications of the embracing couple as Ruth and Naomi and Ruth and Boaz are, in fact, both based on knowledge of the biblical book. Each fastens upon a moment of intimacy in the book of Ruth to supply the context for its interpretation. The one, between Ruth and Naomi, is straightforwardly told, but still gapped[2] (why would Ruth make such a choice?); the other, that between Ruth and Boaz, is related more cryptically and suggestively (the conundrum, what happened between them on the threshing floor?). These scenes have become focal points of biblical interpretation, where comments about Ruth's unusual devotion or the exceptional relationship between mother- and daughter-in-law have become critical commonplaces, and discussion of what did or did not transpire on the threshing floor fills pages of commentary. These scenes are also focal points of appropriation by same-sex and opposite-sex interests. Under the category of same-sex relationships, I am concerned not simply with sexual orientation but with accounts of the strong bond between two women that range from deep and abiding friendship to lesbianism. By opposite-sex interests, I refer to interpretations influenced by the (possibly unconscious) desire to foreground the heterosexual relationship at the expense of the bond between women, which results in a romanticizing of the relationship between Ruth and Boaz. It is not a question of the existence of the heterosexual bond but of its intensity. Again, the issue is not which side is "right," but the fact that advocates for both same-sex and opposite-sex relationships can lay claim to this text.[3]

Calderon's painting vividly problematizes the issue of bonding by giving us an androgynous subject. By virtue of the intensity and tenderness of the embrace, the look of rapture on Ruth's face, and the erotic pose struck by the couple, the painting suggests a sexual dimension to the relationship between the two women. How old are these women? How old are the characters in the biblical story? What effect do readers' assumptions about the ages of the main characters have on the way they visualize the characters' relationships? The older that readers think Naomi is compared to Ruth, the less likely they are even to imagine a sexual relationship. Conversely, the younger she is, the more conceivable is the prospect. Edward Campbell, in his Anchor Bible commentary on the book of Ruth, offers reasonable calculations for the characters' ages:

> If usual ancient Near Eastern procedure was followed, Naomi was probably married in her early to mid-teens, and had had her two sons by the time she was twenty. They in turn would have married by the time they were fifteen or so, to girls a bit younger. Ten years of childless marriage for them would bring us to the mid-forties for Naomi. Given the rigors of life in ancient Palestine, that would be years enough, almost certainly, for her to have reached the menopause. The storyteller will establish that Boaz and Naomi are of the same generation, and we can assume that Ruth was between 25 and 30 when the events in the story took place. (1975: 67)

According to Campbell's reckoning, we *could* have a Ruth nearly 30 and a Naomi of 42.

Boaz is frequently taken to be an older man (the midrash makes him eighty! [*Ruth Rabbah* 3:10]). This involves the male fantasy in which an old man finds new life and fulfillment in a younger woman. That Boaz can easily be older than Ruth for a sexual relationship, but Naomi not, reflects both a heterosexist double standard according to which older men are sexually attractive but older women are not and a related cultural tendency to deny the sexual desire of older women. In his Ruth commentary, Jack Sasson rightly sees "puritanical issues at stake" in the age issue: "It would be much easier to accept the possibility that the threshing-floor involved no sexual activity, if the protagonist were sketched as a wise old man" (1979: 86). If this is true for Boaz, how much more so for Naomi.

On this point, the treatment of the respective ages of the characters in the 1960 film *The Story of Ruth*, directed by Henry Koster, is illuminating. Boaz (Stuart Whitman) is older than Ruth (Elana Eden), but probably not more than ten years or so. Naomi (Peggy Wood) is old enough to be Boaz's mother, and Ruth's grandmother. In the scene where Naomi bids farewell to her daughters-in-law, Ruth is the bitter one (Mahlon has just died, having married Ruth moments before), and Naomi is mawkishly philosophical: "Pain on entering the world, anguish on leaving it. But the interval between is worth it all." When Ruth asks, "Where is Mahlon's invisible god of mercy? Where are his blessings?," a look of recognition mingled with tenderness comes over Naomi's face as she walks toward Ruth and says, "You are one of them." She presses her cheek against Ruth's. When Ruth makes her famous speech, looks of fond devotion pass between them. This is only one moment of tender affection between the two women in the film; at other times they embrace to console each other in adversity or to share their joy. Naomi's advanced age and motherly attitude toward Ruth and Ruth's deferential and protective treatment of Naomi rule out even the slightest suggestion of erotic feelings on the part of either woman. If Naomi had been played by a woman in her forties, their intimacy would make a different impression on theater viewers.

The cinematic version of the story of Ruth finds its point of contact in the works of other painters, those who portray Naomi as noticeably older than Ruth. In William Blake's *Naomi and Her Two Daughters-in-Law*, for example, a young Ruth clings to a wrinkled, aged Naomi (Victoria and Albert Museum, London). Although her head rests against Naomi's breasts and her arms encircle her lower body, the difference in ages, coupled with the solemn expressions and the fact that Naomi does not embrace Ruth in return (her hands are outstretched to each side), render the painting asexual. Similarly, in a triptych by the English painter Thomas Matthew Rooks, a sweet, young Ruth grasps the arm and hand of a haggard and care-worn Naomi (Tate Gallery, London). In Pieter Lastman's *Ruth Swears Loyalty to Naomi*, Naomi is an old crone sitting on a donkey, pushing away a young, appealing Ruth (Niedersächsische Landegalerie, Hannover). Naomi is also an old woman in *Ruth and Naomi* by the Dutch painter Willem Drost (Ashmolean Museum, Oxford). These more common artistic representations have none of the erotic energy of Calderon's painting.

Why do so many viewers whose opinions I've solicited say the couple in Calderon's painting is Ruth and Boaz? Does it have something to do with this erotic energy, or with the ideational difficulty posed by two women embracing passionately? The desire (or need) to see the figures as Ruth and Boaz is so strong that some viewers insist on maintaining this identification in spite of the fact that there is no scene in the biblical story to which it corresponds. This cannot be simply the result of heterosexist bias. Rather, for these viewers the erotic power of the Ruth-Boaz relationship is so self-evident that they assume the painting represents the artist's vision of their relationship—a vision that finds its basis in the source text, but does not attempt to capture on canvas a particular scene from the source text. The heterosexual bond is already considered "natural." My concern is the further naturalizing of the heterosexual relationship by romanticizing it, by which I mean adding a love interest.

This is what we find in Hollywood's adaptation of *The Story of Ruth*, written for the screen by Norman Corwin (Twentieth Century Fox). That in its cinematic version the story of Ruth becomes a love story reflects, on the one hand, a popular belief that it is one, while on the other hand reinforcing in popular culture the perception of the biblical book as a love story. Film is particularly valuable as a metatext because it combines the visual, the narrative, and the interpretative. As a visual medium, the movie, like Calderon's painting, shows us what the characters look like rather than leaving it to our imagination. Peggy Wood's Naomi is old and gray, a sweet grandmotherly type. Elana Eden as Ruth is young, dark, and beautiful, and speaks with a dulcet accent, which serves to remind audiences of her status as a foreigner in Judah. In Moab, Ruth wears clothes that emphasize her erotic appeal (Mulvey's "to-be-looked-at-ness" [1989: 14–26]), but in Judah, she, like Naomi, dresses demurely—though always becomingly. Stuart Whitman is a strong, handsome, and hotheaded (meaning hot-blooded) Boaz with thick dark, curly hair, who wears short, sleeveless tunics to show off his muscular physique (only Mahlon wears shorter skirts than Boaz in this film). I have mentioned the effect that viewers' perceptions of the characters' ages are likely to have on their perceptions of their relationships. By making Naomi old, while Ruth and Boaz are young and attractive, the film effectively defines the one relationship as parental, and the other as romantic.

As a narrative medium, like the biblical book, the film can show the development of character; significantly, it uses this opportunity for extensive development of the love interest. The love interest begins in Moab, with Mahlon, though it is not a very significant love interest. Mahlon loves Ruth, while Ruth is attracted mainly to his beliefs. They are not married for ten years, as appears to be the case in the biblical story; in fact, Mahlon dies the instant they are married—thus Ruth can be a virgin when she marries our hero Boaz.[4] Whereas the biblical story introduces a complication in the plot by suddenly revealing the existence of a nearer next-of-kin, the film uses the next-of-kin to introduce a complication of its own, one designed to make the love angle more interesting. Boaz is given a rival. Tov, the near kinsman, is attracted to Ruth, and while Boaz gets off to a number of false starts, Tov seems to be scoring points. But Tov is not an appealing character, and, anyway, Ruth is falling in love with Boaz. However—and here lies the real obstacle to true love's realization—Tov wants Ruth for his wife, and he, in a rather neat touch, is the one who remembers the levirate law, the law that obliges a man to marry his kinsman's widow.[5] When he claims his right to marry Ruth, Ruth and Naomi are despondent. "I should have remembered the levirate law before we ever reached the banks of the Jordan," bemoans Naomi.

As both a visual and a narrative interpretation, the film is constantly having to fill gaps; in my opinion it does this brilliantly, with much of its gap filling based on midrashic sources.[6] The most incredible cinematic contribution involves Ruth's origins as a Moabite priestess.[7] The effect is to make her "conversion" all the more spectacular. Mahlon starts her thinking about an invisible god of mercy and justice, and after Mahlon's death, Ruth decides to return to Judah with Naomi for theological reasons: "Because I saw a new light in her beliefs, in her god," she tells Boaz later. Some might argue that this cinematic addition makes explicit Ruth's implicit theological motivation in the biblical story. It has serious implications for the audience's understanding of the personal bond between the two women. Unlike the biblical account, the film makes it impossible to see Ruth as motivated by love for Naomi. Indeed, she hardly knows Naomi, having met her only the night before. To be sure, a devoted relationship develops between the two women, but by subordinating Ruth's personal attachment to Naomi to her religious conviction, the film makes plain that the bond between the women, while strong, is not primary.

Clearly the primary bond as far as the film is concerned is the opposite-sex bond. *The Story of Ruth* resolves the question about events on the threshing floor in a way that succeeds in being romantic, while also being moralistic and filling gaps to remove the ambiguity of the biblical story. Though there are hints throughout the film of a developing romantic interest, Ruth and Boaz have their big love scene—not surprisingly—on the threshing floor.

Wearing a fine dress given to her by Tov to mark their betrothal, Ruth follows Naomi's instructions and waits for Boaz to go to sleep at the conclusion of the harvest festival. The film cleverly has her nearly stumble over Tov as she makes her way to the secluded place where Boaz has settled down for the night. She does not lie down beside Boaz, as in the biblical story. Instead, he wakes up with a start to see her standing there, and says, "I was dreaming of you. And you are here." This cinematic addition provides a nice intertextual link not only with Victor Hugo's famous poem *Booz endormi* (discussed by Bal 1987: 68–88) but also with a well-known biblical dream of posterity, Jacob's in Genesis 28. When Boaz declares his love for her with "I love you, Ruth. I've loved you from the day we met in my field," Ruth replies, "It must have been God's goodness that brought me to your field that day. Perhaps he's been directing me to you all my life." Ruth's response offers an explicit affirmation of the "hidden action of providence" that many biblical scholars find in the story.[8]

The moment viewers have been waiting for arrives when Ruth and Boaz kiss, and Boaz tells Ruth he wants her for his wife. Ruth is concerned about Tov and the levirate law, but Boaz assures her that he can get Tov to renounce his claim ("He will come to terms. He likes property"). Unlike the biblical account, the film does not have Boaz ask Ruth to stay the night; on the contrary, he remarks that it is getting light and that she should therefore leave before people will have reason to talk. In spite of the departure from the text, Boaz's admonition does echo Ruth 3:14: "He thought, 'Let it not be known that the woman came to the threshing floor.'"[9] At the scene's end, Ruth touchingly utters the magic words Boaz had spoken to her at the beginning of the scene: "I love you." She runs home, without the burden of all that biblical grain (3:15), to tell Naomi the joyous news.

But the obstacle to the lovers' happiness is not so easily removed, and the romantic interest is thereby heightened. The film introduces a new twist in the plot by having Tov refuse to renounce his claim to Ruth even though Boaz "offered him everything [he] own[ed]." When it appears that there is no way out and Ruth is about to be married to Tov, she tells him that, although she honors his claim, she does not love him. She goes on to say that, on the night of the harvest festival, she sought out Boaz on the threshing floor. Everyone looks on suitably aghast, and Tov, his anger rising, refuses to enter a marriage with a woman of dubious repute.[10] At this point, Boaz steps in to marry Ruth.

What is particularly interesting about this climactic resolution scene is the way the film removes uncertainty about what happened on the threshing floor for the audience only to introduce it for Tov.[11] Tov is tricked into giving up his claim to Ruth because he believes that something sexual did happen on the threshing floor. Lest there be any doubt among the people of Judah, as well as in audiences' minds, Boaz and Ruth swear a "holy oath" that "nothing passed between [them] on that night or any other time except spoken vows of love." Having definitively settled the question of what happened on the threshing floor, the film draws to a close with the happy couple's marriage. Love—that is, heterosexual love—has triumphed over adversity. In addition, by having a holy man introduce the story and bring about the happy ending, the film also suggests that god has been guiding the events to this romantic conclusion. It is a marriage made in heaven.

In Hollywood's version of the story of Ruth, when the romantic relationship between Ruth and Boaz is foregrounded, it is at the expense of the bond between the women. Not only is Naomi too old and nonsexual to be a serious romantic interest for anybody, but also Ruth goes with her to Bethlehem for theological, and not personal, reasons. When it comes to affirming the heterosexual bond over the bond between the women, the film's crowning touch is achieved through the use of the musical score to signal the shift in Ruth's devotion. Early in the film, just after Ruth makes her famous entreat-me-not-to-leave-you speech, we hear her words set to music and sung by a female voice while we watch the two women journeying across the wilderness to Judah. The same musical theme is played again the moment Ruth says to Boaz, "I love you." As she leaves the threshing floor, it is to the tune of "Where You Go I Will Go." The music is repeated at the film's end, when Ruth and Boaz leave the screen as man and wife. By transferring the musical setting of Ruth's speech from Naomi to Boaz, the film has managed not only to *foreground* the heterosexual bond but dramatically and effectively to *replace* the bond between the women with the romantic bond between a heterosexual couple.[12]

I have deliberately not mentioned the title of Calderon's painting, *Ruth and Naomi*. But there are *three* people represented. Although the title reflects the importance of the central figures and the dramatic event the painting represents, the decision to call a painting of three people by the names of two of them inevitably draws attention to the third figure. Once we recognize the central figures as Ruth and Naomi, we are not troubled by the extra person. Just as Orpah is a marginal character in the biblical story, so she is literally marginal in the painting. But if we take seriously the sexual ambivalence of the figure in black and allow for the possibility of seeing the two central figures as Ruth and Boaz, as did many viewers to whom I did not reveal the title in advance, then we are left with the problem of identifying the third person. I mentioned earlier that I find the identification of the figure in blue as Naomi especially suggestive: this misreading of Calderon's painting draws attention to the biblical Naomi's refusal to be written out of the story once the goal—Ruth's marriage to Boaz and the birth of Obed—is achieved.

This brings me to the problem of the third person and the triangular nature of interpersonal relationships in the biblical tale. The third person is a surplus in any romantic equation and is also difficult to account for in terms of bonding. In what follows I want to suggest that the figure of Naomi in the Bible is as sexually ambivalent as the figure in black in Calderon's painting and that this ambivalence, in both the metatext and its source text, challenges our notions of gender by destabilizing our gender categories. In the book of Ruth, there is a striking blurring of gender roles, indeed of sexually determined roles—husband, wife, mother, father— with Naomi symbolically holding all four of these roles.

In Ruth 4:17, the women of Bethlehem say, "A son is born to Naomi." The expression "a son is born to" is normally used of fathers, never simply of mothers.[13] Naomi is thus symbolically in the position of a father to Obed, and, as Obed's father, she is also symbolically a husband to Ruth, who has borne him (4:15). In 4:16, we learn that Naomi "set the child on her breast," as a mother would do,[14] and became his nurse (*'omenet*). How could Naomi, who claimed at the beginning of the story (1:12) to be too old to have a husband, possibly nurse the child? Commentators usually answer this question by referring to the more common and wider sense of *'omenet* as foster parent or guardian. Nevertheless its use to refer to a wet nurse (Numbers 11:12; and possibly 2 Samuel 4:4), in combination with Naomi's placing the child on her breast, reinforces the symbolism of Naomi as a mother to Obed. As Obed's "mother," Naomi is also symbolically Boaz's wife.

Both Naomi and Boaz call Ruth "my daughter" (2:2, 8, 22; 3:1, 10, 16, 18). In addition to making Naomi symbolically a mother to Ruth, this epithet also puts Naomi and Boaz in the position of Ruth's parents— and thus reinforces the symbolic husband-wife relationship of Naomi and Boaz from another angle.

Naomi and Boaz never actually meet in the story, or do they? A fascinating instance of the blurring of roles is created by a *kethiv-qere* problem—fascinating precisely because the problem occurs twice. In her instructions to Ruth in 3:3–4, the vocalized text (the *qere*) reads:

Wash and anoint yourself, put on your finest dress, and go down to the thresh-ing floor. Do not make yourself known to the man until he has finished eating and drinking. When he lies down, mark the place where he lies down and go and uncover the place of his feet and lie down—and he will tell you what to do.

The consonantal text (*kethiv*) reads:

Wash and anoint yourself, put on your finest dress, and I will go down to the threshing floor. Do not make yourself known to the man until he has finished eating and drinking. When he lies down, mark the place where he lies down and go and uncover the place of his feet and I will lie down—and he will tell you what to do.

By having Naomi put herself into the scene twice (a sort of Freudian slip?), the consonantal text conflates Naomi with Ruth as the "seducer" of Boaz on the threshing floor.[15]

Finally, Naomi is also represented on a symbolic level as a wife to Ruth, for Ruth leaves her father and mother and cleaves to Naomi as a man leaves his father and mother and cleaves to his wife (Gen. 2:24; the vocabulary is the same as in Ruth 1:14 and 2:11). In sum, Naomi holds the following symbolic positions: husband to Ruth, wife to Ruth, mother to Ruth, wife to Boaz, father to Obed, and mother to Obed. It would be difficult to imagine a more radical blurring of sexually defined roles.[16]

Ruth is literally Boaz's wife and Obed's mother: she marries Boaz, conceives and gives birth to a son (4:13). She also stands in the position of both husband and wife, daughter and son, vis-à-vis Naomi. As Naomi's "husband" she leaves her parents and cleaves to her "wife," and as the mother of the son "born to Naomi," she stands in as Naomi's "wife." Referred to by Naomi as "my daughter," Ruth fills the role of son in at least two respects: by providing for Naomi after the death of her natural sons (chapter 2),[17] and by being "more than seven sons" (4:15) by virtue of her role in perpetuating the family line—a line traced through sons (4:18–22).

The book's third main character, Boaz, is, on the literal level, the father of Obed, so much so in fact that the genealogy of 4:18–22 ignores the levirate law that would require Ruth's deceased husband, Mahlon, to be Obed's father. He is also in the position of a father to Ruth, whom he addresses as "my daughter." In addition to his role as father, Boaz is a hus-band to *both* women: literally Ruth's husband, he is symbolically husband to Naomi, who sets the child on her breast and nurses him as if she were his mother. Although Boaz does not hold a woman's symbolic position in the story, he nonetheless "accepts being reflected . . . in a female role," as Bal has shown. Boaz takes on a woman's point of view, argues Bal, by acknowledging his dependence on the other, Ruth, in order to establish his subject position, allowing himself to be fulfilled through her (1987: 87).

If all three main characters in the book of Ruth participate in the symbolic transgression of gender and sexual boundaries, it would seem that the book poses a salutary challenge to traditional gender categories, what Judith Butler refers to as our binary frame for thinking about gender (1990: viii). Indeed, if sexuality is a modern construct, as Foucault (1980) maintains, the recognition of it as such might give us a different way of approaching relationships in the book of Ruth, a way that destabilizes our familiar gender categories. Can we refuse to choose between the Ruth-Naomi and the Ruth-Boaz dyad and happily live with an eternal(ly unstable) triangle? By posing this question, I do not mean to suggest that such an intellectual position, should, or could, replace the appropriation of Ruth for same-sex or opposite-sex interests. Appropriations of the Ruth-Naomi and Ruth-Boaz relationships for readers' own interests serve to remind us that we readers have a stake in our cultural heritage, and that, if the only way we can lay claim to our cultural heritage is to reinterpret or, indeed, misread it, then reinterpret and misread we shall. To allow notions of inviolate "original meanings" or "authentic contexts" to prevent us from doing so would leave us impoverished.[18]

The infuence of gender and sexual orientation on reading and viewing needs to be recognized in any kind of reader-response approach to literature and art. At the same time, texts and their visual representations have a way of eluding our attempts to fit them into molds, of destabilizing our interpretations. Relationships in Ruth are not rigidly defined, and gender blurring occurs on a grand scale, with sexually identified roles shared and transgressed by all the major characters. Reading Ruth as an eternally unstable triangle offers a third interpretive option alongside reading in terms of same-sex and opposite-sex relationships, yielding an interpretive triangle analogous to the Ruth-Naomi-Boaz triangle. By destabilizing our gender categories, the book of Ruth, like Calderon's painting with which I began, invites readers to collapse the gender distinctions with which they themselves operate. Or at least to examine them, and perhaps to reconfigure them as well.

Three Local Cases of
Cross-Atlantic Reading

A DISCUSSION ON SPACE AND IDENTITY

Isabel Hoving

Somehow, in doing cultural analysis, one gets caught up in space. Cultural analysis is very much about issues of culture and identity, indeed, but it has become nearly impossible to discuss these without using spatial tropes. These last decades, the postmodern critique of modern concepts of identity as autonomous, as fixed in its proper place, has grown into a deep distrust of the concept of identity itself. Identity is now generally imagined as dialogic, shifting, and unstable. Consequently, a spatial discourse is taking shape in which identity is discussed in terms of shifting relations and positions (Keith and Pile 1993; C. L. Miller 1993: 6–7). "Space" is the key word in cultural analysis: spatial tropes are also used in the reflection of cultural analysis upon its own theoretical position, which can be typically described as "in-between" or "cross-." I like to remember that cultural analysis is born from a commitment to larger debates on value, and that its best moments are characterized by an explicit questioning of the capacity of disciplinary and interdisciplinary academic practices to deal with this issue. This questioning implies a reflection on both the chasms and the possible linkages between academic and nonacademic work on value: in theory, in art, in political movements. In short, cultural analysis creates spatial images of the relation between the academy and its congenial outside.

Space is not only a common issue in cultural analysis; it is also central to postcolonial debates. In postcolonial theory, not only is space thematized in concepts such as displacement, placelessness, and exile, concepts referring to a postcolonial mode of being, but further, the concept of space is sometimes even seen as a postcolonial alternative to the crucial concepts of (linear) time and history, which organize so many Western texts.[1] I do not think such a radical dichotomy useful or defensible, but I think this focus on the importance of place contains a valuable lesson on reading: the need to acknowledge the specificity of differently located discourses. Unfortunately, this is a lesson postcolonial criticism often neglects, for postcolonial theory contains a curious concept of space that stands in stark contrast to that specificity: it constructs the postcolonial condition as a global, transnational space that can be analyzed without reference to the localities in which it is rooted. This concept of space results in a strategy of reading that has been chastised as abstract and appropriating.[2] Inspired by Zora Neale Hurston, literary theorist Laura E. Donaldson has proposed an alternative spatial model of reading. This reading concentrates on the multiplicity of the surface of the text, rather than trying to grasp an abstract, one-sided truth beneath the surface. Donaldson finds the model for this kind of reading in the practice of the hoodoo sign-reader (Donaldson 1992: 19–20). I understand her poetic image as an invitation to oppose the universality of meaning, and to relate different elements of a text to their different localities patiently and precisely, while acknowledging the specific places created by the text itself. Unfortunately, this spatial concept of reading is not exemplary for postcolonial theory. But it can be found as a recurring concern in cultural analysis. What if one were to take the specific concerns of cultural analysis as one's point of departure for an analysis of writings by authors from Europe's former colonies? Could the practice of cultural analysis help to criticize and radicalize postcolonial theory?

The answer this essay will give to these questions runs like this: the focus on the complexity of text or image itself, and the focus on lived experience in cultural analysis, can form an antidote to the universalizing tendencies in postcolonial theory. Where postcolonial theory functions as a European self-critique, using the terms and theories of Europeans, a refreshing understanding of theory as an invitation to engage "discourses we don't know" can form an incentive to confront theories from the South.[3] I like to believe that this concept of theory is characteristic of cultural analysis. If this is so, then cultural analysis certainly forms an inspiration to open up postcolonial theorizing to other discourses.

In the following, I will retrace this argument in detail by offering a precise and concrete discussion of one text by an African-American writer and two by Caribbean migrant writers. I will concentrate on the discourses of spatiality which can be read in these texts, in which an African-Caribbean female identity is outlined. Let me begin by reflecting on the different ways in which one could "frame" one's reading of such a spatial discourse of identity. For there are already highly prestigious discourses of spatiality, which threaten to engulf minor endeavors to articulate such a discourse. First and foremost, I point to Deleuze's and Guattari's nomadology, which is a highly inspiring and catching discourse, as the enthusiasm of its followers affirms. This philosophy of signification is based on a poetic interpretation of a North African nomadic condition of violent mobility. A key concept in this philosophy is "deterritorialization." The term refers to the postmodern movement of continuous displacement of significations, languages, discourses, and identities, a shift which implies constant deconstructions and reconstructions. "Deterritorialization" is the opposite term to "reterritorialization." It is the second moment in a dual movement, by which one positions oneself temporarily, to break away again afterwards. Deleuze and Guattari argue that this nomadic way of traveling/signifying is opposed to the imperialistic one which would aim at settling and appropriating.

This nomadology has been extensively criticized, especially by African and Caribbean scholars (Glissant 1981; Kaplan 1987; C. L. Miller 1993). The French authors are criticized for their failure to localize and relativize their own situated predilection for the notion of nomadism, and their failure to situate the forms of nomadism they refer to. What strikes me most in these comments is the fact that these critics seem to speak from a very intimate and specific experience of a displaced, uprooted identity. Their expertise in the field is hard won, and they criticize the tendency of abstraction in discourses of displacement and nomadology as experts, insisting on the situatedness of concepts such as placelessness (Gooneratne 1986). Deleuze and Guattari's poetics of nomadism is accused of an ethnocentric denial of the importance of place. Indeed, this critique has convinced me that recent postmodern figurations of multiple, migrant identities are not as pioneering as they may seem; comparable notions are deeply rooted in, for example, the experience of the African diaspora, and African epistemologies.[4] To state it polemically, non-Western concepts of multiple and displaced identity came first, and they often seem to address the issue of displacement in a highly concrete and specific way.

Concepts of homeless, migrant identity, then, are always situated. On the other hand, even if the experience of a displaced identity is always specific, in a larger sense it is also shared by at least the many groups and individuals who have been involved in the worldwide processes of migration. My argument balances between two needs: first, the need to articulate those specific, situated spatial concepts of identity in a way that takes full account of their specificity; second, the need to outline general elements in these discourses on identity, and to relate them to other, dominant discourses. I will speak about similarities and generalities without identifying with the contested postcolonial penchant for abstraction and generalization.

To begin my argument, I will concentrate on a recent, black, and feminist articulation of the relation between identity and space which is highly relevant to our discussion. In her rich, very informative study *Black Women, Writing and Identity*, Carole Boyce Davies introduces the concept of "migratory subjectivity" to describe black women's identity. She explains: "Black female subjectivity then can be conceived not primarily in terms of domination, subordination or 'subalternization,' but in terms of slipperiness, elsewhereness" (Davies 1994: 36). This concept insists on the *difference* of black female subjectivity. It should be differentiated from the "nomadic subjectivity" articulated by Deleuze and Guattari: "It is not so much formulated as a 'nomadic subject,' although it shares an affinity, but as a migratory subject moving to specific places and for definite reasons" (Davies 1994: 36–37). In this way, the concept admirably brings together the mobility of black women's identity and its specificity. In addition, Davies's definition (and especially her emphasis on the "elsewhereness" of black women) offers a remarkable guideline for those who wish to listen to and address black women scholars, which I will discuss in some detail. After leafing through many volumes of postcolonial theory, one might exclaim, with Davies (80, 88), where are "the women . . . in the discourses of post-coloniality?" If one presses this question specifically with regard to black and migrant women, Davies's terse answer is, "They are somewhere else, doing something else" (88).

It is tempting to accentuate the outsiderness of black and migrant women's reflections on the self. Indeed, it is quite common to show how black women writers always evade discourses and definitions meant to situate and confine them.[5] This approach, however, doesn't do justice to the complex quality of black women's writing. It implies that black women's writing can only be studied as a critique which inhabits dominant texts in an elusive way.[6] But the force of these texts lies as much in their articulation of culturally specific and gender-specific notions and discourses. They are not merely critiques. It seems therefore wise to refuse to understand all literary expression from the South as reactions to dominant Western discourses. If one does, the following suggestion by Christopher L. Miller, the author of *Theories of Africans*, will be of use: he urges scholars of, say, a specific African literature to learn about the relevant African literary traditions, African epistemologies and theories in which the object of their study is embedded. This, he states, is the only way in which one may encounter the difference of other discourses.[7] In the same vein, black women's discourses of spatiality are not just "outside" and "elsewhere." They often refer to or create some specific *inside* space as well.

With these preliminary remarks about the relation between black women's identity and space in mind, I will turn to a Caribbean text, in which a remarkable discourse on a young woman's migratory identity is articulated. The text seems at first glance the perfect example of a deconstruction of a Western discourse of modern, displaced identity. I will argue that at second sight, however, this text also presents a highly Caribbean notion of modernity and exile. At the same time, it offers a specific example of the bound mobility referred to by Davies.

A Daughter's Journey Out

In *Annie John* (1985), a novel by Antiguan-American writer Jamaica Kincaid, a girl from the Caribbean sets sail for the United States.[8] She sets out on a journey of her own. In addition, however, she also offers a short but effective critique of the journey of Columbus, which played a decisive role in the generation of the modern age. If anyone can be said to have critically inscribed herself into Columbus's dominant narrative, it is this Annie John, a schoolgirl from Antigua. As the location of her inscription, she picks a telling moment in Columbus's life narrative, a lesser-known moment of deep crisis: the episode when Columbus was put in chains. This happened in 1500, at the end of Columbus's third voyage to what he called the New World. A delegation from Spain came to look into the colonists' rebellion against Columbus and his brother on Española, and perhaps into Columbus's political loyalty too. The brothers Columbus refused to acknowledge the authority of the delegation. They were arrested, put in chains, and brought back to Spain. There, Columbus was granted his liberty, but, since it had already become clear that he was a bad governor, he lost the title of viceroy. Under the picture of Columbus in chains in her schoolbook, Annie John writes: "The Great Man Can No Longer Just Get Up and Go" (Kincaid 1985: 78). Here, she repeats the words her mother used to mock her own father, who was slightly immobilized by an illness of his limbs.[9] Annie's act of mocking the disliked patriarch is in line with other acts of defiance of authority, acts in which she and other schoolgirls explore the sensual, vital, and erotic aspects of life. Although this offensive behavior vexes her mother, Annie takes the very words of her anticolonial blasphemy from her mother's mouth, who is the main point of reference for her acts of challenging and escaping (colonial) authority. Annie's adolescent condition of tormented alienation is derived, first and foremost, from her mother. Annie does not refuse or subvert the Western narrative of Columbus's journey for the reason that it would not fit her own sense of Caribbean identity. It is rather the other way round: Annie needs a journey of her own to construct an identity she has not yet been able to claim.

The chapter following "Columbus in Chains" bears the title "Somewhere, Belgium." Reading about cruelly treated girls, Annie envies them for their happy escape: "In the end, of course, everything was resolved happily for the girl, and she and a companion would sail off to Zanzibar or some other very distant place, where, since they could do as they pleased, they were forever happy" (86). Annie, too, longs for an escape to some "very distant place":

My most frequent daydream now involved scenes of me living alone in Belgium, a place I had picked when I read in one of my books that Charlotte Brontë, the author of my favorite novel, *Jane Eyre*, had spent a year or so there. I had also picked it because I imagined that it would be a place my mother would find difficult to travel to and so would have to write me letters addressed in this way:

To: Miss Annie Victoria John
    Somewhere.
    Belgium. (92)

Annie's dreams of exile are indeed self-willed dissociations from the dominant colonial, patriarchal, and matriarchal structures of which she wants
no part. But in her young woman's dreams, her escape is foremost an escape from her mother, whom she can no longer love without hating as
well. Even so, she is caught within her desire for her mother, which becomes clear in the above quotation. She wants to leave home so that her
mother may write to her; the mother's voice must continue to exist as long
as Annie can be the desired, absent addressee. She wishes to be addressed
in writing; a very radical separation is the only way to remodel her relationship with her mother according to the discourse of literature, which
she has found enabling, liberating, and helpful in offering a sense of direction. She is now the absent addressee, of whom no answer is required;
she has won the freedom of the reader.

    When Annie finally leaves home, she does not even do so as a future
reader:

I had made up my mind that, come what may, the road for me now went only in
one direction: away from my home, away from my mother, away from my father,
away from the everlasting blue sky, away from the everlasting hot sun, away from
people who said to me, "This happened during the time your mother was carrying you." If I had been asked to put into words why I felt this way, if I had been
given years to reflect and come up with the words of why I felt this way, I would
not have been able to come up with so much as the letter "A." I only knew that I
felt the way I did, and that this feeling was the strongest thing in my life. (133–34)

She escapes from an oral history which will always place her in her
mother's womb, and thus will immobilize her within the history of someone else. She has no history of her own; there is no narrative to guide her
into exile. The very basics of reading, the alphabet, are now lost to her,
even if she tries to read and write the strongest, simplest elements of her
own story.

    From a blasphemous rewriting of Columbus's narrative, guided by
her mother's parodic discourse, the novel leads to a concept of escape into
a larger postcolonial world in which one can be a happy, unencumbered
reader of even colonial tales (like *Jane Eyre*), which one may consume just

for the pleasure of knowing that one can be a desired addressee; but it ends on the wordless awareness of exile as a necessary zero point, which leads away from stifling histories as well as from (known) language.

Several important points can be made about the relevance of the issue of the journey for the Caribbean women writers' enterprise of constructing their identities. A first remark could be that Kincaid's story can well be read as the story of a girl's coming of age. As Teresa de Lauretis reminds us, Sigmund Freud has offered a Western psychoanalytical model of a woman's journey, although Western fantasy tends to imagine her as immovable place: "Freud's story of femininity . . . is the story of the journey of the female child across the dangerous terrain of the Oedipus complex" (de Lauretis 1984: 132). Simply put, this journey consists of a gradual forsaking of the mother. The girl's destination would be passivity, her reward motherhood. It seems that it is quite common to conceive women as travelers, but only to reach the site of womanhood and motherhood. Once arrived, they are fixed in their identity as passive space. According to this interpretation, Kincaid's story does not really have a bearing on the issue of the journey for Caribbean women. It would be relevant to the adolescent girl's journey in general.

If this interpretation were acceptable, Kincaid's discourse of mobility could not be described as the presentation of migratory identity. However, other readings are also possible. At this point in my discussion, the critical attitude to dominant Western theoretical discourses which is implied in both cultural analysis and in certain strands of postcolonial theory incites me to look beyond psychoanalytical interpretations. I propose to complement the reading suggested above with another reading, which situates Kincaid's narrative within a Caribbean context. To do so, I will emphasize unmistakably post- or anticolonial elements, such as Annie's rewriting of Columbus, and study other elements in the narrative within a Caribbean cultural context. There are two elements I will now examine in particular: one consists of the relation between the notion of identity and that of the journey, and the other bears on her evocation of a Caribbean discourse of the ambivalence of exile.

Kincaid's narrative demonstrates that traveling and displacement can be understood as practices by which one deconstructs or creates an identity as a speaking subject. This kind of approach to identity through a discourse of spatiality and mobility is by no means unusual. It is apparent in Freud; it is common in black and postcolonial writing; and it is apparent in many other writings about Western modern identity. For many historians, the Western modern age was triggered by one specific, paradigmatic journey: Columbus's journey to the Americas is described as the event which inaugurated modernity.[10] Columbus's misled expedition led to radical changes in European images of world geography and the nature of humanity. "Exile," "displacement," and "schizophrenia" are recurring metaphors for the changed human condition in the modern age, and thus for modern identity. In current postmodern, postcolonial, and post-structuralist critical practice, these metaphors of displacement even seem to proliferate.[11] Let us leave the general postmodern and postcolonial discourses aside for a moment and, true to what I would like to be the spirit of cultural analysis, concentrate on a specific Caribbean discourse of exile. Then it will become clear that Kincaid's text contains a specific Caribbean account of Davies's more general concept of black female migratory identity.

European modernity and Caribbean modernity cannot be equated. Simon Gikandi, who has written a book-length study on the forms that modernism takes in Caribbean writing, and whose argument I am following in this section, proposes to differentiate between European and Caribbean forms of modernization.[12] The Caribbean concept of modernity does not come into being by a journey, as the European concept does, but by a complex exile from Africa, the Caribbean, and Europe as well. Gikandi situates Caribbean modernity in the creative schizophrenia embodied in creolization, which he defines as the modernization of African cultures in the Caribbean. Thus, he outlines a split, an inner dichotomy in Caribbean culture, which is akin to the Western modernist experience but must be understood in quite different terms. The ubiquitous trope of "exile" in modernism, for example, receives a specific meaning in the Caribbean context, "because of its overdetermination by colonialism" (Gikandi 1992: 35). This specific exile of Caribbeans of African descent has its beginnings in the Middle Passage. Gikandi shows how Caribbean people of African descent, as well as being exiled from Africa, are also exiled from their own birthplace, because the colonial system does not offer them an opportunity to participate in the community. The home island may be seen as a degenerate and corrupted mother (*Césaire*). And lastly, if Caribbean people leave for the "mother country," that is, the site of colonial power, they will experience yet another state of exile as second-class citizens in hostile surroundings.

Nevertheless, exile can also be seen in a more positive light. A self-chosen form of exile signifies a renouncing of the confinement in the "hole," the assigned birthplace of the modern black man.[13] C. L. R. James and Guyanese writer Jan Carew make clear that leaving one's birthplace means also a dissociation from a dominant, destructive culture, which threatens one's very subjectivity. According to Carew, exile can thus be interpreted as a self-willed entry into history (in Gikandi 1992: 36–42). This understanding lies at the base of Kincaid's story about Annie John: to enter history, Annie had to escape from the place which continually situated her in her mother's womb. On the other hand, Annie already rewrote the script of the history she was entering by refusing Columbus's authority.

Read within this Caribbean context, the continuity between Caribbean narratives of exile and Kincaid's travel story becomes very clear. On the one hand, then, it is perfectly defensible to read Kincaid's story about a migratory identity as a critique of Western discourses. But her text also establishes another dialogue, not with the West, but with the Caribbean. Kincaid rewrites the prototypical Caribbean journey away from the home island, the mother island. For Kincaid, as much as for her Caribbean male colleagues, exile means an enabling escape from immobilizing dominance. Her journey is in part a flight from her mother, which is in itself a traditional masculinist configuration of the journey. However, Kincaid uses this trope while transforming it, for instance by her insertion of the mother's discourse as the source of her own revolt, and of exile as a site oriented towards her mother's discourse. Kincaid's heroine not only chooses exile to "enter history" but does so to maintain a different link with her mother. There is no radical break. Rather than a nomadic subject, Kincaid's narrative offers the representation of bound mobility. The nature of her mobility is modeled after a Caribbean perspective on the journey out, and it testifies to the inescapable ties to the mother. From this point of view, Kincaid's story is also an "inside" story.

A Walking Mother

Women do travel, and they do construct their identities around notions of travel and motion. In so doing, they may put their very gender identities at stake. In the case of the Victorian lady travelers discussed in an essay by Janet Wolff, "their activities positioned them in important ways as at least problematic with regard to gender identification" (J. Wolff 1993: 233). Traveling women of different classes, sexualities, "races," and ethnicity will have to negotiate their identities in their own ways. However, mobility may not always have to be in contrast to their femininity.

This statement may be illuminated by the specific narrative of black women's mobility formulated by one of the best-known women writers in the African diaspora, Alice Walker. In this narrative, Walker links the ability to travel to "race," gender, and a certain form of motherhood. She even articulates the necessity of women's mobility as a part of her definition of black womanhood. In the late 1960s, Walker coined the word "womanist" as a black counterpart to "feminist," giving as the last lines of the second entry of her definition: "Womanist . . . Traditionally capable, as in: 'Mama, I'm walking to Canada and I'm taking you and a bunch of other slaves with me.' Reply: 'It wouldn't be the first time'" (1984: xi). Being a responsible, committed black woman means, among other things, that one is capable of moving oneself and others away from oppression: it means that one is willing to go and to lead into (another) exile. For Walker, this aspect of femininity is quintessential, so much so that her very name testifies to its centrality: "My great-great-great-grandmother walked as a slave from Virginia to Eatonton, Georgia—which passes for the Walker ancestral home—with two babies on her hips. . . . (It is in memory of this walk that I choose to keep and to embrace my 'maiden' name, Walker)" (1984: 142). From this fragment, we learn that Walker is Alice's "maiden" name, that is, her father's name. Even if her ancestor was a mother-in-motion, I detect the suggestion here that women should partly keep their "maiden," maybe androgynous, qualities of unburdened freedom of motion to claim the fullness of black womanhood. Literal, biological motherhood threatens Walker's concept of the mobile female. Nevertheless, women, whether they are artists or not, should have children; but Walker pleads for having one child, and one child only, in a famous essay dedicated to the topic: "'Why only one?' . . . 'Because with one you can move,' I said. 'With more than one you're a sitting duck'" (1984: 363). Mothers bear the curse of being known as the most sedentary variety of women imaginable, and therefore, Walker implies, also the most vulnerable. But this goes only for mothers of more than one. By concentrating on a "light" variety of mothering, that is, the mothering of one child, Walker creates her image of mobile motherhood. In this way, Walker creates a concept of female migratory identity around the notion of a purposeful mobility. I like Walker's image for several reasons. For example, I love her depiction of mobile motherhood. However, the most important point for this discussion is the fact that this representation does not primarily function as a critique of Western representation (though it is possible to read it as such). This image is firmly situated within an African-American sense of space: its points of orientation are Eatonton and Canada.

Again, the text offers a form of migratory subjectivity. Here, however, mothers and grandmothers are represented as strong mobile subjects, who do not travel to claim an independent identity by separating from the community, but who, in contrast, travel to save and strengthen the community. Both Kincaid's and Walker's representations of migratory identity show a mobile form of identity engaged in definite patterns of movement (from a certain place to another place). These representations should be understood in the context of a Caribbean and an African-American cultural context just as much as that they can be read as critical rewritings of Western images. Each in its own specific way, these African-American and Caribbean images fit the definition of a migratory identity remarkably well. However, I do not yet feel the need to speak of the "slipperiness" of these definitions. To explore this aspect of migratory identity, I wish to cross the ocean and read a very specific poem by Grace Nichols, a Caribbean woman writer in Great Britain, which is about the relation between mobility and female sexuality.

A Fluid Woman

My Black Triangle

My black triangle
sandwiched between the geography of my thighs
is a bermuda
of tiny atoms
forever seizing
and releasing
the world
My black triangle
is so rich

that it flows over
on to the dry crotch
of the world

My black triangle
is black light
sitting on the threshold
of the world

overlooking my deep-pink
probabilities

and though
it spares a thought
for history
my black triangle
has spread beyond his story
beyond the dry fears of parch-ri-archy

spreading and growing
trusting and flowing
my black triangle
carries the seal of approval
of my deepest self
(in Cobham and Collins 1987: 29)

Read within the context of the tropes of exile used by black women writers in Britain, this is a remarkable and courageous text. Instead of lamenting her displacement, the poem's "I" concentrates on the sign of her black femininity as the nodal point of the world. Her "black triangle" becomes the point of focalization (overlook) as well as the point which acts on the world (seize, release). Like the mysterious Bermuda Triangle, it seizes and engulfs, not unlike that other greedy black hole, feared by men, the mythical vagina dentate; but it chooses to release also. It wets the world; it spreads, grows, and flows. Contrary to the dry and stable geography of the patriarchal world, it is wet, fluid, and flowing. Its active nature is yet accentuated by its definition as a whole of "tiny atoms."

The poet takes up the old imagery of woman as place by qualifying her body as "geography," but represents this place as multiple. The place consists, firstly, of the "geographic" body, which not only is space but also holds "probabilities," that is, a future; and as such, the spatialized body is itself placed within time, and subject to change. Secondly, the black triangle marks the body's threshold. As such, it is part of the body only to a certain extent; as a go-between between world and body/"I," it does not completely belong to either. The black triangle is a commuter. Seizing, releasing, and flowing, it communicates with its outside. This nodal element of body space, then, is active, mobile, and oriented towards the exterior. It breaks down the image of the body as a unity of spatial passivity. There is yet another spatial reference in the poem: a "deepest self," which, as the ultimate spatial point, counts as an anchoring point. The black triangle can be understood as the active counterpart of this stable center.[14]

The central image of this spatial figuration, then, is the threshold, the frontier. The threshold functions even more strongly as a woman's image, as it separates and links an inside—a home of sorts, traditionally a woman's domain—and an outside. Like black women sitting on their porches or verandas, the black triangle is "sitting on the threshold." But from that threshold, while never really leaving it, it undertakes its very specific journey, and it negotiates the world by spreading, growing, and flowing. Janet Wolff might recognize here another form of "dislocation from a given place." The black triangle reconstructs the site that it commands as "contact zone."[15] The poem plays with the eroticism with which this zone of contact between, say, Europeans and Africans has been invested since the end of the eighteenth century, and which Mary Louise Pratt has described as the "eroticization of the contact zone" (Pratt 1992: 87, 90). This self-conscious black, female journey does not lead to alienation, for it is always connected to a sense of self. Nichols envisions a sense of self rooted in the body, which does not lead to an immobilization in nostalgia, but makes possible an optimistic outward motion. This image of the presence of black women in Britain naturally takes their presence as a given, instead of describing it as displacement or alienation. It rather traces the critical, disturbing effects of its dissenting presence and the displacement it effects itself. Thus, the poem reverses the postcolonial geography (which still organizes a shifting, eccentric empire around a stable cultural center). This reversion makes it harder to read the poem as an internal Western self-critique.

According to Nichols's poem, the liquid nature of the black, feminine self allows it to travel. This moisture is a sign for the richness of black femininity. So, black femininity is no obstacle to this restricted kind of journey. The moisture is presented as an active counterdiscourse, opposed to dry patriarchal discourses of history. It refers to a semiotics of sensuality, governed by the logic of personal desire. Instead of equating female subjectivity with passivity and lack of stability, Nichols sketches an active yet plural black female identity, which defines itself by means of the fluid strategy of a self-conscious sexual desire. The poem plays with a traditional notion of woman as place by blending it with a sensual discourse of the body. This enables the poet to elaborate the specific situatedness of a black woman as a geographical figuration in which black femininity is seen as neither displaced nor immobile. She understands black female identity foremost in its sexuality, which is centered and transgressively active at once.

Nichols's poem is my third presentation in this paper of a black woman's "migratory identity." Again, one notes that its mobility is not nomadic, not free-floating; it is bound and controlled. Is it elusive or slippery? Perhaps, but only if one thinks that women are elusive who take up space, claim the right to speak, claim the independence of their own minds, and refuse to follow dominant norms. I prefer to read Nichols's poem as a wonderful discourse of female identity, which stands in its own right, and which can be understood on its own terms, without situating it between the lines of other discourses. The point I keep returning to is this: I prefer to read black women's discourses as if they form a space of their own, not as if they are present only in the margins of dominant discourse. I stress this fact so much, because many postcolonial studies seem to concentrate on the marginal existence of black women's writing, as if this existence were motivated only by its desire to criticize Western masculine discourses. It seems to me that this attitude is a form of appropriation. In this paper, I have been using the respect for the specificity and the theoretical significance of the literary text itself common in cultural analysis as a means to counter this appropriation, and to free a space for these black female discourses. In the first two cases, I have adopted a somewhat anthropological position. I have tried to relate Kincaid's concept of mobile identity to a Caribbean context, and I situated Walker's notion of the walking (grand)mother within an African-American cultural context. In Nichols's case, however, it is much harder (though not impossible) to situate her imagery. And this difficulty brings me to the last paragraph of my argument.

The many wonderful literary representations of black women's mobile identity urged me to take these representations very seriously, as seriously as theoretical discourses on the same issue. The quality of their force and courage alone deserves such a respect. It is tempting to present these representations as theories, and place them alongside, say, Deleuze's visions. I am not sure, however, whether I should be able to defend such a position in the first place. In the second place, I don't think a static position as an authoritative theory would do them justice.

First, then, it will be hard to defend the authority of these narratives as theory in any traditional sense, because, for example, they have not even been developed into coherent discourses. Nevertheless, one could read these narratives as theory in Jonathan Culler's sense, that is, with respect to their capacity of representing piercing new insights into the interrelation of space and identity. It would also be hard to defend the authority of these narratives with the argument of their authenticity. Even if I have been referring to the lived experience of exile from which much African and Caribbean critiques of postmodern discourses of displacement stem, these representations of black woman's mobile identity can not be described as deeply authentic (that is, rooted in autobiography). In Nichols's poem especially, it is clear that a complex literary image figures in it. These images and discourses have not attained an authority which would immobilize the debate about black women's identity. And I am the happier for that.

To corroborate the second point of my argument: I am glad that Grace Nichols's imagining of women's identity as happily fluid answers British-Caribbean writer Joan Riley's heartrending pictures of the way in which women's bodily fluids attract male violence and sexual abuse and thus immobilize and even kill women. All of these images are eloquent and significant. It seems to me that the cultural analyst's theoretical interest in the local and specific might counter the postcolonial scholars' wish to construct global comparative frames. Only then can a study of the relations between space and identity really begin to take shape. It is a pleasure to imagine that one characteristic of such a theoretical practice will certainly be that it will welcome the voices and discourses of writers, poets, and narrators from outside the academy with the same eagerness with which dominant theories of movement are usually met.

Variety & Standard

SIEGFRIED ZIELINSKI

Translated by Gloria Custance

"In the burial vault of unfathomable sadness to which Fate has already consigned me, into which no rosy, cheerful beam ever enters and in which alone with Night, that dour landlady, I am as a painter doomed by a jeering God to paint, alas, upon the shadows . . ."[1] In Charles Baudelaire's *Les fleurs du mal,* artists operate completely from out of the dark, "in which, like some cook with morbid tastes" they "boil and eat" their own hearts: they are like shadow plants lingering at the edges of the Night. Artists working with advanced technologies at the close of the twentieth century are no light-shunning rabble.[2] They are close to the light and are enlightened by it. They are exposed to the glowing monitors of the programming machines, the editing studios, the workstations from Macintosh to Unix-based. For them, the light-defying blackness of the Night has the status of a luxurious possession existing outside of their work. Their creativity needs electricity as its soul; electronic building blocks fill the cavities of that soul's filigree. The digital is their radiant all-illuminating myth, the new binary polarity (the basal construction on which are built all the great historical mythologies, from the I-Ching to the cabala) from which artists seek to conjure up their visions of the other by teasing out potentially infinite combinations. In the extreme, these artists are pathological cases (in the double sense of being capable of both suffering and passion), manic, with a poorly developed instinct for reality and a strong inclination towards the "nirvana principle"—which Freud understood as "the endeavor of the psychic apparatus . . . to bring every excitation quantity, of outer or inner origin, back to zero or at least to reduce it."[3]

Art with, and through, the latest media technologies is light-dependent; it is tied to power—in the sense of both technical energy and cultural authority. Art hangs on the powerful networks that, ever since the New Media's first take-off period in the nineteenth century, have been so effective in wiring up industrialized society in order to boost its functionality. And art's circuslike acrobatic ascent to the high wires of this network has always been a balancing act, a mincing across Circe's gaping maw: her ambiguous nature makes her a beautiful temptress on the one hand and a repulsive omnivore on the other. In our part of the world, we have known the basic problem at least since the premodern period, which was when the first intensive efforts to achieve a symbiosis of art and technology began.

Creative work with advanced artifacts and technical systems has invariably led the brightest minds to seek the favor and the society of the powerful, since it was only in their palaces, or at least in their spheres of influence, that laboratories could be equipped and operated, libraries could be founded and filled, servants and assistants could be obtained, and meetings could be organized with like-minded and interested circles. (In place of these more or less secret meetings, we now have the more or less closed circles of users coming together at symposia, congresses, workshops, seminars, etc.)

The difference between this feudal, or rather postfeudal, pattern of dependency and the structure prevailing in the pre-twenty-first century is, I believe, less one of principle than one of degree. Today, the distance between heavily funded laboratories and technological facilities can be traversed more easily. When acquiring the materials needed for creative work, artists no longer have to set out on dangerous and strenuous journeys that may last weeks or even months. The fellowships for financing visits between Boston and Montbeliard, Los Angeles and Frankfurt, are no longer bestowed directly by some noble potentate but granted by individual professors or elected bodies and commissions. When artists fail to achieve the expected goal of a project, or, notoriously, show deviancy towards the authorities, they no longer have to fear for life and limb.

However, aesthetic praxis that makes more than infrequent use of advanced technology, and is also in part constituted by it, is bound up with an enormous bundle of forces of regulation, of continual grammaticalization, pressing urgently for universalization. In their everyday form, the phenomena are a practical compulsion to verbalize, the development of legitimization strategies, the integration into the accelerated momentum of the information myth, and the dependencies on highly prestructured applications of machines and programs.

In a culture that is permeated to such a degree by order, and when taking into account that the public debate on culture increasingly stresses the pragmatic and utilitarian, it seems to me that it is an urgent task for representatives of the humanities to focus aesthetic processes ethically, to insist on the indissoluble unity of aesthetics and ethics, and to concretize these for contemporary cultural processes.

Heterogeneity and universalization, understood as a dualistic construct in a Deleuze/Guattari sense, are needed in the interim in order to achieve greater clarity, although ultimately we desire to overcome this opposition. Allow me to state this more pointedly: the efforts and exertions that artists and scientists all over the globe invest in their projects—often verging on self-destruction—may at an individual level be driven by a variety of motives like vanity, ego tripping, careerism, power seeking, sexual gratification, pecuniary benefit, and so on. However, when one is beyond such motives, expenditure of one's energies only has meaning if there exists a decisive vanishing point to which both the academic and artistic pendulum is affixed—like Foucault's—our hectic bustle needs the hope of making a contribution to extending our room to maneuver, needs the potential for realizing our social and individual existence (in the sense of Ludwig Binswanger), and needs the enhancement of living diversity. And constantly resurfacing and reactivating is also that hope of encounters with elements and phantoms of this wild heterogeneity, as a rendezvous with the other, with that which is not identical to ourselves.

To be more precise, with reference to a concern of current cultural discourse, the desire "to get wired" or "to be wired" does have a genuine communicative dimensionality; otherwise it would not be worth the effort to engage with expanded tele-structures at all. It encompasses the need of these separate entities on the Net to encounter the unexpected, the unknown, the alien; to express themselves to this different entity; and possibly to enhance or intensify the mysteriousness of the world. In this I see the noblest endeavor of aesthetic praxis as a specific activity within culture: to sensitize people to the mystery of the world using artistic means, to render people sensible of the other. Or as Deleuze and Guattari might have put it, although in this case it was Roberto Rossellini: "the less human the world becomes, the more the artist is entitled to believe in the relations between humankind and the world and to make others believe."

The central issue that I derive from this is by no means new. However, in my opinion it needs to be reformulated more pointedly: how might it be possible to continue to combine, in a tension-packed way, this trend toward standardizing praxes of expression, codes, and their forms of organization, as well as materialization with the vital multiplicity that is located prior to the effect of the real, of the *Wirklichen* in the sense of *Wirksamen*?

This reformulation includes the search for the utopian potential that resides in the expanded technocultural conditions during their transitional phase to a thoroughly structured order. The global data space is not yet totally organized hierarchically; the many agents already operating in it are not yet all in the pay of state intelligence or the police of private or public service industries and merchants. So how can aesthetic praxis that resolutely evades quantification and statistics, that will generate friction with these, hold its ground in the new networks? Three initial attempts at an answer on different levels follow.

Combining and Letting Collide

First and foremost, there is the opportunity to combine and let collide the highly organized regulation of expression with themes and subject matter that, because of their profundity and complexity, are able to generate friction with the grammatical programs of the new technostructures. Pierre Klossowski's texts, but also his drawings, would be a good example of this.

The way language is used on the Net is terribly affirmative of life. As a principle, the language is positive, animated, apologetic, smart. It bristles with energy. It is an electronic fountain of youth. The computers, their technical designers, and the connections they have cast enable, facilitate, and support (for example, nature). Programs lead, organize, and select.

Landscapes are created, as are populations or generations, which develop dynamically and are at liberty to unfold in (self-)organization. The interfaces have to be interactive and empathic (in the Aristotelian sense) or even biocybernetically interactive; they must organize something alive in the closed circuit. Their secret agents do not have trench coats with turned-up collars to hide their faces; they are not up to anything; as yet you will search in vain for them in the underground; they are tour guides standing in the spotlights, laid back, inviting us to go surfing. The waves of possibilities, in which the quantum truths are now formulated many decades after their discovery by theoretical physics between the wars, exclude the violence of contexts (A. Kluge), and they are waves neither of pain nor of ecstasy. In Chris Marker's "Sans Soleil," we encounter a Japanese man who is always making lists of things, for example, things that make the heart beat faster. I started to make lists of phenomena, phantoms, and modi that I miss on the Net. The speech that thematizes it grows longer by the minute. Only a few of the favorite substantives are: ambiguity—anger—uneasiness—daze—dark anguish of spaces—deviance—incongruence—doubt—excess—hysteria—interruption—irritant—passion—risk—seduction—yearning.

Theory and Heuristics

The most complex mystic praxis with the most complex language that I know is the theoretical cabala: "a technique for exercising reason or also instructions for use of the human intellect. . . , [of which] it is said, that angels gave [it to] Adam . . . after the expulsion from the Garden of Eden as a means whereby to return" (K. Wolff 1989: 10). The ten Sephiroth with their twenty-two connecting pathways constitute a sheerly inexhaustible, networklike store of associations, connections, and punctuation; its construction principle is binary, and it is erected on the basic tensions of theoretical reason (CHOCKMAH) and the power to concretize, to form (BINAH). The only meaningful mode in which the cabala can be read and re-revealed time and again is that of interpretation. In this, the cabala and art are related.

Edmond Jabès's texts are philosophical poems. In a discussion with Marcel Cohen about the unreadable, Jabès was asked what he meant by the "subversion" of a text, to which he replied by referring to the beginning of each and every subversion: disruption/interference. That he operates with grammatically correct sentences and words that retain their connotative meanings is a paradox which he resolves cabalistically:

I have not tried to ruin the meaning of a sentence nor of a metaphor: on the contrary, I have tried to make them stronger. It is only in the continuity of the sentence that they destroy themselves; the image, the sentence, and its meaning, if they are confronted with an image, a sentence, a meaning, that I consider to be just as strong. To attack the meaning by attacking the sentence does not mean it is destroyed: on the contrary, it is preserved because one has opened up a path to another meaning. All this appears to me as though I were confronted by two opposing discourses that are equally persuasive. This results in the impossibility of privileging one over the other and this constantly postpones the control/power of the meaning over the sentence. Perhaps the unthinkable is just simply the mutual suspension of two opposite and ultimate thoughts.[4]

Maybe there is hidden here a key to a possible way of proceeding in aesthetics within orders and structures that, between the Pentagon, academies, and the market, offer but slim possibilities for temporary interference, the filigree weaving of liabilities.

On the Net, there is no art of this kind (yet): it has had no time (yet) to develop a notion of the other, the vanishing point of which would be Death (in the sense used by Emmanuel Levinas). The model for Net culture is life, and because there it has given up its unique existence, it easily becomes a model as a rule. The algorithms used by the engineers and artists, working on a more or less secret order of Circe-Telecom, have been copied from the bio-logical, life form(ula)s translated into mathematics. Genetic algorithms are useful and fascinating because of their proximity to this life. They are bursting with strength and confidence. For the sake of art, it would be well worth the attempt to invent algorithms of (self-) squandering, of faltering, of ecstasy, and of (self-)destruction by way of an experiment. In full recognition and acceptance of the risk that perhaps there would not be much to see or hear, meaning visually and acoustically as we are accustomed to such from art history these algorithms would be transformed into sounds and images. This is the direction in which my third answer is aimed, which I shall give in the form of a brief discussion of an exceptional artistic praxis.

The Work of the Austrian and German Experimental Group "Knowbotic Research" (KR+cF)

In the universal shadow, in the black halo where the strong, light bodies of knowledge of this group move but which prevents them from dispersing, there is a presentiment of this secret.

The composition of the group already indicates the possible way. It works in a highly interdisciplinary, yes, even disciplineless way. Its nucleus is a visual artist (Yvonne Wilhelm), a performance artist (Christian Huebler), and a musician/composer (Alexander Tuchacek). Around this nucleus form and reform changing constellations of computer scientists, programmers, designers, architects, and theorists—specialists from disciplines of planning and construction. The workshop processes that they organize and temporarily demonstrate in installations slide between the praxes of aesthetics, technology, and science, which in the context of art through media are becoming more difficult to differentiate. In this interspace, they try to communicate, to irritate on both the conceptual and the sensory-perceptual level. Their creations and workshop processes are factional, being extracted from both empirical data and the realm of fiction, to which they always seem to want to return. In Circe's net, they strive to guide its visualization (knowledge and its organization) while hinting at seduction, without which art as sensitizing terrain for the experience of the enigma is no(thing) at all. In order to develop this character of the double agent, the "Knowbots" have been assigned a second mode of existence that can take on a form outside of the Net: in an event, in the one-off mise-en-scène of publicly accessible space, they become once again empirical bodies, sensations. The two time-spaces are connected through the idea of expanded operationality: they utilize the new technological infrastructures not as an optional offer that has shifted into immeasurability but as a terrain for practicing interventions.

I must illustrate this with an example. (This is just another example of the compulsion to formulate art in language that I mentioned earlier; without an explanation, this kind of artistic experiment with and through media is almost incomprehensible.) In their project entitled "Dialogue with the Knowbotic South," the group constructs a bizarre hybrid of a place, a "Public Knowledge Space," which is inspired by the idea of the *Wunderkammer* and takes as its actual starting point Jan van Kessels's painting *Amerika* from 1666. In long and painstaking research, Yvonne Wilhelm and Christian Huebler collected material on how present-day research on Antarctica, a continent that in van Kessels's day had not yet been discovered, is conducted and what is studied there. The results were hardly surprising: for the most part, international Antarctic research is not carried out on the spot but via satellite remote-sensing data and computer-monitoring. Over the initial representations of its geography, flora, and fauna, a dense network of symbolic information and processes have gradually been laid down, within which current research operates as a matter of course in a second natural environment. Some of these scientific projects have been taken by the group and condensed into bodies of knowledge—their so-called "knowbots." These are three-dimensional, dynamic, computer-generated graphic constructs that the group implements to expand and rupture the dialogue of the natural sciences with Antarctica.

The group describes the quality of this form of communication as follows:

An extension of the dialogue is achieved not through a recipe for a virtual nature (i.e., its mere perceptually illusive construction) but through the interaction with knowbots in aesthetic fields of the Public Knowledge Space. These fields are generated by the tension between the inadequacy of traditional concepts of nature in the face of technological and cultural developments on the one hand, and the abstract conceivability of a Computer-Aided Nature on the other. The result is a confrontation between the experiences of our historical (physical) presence in nature and the (spiritual) freedom prevailing in the Public Knowledge Space. The detachment from the referent nature is the precondition for the emergence of these specific aesthetic fields. The knowbots outlined by KR+cF represent no static formalization. They can be modified as they interact with the participants present in the Public Knowledge Space. Knowbots are mobile in time and space and become multilocal and multipresent through copying in networks. Processes inside the knowbot can be linked to externally located contextual interests. The Public Knowledge Space thus creates a playground for modifying the possibilities (and hence, the formalization and dynamics) of knowbots as part of an interdisciplinary discourse with a nature that is hypothetical.

In their installations, this extremely abstract playground is recombined with real architectonic space in a specific way. At certain interfaces, the bodies of data are rendered haptically experiential so that they are not only perceived visually but can also be (re)experienced as fluctuations in temperature, acoustic constellations, or air turbulence, as attractions/sensations. Ulrike Gabriel, an artist from the Frankfurt Städelschule who works with similar installation concepts, albeit wholly in acoustic and visual spaces and anterior-Net, has named this the "perceptual arena" a true venue of Circe, training the eyes, the senses, in a preface to a culture of knowledge and feelings that will be fragmentary, hybrid, associative, eruptive, and fluid in its structure.

The use of the same computer codes that are urging on standardization to create radically subjective constructions as offers for interpreting reality—which during the course of their short, temporary existence have need of the activity of the singular—constitutes the ethical-aesthetic vanishing point of these ventures between the disciplines.

Reason only appears to be still meaningful if conceivable in a plural identity, as a multiplicity of possibilities whose relation to one another is marked by creative tension. Reason so defined cannot do without individuals, the very prerequisites of its manifestation. As yet, the telenetworks are still a place where blueprints for such a culture can be explored. This was my motivation, in the first part of my essay, for elaborating on the rulers, administrators, and programmers of the micro- and softculture who are pushing for simplification, categorization, and ultimately the measurability of the Real. These are processes that have precursors in those that took place in the last century, in the founding era of modern media (as in Alphons Bertillon's or Cesare Lombroso's images for technical identification, but also even earlier, in the psycho-physiognomic studies of Della Porta in the early seventeenth century). An inordinate drive to archive that which is deviant, alien, indomitable, with universal methods and to banish it from the center stage of life. But these bodies of images are not easy to read, either. The obsession that spawned them and organized them in vast encyclopedias also admits a deep disquiet, a fear of the other, passion, and the capability of suffering, too.

Heterogeneity cannot be killed off: it stays tough. This hope—sometimes realistic, sometimes with a portion of self-delusion—is what makes me continue to work on the project of an academy of media arts for the next century. Possibly, it could also be a basic motivation for a project like ASCA. In this sense, I would like to see a school where the body of knowledge is in a state of perpetual movement, ideally a nomadic school, without disciplines. It could be in the desert or on the water or ubiquitous. But Amsterdam is a place where such a school could, from time to time, come together and pool its energies.

METHOD MATTERS

Reflections on the Identity
of Cultural Analysis

COMMITTED AS THIS volume is to the practice of cultural analysis, the re-flections in Part III do not claim to propose any "directions for use" or authoritative statements on how to do it. As I mentioned before, this is the reason why the essays appear last and not first. They present a number of different perspectives that indicate the diversity of views that are compatible with, and helpful for, the kind of practice which this book demonstrates in the first two parts. Four of the five essays are arranged in pairs of opposites, representing the kind of fruitful tensions that stimulate debates in and outside classrooms and conferences alike. Their arrangement in such pairs is also meant to indicate that this volume aims at being a teaching tool without being authoritative. Whereas no definite answers are proposed and conflicting views are left in conflict, the essays are similar in that they offer and stimulate, if they do not outright impose by their tensions, a (self-)reflection on cultural analysis, its practices and its underpinnings.

In this spirit, it seems significant to begin these methodological reflections with a critical and self-critical account of the analysis of visual artifacts that both resist and appeal to the categories that the academy is used to analyzing. If art historians know what to do with paintings by Raphael or Picasso, and anthropologists are quite skilled in interpreting a rite of passage in a given culture, then the object that Johannes Fabian, a widely known anthropologist, proposes as a case for methodological reflection consists in paintings, but not by Raphael, and relates to the culture in which it came to be in ways that are far from obvious. Labeling them as "ritual" would be a way to make these paintings politically innocent, while the author claims keen political engagement for them. Thus, the paintings, and the body of work from which they were taken, constitute a great challenge that Fabian meets with extreme care, caution, and self-awareness. The need for self-critical reflection, so obviously great in this case, can thereby come to stand as an emblem or mise-en-abyme for this section.

Through his case study Fabian also challenges cultural analysis as an endeavor. He positions the art between semiotic and material existence, between symbolic overall meaning and specific political comment, and between history and the present in which history is remembered. Neither the semiotic analysis nor the material conditions traditionally called "context"—the question where they are placed and what and how they depict—are sufficient conditions, though both are necessary for an understanding of these objects as a praxis within their culture.

By carefully unpacking the ins and outs of such culturally specific art, Fabian moves from close reading to methodology and back again. Through issues so enormously tricky and complex as popular culture, narrativity, orality, irony, sponsorship, commodification, and authenticity, he is able to demonstrate the pervasive cultural presence of political critique. The essay ends on a thought-provoking note that posits the paradox of aesthetics and politics by pointing at the problematic aspects of both political aesthetics and "pure" aesthetics.

While Fabian's generalizations are methodological, and in the service of a plea for a "local" cultural analysis beyond the dichotomy of universalism-relativism, the second paper in this section starts at the opposite end. Louis Dupré, professor of philosophy of religion and culture at Yale, tries to define culture in general in the face of the increasing fracturing of culture in modernity. Refusing the typically Western tendency to understand others on one's own terms, he aims to develop a renewed metaphysical project as a necessary link or glue between subjectivity and the illusionary absoluteness of local symbolic meaning. The project, not the outcome, is what matters. Dupré cheerfully endorses the circularity inherent in this project, which consists of the attempt to justify the very horizon that the project's existence presupposes. This project, then, includes and indeed derives its coherence from reflection on culture. This reflection is self-reflexive if one endorses the concept of culture on which Dupré bases his definition of philosophy. Cultural analysis thus becomes the primary goal and object of such philosophizing. Between Fabian and Dupré, the tension concerns cultural diversity and specificity.

The second pair of essays in this section can again be opposed as a generalizing speculation and a detailed critical practice, but this time, the tension concerns history rather than cultural space. Indeed, John Neubauer, who teaches comparative literature as well as interarts studies, explicitly draws the analogy underlying this difference between historical and (inter)cultural alterity. Theo de Boer, a philosopher in the hermeneutical tradition, defines cultural analysis as the integration of three distinct and mutually indispensable activities based on three propelling "motors": desire, distance, and insight. Analysis in the traditional academic sense stands in the middle of this triptych, as the distanced, objective activity advocated by structuralism. But this middle position by no means entails privilege or autonomy.

De Boer argues for a systematic contact and support between reason and passion, and in the endeavor, he recalls a quote from *King Lear* cherished by Wittgenstein: "I'll teach you differences." With this quote, the differences, as the target of cultural analysis, are compounded by the teaching, the missionary aspect so strongly present within the humanities. But, perhaps more interestingly for this volume, the I-you interaction is explicit, foregrounded as the axis that requires self-reflection as well as accountability.

In stimulating contrast to Dupré's search for a unifying principle in the face of cultural diversity, De Boer's primary question is, How do we achieve academic distance ("reason") in the face of a diversity that no longer allows for orientation on the unchangeable and general nature, function, and meaning of cultural analysis? He seeks to explore the possibility for a harmonious interplay among the three forces in unconscious reality, daily reality, and fictional reality defined as "intensified." His systematic exploration of the three forces within the three domains of reality yields a typology of activities within cultural analysis and within a perspective that is, if not universal, at least atemporal or, one might speculate, fully based in the present.

John Neubauer, on the other hand, writes as a cultural historian who wants to articulate what distinguishes cultural analysis from cultural history and how we should go about evaluating the contribution of the former to the problems inherent in the latter. This discussion will without doubt be terrifically useful for the many students of culture who see cultural history as the sole viable paradigm and oppose it to cultural studies. Neubauer's essay is itself a great example of cultural analysis in its self-reflexive moment.

Taking his clue from a tension he perceived in the program of the conference on which this volume was based, he confronts the interdisciplinary aspect of the program with its analytical one. The desire to integrate disciplines might be at odds with the endeavor to "take apart" that which analysis, with its emphasis on close, detailed reading, exemplifies. Specifically, he explores the ways analysis can help to keep at bay the tendency in cultural discourse—cultural history and cultural studies alike—to congeal into reified concepts. He takes as his guideline the claim of cultural analysis to give precedence to analysis over historical reconstruction, causal explanation, and aesthetic periodization, analyzing each of these moves through an example from his own practice as a cultural historian. The first case is historical music: how should it be played? Reconstruction of material conditions, which is the cherished object for cultural historians, and in this case includes the musical instruments, settings, and scores, cannot solve the problem. The performer as well as the audience cannot eliminate their musical experience. This posits the integration of the cultural present in any definition of historical inquiry. It is here that the author takes seriously the analogy between cultural otherness and historical otherness, as he uses the concept of cultural analysis as a caution against the illusion of reconstruction.

For his second analysis, causal explanation, Neubauer argues that cultural analysis must propose new models for such explanations, not refuse them altogether. His example here is Goethe's science. Conceiving of cultural analysis as a dialogic discourse on method, he sees that one of its tasks is to work against the tendency of interpretations to monologize and monumentalize texts. In an analysis that resonates with Keller's probing into probing, Neubauer asks why and how different historians come to opposite views of the same phenomenon, and he comes up with a Kuhnian paradigm shift, operated in this case by Kuhn himself. It is only retrospectively, from the vantage point of the present, and self-reflexively that such contradictions can be understood.

The final case concerns the persistence of the "ghost of *Geistesgeschichte*" in Foucault's account of the beginning of biology that so opposes the very reifications Neubauer points out in *The Order of Things*. It is not so easy, he argues, to respect and preserve the heterogeneity of epistemic analysis that Foucault advocated. Again, the argument characteristically reasons with, rather than against, the opponent, so as to conduct a critique from within. This is a useful reminder of how productive the tension between detailed "taking apart" and the cautious integration of disciplines can be. More importantly, this essay provides De Boer's generalizing reflection with some footnotes, and perhaps even challenges. Neubauer shows how specific inquiries—in this case, into historical issues—can reveal those challenges. Together, the two essays provide a dossier for a debate between cultural analysis and its closest relative, which sometimes turns into its fiercest opponent: cultural history. Together, the precious pair, focused on cultural diversity and unity, cover the most pressing disagreements that have been raging in the academy since the advent of cultural studies. It is the ambition of this volume to provide terms for reopening debates that may have been foreclosed by passions and fears anchored in, precisely, diversity parading as unification—differently on both sides, but on both sides no less.

Jon Cook, a literary scholar who is, like many others, also more and more involved in media studies, closes the section by opening it up to a reflection on the future of knowledge in an age of what he calls the "techno-university." He analyzes in particular the institutional aspects of knowledge, an analysis which enables him to predict fundamental changes in what is considered knowledge as a consequence of the institutional changes that he perceives in the university today. In a fine reflection on philosophical implications of practical changes, he discusses such issues as academic freedom and the humanist curriculum, the influence of the generation gap in its interaction with technological developments, and conceptions of performativity in education. His thought, witty and profound, offers just the relevant sharp edge to the preceding discussions and a frame within which the endeavor presented in this book makes continued sense.

—M.B.

Culture and Critique

Johannes Fabian

This essay is based upon ethnographic research conducted in the Shaba region of Zaire from 1972 to 1974, mainly in the two urban-industrial towns of Kolwezi and Lubumbashi. I begin by reviewing a few concepts that are likely to come up in discussions of politics and popular painting. Then, I formulate a series of recurrent research problems and demonstrate my approach on a selection of paintings. Some critical afterthoughts conclude this essay.[1]

While the political significance of popular culture remains the larger issue in the background, it is here approached with a focus on political critique. In Shaba popular painting, political critique is expressed in comments, critical or descriptive, on past and present events, persons, or institutions and organizations that are involved in struggling for, establishing, or maintaining power. Given the history of Zaire, and of Shaba in particular, and also given the social position of popular painters and their public, it is only to be expected that, in their minds, politics is less the art of governing than the experience of oppression and exploitation. Comment is here used in an active, pragmatic sense (rather more like utterance than proposition, to invoke a linguistic analogy). To understand the pragmatics of such comments as are made by popular painting, knowledge is required of actors (producers and consumers of popular painting), settings, situations, social processes, history, and many other conditions that affect communication. Of capital importance are the economics of popular painting (needs, offer and demand, profit margins, market mechanisms). Regarding the actual and potential addressees of the political comment, the most salient characteristic of the corpus to be discussed here was that, at the time when the research was conducted, these paintings were offered neither on the expatriate art-market nor (as a rule)[2] in curio or airport markets.

In identifying what counts as a comment, one first looks at the paintings as material objects and icons. They make their statements by where they are placed and what they depict. But that is only a point of departure. Comment is potentially realized by every imaginable means of pictorial representation (style, composition, arrangement, perspective, colors, inscriptions,[3] materials). Iconic sources (other paintings, printed images, film and television images) as well as cultural symbols (distinctive clothing, posture, gestures, implements, colors, etc.) should be considered among pictorial means of expressing political comment.

If one searches for political critique in popular painting, lack of information on some or most of the above cannot be made up for by semiotic decoding. This point needs to be made because it touches on a frequent, perhaps systematic, misreading for which anthropology may in part be responsible. It regards the tendency to interpret primitive as well as much of popular art as predominantly symbolic, as assembling cultural signs into messages of timeless significance. Semiosis is involved whenever signs are combined. But semiosis is a lower-level conceptualization when it comes to understanding the overall significance of political comment in Shaba popular painting. Painters know that they encode and represent, but that is not what painting is about. *Remembering* is the most important among the higher-level notions that can serve to interpret what occurs in Shaba popular painting. In Shaba Swahili, *kukumbusha* (verb) and *ukumbusho* (abstract noun) are terms frequently used when artists or art consumers reflect on what a painting is supposed to achieve. They are causative derivations from *-kumbuka*, "to call to mind," "to remember." In Shaba Swahili, *-kumbuka* may be used synonymously for *-waza*, "to think," "to reflect." Painters often use the latter term as well as the noun *mawazo*, "thoughts," to describe the nature of artistic work.

Caution is especially in order when it comes to applying semiosis in a narrow, structuralist sense (including the underlying model of communication—sender, message, receiver—as well as concepts such as signifier/signified, denotation/connotation, binary opposition, paradigmatic versus syntagmatic relations). In the past, selective use of such concepts has been shown to have considerable descriptive and heuristic value, but only to the extent that it serves the main goal of understanding the critical, political significance of popular painting in Shaba.[4] Put somewhat differently, while it may be true that a structuralist logic (that is, structural relations articulated in a system) is at work in the process of creating a painting, it does not follow that structuralist techniques of analysis are sufficient to decode its political message.

But neither are evocations of context of the kind that may be collected together with the paintings, or added to their display in exhibitions. To be able to draw on context certainly is better than being faced only with a collection of objects. But availability of information on context should not give rise to the misunderstanding that context is a given. Evocation of context should especially not have the effect of cutting short an investigation of what was called earlier the pragmatics of popular painting in Shaba. "Cutting short" is likely to occur if context is taken to mean primarily con-text, that is, information that is already stored in other texts (printed sources on history, on political, social, and economic organization, etc.). Attention to praxis, that is, to what painters and their customers actually do and say (or don't do and don't say) requires—and delivers—much more. It requires ethnography based not just on observation but on interaction, and it delivers documents of culture-in-action, cultural performances.

Finally, a remark regarding region and period. Since a study of popular painting was not planned when the larger project began,[5] the regional focus, much like the discovery of the phenomenon itself, was a matter of accident. Of course, not at all accidental was the presence of social, economic, and cultural conditions that favored the rise of popular painting. Shaba, the former Katanga, is an industrial and thoroughly urban region. It was always the most important and profitable target of Belgian colonization. When agriculture declined after Independence in 1960, the mineral wealth of Shaba became the country's main source of income. Long-distance labor recruitment until the 1930s resulted in an ethnically mixed population; at the same time, the stability of the labor force and continuity of residence that was characteristic of Belgian colonial policy produced a strong regional identification. People in Katanga/Shaba define themselves as "the ones who work"—against those from "down-stream" (meaning mainly Kinshasa), who are in pursuit of pleasure and the fast buck.

Depending on the characteristic one selects, the emergence of popular painting in Shaba can be traced back to some time between the two world wars. It certainly was fully developed by the mid-1960s. Economic depression following the oil crisis, unrest during the Shaba "invasions" of 1976 and 1978, and especially the punitive political and economic measures imposed on the region by the central government seem to have removed the material as well as political conditions that favored popular painting. During extended visits to Shaba in 1985 and 1986, I had the impression that the production of paintings had ceased. People could no longer afford even small luxuries, and most of the expatriate academics who collected popular art in the mid-1970s had left.

Issues

Popular culture.   Generally speaking, popular production of images should be seen as part of a larger process which, for lack of a better word, may be called popular culture.[6] The critical, political comments made by paintings get their full meaning in connection with those that are formulated in other media, notably popular music, theater, and modern, urban folklore, including folk historiography (see Fabian 1990a and b). The material from Shaba shows that finding such connections between different media is not just a matter of comparison and analysis after the fact. Connections between popular song and popular painting are consciously made by the artists and perceived by their public. The same goes for tales, proverbs, and popular theater.

Narrativity.   A foremost characteristic of popular painting in Shaba is its narrative intent, organization, and reception.[7] With some confidence we can extrapolate from many sources a general rule guiding the appreciation of a painting: it must tell a story. This is often contrasted with paintings that don't, mainly the decorative and in various degrees nonfigurative productions of painters that came out of colonial art schools or are derivative of Western modern art. However, the contrast that is made in these judgments is only in part coextensive with conventional distinctions between abstract and figurative, or symbolic and realistic painting. Several Shaba painters stated explicitly that they perceived their work as a continuation of traditional plastic arts; not one of them hinted at a contrast between figurative representation in their work and a tendency toward abstraction and decorativeness in that of their predecessors.

Orality. Narrativity is in this society closely linked to orality. Neither the painters nor their public are illiterate; far from it. But their literacy is one that, through connection with orality, remains performance oriented. It has been shown that this is an important consideration when it comes to reading popular texts (Fabian 1990a). Analogously, it applies to the reading of paintings. On the side of the consumers, for instance, selecting a painting for purchase and displaying it is an occasion for (repeated) performative statements. It is not their oddity or curiosity that makes popular paintings conversation pieces, but their narrativity. Because of this orientation toward orality and narrativity, many, perhaps most, paintings actually involve recourse to an active repertoire of mostly urban lore: stories, proverbs, memorable statements, and anecdotes. This can be demonstrated in cases where recorded conversations with painters show that a painting's message derives its meaning from a story evoked by the artist. It is in the nature of the beast that, on the side of the public, such direct evidence for connections between elements of lore and paintings is not easily detected. The problem of documenting reception of popular art is always a difficult one. Still, given the social position of painters in Shaba, where they are in daily life thoroughly part of the society for which they work, it is safe to assume that the specific stories a painter evokes are shared by his public.

Irony. Realistic representation in popular painting should not be mistaken for literal meaning. Lessons that we have learned from other expressions of popular culture also need to be applied to the appreciation of popular painting. The understandable inclination among outsiders to classify these painters as naive, guileless, and therefore basically harmless is inappropriate, and not only for aesthetic reasons. Even a positive characterization of the political comments in these works as stark or poignant does little justice to something which Zairean painters share with singers, actors, and storytellers: an unlimited capacity for irony, allusion, dissimulation, double entendre, and outright misdirection. I had, among other things, these aspects in mind when I mentioned the need for ethnographic research on the performative character of popular painting.[8]

Expatriate sponsorship. The fact remains that this contribution to an understanding of popular political criticism is an academic exercise. As is the case with interpreting any corpus that exists mainly in collections in the West, there is always the danger that standards are derived from the oeuvre of a few painters who escaped anonymity. In Zaire, I believe that such biases were introduced right from the beginning with, say, the works of Djilatendo and Lubaki; it certainly happened again with Tshibumba and has reached its current apogee with Moke and Chéri Samba.[9] Tshibumba, probably Moke, and certainly Chéri Samba produced their best-known works for expatriate researchers and/or collectors. This does not as such discredit their paintings as documents of popular art, but it changes the communicative and pragmatic conditions of art production that need to be understood.

Commodification. Commodification and globalization of images and meanings is involved whenever popular painting is transported into the realm of international art. This raises the question of the extent to which political comment can be made at all by such transported painting—except in the most trivial sense of depicting political subject matter and, as is often the case, by literally inscribing political messages on the painting. What we need to appreciate (and can appreciate on the basis of ethnographic information) is the different degree to which rhetorical devices such as metaphor, irony, hyperbole, and others become reproductive stereotypes and cease to be productive statements. What is critique and what chic in Chéri Samba's recent paintings?

Authenticity. These remarks on the transportation of popular art should not be understood to say that expatriate sponsorship and collecting removes popular art from its context, or from an inside to an outside, and thereby makes it inauthentic. We cannot postulate a world system and then turn around and make popular painting a purely ethnic phenomenon. In varying degrees, the expatriate researcher/collector becomes part of the artist's audience. The world outside which the researcher/collector is said to represent is in fact always already inside the artist's world; what is not always given to the popular painter is the opportunity to address his message to the world at large. I suspect that the expatriate sponsor is not so much the addressee as only a catalyst, a provider of occasions (and, not to forget, of the means to paint an oeuvre that could not be sold on the local market). Often a relationship is created which produces for the popular artist extraordinary freedom (from the daily fight for survival), a sense of exhilaration as well as urgency, and at any rate an intensification of creativity. Politically, this can turn comments, provided by the work of popular painters working under conditions of political oppression, into outcries—messages smuggled from a prison.

Evidence: Paintings and Recordings

Let me now attempt to give empirical plausibility to the conceptual distinctions and general assertions made so far. I shall draw mainly on a work by one painter, Tshibumba Kanda Matulu's *History of Zaire*, as told and depicted in one hundred paintings. He happens to be the one Shaba painter who has received the most attention in recent writings. While he certainly deserves that attention, his oeuvre is of a rather special kind and cannot simply be taken to stand for Shaba popular painting in general. But neither is it necessary to disqualify Tshibumba as an idiosyncratic exception. In form, content, and pragmatic intention, his work was part of popular painting in Shaba and puts in perspective much that otherwise would remain an incidental collection.[10]

Contacts with other popular painters were less intensive; in a few cases only a picture or two was collected, sometimes second-hand. However, conversations with about a dozen popular artists were eventually recorded. These contained, apart from biographical, social-economic, and historical information, detailed discussions of genres and of the paintings offered for sale. In these exchanges, political comment was a less prominent topic than in the conversations with Tshibumba, which is not to say that political and critical implications were lacking.

Critical Comment in Popular Painting

It would be easy to select from my collection dozens of examples illustrating manifest political comment. But following an approach that I have taken before (on popular historiography and popular theater), I

FIGURE I. B. Ilunga (genre painter), *Attack on the Lubumbashi Copper Smelter by United Nations Fighter Planes* (1973). From the collection of Johannes Fabian. May not be reproduced without written permission of Professor Fabian.

want to pursue a more ambitious aim. By juxtaposing several paintings, or images and verbal information, and by confronting political comment in popular painting with other kinds of cultural and historical information, I want to show how critique is constituted as a pervasive praxis.

Politics and genre painting. Socioeconomically and aesthetically, popular painting is genre painting.[11] In Shaba, genre painting has two major functions. One is, as it were, material and decorative: demand for paintings derives from the differentiation of living space which is expressive of a process of urbanization and emergence of a petit embourgeoisie. Genre paintings are bought to be displayed on the walls of living rooms (salons) in private dwellings, as well as in shops and places of entertainment. The other function is intellectual; it responds to the wish to remember or think, as explained above. Paintings that evoke colonial and postcolonial experience are especially appreciated. Without being rigidly defined, genres structure memory in terms of a limited set of recognized topics or *sujets*, executed in a certain manner. Where, then, can we locate political comment in genre paintings? The two principal functions that I distinguished are a starting point in that they set up an interesting contradiction. The material-aesthetic function seems to make any political intent rather doubtful. Decorative objects hung on living-room walls are in no obvious way political. But then there is the requirement that they serve memory. Political comment is thus generated already by the mere contrast between being settled in (relative) comfort and visible memories which are unsettling.

Furthermore, several of the twenty or so genres painted in Shaba are of an explicitly political nature. Take, for instance, the popular war scenes. Our example (Fig. 1) shows United Nations war planes attacking the Lubumbashi copper smelter during the secession of Katanga (as Shaba was called then). A battle scene is by definition political; but is it critical? If one considers the moment when these paintings were sold, at the height of Mobutu's regime, then it is easy to see that a war scene from the Katanga secession can be experienced as a local gesture of defiance against a remote but nevertheless oppressive regime. "We survived bombing and strafing by UN foreigners; we will survive oppression by the people from Kinshasa"—this is the message that memory of the past has for the present.

What about two genres that are even more popular than scenes of war and other reminders of political events? Can a *paysage*, a landscape, make a critical comment? I believe it can if one considers that critique may express itself in a pervasive mood rather than in pointed statements. Within the repertoire of genres, the landscape helps, as a reminder of things past, to generate the kind of generalized memory that makes specific gestures of critical distancing possible.[12] That landscapes are also appreciated because of their prettiness and their capacity for evoking nostalgia need not be denied. These traits are valued by expatriates and the Zairean middle class. This is why landscapes painted by popular painters seem to have been sold now and then to customers more affluent than the usual buyers of genre painting. But the type of a pure or mere landscape is relatively rare. In most cases, *paysage* paintings include villages and scenes depicting rural activities. It is not nature and culture that are contrasted here, but rather village past and urban present.

I can be brief about *mamba muntu*, the mermaid (Fig. 2). On the

FIGURE 2. Kabuika (genre painter), *The Mermaid* (1974). From the collection of Johannes Fabian. May not be reproduced without written permission of Professor Fabian.

surface, this genre appears to belong to the realm of fantastic lore and possibly magic, whose potential for social and political critique may be hard to imagine. Since it is probably the most popular of the genres (measured by the sheer quantity of paintings), it would appear to weaken the case that I am trying to make for a critical function of genre painting. Yet analysis of a sizable corpus of paintings has shown the mermaid to be a kind of synthetic key symbol commenting on the predicament of the urban masses in Shaba, who desire wealth but see it being accumulated in strange, unpredictable, and incomprehensible ways. This is what is evoked by the most striking feature of mermaids, their being non-African females dwelling in the deep and appearing only by chance.[13]

Propaganda and myth.   Now to a tougher test. It would seem that the next example, a painting commemorating the founding of Mobutu's party (Fig. 3), represents the opposite of political critique. Especially when the images are taken together with the inscriptions, this painting appears to be propaganda for the regime, a sort of praise painting, analogous to the praise songs that party propaganda, animation, copied from traditional song and dance. It was painted by Tshibumba to be sold on the genre market (it was among the batch of pictures he carried when I first met him), but eventually he included it in his *History of Zaire*. The problems that this and similar paintings pose for me, with regard to their critical intent, are resolved when one assesses their place in the whole series of which they are a part (the system of remembering in genre painting, and the *History of Zaire* in this particular case). It then becomes clear that *24 Novembre* is, to say the least, ambiguous. On the one hand, it looks like a gesture made by the artist in order to ingratiate himself with the regime (and perhaps to reach customers among its supporters). In our conversation, Tshibumba reminded me that Mobutu brought calm and peace to the country. On the other hand, pictures like *24 Novembre* acquire an ironic function in the light of other explicit and implicit statements made by the painter in other pictures or in other oral comments. No one who is familiar with the context of this picture—Tshibumba's narrative, comments, and the other paintings—would suspect him of being an ardent supporter of Mobutu's regime.

FIGURE 3. Tshibumba Kanda Matulu, *24 Novembre* (1973). The artist marketed the painting as a New Year's present for 1974. From the collection of Johannes Fabian. May not be reproduced without written permission of Professor Fabian.

An ironic interpretation of what looks like propaganda becomes more plausible when we consider paintings depicting the "passion of Lumumba." One of them shows the deposed leader in front of a house near the Lubumbashi airport shortly before his murder/execution. The inscription presents Patrice Lumumba as a national hero, "thanks to the MPR" (Mouvement Populaire de la Révolution, Mobutu's party). The image shows him tied, suggesting a victim of oppression more than intimating that he is now being glorified by the very regime that may have been involved in his removal from power and eventual death. The point is that, given oppression in the present, any evocation of past oppression denounces present oppression[14] and is therefore potentially dangerous. In this case, an incident supports our reasoning. Tshibumba was once actually arrested and manhandled by police or soldiers for carrying a painting on which Lumumba was depicted in a torn undershirt.

Among the genre paintings that Tshibumba included in his *History of Zaire* there was also a nativity scene: The three Magi visiting the newborn child. If we had to select an example of naive, apolitical painting, quaint and perhaps unintentionally funny, this would be it. Again, appearance can be deceptive to an outsider who has nothing to go on except the painting itself. From its position in the historical series (it marks the transition from ancestral to modern history), and from Tshibumba's oral narrative, as well as from his detailed comments, we know that this painting has a crucial function in his critical historiography. It turns out that the trigger of memory is in this case not the birth of Christ but the presence among the Magi of a black king. In the recorded account that went with this picture, Tshibumba first told the story of Noah and the curse he put on his son who became the ancestor of the Africans, forever condemned to be poor and ignorant. Holding this painting up as evidence, he said that the story was a lie: Africans, even African kings, were there when Christ was born. Then he explained the point that this painting was to make:

Because—it is the story of the black man himself which I am explaining to you, right? He was lost long, long ago. I took my departure with the three Magi because one among those three men was a black man. He did not return. They killed him and he perished. Up to this day he cannot come back. I believe this is the story of the black man right there, it was lost. It was only later that we accepted things like [the story of Noah,] the man who was asleep in his house, and what not. No, it was at that moment that the story of the black man was lost.[15]

Notice that this anchoring of the history of Zaire in Christian myth actually results in its being lost by an act of violence, and that summarizes the critical view Tshibumba has of colonial history, especially also of the role of Christianity.

History and legend. Leopold II, founder and owner of the Congo Independent State, occupies a prominent place in Tshibumba's history. I don't recall ever seeing a painting by another genre painter representing Leopold. Does Tshibumba, here, leave the realm of popular imagination and work as the illustrator of a history that is of no interest to the people? Should one, therefore, assume that paintings of Leopold II, although manifestly a political *sujet*, are of no critical political significance? Not at all, if we listen to Tshibumba's story and explanations. We know from other sources[16] that Leopold is very much present in popular lore. Around this towering figure there developed at least two types of story that seem to convey contrary messages. On the one hand, the bearded patriarch embodies the "good old time" of the beginning of colonization "when Africans were not yet treated as slaves and Europeans took good care of their black workers."[17] The second kind of story is of great local significance. It is built on a striking resemblance between Leopold II and Monsignor Jean-Felix d'Hemptinne, a founder of the Benedictine missions in Katanga and later bishop of Elisabethville. People are convinced that d'Hemptinne was the son of Leopold (illegitimate, it is rumored, apparently also among Belgian colonials). Tshibumba actually went as far as to speculate that Leopold never died but was reincarnated as d'Hemptinne. People slightly older than he remembered d'Hemptinne as a rather brutal racist and colonialist. The *Vocabulary of the Town of Elisabethville* and Tshibumba, as well as other people with whom I have spoken, maintain that he gave his blessings to a massacre of striking mine workers in 1941. With that kind of background knowledge it is easy to see that legends may have a political function, and that evocations of Leopold II in Tshibumba's *History* qualify as critical comment on colonial experience.

Politics and ethnicity. The political perspective of Shaba popular painting is always informed by the common experience of colonial oppression. Being widely shared, these memories suggest that their critical intent is indeed part of a "political culture of criticism." But there are among the genre pictures some that make statements whose critical function becomes

FIGURE 4. Tshibumba Kanda Matulu, *Attack on a Refugee Train* (1974). From the collection of Johannes Fabian. May not be reproduced without written permission of Professor Fabian.

doubtful because they seem to be informed by particularist concerns, such as ethnicity. Tshibumba is a "Luba Kasai," an ethnic category with complex colonial origins. Though born in Shaba, he is a descendant of labor migrants from the Kasai region of Zaire, and so are many, perhaps most, of the genre painters and also many of their customers. For demographic and socioeconomic reasons, it is likely (but not demonstrated) that people from the Kasai may be the largest group among the petit-bourgeois buyers of genre painting. This does not, however, justify the conclusion that popular painting in Shaba is ethnic in nature.[18] Take one of the popular genres Tshibumba included in his *History*, the attack on a train, or simply *The Train, mashua*, as it is usually called (Fig. 4). On the surface these paintings commemorate the times of "troubles" following Independence, before, during, and after the Katanga secession. It is never stated, but known to everyone, that the historical events depicted here were attacks by youthful Luba Katanga guerrillas (*baJeunesse*) on trains carrying Luba

Kasai refugees on their way from Katanga to the Kasai. There is no doubt that, as a Kasaian born in Katanga, Tshibumba identifies with the persecuted Luba Kasai. But then it could be said, on the basis of other pictorial evidence from his oeuvre, that he identifies with Katanga as against the lower Zaire and the oppressive regime located down there. The point is that both identifications are embedded in a critical reflexivity that transcends regional and ethnic perspectives and makes possible some of the most moving critical comments in his paintings, such as one that shows the death of Banza Kongo, as Tshibumba calls the ruler of lower Zaire who first encountered the Portuguese in the fifteenth century. (Kongo is an ethnic label attached to Kikongo-speaking populations in lower Zaire.) In his account the painting marks the moment when the royal force that unified African culture and social life in Zaire was extinguished: Banza

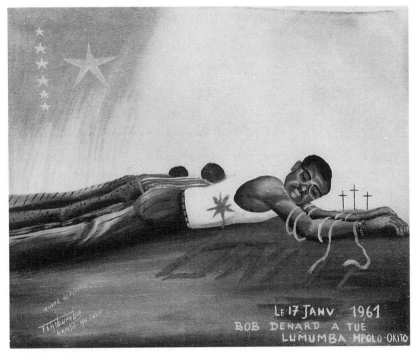

FIGURE 5. Tshibumba Kanda Matulu, *The Death of Patrice Lumumba* (1974). From the collection of Johannes Fabian. May not be reproduced without written permission of Professor Fabian.

FIGURE 6. Tshibumba Kanda Matulu, *Happiness, Calm, and Enjoyment of Life in Peace* (1974). From the collection of Johannes Fabian. May not be reproduced without written permission of Professor Fabian.

Kongo is said to have been poisoned by King Leopold's envoys. And when Tshibumba depicts the death of Lumumba (Fig. 5), another person who was neither Luba Kasai nor from Katanga, the true victim, written by the blood that flows from the hero's chest, is *unité*, the unity of Zaire.

Critique and despair.   Originally, Tshibumba had his series—and thereby history—end with a sort of apotheosis of Mobutu (Fig. 6). Did he mean it (that is, was the picture a mere submission to the regime or did he want to make a critical statement)? Yes, he meant it, but the question is how he meant what he showed. In a study based on work with popular theater, I suggested that a play about power only appears to end with an affirmation of the political status quo. In reality the ending evokes despair rather than accommodation (Fabian 1990b: 260–61). I would argue that the same is true in this case. At any rate, when Tshibumba continued his account into the present and future, the first picture that followed was dedicated to the "Martyrs of the Economy," commemorating the victims of an accident in the Kipushi mine, reminding us that someone, the African worker down in the mine, is paying the price for "happiness, calm, and enjoyment of life in peace" (which is the inscription on Fig. 6). That his inscription quotes a party propaganda slogan coined by the regime takes nothing away from Tshibumba's critical intent. Here and on numerous other occasions he is using a rhetorical device of popular criticism: the phrases, slogans, and catch words spread by the regime only need to be repeated to reveal and denounce their hollowness. This is how *citoyen*, the prescribed term replacing *monsieur*, came to be applied to a category of people perceived to be at the bottom of the social scale, for instance, the Pygmies. *Authenticité*, Mobutu's political doctrine, became a code word for corruption and mismanagement; *encadrement*, a key word in party jargon, stood for political control and oppression; and so forth.

Finally, I want to take a look at the painting that follows the one just discussed (Fig. 7). Artistically, it is perhaps not very impressive. Given that it was said literally to record a dream, it appears strangely poor or sparse in its imagery. It seems to hover, undecided, somewhere between the iconic and the graphic. Taken together with Tshibumba's recorded comments, however, it is one of the richest and most powerful documents in this series. In these brief remarks it is impossible to do justice to its many explicit and implicit meanings. Let me note just two observations. The first one regards what is presented graphically. It is one of the few paintings on which Tshibumba not only inscribes his signature but also leaves, as it were, the artist's place backstage. He confronts the viewer on the surface of the picture by means of a kind of second signature. Moreover, when he thus identifies himself, he does this in contrast to the painting's other prominent inscription, "100 Years for Mobutu," a line from one of the chants performed during animation. The meaning of that contrast—apart from what is obvious in this counterposition of the individual artist and the embodiment of the regime—finds its exegesis in the visual imagery. A compact, domed building, festooned by Party flags and radiating some kind of force from a ball of energy visible through

FIGURE 7. Tshibumba Kanda Matulu, *Key to the Future* (1974). From the collection of Johannes Fabian. May not be reproduced without written permission of Professor Fabian.

its open doors, appears to be guarded, or haunted, by skeletons, two of them bent over and crouching along the facade, one of them erect in the foreground. Read on a horizontal axis, the large skeleton is linked to Tshibumba's dream by the painting's title, *Key to the Future*. This suggests an intensely personal interpretation, a foreboding of the artist's own fate. From all we know he is dead, probably a victim of the upheavals following the 1978 "invasion" of Shaba. Considered vertically, the elements of the picture amount to a powerful prophecy, an ultimate gesture of critique. Remember that the painting was produced during the few "golden years" of post-Independence Zaire, when relative prosperity contributed to veritable explosions of artistic activity, among which popular genre painting in Shaba was one sort. In 1974, the end of the golden era was not obvious, and today's hopeless pauperization of the masses, starvation, and the ravages of AIDS and other diseases were still a thing of the future. Tshibumba was getting desperate, he told me, when despite many attempts he had not come up with a dream; despair is the "key" to his *History of Zaire*.

Afterthoughts

This paper is informed by a conviction that power relations and the experience of oppression, hence politics, pervade the subjects as well as the products of artistic imagination in Zairean popular painting. Like any other strong position one takes in interpreting art, mine has its intellectual problems and puzzles. What is consciously, deliberately political and critical, and what acquires such meaning in effect, that is, as the result of circumstances in which a given statement appears? Underlying that question are others that are more fundamental and may have to be faced first: Does painting depict consciousness? Should one assume that consciousness as an intellectual construction preexists painting, that it is perhaps more consistent and coherent than the fragmentary pictures produced for and sold on the popular market? Or should one, conversely, approach this problem by positing that consciousness exists only in objectifications such as painting and oral lore? There is no doubt in my mind that, empirically, the latter position is a sound one. At any rate, it was the one that I followed in this attempt at interpretation. Whatever its problems are, it seems preferable to an approach whereby insights, in our case into political critique, are derived from other sources and then simply illustrated by cleverly selected paintings.

However, I am not about to suggest that there is such a thing as simple induction from empirical data. Epistemologically, to interpret political popular painting requires, like any other critical hermeneutic, a dialectical stance involving at least two activities: confronting material objectifications and a constant back-and-forth tracking from individual object to a whole world of which it is a realization (evoking the well-known hermeneutic circle). But that is not all. Methodologically, or better, practically, what I called back-and-forth tracking is most often accomplished by starting with contradictions, by examining contrary possibilities, by confronting resistance to understanding, by setting up interesting puzzles, and by other interpretive strategies that have in common the idea that meaning is never simply stored in symbols, nor consistently stated in texts, nor logically constructed by underlying cognitive schemes. Every one of the examples that I have discussed was initially presented as an actual or potential contradiction to the overall thesis, arising from the ethnographic record that we have. I hope to have shown that staying close to the very materiality of political consciousness—as it is embodied in objects and voices—is one of the most interesting avenues to follow if the task is to understand institutionalization of political culture.

The dialectical approach that I advocate requires thinking in terms of particulars as well as totalities. Furthermore, these totalities are arrived at, not by classification and generalization, but by historical identification. Popular painting in Shaba is not treated as an analytical category abstracted from observations on the behavior of people; it is identified as a concrete, collective praxis. In that sense my approach is historical rather than sociological. Like any other theoretical and methodological choice, mine is not without its dangers. Even sympathetic critics have in the past expressed concern that my views on popular culture in Zaire, especially on its political, critical potential, tend to romanticize the African masses. This global allegation does not disturb me much. I know my feelings regarding the postcolonial predicament. They tend to be desperate, or cynical, but certainly not romantic. But, staying with the subject at hand, there are two problems that need to be faced again and again. One is posed by presenting a collective practice as a coherent, integrated, and somehow balanced system (remember the systems of action and belief that we used to study, and find, almost everywhere). Neither oppressive regimes nor popular resistance have been coherent, especially not resistance. It occurs ad hoc, in leaps and bounds. It is always revolutionary rather than evolutionary. Its themes and topics are, as I have argued in the past (drawing on a notion proposed by M. Foucault), always dispersed in many different forms of expression (Fabian 1978: 318–19).

Awareness of the precariousness and contingency of popular culture should counteract another danger that is always present when attention concentrates on artistic forms of expression, especially visual representations such as painting. This danger is the possibility that political experience, as well as critique, may be aestheticized and thereby removed from practice on the ground level. Actually, this raises two questions. One is whether a given interpretation aestheticizes expressions of popular culture, and the other is whether popular culture itself aestheticizes experience. As I see it, it is necessary to voice such concerns, but it would seem that the lessons we have learned, say, from studies of fascism and its aesthetics should make it impossible to entertain notions of pure, apolitical aesthetics (or art, or culture). Conversely, it does not follow that political critique aesthetically expressed and institutionalized in the medium of popular painting is politically of no consequence.

Cultural Variety and Metaphysical Unity

Louis Dupré

There appears to be no immediate evidence that culture needs any philosophical justification or that philosophy is able to contribute to it any essential quality it lacks. Being essentially a reflection on *what is already there*, philosophy seems, in this case as in others, dispensable to a reality that existed long before the philosopher entered the stage. The relation between philosophy and culture *is* different, however. Philosophical speculation has from an early stage in the development of our civilization formed part of its culture and, in this writer's opinion, significantly assisted it in performing its primary purpose: the conveyance of meaning to existence.

Culture consists of the symbols that preserve and direct the life of a society. Through culture, humans subdue the otherness of nature, rendering "present" what previously had been absent. Incorporating all things within a single temporal vision, culture integrates them with human existence. Emmanuel Levinas's formula captures the essence of all cultural activity: "La culture c'est le sens venant à l'être" ("Culture brings meaning to being") (Levinas 1986: 75). But meaning may be conveyed in many ways. The first domestication of primitive otherness occurs when we name things, as Adam did in Paradise. One unduly restricts the meaning of culture, however, when defining it in purely theoretical terms. Being part of nature, humans have to conquer their own place in a whole that nurtures as well as threatens them. Like other animals they are forced to pick their way between yielding and resisting, between circumventing nature's dangers and feeding on its resources. What distinguishes humans is their ability to outwit nature by means of *technē*—craft or art.

Culture does far more than equip a society with the norms and values needed for coping with the material conditions of its existence. It holds out a spiritual surplus that urges humans beyond the satisfaction of immediate needs. Georg Simmel commences his seminal essay "On the Concept and the Tragedy of Culture" with the following statement of principle:

Man, unlike the animals, does not allow himself simply to be absorbed by the naturally given order of the world. Instead he tears himself loose from it. . . . The ripening and the proving of the human spiritual powers may be accomplished through individual tasks and interests; yet somehow, beneath and above, there stands the demand that through all of these tasks and interests a transcendent promise should be fulfilled, that all individual expressions should appear only a multitude of ways by which the spiritual life comes to itself. (1968: 27–28)

Cultural models raise the phenomenally transient to ideal permanence. Through the symbolic meaning we attach to it, human existence escapes the drudgery of the ordinary. Without the luxury of cultural symbolism, life would become unbearably poor. What Alfred Whitehead once wrote about art holds for the entirety of culture: "The mere toil for the slavish purpose of prolonging life for more toil or for mere bodily gratification is transformed into the conscious realization of a self-contained end, time-less within time" (Whitehead 1954: 348).

A philosophical reflection on culture must start from the fact that culture is *not* a homogeneous system of symbols. It consists of an irre-ducible plurality of symbolic systems. Even elementary, prehistoric cul-tures do not limit their universe of meaning to a *single* set of symbols. They may integrate their systems more tightly than we do, but, as Malinow-ski and Lévi-Strauss have shown, they maintain clear distinctions between various levels of reality, as for instance, between ordinary-practical and magical or religious levels. Philosophy's primary task in justifying the symbolic complex of which a culture consists is to clarify the nature and the distinct modes of symbolic signification. Cassirer did this outstand-ingly in his *Philosophy of Symbolic Forms*. He described symbols in terms of a simultaneous presence of what appears and absence of that to which it refers. Philosophy investigates the relation between this appearance and its intentional object.

Why should there be a need for philosophical justification of symbolic systems that so obviously seem to justify themselves? Shortly put, because each mode of symbolization in its own way invites critical reflection. In the case of science the question soon arises: What enables a system of abstract, mostly mathematical symbols to disclose the nature of physical activity? This question, at the root of Kant's thought, has intrigued both scientists and philosophers of science ever since. The invitation to further reflection may appear less obvious but is in fact no less urgent in the case of art and of religion. Are they more than subjective, emotional expressions? How can the artist pretend to convey meaning by forms that, from a perspective of ordinary perception, appear either derivative of the real (Plato's "imitation of an imitation") or an arbitrary substitute for it? Least acknowledged by believers but most pressing is the demand for critical clarification of religious symbols. Are religious representations, rituals, and sacraments more than expressions of the prerational mind? Such are the questions confronting philosophies of science, of art, and of religion, all of which investigate specific modes of symbolization.

The problem raised in this paper is whether these specific reflections suffice for a philosophical justification of culture, or whether, in addition, a more comprehensive reflection may also be required to show how the multiple, symbolic systems relate to each other in establishing that more or less coherent totality which we call a culture. Without a critical awareness both of the relativity of each of these systems and of their relation to one another, each one separately will easily be mistaken for the *entire* expression of cultural meaning, or at least for the principal one to which all others are subordinate. Such a possibility is no idle hypothesis. In much of medieval thought religious symbols came to be regarded as independently, unqualifiedly true and defining the truth of all others. Without critically viewing them within a cultural totality that includes various symbolic systems, the believer may easily mistake religious symbols for the absolute itself to which they refer, thus converting icons into idols. Again, did not the success of the physical sciences for more than a century dominate the cultural climate to a point where scientific descriptions came to be regarded as the very essence of the real? Even art, when detached from other modes of symbolization, degenerates into an aestheticism. All symbols articulate meaning, but they do so within a larger complex of signification which enables humans, even of different generations and varying backgrounds, to communicate with each other across symbolic discrepancies. It is precisely to this multiform complex that we refer as culture.

In the latter part of this paper we shall raise the question whether a philosophical reflection on culture does not itself call for what Plato and Aristotle already referred to as a reflection on ultimate principles—later to be known as metaphysics. But before this question could even occur, philosophy, in whatever way it is understood, had to recognize that the sheer multiplicity of which each single culture consists formed an organic unity in its own right, worthy of its critical attention. This took a long time! The mechanistic philosophies of the early modern age were obviously incapable of accommodating the concept of an ideal complex functioning as a distinct, self-directed entity with a teleology of its own. The teleological principle, indispensable to the understanding of culture, was overruled by efficient causality. The turning point came when Leibniz redefined substance as an autonomous unit endowed with a purpose of its own, yet contributing to the overall purposiveness of the universe. At this point yet another obstacle had to be removed, namely, the rationalist principle of the Enlightenment according to which history (and by implication, culture) contains nothing but contingent events. Its knowledge yields no more than factual truth (*vérités de fait*), while philosophy deals only with the necessary truths of reason (*vérités de raison*). Kant accepted Leibniz's distinction. Facts convey only what *is*, not what *necessarily* is. All that history teaches is particular. Instead philosophy is the science of the universal. It was all the more remarkable, then, that Kant was among the first to recognize history as a new object of philosophical reflection and thus to lay the basis for a philosophical study of culture. As a moral being, the person is distinct from the realm of nature to which he or she belongs in other respects. The exercise of moral powers constitutes a realm of freedom that purposefully links the natural being of the world with a moral vocation beyond the world. Culture, the outcome of this historical endeavor, throws a bridge between nature and the person's moral vocation. It paves the way to that ideal of full human dignity (*Humanität*) which is the very purpose of reason. The older Kant distinguished culture from mere civilization: "We are *civilized*—perhaps too much for our own good—in all sorts of social grace and decorum. But to consider ourselves as having reached *morality*—

for that much is lacking. The ideal of morality belongs to culture; its use for some simulacrum of morality as the love of honor and outward decorum constitutes mere civilization" (Kant 1963b: 21). Kant drew attention to a new field of philosophical investigation, but he himself never succeeded in perceiving the universal *within* the particular. We may be able to distinguish a regular movement in the historical processes through which cultures are formed, but "no conscious purpose comparable to the teleology in nature is manifest in this idiotic course of things human" (ibid.: 12). Herder, Kant's admiring but wayward disciple, provided the missing link. He understood that each culture in its own way presents the organic universality of the human spirit and uniquely contributes to the complex variety of ways in which we express our universal humanity. A culture is an organic unit directed by its own internal teleology. Each people's artistic, scientific, and philosophical achievements constitute an ideal unity that bears the mark of its national genius. Having thus reunited the particular with the universal, Herder removed the main obstacle that barred the road to a philosophy of culture. All through the nineteenth century a succession of thinkers were to build on the terrain he prepared.

The view that history was a process with universal significance enabled culture to become an object of philosophical investigation. No one perceived this more sharply than Hegel, for whom the process of cultures, "the slow-moving succession of spirits, a gallery of images, each of which endowed with all the riches of Spirit" (Hegel 1977: 492), constituted in fact the very development of the ultimate, all-comprehensive principle of *Spirit.* Having expressed itself objectively in technology, law, morality, and politics, Spirit reincorporates these objective expressions within its own self-conscious interiority in art, religion, and philosophy. This occurs in art, religion, and philosophy. The mind passes through a dialectic that first moves outward and then returns to itself in the higher forms of culture. This process is not merely one through which individual minds, or even entire civilizations, attain cultural maturity. It describes the development of reality itself as it moves from purely physical subsistence to animal life and gradually becomes assumed in the life of mind. Mind, Hegel shows, is as real as matter; in fact, we can define matter only through mind. He therefore refers to the real in its full comprehensiveness, where it absorbs all oppositions in an all-encompassing process as "Absolute Spirit." That spiritual process culminates in culture. His critics have questioned whether the diverse aspects of each culture and, even more, the diversity of various cultures allow such a tight integration within a single ideal unity. Is it really possible to rank the succession of cultures in a logical order as Hegel did in his *Philosophy of History*? Or to compel the variety of religions, or of artistic expressions within a hierarchical structure, as he did in the *Philosophy of Religion and the Philosophy of Art*? Or even to subordinate the different manifestations of one cultural complex under a single nomer, however comprehensive? Most of those who later reflected on the philosophical significance of culture (including this writer) think not.

But that raises further questions: Is it possible to find ideal concepts comprehensive enough to include the various aspects of culture without forcing them within a philosophical straitjacket? Moreover, can we still relate the various cultures to a single concept? But if this is impossible, can we still turn to so-called ultimate principles of reality for a philosophical justification of cultural activity? Let us begin with a simple description of the phenomena as they present themselves to us. Do we find any meaningful unity in cultural diversity? Intercultural communication does not reconcile the opposition among cultures. The inner coherence of one culture remains largely impenetrable to another. The comparative study of culture has mainly revealed a typically Western desire to understand others on their own terms. Even if ethnologists would fully succeed in divesting themselves of their native prejudices, the problem of how cultural multiplicity relates to metaphysical unity remains unresolved. Such reductive concepts as "Greek culture" or "Roman culture," still popular in nineteenth-century thought, unduly universalize specific traits where there are only related characteristics. When we arrive at what we have come to call "modern culture," even that coherence no longer exists. The term "modern culture" has hardly any definable content beyond an almost universal aversion of traditional attitudes and values. As a society develops, culture diversifies to a point where the same society may display different, often incompatible cultures. In modern society, we witness a proliferation of subcultures barely able to communicate with one another (Eliot 1948: 25).

The contingency of cultural symbols constitutes the principal obstacle to any philosophical integration. They possess none of the universal necessity of Aristotelian or Kantian categories. "*There are* symbols; I encounter them. I find them."[1] I do not know why they are there, nor shall I ever know them all. What I find depends on my own contingent time and place in history. Those who explore cultures at other times from different perspectives will discover different symbols. The hermeneutics of culture never yields the kind of certainty and completeness philosophers are wont to require. We are simply gambling on the faith that the always hazardous interpretation of cultural symbols will pay off in some coherent understanding of human existence and, through it, of the very nature of reality. The modesty of the promise appears acceptable only because of our present awareness that the certainties of the past rested upon the illusion that being is directly accessible to philosophical investigation. Modern thought has lost that unmediated certainty. Ultimate understanding must be mediated through a hermeneutic of symbolic expressions.

Instead of certainty contemporary thought stresses communication. It often does so with an antimetaphysical bias. Thus, Richard Rorty reduces the philosophical enterprise to an intellectual conversation that has given up such "meaningless" universals as "being" and "truth" (Rorty 1979: chaps. 4 and 6). Jürgen Habermas hopes that uninhibited communication may result in a truth "by agreement" (Habermas 1987). He also has abandoned the concept of a "metaphysical" truth. For others, such as Karl Jaspers, to the contrary, communication is possible only on the basis of a metaphysical synthesis. Cultural hermeneutics, from that viewpoint, results in a "fusion of horizons" that invites a metaphysical integration. Those who accept this position need to add that philosophical reflection itself presupposes a hermeneutics of culture. Past philosophy did, of course, always reflect the conditions of the culture in which it originated, but remaining mostly unaware of that dependence, it speculated *sub specie aeternitatis*, as if it were not culturally conditioned. In fact, wherever it has existed, philosophy has functioned as the final, most comprehensive factor of culture.

Precisely at this point, our age encounters a more complex situation. Not only has philosophy become aware of the culture that conditions it, but philosophy confronts a different cultural situation altogether. In the past the philosophical synthesis could build on an already established cultural integration. People mostly shared a common value system as well as a basic outlook on reality. They might violently disagree on its implications, but they remained capable of understanding one another as they spoke a common cultural language. Until the eighteenth century Westerners related to the basic ideas of world, person, transcendence in accordance with a common worldview. Philosophy built on that agreement. But the symbolic systems operative in the present cultural situation have ceased to agree with one another. Philosophy can no longer perform its traditional task of providing the ultimate theoretical justification of an already existing cultural integration, for that practical integration no longer exists. What has caused this fragmentation?

In ancient Greece the cosmos incorporated all reality: it included humans and gods as well as physical nature. Jews and Christians separated God from cosmos, yet they nonetheless kept the three fundamental principles (more loosely) united within the idea of creation. The nominalist theology of the late Middle Ages virtually broke them apart by presenting the Creator as inscrutable, totally remote, and not providing or guaranteeing the principles of intelligibility for the understanding of nature and person. Whereas for Greek philosophers and Roman Stoics the source of intelligibility had been the cosmos or nature, and for Jewish, Christian, and Muslim thinkers the Creator who had made all in wisdom and measure, that source had suddenly dried up. Of course, there still was the bond of causal dependence on the Creator, but since that transcendent principle was now seen as inscrutable in its effects, one could no longer rely on the intrinsic intelligibility of things. The task of establishing the intelligible fell entirely upon human reason. Henceforth the sole source of meaning became the mind. The human mind alone set the boundary stones of the intelligible and defined what was "real."

The cultural impact of this intellectual revolution, here so briefly sketched,[2] did not fully appear until much later. The synthesis that had integrated Western culture became fragmented into isolated spheres: an opaque nature subject only to blind causality, a meaning-giving mind, an inscrutable God. The transcendent component gradually withdrew from it—a process that appears to have become complete in our time. It is not, of course, the case that contemporary culture denies the existence of God or of the divine. But transcendence plays no essential role in the self-understanding of our culture, certainly not one sufficient to integrate its disparate elements. Once the human subject became solely responsible for the constitution of meaning and value, tradition also lost its former authority. Individuals were forced to make sense of things as well as they could, ransacking the tradition for spare parts. Each one came to develop symbolic systems of his or her own, integrated or not integrated with each other, and loosely related to some general patterns, accepted ideologies, and vaguely shared values of society at large.

The emancipation from a preestablished order and a rigid onto-theological hierarchy has resulted in a "big bang" of symbolic creativity. The autonomous systems it creates are subject only to self-given rules. The fragmentation has given contemporary culture a kaleidoscopic fasci-nation. Each of these symbolic structures—literary, artistic, social, politi-cal—tends to spawn a small universe of its own. Nor can we truly share these "miniverses" as common possessions. In much of contemporary art, for instance, the reader, viewer, or hearer is invited, often required, to re-create the artist's private world into a private world of his or her own. Even literary or artistic criticism, rather than bridging the gap between creator and receiver, merely expands the number of private possibilities, eclipsing original meanings in favor of equally private new ones of its own making. Postmodern culture, the consistent heir of the fundamental principles of modernity (despite its family quarrels with it!) presents an exciting spec-tacle. Yet its unrestricted creativity exacts a toll. Symbolic structures inte-grated within a coherent culture have traditionally functioned as beacons of meaning on our journey through time. If we abandon the attempt to integrate them into some kind of coherent synthesis, both private and general-cultural, they cease to provide guidance. They then turn into mere games—words or forms with all the glitter of glass beads (Hesse's *Glas-perlenspiel*)—that cease to provide meaning to existence. This, I take it, is what Daniel Bell meant when he wrote: "Modernism has beyond dis-pute been responsible for one of the great surges of creativity in Western culture. . . . Yet there has been a price. One cost has been the loss of co-herence in culture, particularly in the spread of an antinomian attitude to moral norms and even to the idea of cultural judgment itself" (Bell 1978: xxii). Today science, art, and religion have turned into private domains; they are no longer integrated with one another. What remains is what T. S. Eliot terms "a heap of broken images," wobbling beacons in an un-stable universe. Once the cultural synthesis was broken up and the human person became the sole source of meaning, this fragmentation became inevitable. It was only resistance to change that prevented culture from forthwith splintering into the unlimited diversity we are witnessing now.

The present condition has resulted in what we have come to call our cultural "alienation." Rousseau, Hegel, Simmel, and others assumed that culture by its very nature estranges humans from an original state of immediacy. In any society, conflicts arise between social institutions and cultural artifacts on one side, and the search for meaning which these objective forms were meant to satisfy on the other. Every culture creates objective forms which its creators no longer recognize as their own. No culture, then, escapes alienation altogether, and as Sigmund Freud observed, the more a society becomes cultured, the more painful restrictions it exacts and the more demands it makes (Freud 1962a). But in comparing our own complex cultural condition with that of earlier generations, we cannot but wonder whether our experience of the inadequacy of contemporary culture in conveying meaning to our lives differs from past dissatisfaction merely in degree. As Marx pointed out, some forms of alienation occur only in some societies and not in others. In his *Philosophy of Money*, Simmel had referred to modern monetary exchange as "reified." Nevertheless, he claimed (following Hegel) that any culture creates objective forms in which the human creator no longer directly recognizes himself. Capitalist reification forms an extreme case insofar as the worker on the assembly line ceases to identify altogether with the products he turns out. But different economic systems result in comparable forms of reification. Lukács rejected Simmel's timeless model of human relations in general. Reification for him is a *specific* problem of our society, of which it has become the structuring principle. It has penetrated all aspects of culture: human relations have become objectified, language formalized, theory detached from praxis (Lukács 1971: 125–31).

Interpretations such as Lukács's, and Marx's own, oversimplify a complex situation. Economic conditions represent only one facet of a much wider problem. But their idea that each culture possesses a unique character leading to unique forms of alienation may help us to understand why one particular culture may experience greater difficulties than another in integrating its diversity into an acceptable synthesis. After the fragmentation of the classical synthesis in the late-modern epoch, meaning, once held to be inherent in the very nature of things, became the exclusive attribute of the human mind. The mind alone imposes rationality on the real. The idea of an established world order and of a tradition based upon that order has lost its authority. The intrinsic teleology of nature has given way to an extrinsic one determined by the human subject.

Here then lies the main obstacle to a philosophical integration of culture in the modern age. Where the component principles of culture have become disrupted, the real no longer appears as a coherent totality. Can modern culture ever reunite those *disjecta membra*? The fragmentation of culture coincided with the modern shift of meaning toward the subject. That shift to the subject, however, is not necessarily fatal to a cultural integration. The principle of subjectivity as source of meaning cannot be abandoned. Trying to do so is like attempting to de-invent science. But the crucial issue is whether subjectivity is compatible with the more fundamental givenness that includes the creative subject itself. The immediate givenness of the cosmos in Greek thought, or of created nature in medieval theology, is no longer available in modern thought, of which the human subject must mediate all conditions. But the idea of a meaning-giving subject does not in principle exclude the essential givenness of that subject itself. Such a givenness of the subject appeared real enough to such early-modern thinkers as Nicholas of Cusa, Erasmus, Pascal, and Malebranche. All of them succeeded in securing the self a central position within a reality conceived as fundamentally given.[3] The brokenness of the modern worldview directly results from the axiomatic position of the subject as ultimate. A primary condition for any reintegration of modern culture is that the creative subject be rooted in a comprehensive givenness without thereby losing its own meaning-giving function. An integrated conveyance of meaning is ruled out only when that subject ceases to be part of a more comprehensive totality.

If subjectivity no longer forms an integral part of an all-inclusive reality, metaphysics, the science of the ultimate principles of the real, has no proper object left: it lacks what Clifford Geertz has called the image of a cosmic order projected unto the place of experience (Geertz 1973: 90). If, however, the subject has its place within the comprehensive horizon of a reality viewed as integrated, rather than dualistically opposed to the mind, metaphysics becomes possible again and capable of providing the final, theoretical integration of culture, however diversified its components may be. Of course, such a metaphysics would no longer be the timeless speculation *sub specie aeternitatis* it once was. It must be aware of its essential link to a particular culture, and it must recognize that ultimate principles are accessible only through the mediation of the human subject's manifold and forever unfinished symbolic expressions. Moreover, the absence of a direct apprehension of ultimacy would give to the ultimate principles of the new metaphysics a quality of mystery, not unlike the one they possessed in the Neoplatonic tradition of Plotinus and Proclus, who raised the ultimate above the known.

In the preceding pages I have tried to show why some integration of the many aspects of culture is desirable. A primary function of cultural symbols is to introduce some meaning into the intolerable arbitrariness of life's contingency. Even the simplest symbolic systems functioning as ordering principles are already syntheses in their own right. Culture, taken either in a general sense (such as Western culture) or in a particular one (e.g., the aesthetic culture of the Enlightenment), always implies a dynamic integration of a plurality of elements. Its synthesizing activity by no means imposes an all-encompassing, rigid unity: it may in fact be a very limited unity, juxtaposed to other, equally limited syntheses and even incompatible with them. The present difficulty of achieving an integration of these partial syntheses within an ultimate, comprehensive one came in the wake of the cultural fragmentation of the early-modern age. Ever since, we have increasingly done away with "les grandes histoires" accepted by earlier generations. Yet we cannot simply dispense with the impulse to overcome sheer multiplicity, for that impulse is the driving force behind culture itself!

Those who agree with that interpretation may still wonder how culture should profit from the kind of theoretical synthesis that philosophy provides? Why should a practical integration such as each individual achieves with varying degrees of success not be sufficient? The reply must be, I think, that the issue is not only whether individuals personally achieve some synthesis of meaning but whether the cultural diversity within which the individual lives can itself be unified. The reflective mind, even if capable of achieving a personal integration, refuses to be satisfied with multiplicity as an ultimate, unjustifiable datum. Metaphysics merely follows the cultural impulse toward unification to the end. It reduces the multiplicity of phenomena to the ultimate principles of the real as such. Unless the diverse symbolic units of culture are grounded in a synthesis sufficiently comprehensive to assign to each its own place in an orderly totality, our partial syntheses tend to inflate their relativity into ideological absolutes. It is just such a comprehensive, theoretical synthesis that metaphysics provides. But if it is true that culture receives its ultimate integration from metaphysics, it is also true, as I have argued, that metaphysics requires a certain cultural coherence as a necessary condition for its existence. The argument is circular because their relation is mutual. Metaphysics presupposes cultural coherence, but it also functions as a primary factor in achieving that coherence. The search for cultural integration goes hand in hand with the search for metaphysics.

Desire, Distance, and Insight

Theo de Boer

De pudding van het brein
gaat verdragen aan met de karbonade van het hart
—Lucebert
(The pudding of the brain
enters into treaties with the cutlet of the heart)

Culture and Cultural Analysis

What is culture? What is cultural analysis? Johan Huizinga complains that culture is difficult to define. It is like time. "We know *approximately* what we mean by it," but it "cannot be analyzed."[1] However, by taking his scattered remarks and putting them together we can arrive at a definition of culture. In his last work, *Geschonden Wereld*, he writes: "Test yourself by asking yourself what you consider the essential thing about civilization. Suppose culture collapses, but you alone can save, as from a fire, one element of your choice from the treasure-house of civilization. What do you choose?" Huizinga's choice falls upon what he calls "the treasures of the mind and the heart" (1950: 579). On closer inspection, he counts among these religion, the system of law, and ethics, on the one hand, and the arts on the other.[2]

To tie into Huizinga's metaphor, we might say: culture is the flower of civilization. Naturally, we know that the flower grows from a ground, a soil. But it is also useful to look at the flower itself, not just to study it by starting from the bottom. I shall therefore completely ignore economics, technology, and politics. What I want to talk about here is a lifeview (ethics and religion) and liberal arts, which Huizinga sometimes calls *bonae litterae*.

Culture in this sense is the subject of hermeneutics and semiotics. These are sciences which study not only texts but also anything that can be interpreted by analogy with texts. We can distinguish between semiotics and hermeneutics, in the manner of Ricoeur, as structural analysis and situational interpretation. I do not propose to go into this distinction here. For the time being, I shall lump the two approaches together as "cultural analysis."

My concern is first and foremost that cultural analysis, viewed philosophically, should be taken as something broader than what at the university is generally understood by the term analysis. Cultural analysis, in the current academic sense of the term, is in my view, merely the central panel of the far broader triptych that is the process of culture. Something precedes it and something comes after it. Usually all attention is focused on the central piece—analysis in the narrower sense—but this is flanked by two side panels: desire and insight. It is these that determine the *sense* of cultural analysis. They give us an indication of why we analyze and why cultural analysis is a cultural good. Desire is the mainspring, but it does not automatically coincide with the desire for knowledge. Insight is more than the result of research that is recorded in research reports. Insight is scholarly knowledge *integrated into desire*.

What are we to understand by desire? Although that can only become clear gradually, I will define it now as follows: desire is the desire for reality. Spinoza spoke of the *conatus essendi* as the driving force of every substance. The French philosophers, such as Sartre and Ricoeur, use the expression *désir d'être*, which must be seen as a subjective and objective genitive. The desire wishes to be, but can only realize this aim by matching up to the being that it itself is not. Desire always has something of a totalitarian intent. Basically, it wishes to embrace the whole of existence. It is part of the *condition humaine* that this desire can never be fulfilled directly. That would lead to accidents. Desire needs insight, and that calls for distance. It is in the space of that distance that cultural analysis has its place. It reinforces the necessary detachment and teaches us how to exploit it.

By this distance, I do not mean merely that desire cannot achieve its goal directly and without intermediate steps. It has to follow a path, the path of the formation of culture. But that path is also strewn with barricades, which desire is unable to clear aside by its own efforts alone. What is needed, then, is some agency that can lift desire over these hurdles. This agency is what we call reason. Passion and reason are not opponents, and they are not natural enemies as in the metaphysical tradition; they come into "contact" with each other in poetry, as the Dutch poet Gerrit Achterberg puts it, that is, in a work of culture. It is in culture that desire tries to appropriate reality. Reason is necessary to bear the reality for which desire longs. Desire—for reasons which we do not know—is itself frightened and blind (or frightened and therefore blind) and needs the light of reason to be able to stand up to reality. "Humankind cannot bear very much reality," wrote T. S. Eliot (1974). The curious thing about desire is that it fears the very reality it desires. It is afraid of the other, which by its very existence puts a question mark against the self-evident nature of the self. Desire must force itself through the bottleneck of its own fear. Reason can contribute to relieving that constriction.

From what I have said so far, it follows that the mainspring of research, the thirst for knowledge, is embedded in a broader desire. It has an existential horizon. The *sense* of cultural analysis is more than knowledge for the sake of knowledge.

Before I turn to the central panel, cultural analysis in the narrow or proper sense, first let me say something about the second side panel, insight. Scholarly knowledge, as I see it, only becomes insight if and when it is bent back to desire. Without this re-flection it is no more than erudition, a collecting of curiosities. The thirst for knowledge that characterized nineteenth-century historicism sometimes degenerated into this. The paradigm of empty knowledge of this kind is the research conducted into the Marquis de Rollebon in Sartre's *La nausée*. The transition from this historicist, rudderless hermeneutics to present-day hermeneutics has been termed a transition from a hermeneutics of meaning (Dilthey) to a hermeneutics of truth (Gadamer). In the latter case, it is the application that is central, and the question that is asked is what is the significance for one's own life of what one has discovered through one's study. This hermeneutics ties in with the long tradition of the *artes liberales*, which also had a practically educational purpose: the widening of knowledge, the broadening of the horizon, and even, as John Henry Newman put it, an ennobling of sentiments. All this was designed to create and nurture a humanistic outlook of understanding and tolerance towards other cultures. Because this sounds perhaps too "intellectual," I would add that insight also contributes to our awareness of reality, to our ability to bear the burden of existence. How it can do this is what I hope to make clear in what follows.[3]

Cultural analysis, the central panel of the process of culture, is characterized by distance and discipline. Here the rules of scholarship apply. Adherence to the method, the striving after pure scholarship, is the intrinsic purpose of reason (albeit, as I have explained, with a broader, existential horizon).

In science and philosophy there is a classical tradition which links reason (*logos, ratio*) and rational knowledge (*ēpistēmē, scientia*) to the unchangeable and the general. Hence the saying *individuorum non est scientia*. In this tradition, knowledge is achieved in a kind of contemplation (which we find in the intuition of essences of Husserl, the last great representative of the classical tradition). People have never known, however, what to make of history as a science. Knowledge, it was felt, could have no grasp of the particular and the contingent. I see the efforts of the human and cultural sciences to imitate the natural-scientific method as a legacy of that tradition. Those efforts are, after all, concerned with general laws under which the individual can be subsumed as a case—we speak of the nomological or subsumption-theoretic method—whose laws, in turn, would have to be deduced from a theory. I have no wish to cast doubt on the legitimacy (within certain limits) of this method, but cultural analysis is concerned with something else. Cultural analysis is the analysis and interpretation of individual entities and the exploration of particular contexts. The words of Kent in *King Lear*, which Wittgenstein wanted to use as the motto for his *Philosophical Investigations*, are applicable to cultural analysis: "I'll teach you differences." What cultural analysis can teach us is to think more precisely, that is, to see the differences.

This certainly applies to the area that I referred to earlier as the flower of civilization. It can be regarded as the most ephemeral and changeable aspect of it, and hence as that which, according to classical standards, would be the least appropriate subject of science. The question facing us is what, in this science of the contingent and particular, should we understand by reason and distance if there is no longer an orientation on the un-changeable and general. How, within a special and changeable culture, can we adopt an "objective" standpoint? How can we avoid, here, becoming bogged down in cultural prejudices and particularisms? The knowledge we are looking for must have an inner link with time and changeability.

Despite the change of knowledge paradigm, what I am about to sug-gest should not be regarded as newfangledness. In Aristotle's *Nicomachean Ethics*, book 6, we already find a form of knowledge that can stand as a model for our own design. Alongside *ēpistemē*, Aristotle discerns several other forms of knowledge, including *phronēsis*, which is generally trans-lated as "prudence." This prudence, or sensibleness, has three qualities, which correspond to our triad of desire, analysis (distance), and insight. It is not a knowledge of the unchangeable but a knowing of that which concerns me (*to to hautou eidenai*). It relates to the special of concrete situations (*ta kath' hekasta*), and indirectly, as a dianoetic virtue, it also contributes to the desire for a "good life" (*to eu zen*).

In what follows, I wish to investigate the function, nature, and meaning of cultural analysis in three areas that we may see as three levels of reality: unconscious reality, daily reality, and fictional reality. Or again, anticipating what follows: diminished reality, "real" reality, and intensi-fied reality. In fact I shall be talking successively about psychoanalysis, phenomenological analysis—in particular the phenomenology of the reli-gions as the successor to natural ethics and natural theology—and literary analysis.

For the first of these, psychoanalysis, the model is the dream. The dream represents a domain beneath everyday reality. Desire has the form of a drive. The dream, Aristotle says, is the hope of someone who sleeps. It is therefore in a way an unreal desire that requires much correction by reality, by what Sigmund Freud termed the "reality principle."

Daily desire looks fairly sober, but it can sometimes be drunk, par-ticularly when it relates to religion and worldview. Here again, civilizing knowledge is required so that desire, by using reason and suspending the usual evidence, can arrive at insight.

Fiction is a stylization of reality. In Aristotle we find the remark that poetry is philosophically more important than knowledge of every-day reality because it has to do with the possible and the probable. Here reality has been passed through a sieve to render essence. Ricoeur uses the expression "elevated reality" or "enhanced reality." Fiction, paradoxically, brings about what Germans call a *Potenzierung*, a squaring of reality. So we are dealing here with three manifestations of desire, each of them coupled with its own form of analysis and insight.[4]

Psychoanalysis

Psychoanalysis has to do with cultural analysis on two levels. It is a particular approach to works of culture which reveals their roots in an infantile longing (and the aggressive converse thereof). But in the first place, as a therapy, it is an analysis of the way in which the subject enters the culture, and of the subject's attitude towards culture; it concentrates chiefly on the ethical (and religious) component of culture as precipitated in the superego. Psychoanalysis dwells in the vestibule or portals of culture, a "preworldly sphere," and precisely because it does so, it can shed a sharp light on the culture in which we live. In this sense, psychoanalysis is cultural analysis. Its importance in our trio of sciences of culture is that here desire has a pronounced place (just as analytical distance has in phenomenological analysis and insight in literary analysis).

The world that desire projects here is an imaginary world. What does this desire want? Desire is double. It has an ambiguity that can never be entirely overcome and that, in another guise, returns in higher forms of desire. On the one hand, it wishes to remain in its own imaginary, comfortable world, but on the other hand, it also wants to take part in harsh reality. It is the purpose of psychoanalysis to accompany some along that difficult path. Insight here has the shape of awareness of reality.

Desire.   Freud called unconscious desire the primary system. Characteristic of this is the absence of public rules to link unconscious feelings and thoughts with the outside world, whether directly or indirectly, by way of connectedness with utterances and actions (Mooij 1991: 23, 25). The public field of symbolizations, culture, which is opened up by common rules, is the secondary sphere of adults-to-be. The primary system tends towards unity and immediacy. In the secondary sphere, by contrast, differences and distance prevail. The child is gradually initiated into the framework of language rules and into the thoughts and sentiments that prevail within a culture. The other is then no longer clothed in projections from the preworldly sphere, but is met in its being different.

Distance.   All this has already led us to suspect that in psychoanalysis we cannot expect much good to come out of inductive generalizations and a gradual climbing towards ever-higher abstractions. Psychoanalysis is not a part of functional psychology, which concerns itself with that which remains the same; rather, it is cultural psychology, psychology of self-culture. The problems do not lend themselves to a nomological treatment. In fact, as Habermas observed, all we can do is work with general, rather monotonous narrative schemes, always with the same problems. These schemes must not be applied but filled with greater detail. Even if there is regularity, this is because in our culture many young people are damaged in the same way, and in that sense are equally (made) mad. A regularity that we prefer not to fix in laws and then apply.

Nothing is more changeable than humanity. How are we to get a grip on it? Must we abstract from time? A closer examination shows that time is precisely what we must see as our frame of reference. We cannot see changeability in people as an inconvenient side effect. The perception of time is the basis of the experience of coherence of meaning. Meaning is on the one hand, in the present, the horizon of expectation. On the other hand, the presence itself is the meaning of the past. A moment in time can only be meaningful in relation to another moment in time, whether that later moment has already passed or not. Without the passage of time it is impossible to tell a story. That 1939 marks the beginning of the Second World War was not something that was realized at the time; it can only be said from within the future that has meanwhile become the past. A timeless observer would be dumbstruck by this phenomenon (and would thus rightly observe that there is no science of the changeable). It is only treacherous time, the metaphysical spoilsport, that makes links of meaning possible. Psychoanalysis analyzes those links. It looks for the meaning of the past in relation to the present, but also in relation to an anticipated time as a perspective of the future. The difference between this and a purely historical analysis is that an attempt is made to fill in gaps, to eliminate discrepancies. "Apparently meaningless utterances, actions that cannot be rationalized and experiences that cannot be articulated are put into a meaningful context. The field of symbolization or articulation becomes larger" (Mooij 1991: 27).

Filling in the schemes, to which I have referred, is in effect a learning of differences. The "working through" (*Durcharbeiten*) that is done consists of a process of differentiation and distanciation. In transference, the psychoanalyst, who does not play into the game of seduction initiated by the patient, tries to bring about small changes in the behavior pattern. This calls for a distance that the analyst has learned to create during the course of a lengthy training. The analysand is surprised to find that there are differences. The imaginary world that is also constructed around the analyst is broken. The analyst introduces reality. Desire laboriously learns to relinquish illusions of unity.

One example of the method is what happens to the dream. We do not collect large numbers of dreams in the hope of discovering some kind of law or regularity in them. A particular dream is provided with contexts. In the analysis of dream fragments, the patient is asked to establish the place of the fragment in the context of the whole dream or in a series of dreams. He or she is then asked about associations. To the answers, the analyst then adds his or her interpretations, which are then incorporated into the discussion as it continues. The model is not that of an upward, stepwise progression but one of concentric circles. The particular (*to hekaston*) remains the pivot upon which all turns. It proves not to be ineffable. On the contrary, there is a great deal—too much!—to be said about it. The time comes when the analysis has to be broken off, not because the phenomenon has been exhausted but because ordinary life awaits, which is much more inexhaustible still. The point is whether sufficient distance has been learned to make further life possible. And that is ultimately the criterion of truth. Here Gadamer's general observation applies: "Completed experience is not a completion of knowledge, but completed openness for new experience" (1971: 311). It is not the predictive power of analysis that counts but the adequacy of the network that is woven in the analysis and which must ultimately lead to the insight of the analysand that we call awareness of reality.

Awareness of reality. Finally, desire demands reality, the *res* that is mentioned as the referent in the classical definition of truth (*adequatio rei et intellectus*). That is the paradoxical basic assumption upon which the entire enterprise of analysis rests. It is really a normative starting point, but it is a very curious one. A. Van Dantzig once observed that it is a ground rule of psychoanalysis, and evidently of life too, that feeling is better than not feeling. To choose not to feel is to choose to exist as little as possible (Van Dantzig 1990: 36, 182). Thus, when a child is humiliated it is better for it to feel anger than not to feel it and hide in a feeling of guilt. This is in spite of the fact that it may appear to be "functional" to suppress the anger. "Humankind cannot bear very much reality." It seems wise to keep a low profile in the face of virtually omnipotent parents, but time and experience show that this is counterproductive. It is therefore, as A. W. M. Mooij puts it, an "appropriate reaction" to display indignation (1991: 91–93). It may be true of emotions that they can only have a function if they are not themselves understood in terms of a function. Emotions teach us to recognize the gravity of reality, or reality in its gravity.

If we use the term "normative," the norm has nothing to do with an ought but rather with an is. Mistakes are made if reality is not respected. That is not to say that the patient is brought up to realism or opportunism. The therapy aims to achieve a form of "good life," of well-being, so that someone is again able to ask ethical questions in real life. That is why it is not pragmatism when we say that here the truth lies in the possibility of continuing to live. Life may then be termed "good" in the Aristotelian sense because it allows for reality. Desire can only permit itself this when it has distanced itself from itself, from its primary imaginary form.

So far I have said nothing about the desire of the analyst. This is a derivative of the analysand's. Somewhere Georges Simenon refers to his inspector, going around as a sort of pipe-smoking therapist in his little world full of the slightly cracked or completely potty, as a "raccommodeur d'existences," a "life mender" or "life repairer." The analyst's desire consists in restoring the desire to exist.

Phenomenological Analysis

As I said in the introduction regarding the analysis of culture, I would be mainly looking at what Huizinga called the "treasures of the mind and the heart"; that is, besides the liberal arts: religion, the system of law, and ethics. In the Enlightenment, these three things were the subject of a classical, rational science: natural ethics and natural theology. What was sought was a hard, universal core in the great diversity of religious and moral traditions, and it was thought that this immutable essence could be arrived at from insights of reason. This way of thinking, which we now call foundationalism, has since lost its cogency. Historical investigations and cultural anthropology have erased the rational constructions of natural ethics and theology. Their place has been taken by the empirical description of a deluge of religious myths and rituals. The work of the Dutch historian of religions Gerardus van der Leeuw, *La religion dans son essence et ses manifestations"* (1955), is a document of what has been achieved in this school of the phenomenology of religion. Searching for a common denominator has made way for revealing differences. The same kind of development has taken place in thinking on natural law and ethics. The axiomatic system is replaced by a great diversity of narrative traditions. Typical of this is Ricoeur's last work, *Soi-même comme un autre* (1990), in which the design of a universal ethics of the Enlightenment—which is something that Ricoeur takes very much to heart—has shrunk to a thought experiment that nourishes itself from the traditions and also, if it is not to cause totalitarian accidents, has to be re-embedded in a narrative ethic.[5] Both of these concerns, the concern for religion and the concern for moral law, nowadays come together in the interest in civil religion as the cement of society. What is the impact of cultural analysis in this context?

Desire. When the subject enters the field of public symbolizations, it arrives in the world of grown-ups. There it encounters a variety of forms of adult desire. Kant summarized them as the lust for property, power, and honor. A good comprehensive term is the effort to exist (in Spinoza, *conatus essendi*; in Ricoeur, *effort pour exister*). As agreed, however, I shall confine myself here to the more ethereal part of civilization. A good term for desire here may be the English word "interest," which does not yet, like its German equivalent, have the meaning of self-interest. What we are talking about here is the way in which self-maintaining subjects try to regulate their mutual relations without violence and, if possible, even to display some interest in each other. The desire-to-be of the one imposes restrictions upon itself for the sake of the desire-to-be of others. It can assume the civilized form of interest in the public weal, civic sense, and civic duty. The postmodern effort to exist even presents itself as an inquiry, subsidized or otherwise, into the meaning of life. It is in that context, it seems to me, that we must also see the civil importance of cultural analysis.

Distance. In the nineteenth century, classical natural theology and moral law were replaced, as I have said, by empirical sciences of religion. That also meant a not always sufficiently recognized turning point in the view of rationality. Whereas in the classical conception the particular and individual was seen merely as an exemplar of the general, which added nothing to our knowledge of it, historicism brought a thorough reappraisal of the individual, the factual, and, as the basis of this, time. Time was now valued as the parent of diversity, not merely as a factor of dispersion. The individual was not merely the bearer of the general, as it is, for example, in Russell's theory of universals, but embodied the general and thereby endowed it with its own color and shading. The challenge to the new human and cultural sciences was to trace this diversity. In this situation the philosophy of religion, which succeeded rational theology, saw itself more as an attempt to explore the meaning of religious utterances than to determine their truth. Science, in the cultural analytical sense, tries not to abstract from differences; on the contrary, it attempts to cultivate them. Rationality lies in the particular self as an inherent coherence (whether as a structural relation after the model of linguistics or as an internal connection in hermeneutics). In the former section, we called these rational relations of temporal phenomena coherences of meaning.

In the modern philosophy of action (Dray, Winch, Von Wright), much attention has been paid to the "rational analysis" of contexts. Arthur Danto spoke of a "metaphysics of everyday life." Huizinga, from his own practice as a historian of culture though perhaps not a great philosopher of science, could sense very clearly what was going on here in terms of the theory of science. According to him, "no truly historical analysis is possible without the continuous elucidation of meaning" (1950: 43). Historical knowledge seldom, if ever, means identifying a causality. It is the understanding of coherence that is always open; "that is, it must never be presented as links forming a chain, but only as a loosely bound bundle which remains open for the addition of new twigs." More appropriate than a bundle of twigs, says Huizinga, might be the image of a bunch of wild flowers. Elsewhere, he repeats this metaphor, saying: "Each new notion that is added changes the appearance of the entire bunch" (56, 131). Essentially, in Huizinga, we already find Karl Popper's later argument against applying laws to history. His imagery also makes it perfectly clear that the passage of time always enriches the coherence that has been found and hence necessitates continuous reinterpretation of the past.

To discern connections—this is something that early phenomenology failed to realize fully—is more than mere description. There is always an element of interpretation and/or "application" (*applicatio*) in it. This means not giving up objectivity but redefining it. Objectivity is sought not in a standpoint outside time but from a point in time by observing distance. Max Weber puts it like this: the beam of light that we cast on culture is directed by our values, and within that beam we try to arrive at an objective determination of what we can see (Weber 1968: 163). In a moment I hope to be able to show how, in cultural analysis, distance, coupled back to desire, can produce something like sensibility or prudence.

Insight. The situation that we find in empirical research is, as I have said, one of great diversity. To adopt an all-embracing viewpoint, a *regard survolant* as Maurice Merleau-Ponty calls it, or a "bird's-eye view," is beyond our capability. We cannot lay a rational grid across this diversity and in that way sift out what is special. Nor can we regroup it into an orderly row governed by a Kantian regulative idea in which an asymptotic approach to the truth would become visible. That too would be a form of the totalitarian thought criticized by Emmanuel Levinas and would lead to the exclusion of whatever failed to fit into the rational idea. It would be a denial of the fact that it is only from a standpoint within time that a context can be established. An Ideal Witness who would ascertain the naked facts in an Ideal Chronicle would be able to say nothing at all (Danto 1968: 151, 167). But in that case, what does distance mean here?

There is only one way of thinking that is consonant with historical thought and the fundamental recognition of the right to diversity with all that it implies. It entails, in the first place, a different view of rationality, as set out above. The alternative of classical rationalism is not irrationalism, even though there have been philosophers who believed that it was (the early Nietzsche, for example). There exists another kind of reason. This becomes manifest in analysis and interpretation. This other reason entails a pluralization of reason. It is a rationality without an all-embracing overview or control center, and hence without a monopoly. Giving up the ambition of the one rationality for all implies that the claims of all to a rational form of life are in principle equal. Each philosophy is, to use a term coined by Ricoeur, a *proposition de sens*, a proposition and proposal of meaning which is open to debate. Reason in the plural means: the other reason is also reason, or the other-of-reason is another reason. The same thing can also be put like this: after the loss of the rationalistic idea of a single truth, we do not fall back on "opinion," the doxa as the traditional counterpart of the *épistemē*, but on emancipated opinion, an opinion which is no longer automatically placed under the governance of rational truth. The truth of opinions, or rather their tenability, can only be determined by a dialogue.

What does all this mean for the treasures of mind and heart: religion, ethics, and the system of law? Have we returned to the stage of polytheism, as Weber believed? Have we been turned over to relativism or an uncommitted postmodernism? The new situation means, first of all, a high level of expertise that is indispensable in a multicultural society. Second, it means taking those traditions seriously. Analyzing is a clarification and articulation of meaning, and after an initial descriptive phase it is possible for a discussion about the truth to take place. (See the opening section on the "hermeneutics of truth.") But it seems to me that the most important implication is that a new form of distance has been acquired. With emancipated opinions, having a standpoint does not cut off openness to other standpoints. We judge, but with caution. Conversely, this openness does not mean a lack of standpoint. The standpoint of the emancipated opinion is, obviously, no simple matter, witness the attractive power of fundamentalism. Nor is it a cheap option, for acknowledging the other opinion, or acknowledging the other with its opinion, means, at the very least, that we have to place a question mark against the rightness of our own opinions. Thinking historically means suspending beliefs that we have considered self-evident; it means breaking with the accustomed, the wished-for, and the familiar. And, here again: "Humankind cannot bear very much reality." It is precisely cultural analysis that can increase this bearing capacity by its distance, by going through the learning process of distanciation. Bearing reality, in society, we call tolerance. This is the purport or import of cultural analysis, a heritage to be cultivated. Why is it good that we should be taught differences? Seeing differences is, as Levinas says, a form of non-indifference. Erasing differences leads easily to the unconsidered positing of what belongs to the self. That is why deepening one's own view of life is not, as people often think, a form of seclusion. Analyzing what is our own teaches us to see its limits. To put it another way: it teaches us to be aware of the limits of the self. This is the insight of which it may be said that complete experience is complete openness to new experience (Gadamer). Superficiality, by contrast, leads to myopia.

What does desire want? Here again it is divided. That passion wishes to make contact with reason is definitely not a matter of course. How can desire discover that when it flees from reason it also flees from what it really wants: reality? In the public world, fleeing from the other reason means fleeing from the reality of the other to whom, on the other side, the desire is after all directed. Can literature and literary analysis contribute to the attempt to bring desire to reason?

Literary Analysis

In the previous two sections we were concerned with the analysis (and interpretation) of reality; here we shall be looking at the analysis of fiction. The jump from the one to the other is not so large when we realize that literature is also a form of investigation. Milan Kundera says that in the modern age, the novel was the instrument of investigation of the life world when philosophy gave up and concerned itself solely with science. In his last book, Ricoeur calls literature the laboratory of ethics (1990: 176, 188, 194). In it we can institute an investigation of ethical situations that would not be possible in reality. Literature has been called a "continuation of science with other, considerably better resources."[6]

Desire. If desire is a desire for reality, then in literature it seems to take a curious detour. On the surface, it appears to be a form of regression in which fantasy takes the place of experience. But literary fiction is rather the opposite of the imaginary phantasm or of fancy. Reality is not fled from, but tested more radically by eliminating all coincidence. To come back to what I said in my opening section, this is why we can speak of an intensified or squared desire for reality, or of passion. It is argued in public discourse today that the modern writer lacks this passion. He is accused of a lack of engagement. Writers should be writing about the state of the world. Quite rightly, however, it has been pointed out that perhaps the writers who have plumbed the world the most deeply are precisely those who have kept themselves the most aloof from current problems. In this view, Kafka comes closest of all writers to the chill reality of twentieth-century bureaucracy. This means that desire achieves its goal precisely by abstinence. I have already mentioned Aristotle's saying that poetry is more philosophical than the writing of history. Historical writing tells us everything about what happens to happen, but poetry confines itself to the possible and the probable. This implies that—considering not only the literary character but also the writer—we must speak of a certain recognition or anagnorisis, to use a term of Aristotle's. Desire has passed through a crisis. It has distanced itself.

Distance.   How can fiction be an instrument of investigation? According to Max Weber, imagination already plays a fundamental role in historical analysis, that is, in the science of facts. It is only when we place what has actually happened against the background of what could have happened that we gain insight into history: "To see through the real causal relations we construct unreal ones" (Weber 1968: 147). It is not the reproduction of the facts but the distance in the imagination and the mental representation of how things might have been otherwise that create insight. Likewise, Huizinga says: "The imagination is at work even on the most sober presentation of the simplest historical fact" (1950: 167). In literature, which is not a science of factual reality, then, the imagination must play a double role.

In literary imagination we enter the territory of a possible world, but that is something quite different from a possible variant of the real world, which is what Weber is talking about. After all, in a work of fiction things happen that would be impossible in reality. In his or her auctorial capacity, the narrator has an overview that no one in the real world can have, and from the personal perspective he or she has an insight into persons that is granted to no one in that world—which is why we refer to characters in a novel as characters rather than persons. Changes in time perspectives, for instance, take place in a way that is impossible in everyday life. Yet the view of the narrator is not a *regard survolant* in the classical sense; it is not outside time. Rather, what happens in the novel is an intensification of time which brings about a concentration of meaning. Concentration is not only one of the main characteristics of poetry, as Simon Vestdijk says (1991: 27, 205); it is also a principal characteristic of literary prose as compared with nonliterary prose.

It seems paradoxical, as I have already observed, that fiction should intensify reality. In fiction we are in a sense discharged from the burden of reality. In the theater we can endure realities which we would be unable to stand in real life. The theater appears to meet the inclination of humankind to flee from reality. Yet the connection with reality remains intact.

Tragedy, after all, is mimesis: if it is not an imitation of real life, then it is at least a representation of it. It would be unable to evoke sympathy and fear, which, according to Aristotle, bring about catharsis, if it were otherwise. By the "unbearable lightness of being," Kundera means, I believe, the feeling that arises when life itself is experienced as a stage play. The lightness of the theater, the lightness of literature in general, does not break the bond with reality. It does, however, create space, distance. That distance is used to establish a more thorough investigation of reality than would be possible in real life. What is lost in actuality is regained in the area of meaning. The radicalization of the question of meaning must culminate in the catharsis that arms the reader against actual reality. To the question What is poetic imagination?, the German poet Reiner Kunze answered: "The ability to use language to create in our imagination a new reality through which actual reality may be more readily experienced" (Kunze 1994: 237).

Fiction works with the changes of times and perspectives to which I referred earlier, that is, with the processes of style. Writing is, accordingly, a form of labor or craft. Upon the author rests the full seriousness of the creator. As the novelist W. F. Hermans once remarked, he or she must not allow even a sparrow to fall to earth without consequences (Hermans 1983: 108). Nor can the author identify with one perspective or one character. This gives rise to what in Fyodor Dostoevsky is called "polyphony." It is not clear at the outset whether Ivan or Dimitri or Alyosha is right. The writer of a novel cannot simply give vent to his or her own prejudices, which is so easily done in an essay, diary, or pamphlet. That is why we can say that it is precisely fiction, with its doubled imagination, that admits of greater reality than daily experience. Imagination, thus, also means distance. The experience transformed by imagination is purified experience, suspended experience (just as phenomenology suspends the relationship to reality precisely in order to know it better). Viewed in this way, it is precisely the medium that Plato rejected, on account of its deceptiveness, that brings about the most concentrated view of reality. By intensified reality, then, we mean a reality whose meaningful content has been enhanced at the expense of factuality, but not at the expense of truth.[7] After a sojourn in this possible world the reader can return to the ordinary world with a whetted insight.

Insight. What does the return from fictional reality to real reality mean? What has happened to the desire to be? I have already used the term catharsis. Following Aristotle, however, I ought to be more precise and distinguish between catharsis and anagnorisis. Anagnorisis is part of (the character and) the writer, catharsis part of the reader (including the practitioner of literary analysis). It is illuminating, it seems to me, to put both terms in the context of style or composition (Ricoeur 1975: 55–56). What is at stake here is not a matter of psychological, or moral, processes but of aesthetic experience. In either case, "purification" has to do with the transparency or concentration that comes about in the work of art (for which I have already used the terms purification and suspension).[8]

Arriving at wisdom or recognition is a painful process. Desire must once again work against itself. There is a lucid description of this process to be found in the work of the Dutch poet Martinus Nijhoff. In his *De pen op papier* (The pen on paper), he points out that the direct expression of feelings is not a good starting point for poetry (Nijhoff 1982: 1073–75). If you wish to pour out your feelings, it is better to do it in a diary. Poetry calls for a degree of hardness. In a dramatized meeting with the Pied Piper of Hamlin, the piper tells him that the emotional way of writing is wrong. "You are soft with emotion" is his rebuke. If the verse form is taken up, the poet must "constrain himself to a certain objectivity." And this implies in turn that the poet must write about "the feelings of others." How does Nijhoff see this interrelation between style and the ethos that we have already come across in the last section as non-indifference?

Choosing to write in verse, he says, brings with it a certain distanciation from the writer's own personality. The author becomes a stranger to him- or herself. The form creates distance from the natural sentiment and the direct content of the poetry. Ultimately, the content as content of life, as it is immediately experienced in the life of the poet, cannot be the content of the poem as work of art. When the experienced content has passed through the sieve of form, a new, second content is created: the content of the form. This, to put it another way, is not expressed but created (De Boer 1993: 195–96). This concept of "content of the form" is a sharp definition of what we have already come across as "enhanced" reality or purified, intensified experience.

Form evidently has a sobering but, at the same time, concentrating effect so that the writer, as it were, "exists more." He or she is forced by the form to adopt an outside standpoint as an empirical person: the standpoint of the fictional narrator. This is not pure speculation; it is confirmed by experience. I have already referred to the polyphony of Dostoevsky's novels, and it is in this sense that they differ from the one-dimensionality of his diaries, in which he does indeed express his Russocentric sentiments. Another example is Louis-Ferdinand Céline, who ventilated sentiments in his pamphlets, but in his novels, or at least in those of his early period— I am thinking of *Journey to the End of the Night* and *Death on the Installment Plan*—there is none of that primitive thinking. The form, the artistic style, has, as it were, lifted the writer out of himself. This is despite theories put forward by Céline himself, who believed that a writer should express himself in a spontaneous, direct way in order to reproduce the lyricism of the full life (Van Zoest 1994: 41; Kummer 1994: 46–48). However, we know that his novels are far from being the result of direct expression; they are the products of a refined stylistic process. In fact, he himself says that there is nothing more difficult than writing that spontaneous language of feelings, and that it calls for a terrible "technique" a thousand times more difficult than the so-called sober style. Céline was another "linguistic laborer," endlessly crossing out and changing things around.

Novels can be analyzed for their style, but when it comes to "ego documents" like diaries, the only thing that is really possible is the application of psychology or possibly psychoanalysis. That is the result of the distance of the form. It also indicates the difference between the diminished reality, to which I referred in my opening section, and the intensified reality of literature. Following on from what I said earlier about rationalism and irrationalism, I can now say that precisely because of the distance—brought about by the labor and the style—the message of the novel (the content of the form) is rational. The pamphlets, on the other hand, are irrationalistic.

There is the case of Nijhoff, who over a period of sixteen years wrote five new versions of a poem ("De nieuwe sterren"). It is a romantic misconception that this kind of effort in some way conflicts with inspiration. The process of crystallization means that, on the contrary, the experience is intensified, for the emotion felt becomes an aesthetic emotion. The "constraining oneself to a certain objectivity"—the suspension or *épochē*— creates the distance that leads to insight. Here we see once again, but on a higher level, that excavating the depths of the self creates space for the confrontation with the other. That contact arises not through a leveling

off and dilution of the author's own standpoint but through delving down
to the depths, by digging out one's own heritage, to use an image from the
Irish poet Seamus Heaney. When the experienced content is represented,
given form, it can discern and allow other voices alongside it. Polyphony
is the aesthetic counterpart of what on the social plane is called pluralism.
By contrast, superficiality, which is what Osip E. Mandelstam calls "lyri-
cal laziness," remains bogged down in "the general mess of imprecision
of feeling, / undisciplined squads of emotion" (Eliot). Sentiments which
have no limits fail to descry what is beyond the limit. This, I believe, is
the underlying reason for Nijhoff's conviction that the laws of language,
or the laws of the verse form, lead to the feelings of others.

I have said little about the desire of literary analysis itself. It seems
to me that this too is derived from the desire that it analyzes (as with
psychoanalysis). The passion of literary analysis shares, on a higher plane
of reflection, in the passion of writing, which is itself a form of investigation. This applies to cultural analysis in general. The investigation exploits
the anthropological possibility open to humans of distancing themselves
from their desire, but that is not a break with desire. Desire itself desires
the light of reason. And with this in mind, I cited the poem of Gerrit
Achterberg's at the beginning of this essay: "Begrip en lust bewegen naar
elkaar. / Hartstocht en rede komen in contact" (Understanding and desire
move towards each other. / Passion and reason come into contact).

Cultural Analysis and
the Ghost of 'Geistesgeschichte'

John Neubauer

I wish I could follow the example of Molière's Monsieur Jourdain, who spoke prose for forty years without knowing it. I could then claim that I have always practiced cultural analysis without knowing it. But I started out as an intellectual historian and cannot make such a claim. I was, and still am, fascinated by the task of writing choreography for the dance of ideas and discourses on the stage of history, even though I have become increasingly concerned with the question of how dance and choreography relate to the theater and other institutions.[1]

Does that make me a cultural analyst? Let me entertain the question by considering the introductory words to the workshop titled "The Practice of Cultural Analysis," out of which this volume emerged: "A focus on culture implies that boundaries between disciplines are bracketed, ignored, or subordinated to the larger vision that binds the different disciplines in the humanities together. Similarly, the word 'analysis' gives precedence to detailed examination of cultural objects as they exist and function today, over historical reconstruction, causal explanation, or aesthetic periodization" (Bal 1995: 4). This is admirably put and revealingly reflective of problems and tensions that probably all of us face in "doing" cultural analysis, regardless of whether or not we agree with the specifics of what is proposed here. For the two sentences, one pertaining to "culture" and the other to "analysis," are clearly working at cross-purposes: if thinking about culture is a synthetic activity that breaks down barriers as it strives for "the larger vision that binds the different disciplines in the humanities together," then analysis detaches and takes apart, isolating the individual text or event. And if we strike a balance between these two components of our work, we may be modern-day Penelopes, taking apart at night what we knitted together in the daylight before (or more appropriately, the other way around).

I have no recommendation for the ideal mix between synthesis and analysis, but it is my impression that in spite of our skeptical, anti-essentialist, and corrosively postmodern temper, we are engaged in much more synthesizing and holistic thinking than we are likely to admit. Indeed, I speak of "The Ghost of *Geistesgeschichte*" to call attention to the fact that while we tend to be interested, as Mieke Bal writes about her own work, in "the fractures and breaks within a culture," denying that the whole is unified (Bal 1995: 10), we continue to incorporate into our discourse traces of holistic thinking (transmogrified versions of zeitgeist, development, and organicism). Witness the remark that we strive for a vision of interdisciplinary study of culture that "binds the different disciplines in the humanities together" (Bal 1995: 4).

I regard it as one of the central tasks of "analysis" to keep us on guard against the tendency of cultural discourse to congeal into reified concepts. But how is that to be accomplished? I shall try to answer this question by considering the definition of "analysis" in the preamble to this conference in light of my own work: "analysis," we read, "gives precedence to detailed examination of cultural objects as they exist and function today, over historical reconstruction, causal explanation, or aesthetic periodization" (Bal 1995: 4). I shall discuss instances of my research in view of the three activities—historical reconstruction, causal explanation, and aesthetic periodization—over and above which the "detailed examination of cultural objects" should take precedence.

Historical Reconstruction

Among the many treats that Amsterdam offers to melomaniacs like myself are wonderful performances by Gustav Leonhard, Ton Koopman, Frans Brüggen, and others on reconstructed historical instruments. The revival of interest in historical instruments and authentic "historical performance practices" in music, which is several decades old by now, has somewhat mellowed its original radicalism, but it has not surrendered its basic premise that older music ought to be played the way it was conceived and originally performed. To what extent a past performance can be reconstructed "the way it really was" has been a matter of intense discussion among performers and musicologists, but the arguments have seldom made use of the analogous debates among literary historians and theorists. It should be one of the tasks of cultural studies "to mediate insights from one field to another, taking, of course, into account the unique features of the separate fields" (see Neubauer 1992a).

A careful cultural analysis of the problem of how to play earlier music will avoid a summary choice between historical reconstruction on the one hand and contemporary meaning and use on the other, for there are several different cultural objects involved, each with a differing historical specificity. On one end of the spectrum are the instruments, which, at least for Renaissance music and beyond, have indeed been reconstructed with remarkable historical accuracy as to material and shape—with the exception of one extraordinary case that has attracted much attention lately: the body of the castrato.

Next to the instruments, one must consider two additional types of material objects necessary for the performance of music: the setting (buildings, parks, churches, rooms in private homes) and the scores. The former are, like the instruments, largely reconstructible, and many contemporary performances of older music do indeed take place in reconstructed settings, which are often given a contemporary function this way. The matter becomes more complex if we turn to the scores, which present a philological problem that transcends its literary version because Renaissance and baroque scores are notoriously meager and leave much of the "filling in" to the performer. How Bach or Mozart intended their music to be played occupies much musicological attention, and although some questions can never be resolved, others have been answered in a historically reliable manner.

However, the greatest obstacles in the way of reconstituting historical performances are human minds rather than material objects. However admirably musicians may succeed in *re*constructing historical instruments and older techniques of playing, they can never arrive at a pristine reconstitution of "how it really was," for neither they nor their audience can ignore their musical experience, which includes, next to Monteverdi, Bach, and Mozart, also Beethoven, Mahler, Schoenberg, and Cage. In many respects the very attempt to *re*construct earlier performance practices is a cultural manifestation of *our* age, a late-twentieth-century cultural practice comparable to the interest in "primitive" art around 1900.

One of the tasks of cultural analysis should be both to caution us against the illusion that the historical or cultural other can be "fully" represented within our cultural practices and to counter the dogmatic historicist position that contemporary performance must always aim at the reconstruction of original intentions. In doing so, cultural analysis may remind us that many great revivals of the past were creative misprisons that we treasure not for the accuracy of their reconstruction but the vigor of their innovation. The late-Renaissance attempts to revive Greek theater led to the development of the opera, which turned out to possess enormous future potentials but was of no documentary value about classical antiquity. While historical performance practices are historically more reliable than the historicist blunders of the late Renaissance, their value too transcends their antiquarian achievements: their historicism is a way to make familiar music sound different.

Having criticized the ideology of historical reconstruction, I want to add that such attempts are of great value as long as they do not try to lull us into comfortable dogmas about the past and our ability to grasp it. If we remain conscious that every attempt at *re*construction is always and inevitably also a *construction*, then reaching out for the other, including the historical other, is both possible and ethically desirable. The cultural analyses of *historical* objects must be as sensitive to their "otherness" as *intercultural* analyses are to theirs. An openness to alien discourses is both a gesture of respect and a defensive move to avoid solipsism.

Causal Explanation

Does a consideration of historical performance practices confront "analysis" with "causal explanation"? I do not think so. We need cultural analysis to find out how people listen, but we cannot but help developing causal explanatory models, even if we shall find musical listening overdetermined by a number of alternative and complementary causal mechanisms. Whether we claim that the experience of music is related to the rhythm of heartbeat (a biological model) or whether we trace our playing and listening to our earlier musical experiences (a cultural one), we evoke causal models. The function of cultural analysis is, in my view, not to replace causal mechanisms with something else (what would that be?) but rather to propose new, alternative explanatory models, indicating thereby that causal models are our constructions rather than entities inherent in the objects themselves.

The traditional concatenation of ideas in intellectual history is, for instance, one of several modes to enmesh them in causal networks. The interdisciplinary instrumentarium of cultural analysis may embed ideas in alternative and complementary psychological, national, social, institutional, gendered, and other frames, none of which can claim exclusivity.

I want to illustrate this second point with remarks on Goethe's science, developing my position, as in the first case, by means of critiques. For me, cultural analysis is largely a dialogical discourse on method. This time, my partners will be Charles Coulston Gillispie, a leading historian of science of the 1950s and 1960s, and Stephen Jay Gould, a biologist, historian, and popularizer of science.

Gillispie writes in his highly regarded study of the scientific tradition, *The Edge of Objectivity*:

Goethe's nature is not objectively analyzed. It is subjectively penetrated. His is the continuum, not of geometry, but of sentience, not to say sentimentality. Nor does this vision of flux and process lead on to evolution in the proper sense. On the contrary, the unity of nature triumphs over the diversity of experience in universal metamorphosis. Man is neither product nor observer of nature. Instead, he is participant. He is communicant. (Gillispie 1960: 198)

In turn, Gould, who is a generation younger, praises Goethe's *Metamorphosis of Plants* (1790) as a historically influential work that must be understood in the morphological tradition called *unity of type*:

[Goethe] longed to find an archetype—an abstract generating form—to which all the parts of plants might be related as diversified products. . . . In his most fascinating intellectual move, Goethe produces a complete account by grafting two additional principles onto the underlying notion of leaf-as-archetype: the progressive refinement of sap, and cycles of expansion and contraction. We may regard these principles as ad hoc or incorrect today, but the power of their conjunction with the archetypal idea can still be grasped and appreciated with much profit. (Gould 1993: 159–61)

My immediate reaction to Gillispie's and Gould's approaches to Goethe's morphology was disagreement. For present purposes I want both to summarize my reactions and to reflect on them.

In 1792, two years after publishing *The Metamorphosis of Plants*, Goethe wrote his most important essay on methodology, *Der Versuch als Vermittler zwischen Objekt und Subjekt* (The experiment between object and subject), which opens with the following words:

As soon as we become aware of the objects around us, we relate them to ourselves, and justly so. For our whole fortune depends on the question whether we like or dislike them, whether they attract or repulse us, whether they are useful or harmful to us. . . . Those who are urged on by their quest for knowledge to try to observe the natural objects in themselves and in their relation to each other are facing a much harder task, for . . . they lose the yardstick that was useful to them in relating things to themselves, that yardstick of liking and disliking, attraction and repulsion, benefit and harm. They must give this up completely: like divine beings, they are expected to seek and investigate what exists and not what pleases. (Goethe 1985: 4.2: 321–321f)

This objectivism and empiricism, which in many respects resembles the "edge of objectivity" that Gillispie holds up against Goethe's presumed subjectivism, was Goethe's first reaction to Newtonian science, more specifically to Newton's claim that a single key experiment, an *experimentum crucis*, could decide between rival theories (in this case in favor of his corpuscular theory of light). For now, the important point is that Goethe accuses Newton of subjectivism, just as Gillispie accuses Goethe of the same. Anticipating Karl Popper's theory of falsification, Goethe believed that no theory is ever definitively confirmed, that "one can never be cautious enough to refrain from rashly deducing something from experiments, from proving something directly from experiments, or from verifying a theory by means of experiments" (Goethe 1985: 4.2: 326). Since "a single experiment or even several experiments interlinked do not prove anything" (4.2: 326), he declared that the "actual duty" of scientists was the "multiplication of each individual experiment" (4.2: 330). Newton may have claimed that he did not invent the hypothesis, but in Goethe's (and not only his) opinion, Newton's treatise on optics was full of unconfirmed hypotheses, which reified into truth what were once rhetorical, authoritative, and professional interests, and thereby institutionalized the hypothesis. In short, Goethe would have answered Gillispie that Newton's science, rather than his own, was subjective; he would have thanked Gould for praising his appeal to hypotheses, but he would have added that he, Goethe himself, had a low regard for scientific hypotheses.

This line of argument, worked out more thoroughly and with more relevant passages from Goethe, would be a response to Gillispie as well as to Gould within *Geistesgeschichte* or the history of ideas. The response calls attention to texts and textual passages that the others neglected or mis-interpreted, but responses of this kind must usually admit that the oppo-nents can also marshal a battery of quotations in support of their view. In most cases it is difficult to determine which side has the better cards.

Can cultural analysis help us to overcome the dilemmas of *Geistesge-schichte*? No, I think; not if by overcoming we mean reaching a definitive resolution. But it can point out that notoriously vague terms like "sub-jective" and "objective" can only be meaningful if we specify from which angle and in which context we look upon a matter; it can provide new perspectives, new frameworks in which to analyze the issues; and it can work against the tendency of interpretations to monologize and monu-mentalize texts.

How, concretely, can cultural analysis contribute to the issues raised with respect to Goethe? Note first of all that I have used a single text by Goethe to criticize both Gillispie's and Gould's readings. This indicates that their views significantly overlap, even if their judgments differ; or, to put it more pointedly, they see the same thing but attach opposite values to it because they speak from different scientific paradigms. What Gillispie disparagingly calls "subjective" is "bold" for Gould. The difference lies not in *what* they ascribe to Goethe but what value they attach to it: within Gillispie's objectivist notion of science Goethe's presumed excessive use of hypotheses is a sign of romantic subjectivism; within Gould's more imagi-native view of science, hypotheses fulfill a salutary role.

Cultural analysis of Goethe's science could then start by asking why and how is it that different historians come to such opposite views of the same phenomenon, and it may seek an answer in the intellectual, insti-tutional, and social context of these historians. Gillispie's objectivist and Gould's hypotheses-friendly approach are separated by a revolution in the philosophy of science. Gillispie's reading of Goethe was conditioned by notions of romanticism he adopted from Whitehead and M. H. Abrams, and neopositivistic notions of science still dominant toward the end of the

1950s. Two years after the appearance of *The Edge of Objectivity*, Gillispie's new colleague at Princeton, Thomas Kuhn, blunted so to speak the "edge of objectivity" with his theory of scientific revolutions. Gould is on the other side of the watershed, not because he is at Harvard, but because he belongs to a post-Kuhnian generation. The difference between Gillispie's and Gould's visions of Goethe is to a considerable degree conditioned not by the text they look at but by the different notions they have of what constitutes good science. Note that in arguing this way I am not abandoning causal explanation; I merely introduce another explanatory mechanism.

This is, of course, only one side of the coin. Cultural analysis must also concern itself with the psychological and cultural forces operating both within Goethe's scientific texts and within successive generations of culture that received them. If one does this, as I have tried to do in a series of publications, it becomes evident that the cohesive meanings that Goethe's science assumed during its now two-hundred-year-old history of reception were mostly monumentalizations of a textual body that is full of cracks and fissures and that underwent substantial revisions during Goethe's life.

Concerning Goethe's own revisions, cultural analysis can show that Goethe's science, and science in general, is shaped by psychological and institutional forces. Goethe didn't change his scientific ideas and his ideas on science simply as a result of reasoned reflection. In his later writings, he wove morphology into an autobiographical discourse and into personal reflections on the sociology and history of science because he no longer believed that disciplinary thought alone determines morphological science. He reflected on the metaphors of science, and he emplotted morphology by means of his autobiography, the history of institutions, and anecdotes about scientific quarrels.

In order to make sense of this, to grasp Goethe's science in terms of his growing hostility toward the professionalized science that disregarded his contributions or put them down as inventions of a poetic temper, we have to go beyond intellectual history, out into the psychology and sociology of institutional history, including the history of how science and literature became professionalized and institutionalized. It is not "incorrect" to consider Goethe's critique of Newton and Newtonian science as an intellectually reasoned response, though today I myself prefer to see that critique as an amateur outsider's response to the historical institutionalization of science. The cultural analysis of this case involves the construction of a new explanatory network by means of reconstructing the historical professionalization of science and Goethe's ambivalent reaction to it.

To the analysis of the cultural forces active in the making of (Goethe's) science, we have to add the analysis of its subsequent cultural history. Goethe, together with Schiller, has been one of the most systematically monumentalized authors of world literature, whose enshrinement as a national monument was crucial for the construction of a German national identity in the nineteenth century. The monumentalization meant valorizing his literary works over his scientific ones, but since the end of the nineteenth century, the scientific writings have been repeatedly monumentalized into a "Goethean alternative science" by subsequent waves of protesters against modern science, including Rudolf Steiner and his anthroposophic followers, Oswald Spengler (Spengler 1981), various right-wing irrationalists of the 1920s, and holistic environmentalists of all stripes today. Furthermore (see Neubauer 1988), Goethe's morphology gave rise in the first half of our century to an ideologically tainted German "morphological poetics" (Günther Müller, André Jolles, Horst Oppel, and, by indirection, Eberhard Lämmert); it also served as a motto for Vladimir Propp's morphological analysis of Russian folktales. A cultural analysis of this tradition would show that the function and meaning of Goethe's science today cannot be separated from its history of reception; at the same time, such an analysis would have to make subtle judgments about the line one ultimately has to draw between reasonable and unreasonable misprisions.

Admittedly, this is a messy business. How are we to find the chips that were discarded when the monuments were chiseled out of the amorphous masses of Goethe's writings? Who is to decide, and how should such decisions be made, as to which chips and which parts of the monument are to be assembled? How are we to avoid the misprisions that celebrate their own ideological purposes? Will my Goethe not be another constructed monument, in spite of my intention to reconstruct? While I have no secure answers to these questions, I do expect cultural analysis to keep asking them instead of leading me beyond them. To ask questions and to try to answer them means to stay within the domain of causal explanations—but I see no alternative to it.

Aesthetic Periodization

That the detailed examination of cultural objects should have precedence over "aesthetic periodization" is a desideratum that may need broadening in view of "culture's" inherent thrust to propel us from "aesthetic"
periodization towards holistic cultural entities. I speak of a "Ghost of *Geistesgeschichte*" to remind us that while we confess to be nominalist and
anti-essentialist, our discourse, perhaps involuntarily, remains realist in the
sense of imputing reality to generalizing abstract terms. I want to illustrate
this final point with two examples, one from the rising tide of cultural
studies of music, the other from Michel Foucault's *The Order of Things*.[2]

Formalism and modernism sternly rejected representational interpretations of instrumental music, but their injunction flew in the face of
musical listening by nonprofessionals, which tends to associate images,
words, and stories with "absolute music." I side with those who link music
to culture by claiming that pure music is culturally semanticized, but unfortunately I have to disagree with several recent approaches that try to
establish the link between music and culture by means of codes exclusively
extracted from the culture in which the composition was created.

Anthony Newcomb's term for that code is "plot archetype" (Newcomb 1992: 119). Analyzing Mahler's Ninth Symphony, he disagrees with
those who regard it as the composer's swan song and shows that instead of
premonitions of death it portrays an adolescent entering adult life. Newcomb gives to this fascinating, if somewhat implausible, interpretation a
cultural support by linking the musical adventures of the young hero to
a "spiral or circular" romantic plot, adopted from M. H. Abrams and
others. My trouble with this cultural approach to music is not just that
I do not care for spiral or circular archetypes, but that I am skeptical of
paradigms that span more than a century. Above all, I disagree with Newcomb's two methodological assumptions, namely that cultural archetypes
can somehow anchor the interpretation of individual works and, secondly,
that the cultural archetypes around the compositional process determine
the work's future meaning. In my view, the archetypes of the cultural
context are less securely established than individual interpretations and
just as much subject to reinterpretation. Indeed, since music is weakly semanticized, it is more frequently and more radically reinterpreted than
literature. Cultural approaches to music that do not leave room for this

fall back into positivism: Newcomb's cultural archetypes are spawned not only by Hegel but by Ranke as well.

Michel Foucault's *The Order of Things* is indebted to the same ancestors in spite of Foucault's vehement critique of *Geistesgeschichte* in *The Archeology of Knowledge*. Like Thomas Kuhn, who claims that scientific paradigms are "incommensurable," Foucault speaks of formations of epistemic discourse, separated from each other by radical breaks unbridged by developmental links. Skirting the difficult question of how the discourse formations of *The Order of Things* are related to the social and institutional power that Foucault analyzes in several other works, I want to focus on the discursive space that Foucault believes appeared around 1800. He shows with great force that the classical episteme of representation (with its discoures on exchange, natural history, and speech) was replaced at that time by the new discourses of labor, biology, and historical linguistics. Whether these discourses are paradigms of epistemic discourse in further fields is unclear but unimportant for my topic here.

Let us examine then how Foucault deals with the epistemic discourse of a single field, biology. As is well known, his archaeology moves discourses from the personal into the public sphere; by detaching these cultural objects from their makers he is surely one of the intellectual inspirations of cultural analysis and of the way analysis shifts its focus from individual speech, psychology, and biography to discourse and social formations. It is surprising, therefore, that the heading of Foucault's chapter on biology (as indeed on labor and linguistics) is a proper name (Foucault 1973: 263). Although Foucault disdains histories of personalities and person-bound theories, he attaches the new biological discourse to the name of a single figure, Georges Cuvier. It is Cuvier's structuralist approach to organisms that becomes the biological discourse of the episteme.

What are the epistemic features of Cuvier's discourse? Biology replaces the classical system of "natural history," which established classificatory systems by means of "characters," that is, visible structures "selected to be the locus of pertinent identities and differences" (Foucault 1973: 140). The characters of Linnaeus's botanical system, for instance, were the organs of fructification. When the classical system reached "the limits of representation" between 1775 and 1795 (Foucault 1973: 217), it continued to aim at classifying characters but arranged these characters now hierarchically, so that the highest, often invisible ones, pertained to the vital functions of eating, breeding, breathing, and locomotion.

In Cuvier's comparative anatomy, characters acquired a new, organic function. The interest shifted from the comparison and classification of individual characters to the internal structure of organisms and the comparison of complete organisms. As Foucault writes at the beginning of his Cuvier chapter: "Cuvier freed the subordination of characters from its taxonomic function in order to introduce it, prior to any classification that might occur, into the various organic structural plans of living beings. . . . It is this displacement and this inversion that Étienne Geoffroy Saint-Hilaire expressed when he said: 'Organic structure is becoming an abstract being . . . capable of assuming numerous forms.'"[3] This undoubtedly captures something of Cuvier's achievement, but one is disturbed that in defining it Foucault appeals to a quote from Geoffroy. The passage that is to reveal the epistemic break between natural history and biology unwittingly indicates a double voice within Foucault's presumably coherent episteme: Cuvier's new epistemic discourse is conveyed via the voice of Geoffroy Saint-Hilaire. To complicate matters further, Foucault quotes Geoffroy from Théophile Cahn (1962: 138).

Filtering Cuvier via Geoffroy and Cahn, Foucault abandons his own methodological principle of letting the historical documents speak in their own voice. A minor blemish? If one checks Cahn's book, one discovers why Foucault did not cite Geoffroy directly: no references are given in Cahn's otherwise conscientious and scholarly book. Foucault and his readers are unable to check the correctness, the pertinence, and the context of the quote from Geoffroy.

All this would be pedantic academic nitpicking if larger issues didn't depend on it. One is disturbed not only by the fact that Cuvier's epistemic discourse is introduced by means of another voice, but more importantly by the subordination of Geoffroy's voice to Cuvier's concept of biology. Foucault's books contain no other quote from Geoffroy, even though it was he who hired Cuvier at the Jardin des Plantes, who collaborated with him for several decades, and, most importantly, who finally clashed with him frontally in a debate within the French Académie in 1830, one of the great scientific debates of all times. By positioning Geoffroy as a stand-in for Cuvier, Foucault suppresses Cuvier's great countervoice within the epistemic discourse.

Foucault would presumably have answered this objection that the debate belongs to the "more visible level of discoveries, discussion, theories, or philosophical options" (Foucault 1973: 274) which does not reveal the archaeological depth of epistemic space and discourse formation. But while it is true that the debate was muddled and inconclusive, the differences were profound and paradigmatic. As Toby Appel has put it recently: "Brought to a head in the Cuvier-Geoffroy debate of 1830 was a fundamental division in the biological sciences: whether animal structure ought to be explained primarily by reference to function or by morphological laws" (Appel 1987: 2).

Simplifying a very complex opposition, I would add that Cuvier's functional biology was teleological, because Cuvier believed that "every structure was created by God to fulfill a specific purpose" (Appel 1987: 203), whereas Geoffroy believed that animals possessed a common organic plan, an *unité de composition*, and he sought accordingly morphological laws that transcended Cuvier's four classes of vertebrates. In search of that unity, Geoffroy boldly claimed that bones with disparate functions in different animals were often morphologically homologous (analogue). Since Geoffroy's morphology was highly dependent on visual inspection, it is misleading to make him a spokesman of Cuvier's biology, which Foucault characterizes by a turn to invisible characters and internal functions.

A traditional historian of ideas could defend his neglect of Geoffroy by saying that it was Cuvier, and not Geoffroy, who anticipated Darwin and the future development of biology. Foucault claims something similar when arguing that Cuvier, and not Lamarck, is Darwin's avatar (Foucault 1973: 274–75), but this option is actually closed to him since in *The Archeology of Knowledge* he severely rebukes histories written in terms of avatars and successors, winners and losers. This to him amounts to an injection of teleological thinking into history.[4]

A bare scratch of the surface dissolved the apparently homogeneous epistemic discourse into a crisscross of conflicting voices, which strongly suggests that there is more than one way to stage the birth of biology. While it is legitimate to foreground the role of Cuvier, it is impermissible to monumentalize his voice into the discourse of biology and to suppress his countervoices. Foucault totalizes, homogenizes, and monologizes the first biological discourse-network; he papers over the tensions, divisions, and ruptures within it, in order to set off the episteme against its equally homogeneous predecessor. The foregrounding of epistemic space reduces the dialogue within it.

Note that we have so far remained totally within discursive space, for Foucault's description of the new biological discourse, like classical *Geistesgeschichte*, makes no references to biography, social history, and institutions. And yet, as the following anecdote indicates, the biological discourse was enmeshed in politics and power.

When news of the abdication of Charles X and the flaring up of the Cuvier-Geoffroy debate reached Weimar in the first days of August 1830, Frédéric Jacques Soret rushed to Goethe, and the latter greeted him by exclaiming: "What do you think of this great event? The volcano has erupted; everything is aflame, and there are no more dealings behind closed doors!" "A frightening story," Soret replied, "but could we expect anything else under the well-known circumstances and under such a ministry than that it would end with the banishment of the reigning royal family?" "My dear," said Goethe, "we don't seem to understand each other. I am not speaking about those people at all. . . . I am speaking about that immensely important scientific strife between Cuvier and Geoffroy that came to a public outburst in the Academy" (Goethe 1985: 19: 675; Appel 1987: 3).

Soret was baffled to see the conservative octogenarian poet display Jacobinical revolutionary fervor on account of a debate in biology. He did not fully understand that for Goethe the assault on the gates of the monarchy was less important than the presumed attack on those closed doors of institutionalized science that had kept him out of the sanctuary he so desired to enter.

Goethe preferred Geoffroy to Cuvier, because he was the one who appealed to the broader public with a booklet on the debate (Geoffroy 1830), and, more importantly, because Goethe's neglected morphological ideas resembled those of Geoffroy. The debate did actually bring publicity to Goethe and his morphology: when he wrote a favorable, though by no means uncritical, review of Geoffroy's booklet, his theory, and the debate (Goethe 1985: 18.2), the latter discovered in Goethe a precursor and started to lavish praise on Goethean morphology in order to boost his own cause (Geoffroy 1831). It is probably true "that the members of the Académie for the most part did not share Geoffroy's high estimate of Goethe as a scientist, and that Geoffroy did little to further his cause among academicians by his continual references to the German poet" (Appel 1987: 167), but Goethe's morphology did win favor with Balzac, George Sand,

Edgar Quinet, and other French writers and intellectuals, almost all of whom sided with Geoffroy. Balzac, for one, described the social universe of the *Comédie humaine* in terms of Geoffroy's *unité de composition*. Adopting Geoffroy's idea that all vertebrates were built on a common schema which then became modified by their particular environment, Balzac proposed to show the emergence of human variety under specific historical and cultural circumstances. He thanked Geoffroy for the idea of the *unité de composition*, and thought that Geoffroy's victory over Cuvier was "saluted in the last article that the great Goethe wrote" (Balzac 1976: 8). Goethe's article contained no such salutation, but Balzac's interpretation determined the way in which Goethe's morphology and his role in the debate came to be understood in France. What looks like a coherent discourse in Foucault has by now become a cacophony of voices—voices that utter (biological) ideas out of professional jealousy, desire for power, disciplinary interests, ideological convictions, sheer misunderstanding of what others have said, and countless other nonbiological and nonintellectual circumstances.

Let us return for a final point to the quotation from Geoffroy: "Organic structure is becoming an abstract being . . . capable of assuming numerous forms" (Foucault 1973: 264; the elision comes from Cahn). It is general enough to cover Cuvier's as well as Geoffroy's system, and one cannot exclude the possibility that in its original context it does indeed refer to Cuvier's notion of organic structure. But Foucault could not trace the passage and knew only about its place and function in Cahn's book— and this gives extra piquancy to the matter, for Cahn uses it in a short chapter on German *Naturphilosophie* in order to show how close Geoffroy was to it. According to Cahn, the sentence quoted from Geoffroy strongly resembles Lorenz Oken's remark that "the whole of the animal kingdom corresponds to humanity stretched out."[5] He further mentions Schelling, Karl Friedrich von Kielmeyer, Oken, Goethe, Johann Friedrich Blumenbach, and others to forge an analogy between Geoffroy and German.

We need not worry about the question whether such an analogy really exists (it actually does). What matters is that Cuvier, who studied with Kielmeyer and continued corresponding with him, violently opposed German *Naturphilosophie*, which he accused of pantheism, irreligion, and lacking in scientific rigor. Thus, the sentence that Cahn quoted to show Geoffroy's proximity to *Naturphilosophie* is in Foucault's text made to serve Cuvier, the great opponent of *Naturphilosophie*. Foucault doesn't just violate the integrity of Cahn's and Geoffroy's texts (which is bad enough); he once more overlooks (deliberately?) a whole set of religious, methodological, ideological, and national differences in order to forge a discourse that is both homogeneous and free of societal interference.

I want to conclude, then, that cultural analysis must be sensitive to all those twists and turns, misprisions, and conflicts that arise out of the religious, political, national, and institutional connections of literature and science that Foucault's sanitized and homogenized account suppresses. We must scrutinize not only the historical objects of culture but also the texts about them. Cultural analysts can learn much from some of Foucault's works. But if culture is to be more than epistemically clean and homogeneous discourse they better not take *The Order of Things* as their model of inspiration.

The Techno-University and the Future of Knowledge

THOUGHTS AFTER LYOTARD

Jon Cook

The future role and purpose of universities have become matters of widespread discussion in the Western democracies. A rhetoric of impending crisis is matched by a sense of intractable problems. These are so many symptoms of what I take to be a major change in universities, their transition to what I have chosen to call "techno-universities." In what follows I set out some of the evidence for this assumption, establish a contrast with a different and historically precedent idea of the university, and then reflect on some of the consequences of these changes for the identity of cultural studies and cultural analysis. My assumption is that what we understand by knowledge, although not simply reducible to institutional forms, has an institutional dimension, and therefore, institutional change of the kind summarily described in what follows will, over time, alter the consensus about what is to count as knowledge in different domains.

One authoritative sign of change comes from two recent reports by the Organization for Economic Cooperation and Development (OECD). A 1983 intergovernmental conference identified a "crisis of performance" in universities. A more recent publication, from 1987, *Universities Under Scrutiny*, provides a detailed account of that crisis and what is needed to resolve it. What is required is more "career-oriented study" among students;

a greater emphasis on "applied research and development"; planning for "effective technology transfer and knowledge diffusion"; "a continuum of functions which cut across and break down the categorical distinctions of the past"; "greater government involvement and more responsiveness and accountability by the universities" (Peters 1992: 124). These confident abstractions are not difficult to decipher. Universities are being called to account because they are not offering a good return on investment. Their value as autonomous institutions, however much this may be referred and deferred to, has become increasingly redundant. Universities need to be reminded of their heteronomy and, therefore, of their subordination to the requirements of economic efficiency and performance. The publication date of *Universities Under Scrutiny* also deserves note. This is an example of forward planning for a post–Cold War world in which universities lose their role and justification as minor icons of cultural and intellectual freedom. Stripped of the protection afforded by this role, they can now be exposed to a healthy dose of the iron laws of the marketplace. The question of their cultural value, always doubtfully qualitative and nebulous to hardheaded economic reasoners, can be set to one side.

Different nation-states have responded to the future envisaged by the OECD report at different rates. Certainly the British state has not been slow into the field. The last sixteen years have seen persistent cuts in the state funding of universities with the purpose of making them "leaner" and "fitter." This has been accompanied by an ever more detailed scrutiny of what universities do and how much they cost. Performance is monitored by regular "Teaching Quality Assessments" and "Research Appraisal Exercises." It is now possible in some universities to track how much an individual faculty member "earns" in terms of number of students taught and income generated through research productivity. The terror of numbers has never been more in evidence. The requirements of performativity, of "efficiency gains," of "total quality management" provide the context for judgment and legitimation.

This more abrasive relation between universities and their paymasters is one condition for the emergence of the techno-university. The technicity at stake here has to do with the assumption that universities are instruments to increase economic efficiency and that the knowledge they impart will be technical in a sense that echoes Aristotle's account of *technē* as a knowing how to do things.[1] Knowledge is justified by what it enables its possessors to make or perform in a rapidly changing labor market. Hence the increasing stress in British higher education upon "transferable skills," something that manifests itself in humanities departments by a concern to show that learning about Shakespeare can directly or indirectly make people into better managers or entrepreneurs. The ordinary activities of humanist inquiry—seminar discussion, using libraries, writing essays and research papers—become valuable because they can be cashed in as marketable skills.

Education policy, or what passes for it, forms only one part of the picture and may itself be symptomatic of a more far-reaching change. Universities are being transformed by the computer technology they did so much to invent. Computers are no longer machines apart, housed in specialized laboratories or faculties of systems engineering. As in other areas of daily life, the presence of information technology is increasingly taken for granted in work across a broad range of university disciplines. University libraries, once dedicated to books, now contain computer workstations which punctuate the traditional silence of study with the discreet chatter of digital processing.

What effect, if any, this change will have on existing economies of knowledge has already been much discussed. I shall comment on some of that discussion later in this paper. For the moment it is worth noting that the scrutiny of the cost-effectiveness of universities can go hand-in-hand with a call for the use of computers to either replace or supplement existing modes of teaching. Computers can mediate the increasing demand for university education and the decreasing willingness to fund it at levels established in the 1960s and 1970s. Caught in the pincer movement between demands for ever greater efficiency and the increasing use of the computer as a means of information storage and retrieval, traditional university departments may well feel that their future survival is in question.

Universities are being reshaped by new factors of power. In the process a particular idea of the university is becoming obsolete. It is as though a way of talking comes to seem irrelevant or difficult to recognize or merely nostalgic. This idea of the university is itself a historical creation. Its legitimating rhetoric can be discerned in a range of texts written in Europe and the United States in the nineteenth and twentieth centuries. These texts form a subgenre which includes John Henry Newman's *Discourses* and his *The Idea of the University*, Matthew Arnold's *Culture and Anarchy*, F. R.

Leavis's *Education and the University*, Heidegger's notorious Rector's Address, and Karl Jaspers's work of 1946 which has a recurrent title within the subgenre, *The Idea of the University*. These texts are not homogeneous in any simple way. Each bears the imprint of specific historical and national circumstances. But they do bear a family resemblance which manifests itself in the recurrence of four figures of thought: the figure of tradition, of unity, of the elite, and of homosociality. I call them figures of thought rather than ideas or concepts because their effects cannot be adequately encompassed by providing dictionary definitions of their meaning or subjecting them to logical analysis. The figures work interdependently in a discourse. The terms I have provided for them are in some cases labels. What I intend to summon by them is as much a cultural mood about universities as an argument in their defense. Both mood and argument are important for understanding how the discourse in which they are embedded make its bid for legitimation.

Heidegger's Rector's Address sets out the importance of tradition to the conduct of an "authentic science" in the university. It can arise "only if we again place ourselves under the power of the beginning of our spiritual-historical being. This beginning is the setting out of Greek philosophy. Here, for the first time, western man raises himself up from a popular base, and by virtue of his language, stands up to the totality of what is" (Heidegger 1985: 471–72).

The university is the place of an encounter with tradition which in Heidegger's phrasing takes on hieratic power. The encounter with the "beginning of our spiritual-historical being" has a ritualistic as well as an intellectual meaning (1985: 471). Knowledge is not bound by concept or quantification, but is located in a reenactment which places the knower in the space between an originary act and its mediations. This is the basis for a form of heroic self-definition which is in line with the task of national affirmation seen by Heidegger as one of the crucial tasks of the university (the full title of his address is "The Self-Assertion of the German University").

F. R. Leavis, although presenting his ideas less portentously, identifies the university, and particularly its English faculty, as similarly obligated to tradition. Universities, and for Leavis this means especially the "ancient universities" of Oxford and Cambridge, are preeminently the place where tradition is incarnate. Leavis makes clear that this is not, in his ambitious conception, a sideline in nostalgia or part of what we have come to know as the heritage industry. Tradition is hegemonic. It is to act as a "directing force." Anticipating the objection that tradition "may seem a vague concept," Leavis engages in an exercise of pointing to what he takes to be "there": " 'Humane tradition' may seem a vague concept. I don't think that an attempt to define it by an enumeration of its contents would help. It seems to me better to point to English literature, which is unquestionably and producibly 'there,' and to suggest that the 'literary tradition' that this unquestionable existence justifies us in speaking of might also be called a vague concept" (Leavis 1979: 16–17).

The argument works upon a trade-off between the conceptually vague and the empirically self-evident. This indicates again that the knowledge born by tradition is not necessarily frameable in a conceptual form. It may be received by a particular witnessing of words (as in Heidegger) or an apprehension of the significance of literary form. But vagueness is also strategic. It creates a space in which Leavis can powerfully invent a tradition, and yet disavow the fact of its invention by producing it, Svengali-like, as if "there." And the same holds true for Heidegger's oracular return to the "setting out of Greek philosophy," which will, in practice, consist in Heidegger's compelling etymological inventions around Greek philosophical words.

The figure of unity is closely allied with that of tradition, as in this quotation from Karl Jaspers: "Still the university with its aura of tradition represents to [the student] the unity of all branches of learning" (Jaspers 1960: 52). In the preface to his *Discourses on the Scope and Nature of University Education*, Newman describes the university as "a place of *teaching* universal *knowledge*" (Newman's emphasis on teaching is linked to his insistence that universities are not primarily places of research) (Newman 1957: 355). Leavis acknowledges the inevitability of specialization but goes on to claim that the central task of a university is "to bring the special sciences and studies into significant relation—to discover how to train a kind of central intelligence by or through which they can, somehow, be brought into relation" (Leavis 1979: 25). Heidegger gives his variation on the figure of universities and unity. Once questioning is understood as no longer a preliminary step to knowledge but itself "the highest form of knowing," then "such questioning shatters the division of the sciences into rigidly separated specialties, carries them back from their endless and aimless dispersal into isolated fields and corners, and exposes science once again to the fertility and the blessing bestowed by all the world-shaping powers of human historical being" (Heidegger 1985: 474).

Heidegger's metaphors suggest a moment of violence which is also a moment of recuperation. The university is to have a redemptive or curative role. If there is a logic in the progress of knowledge which produces specialization, the university will bind knowledge back into a unity which is provided by tradition. Hence the university is presented as a place at odds with its surrounding society and the effects of that society within it. The return to tradition is set against what Leavis describes as "the blind drive onward of material and mechanical development." It represents a "wisdom older than modern civilisation" and a "check and control" on the slavish impulses of modernity (Leavis 1979: 16). In Jaspers's argument, "the growing emptiness of modern life," produced by the fragmentation of knowledge into diverse specialisms, has to be countered by the university's power to produce a kind of knowledge which is *universally valid* (Jaspers 1960: 24).

Access to tradition and unity are only available on a selective basis. The idea that a university education is the education of an elite pervades these texts. Heidegger claims that the university educates and disciplines "the leaders and the guardians of the German people" (Heidegger 1985: 471). Matthew Arnold, in *Culture and Anarchy*, is not directly concerned with the idea of a university, but he envisages the creation of a new minority class of "aliens" identified by their devotion to cultural tradition and its dissemination (Arnold 1993: 110). Jaspers argues with an interesting duplicity that the university addresses itself "outwardly to all, intrinsically to the best only" (Jaspers 1960: 112). The implication of this duplicity is evident. Jaspers is indicating the process whereby a university does not simply recruit an elite, but actively forms its identity. The university is the place where the "best" are selected out from the "all."

The elite identified and shaped by their access to tradition and the unity of knowledge is a society of men. The assumption within the discourse here is so embedded, so naturally taken for granted, that it rarely if ever surfaces as something in need of explicit justification. Newman, in his *Discourses*, arguing against religious sectarianism, presents a new ideal of the "gentleman" as a type the university should produce (Newman 1957: 544–46). Heidegger's "guardians" are men, as are Leavis's students at the "English School." These writers ignore or regard as peripheral the fact that they wrote at a time when women were beginning to gain access to higher education. The point here is not to note this with a Whiggish scorn, but to register the importance for an idea of the university of knowledge as a gendered gift to be passed on from the old to the young.

How are these four figures of thought to be interpreted? And how do they stand in relation to what I earlier described as the development of the techno-university? The texts informed by these figures convey a powerful sense of a reference backwards in time. This does not necessarily have to do with the persistent invocation of tradition, the sense of swimming against a tide of modernization, which is stated within each of the figures and reinforced in their repetition. Nostalgia is often a matter of updating something, and in this case, it is a classical topic of educational theory: how to educate a ruling elite. Founding texts here include Plato's *Republic* and Aristotle's *Politics* and his *Nichomachean Ethics*. The tradition of civic humanism reworks some of the main ideas in early modern Europe. When, for example, Arnold proclaims the importance of "seeing things steadily and seeing them whole," or Newman describes a process of training which will lead to a connected view or grasp of things, or Jaspers states that his ideal student "wants to gain a clear view of the world and of people," they all repeat a claim about the centrality of a kind of knowledge appropriate to a sovereign citizen or a philosophically educated ruler. This sets a comprehensive view of the social good, a generalizing reason, or a capacity to know the underlying, eternal forms of true knowledge against the knowledge of and immersion in particulars which is thought to be characteristic of artisans and slaves. The capacity to "see things steadily and see them whole" is a necessary qualification of the governing individual. Hence Newman's concern that universities should not educate students simply for particular vocations or professions. This runs the risk of confining them to partial and interested perspectives which will unfit them for leadership. To adapt a term from Foucault, the purpose of a university education is to create panopticians.[2]

This endowment is a condition of a negative and a positive freedom. The freedom is negative because the knowledge that rises above particularity frees its possessor from the confinement of partial perspectives or illusions masquerading as knowledge. Its positive character is legislative. Comprehensive knowledge enables its possessor to determine laws, limits, and what lies beyond them. In Heidegger's Kantian formulation, "To give the law to oneself is the highest freedom" (Heidegger 1985: 475).

These texts restate another theme that runs through discussions of the education of rulers from the time of the Renaissance. The study of the humanities is the route to the knowledge and the moral virtue necessary for a good governor. In the Renaissance this would typically include the study of grammar and rhetoric and culminate in the study of philosophy. This version of the appropriate humanist curriculum does not, of course, remain stable over time. In my examples of nineteenth- and twentieth-century argument, the general agreement about the value of an encounter with tradition is inflected by differences about what is to count as the humanizing core of a university education. For Leavis it is the study of English literature, for Heidegger a return to the founding texts of philosophy, for Jaspers an overcoming of the division between the humanities and the natural sciences. And if this study carries both an epistemological and a moral benefit of a kind that links it to earlier classical and Renaissance discussions of the appropriate education for the good governor, the idea of what it means to be a ruler has been changed. The requirements of the Athenian polis or the Renaissance court are markedly different from those of industrial nation-states. The authority proposed as the best outcome of a university education is as much cultural and social as political. What was once focused in the idea of the Athenian citizen or Renaissance prince has now become more widely dispersed. Heidegger's "guardians" or Newman's "gentlemen" are not, at least in thought, destined to be invisible bureaucrats. They are the visible exemplars of the authority bestowed on them by their education. They manifest the presence of leadership across the varying and complex surfaces of modern society.

The countertime of the university requires, then, the restatement of certain classical themes: an ideal of a comprehensive and unified knowledge beyond the specialized and limited knowledge of professional or technical experts; a submission to the authority of a wisdom contained in texts as opposed to the experimental manipulation of material; a purpose in the education of leaders. Taken together, these constitute the necessary, although not always sufficient, conditions for making higher education high. They also indicate that the very modernity of these texts lies in their hostility toward modernity.

Some signs of this hostility have already been noted: Leavis's opposition to "the blind drive onward of material and mechanical development," or Jaspers's concern about "the growing emptiness of modern life." Modernity is mapped through a range of terms, all of them associated

with ideas of uncontrollable development, aimlessness, and inauthen-
ticity. Among these technology plays a central role. Heidegger refers to the
"mathematical-technological thinking" which has separated science from
the necessary knowledge of its beginnings in classical Greek thought (Heidegger 1985: 473). In an extended reflection on the place of technology
outside and inside the university, Jaspers identifies technological development as the defining moment of modernity:

Although technology is ages old, and has developed through thousands of years,
until the end of the eighteenth century it remained a part of handicraft. . . .
Then, during the last 150 years, technology made an incision deeper than all the
events of world history over the past thousands of years, as deep perhaps as that
caused by the discovery of tools and fire. Technology has become an independent
giant. . . . Trapped in the spell of technology, men seem no longer capable of
controlling what originated as their own works. (Jaspers 1960: 104–5)

There is a paradox implied by Jasper's language: the epitome of the
modern, technology, is phrased in terms of the archaic, of giants and
spells, of something that has yet to come under the legislation of a reason
appropriate to its nature. In a quasi-Hegelian dialectic Jaspers thinks of
technology as a matter whose form or spirit awaits realization: "It seems as
if there is something that is bound to awake even though still half asleep,
something that until now has remained silent behind the great mass of
ingenious technological devices" (1960: 106).

This interpretation sets the stage for the university's humanizing
and regulative encounter with technology. Jaspers is tentative about this
prospect, but the "meaning and purpose" bestowed on technology by its
presence within the university is not simply to the benefit of technology.
The university, in its turn, will be modernized by the encounter; but such
is the contortion and uncertainty of Jaspers's argument at this point that
the emphasis shifts again to the importance of reviving the "old idea" of
the university as a place of comprehensive knowledge before this modernizing encounter with technology can properly occur.

The hesitations in Jaspers's argument are symptomatic. What is at
issue is not a "policy decision" about the place of technology within or
without the university, but a discursive form which identifies technology
as monstrous, however that monster might subsequently be accommodated. If the assertion of the university's relation to time occurs through
the figure of tradition, in this discourse technology means something more

than the invention of new materials and artifacts. It is a crucial aspect of the disordered or sinister form of time itself. Technology threatens to destroy the time of tradition. It also imposes a particular (dis)order of space: Jaspers's "great mass of ingenious technological devices," for example. In Heidegger a similar process, if not controlled by the self-assertion of the German university, will produce a crisis in which a "moribund semblance of a culture caves in and drags all that remains strong into confusion and lets it suffocate in madness" (Heidegger 1985: 480). Either space is crowded with technical artifacts, or, in Heidegger's apocalyptic excess, it implodes and suffocates. The pure air of tradition evaporates.

The imagination of technology in this discourse is continuous with other threats to the time and space of tradition. In Arnold's *Culture and Anarchy* the "populace" or proletariat are similarly blind, disordered, and threatening in their crowdedness (Arnold 1993: 88–89). By contrast, the university preserves what Walter Benjamin described as the experience of "aura." Benjamin's formulation of the concept is principally associated with his writings on art, notably his essay "The Work of Art in the Age of Mechanical Reproduction." The aura of a work of art resides in its uniqueness, its location in a tradition, and its literal and psychological distance from its viewers and their everyday reality. When the auratic work is available to sight, viewers travel to it; the work does not travel to the viewer. According to Benjamin, all these qualities are threatened by the powers of technological reproduction, both in terms of what that technology does to traditional forms of art and in the new art forms it makes possible. But, as Benjamin makes clear, the power of technological reproduction which threatens the auratic work of art is "a symptomatic process whose significance points beyond the realm of art" (Benjamin 1973: 223). The crisis of value identified by Benjamin finds both an anticipation and a resonance in the anxieties of Heidegger, Jaspers, Leavis, Arnold, and Newman. The auratic university, like its equivalent in the sphere of art, is embedded in the authority of tradition. Its value resides in its metaphoric, or literal, distance from what is around it. It gives a monumental value to the past, and is threatened by the same technological and social changes that undermine the auratic work of art: "It [the contemporary decay of aura] rests on two circumstances, both of which are related to the increasing significance of the masses in contemporary life. Namely, the desire of contemporary masses to bring things 'closer' spatially and humanly, which is just as ardent as their bent toward overcoming the uniqueness of every reality by accepting its reproduction" (Benjamin 1973: 225).

The desire for closeness and the acceptance of reproduction are intimately linked. A Picasso on a postcard can be held in a hand or be incorporated into a domestic collage of reproductions. Television brings distant events into the "close" space of the sitting room. The dissolution of the boundaries of the unique event or object this entails has consequences for the value of time, as another of Benjamin's sentences makes clear: "Uniqueness and permanence are as closely linked . . . as are transitoriness and reproducibility" (1973: 225). This, in turn, illuminates the economy of knowledge proposed in my chosen texts about the university. Heidegger's return to the "beginning" in the "setting out of Greek philosophy," Leavis's "wisdom older than modern civilisation," and Arnold's aptly named "touchstones" assert the value of a knowledge which is at once unique and permanent (Arnold 1888: 17). Its uniqueness and permanence, in the prolonged crisis of modernity, depends upon its preservation and transmission within the milieu of the auratic university.

What is at issue here is something clearly more complex than a simple rejection of technology. But technology, equally clearly, exists outside the charmed circle created by the figures of tradition, unity, the elite, and the homosocial society. Discursively placed on the outside of the university, or in some uneasy intermediate zone, technology poses a risk that its incorporation will destroy the body of the host. If we follow the arguments of a more recently published text, Jean-François Lyotard's *The Postmodern Condition: A Report on Knowledge*, it may well appear that this is precisely what has happened.

The Postmodern Condition may be a text that is now worn out by overuse. It has been a source or focus for some stock ideas about postmodernism. But, like the texts discussed earlier, it is also about the idea of the university. The first hint comes in Lyotard's introduction, where he links together the by-now-familiar postmodern "incredulity towards metanarratives" with "the crisis of metaphysical philosophy and of the university institution which in the past relied on it" (Lyotard 1984: xxiv). This crisis is a consequence of a new economy of knowledge which has been brought about by sciences of language and code, the invention of "intelligent" machines, and digitalization of information. This produces a research culture oriented towards questions of the complex ordering, transmission, and transformation of information (genetics and neuroscience, for example). It produces an educational culture informed by a new kind of machine power: "the miniaturization and commercialization of machines is already changing the way in which learning is acquired, classified, made available and exploited" (1984: 4). In this environment, the survival of knowledge depends upon its translation into "quantities of information" (1984: 4). Or, to make a blunt paraphrase of Lyotard's argument, knowledge that cannot be stored on a computer won't count.

Lyotard traces the effects of this new economy of knowledge upon the traditional or auratic university. These can be briefly summarized in relation to the four key terms or figures of tradition, the unity of knowledge, the creation of a ruling elite, and homosociality. It hastens the obsolescence of the principle of *Bildung*, the idea that the "acquisition of knowledge is indissociable from the training of . . . minds, or even of individuals" (1984: 4). This in effect undermines the authority of tradition insofar as a crucial realization of the principle of *Bildung* occurred through a student's encounter with a wisdom drawn from the past. It was this kind of knowledge that forged the link between what you know and who you are. Similarly, the university's claim to be the locus of a unity of knowledge is abandoned in the face of what Lyotard describes as "a multiplication in methods of argumentation and a rising complexity in the process of establishing proof" (1984: 41). This "multiplication" produces an idea of knowledge as a proliferating and heterogeneous set of language games, each with its own procedures for establishing validity. Hence the development of inquiry is now thought of in terms of the analogy of a move in a game. These can be moves within what is accepted as the rules of the game, or they can be moves which establish a new game. The university's role in the creation of a ruling elite has also undergone significant transformation. The functional requirements of a system have replaced elevated claims to educate the shapers of national destiny. These requirements include training both for traditional professions (law, medicine) and for the new (systems engineering, organizational management, biotechnology). In addition, universities become the gathering places for young people who would otherwise be registered as unemployed. Their situation is ambivalent. Like their professionally trained counterparts they can acquire skills which will prepare them for work in the media or the educational system. But Lyotard regards them as the first representatives of a new kind of student who makes use of the university as a resource for continuing education. The traditional timing of the relation between study and economic activity changes as does the student's relation to knowledge:

Knowledge will no longer be transmitted *en bloc*, once and for all, to young people before their entry into the workforce: rather it is and will be served "à la carte" to adults who are either already working or expect to be, for the purpose of improving their skills and chances of promotion, but also to help them acquire information, languages, and language games allowing them both to widen their occupational horizons and to articulate their technical and ethical experience. (Lyotard 1984: 49)

Hence the university's generational shape is altered. It is no longer predominately a place where the older initiate the younger in the wisdom of tradition, but an intellectual service industry adapted to the needs of its different clients. And this change is accompanied by another. The university ceases to be a homosocial community. This is not to argue that it then becomes an order dedicated to the interests of women in the way it once was to the interests of men. The performativity criterion, which constantly seeks an "optimization of the global relationship between input and output," is indifferent to gender (Lyotard 1984: 11). The kinds of knowledge and skill required do not depend upon the maintenance of a bond among men.

If the traditional time of education changes, so does the sense of the university as a place, or place apart. The mystique of place plays a role in what I have called the auratic university. Matthew Arnold invokes this in his account of Oxford in *Culture and Anarchy*: "Yet we in Oxford, brought up amidst the beauty and sweetness of that beautiful place, have not failed to seize one truth—the truth that beauty and sweetness are essential characters of a complete human perfection. When I insist on this, I am all in the faith and tradition of Oxford" (Arnold 1993: 73).

A similar, if more austerely phrased, fascination with place can be found in F. R. Leavis's love/hate relation with Cambridge as a university at once uniquely qualified to realize his ideal of the "English School" and to prevent it. The mystique which unites spirit and matter, values and architecture, in this way carries within it the trace of a material circumstance, the creation of the university library. In the medieval period the physical scarcity of books required the creation of institutions where they could be preserved, consulted, and created. This technology of information storage and retrieval required the student to travel to the source of knowledge. The invention of print and then of information technology has reversed this process. Knowledge can travel to its user rather than the other way around. These technological changes do not in and of themselves determine one particular cultural result. But they do and will continue to have consequences for the cultural perception of the university as a physical place. These will probably include an increasing pressure to distinguish between those kinds of learning that require human contact and those that do not. Catastrophe addicts are already vying with optimistic visionaries about the significance of these changes for a human future. What is certain is that "going to a university" will be increasingly a technologically virtual event as well as a physically actual event.

As Lyotard makes clear, the techno-university is just one player in the new economy of knowledge. Digital technologies provide new forms of information storage, retrieval, and manipulation. Echoing Marx's analysis of the commodity form, Lyotard argues that these technological changes facilitate a new market in knowledge: "Knowledge is and will be produced in order to be sold, it is and will be consumed in order to be valorised in a new production: in both cases the goal is exchange. . . . Knowledge in the form of an informational commodity indispensable to productive power is already, and will continue to be, a major—perhaps the major—stake in the world-wide competition for power" (Lyotard 1984: 4–5).

This gives a dramatic, perhaps melodramatic, overview of the transformation of knowledge by technology. The apodictic terseness of Lyotard's sentences derives from a critical confrontation with two nineteenth-century "illusions": the speculative idealism which sees knowledge as a subject in itself with its own laws of development, uncontaminated by national or global economic imperatives; and the humanism which maintains the possibility of a knowledge dedicated to the general human good, a thinking that is ethically distanced from particular ideological or political interests. Ironically, capitalism has worked more effectively than a Marxist ideological critique in undermining the credibility of either of these two stories about the growth and purpose of knowledge. Technological change and market forces are always at least one step ahead of the critical intellectual.

It may be that in famously announcing the end of historical master-narratives—exemplified by stories about the growth of knowledge, the triumph of the proletariat, or the emancipation of humanity—Lyotard is compulsively attracted to master narratives of his own, including stories about the commodification of knowledge and the emergence of a global politics with knowledge power as its principal stake. Where his argument does seem prescient is in its recognition of the new subjects and locations of knowledge associated with digital technologies. Knowledge machines are not the preserve of a technological elite. They are part of popular culture. Evidence for this includes the growth of computer supermarkets; the proliferation of magazines devoted to different aspects of computer use; the elaborate information mosaic of the Internet, where you can, according to taste, and among many other things, find out about the latest developments in astronomy, consult the European Railway schedule, join in the musings of Pynchon freaks, or read Shakespeare.

The cultural implications of these changes are far too complex and various to be discussed in any detail here. But two points are worth noting. One is that we may be witnessing a significant transformation in the identity of contemporary popular culture, one that moves away from a focus on escapism or subcultures or consumerism to a fascination with expertise, games, and risk. A premium is placed on certain kinds of intellectual skill: the ability to anticipate moves in a game, for example, or to communicate information effectively on the Internet. The second is that these developments can constitute another culture of education. A recent advertising campaign for Microsoft Encarta provides a telling example. A series of double-page advertisements play variations on the same theme of the intellectually precocious child. Informed by Microsoft Encarta, children now demand bedtime stories about Sartre and existentialism instead of Goldilocks and the Three Bears. On one page, two children look out with determined smartness at the reader. On the other page, the text of the advertisement simulates the children's collective voice:

We click the mouse and we hear Martin Luther King Jr. or Fidel Castro speak. (Castro is sort of hard to understand.) We can see the Berlin Wall being torn down or the propagation of a nerve impulse. We can rock out to Belgian guitarist Django Reinhardt or Classical Patt Waing of Burma. Alas (a word we learned from our Microsoft Bookshelf reference library), if we told you every single great thing Encarta does, we'd be up all night and there'd be no time for Dad's bedtime stories about Sartre and the existentialists. (*Wired*, U.K. edition, June 1995: 12–13)

The basic organization of this text may seem simple enough. Behind the child's voice is the voice of a high-tech corporation telling us, in case we didn't know, that Microsoft Encarta is a multimedia encyclopedia, combining the resources of print with sound recording and moving images. Through the technology a world of knowledge is presented to the child which cuts across the traditional disciplines of history, politics, biology, and philosophy. Knowledge is acquired according to curiosity, not according to the requirements of a discipline. The thematics of Rousseau are displaced into the world of interactive technology. The notion that some kinds of knowledge are difficult, beyond the comprehension of a child, is dissolved in a jokey text which turns existentialism into an intellectually sophisticated bedtime story.

The advertisement for Microsoft Encarta coyly unsettles two kinds of assumptions about education and its institutional forms. One kind is temporal, having to do with when someone is supposed to know what they know. The very idea of a curriculum is based upon an order which establishes a gradation of knowledge over time, discriminating between what is basic and advanced, simple and complex, general and special. The second is spatial, having to do with where learning occurs. In the world of the advertisement, and in the land of knowledge machines, the learning that counts is as likely to occur in the home as it is at school. The child's knowledge, born out of human/machine interactions, produces new moves in the game of the relations between children and parents. It is this game-playing quality in the whole text of the advertisement that establishes the oscillation between lighthearted family fun and something more threatening, the demands of a technologically mutated humanity which works off the resources of machine knowledge. The advanced student speaks out of the body of an eleven-year-old child in a cute version of American English.

This example is no more than a minor episode in the cultural imagination of the "new" technologies. What it indicates can be applied, *mutatis mutandis*, to the situation of universities, caught uneasily between the great commercial power of knowledge corporations and an exponential growth in the informal cultures of learning. The question I want to take up in conclusion is what the place of cultural studies or analysis might be in such a conjuncture.

Lyotard's *Postmodern Condition* suggests one possibility. Its style and mode of argument place it between the blunt prescriptions of the OECD reports quoted at the beginning of this paper and the anxious defense of tradition and the unity of knowledge conducted by Heidegger, Leavis, and

others. On the one hand Lyotard accepts the reality of the instrumental-
ization of knowledge, the integration of science and economic production,
and the emergence of knowledge industries which underpin the arguments of the OECD reports. He acknowledges the effective power of the
performativity criterion which seeks to increase the efficiency of a system
by minimizing inputs and maximizing outputs. Paradoxically, this can be
realized not just by the use of a means-end rationality or by the repetition
of previous examples of successful performance, but by something that
Lyotard calls "imagination," the capacity to connect together "series of
data that were previously held to be independent" (Lyotard 1984: 52). In
this view performativity requires that knowledge be put into new configurations and hence that education include "training in all of the procedures
that can increase one's ability to connect the fields jealously guarded from
one another by the traditional organization of knowledge" (1984: 52).

Lyotard's argument would seem to provide a rationale for cultural
studies or cultural analysis which accords with the requirements of performativity: cultural studies as the subject of imagination, the art of connecting together what had previously been held separate, the mobile "in
between" driving the traditional disciplines forward. However, this bright-
eyed view does not acknowledge another story about performativity that
Lyotard tells, a story that may constitute an aporetic moment in the argument of *The Postmodern Condition*. Performativity carries a kind of violence within it. It rewards any moves which facilitate the efficiency of the
system according to measures of input and output. It has a momentum
which does not serve human interests in any self-evident way:

> The system seems to be a vanguard machine dragging humanity after it, de-
> humanizing it in order to rehumanize it at a different level of normative capacity.
> The technocrats declare that they cannot trust what society designates as its
> needs; they "know" that society cannot know its own needs since they are not
> variables independent of the new technologies. Such is the arrogance of the deci-
> sion makers—and their blindness. (1984: 63)

Lyotard's sentences move rapidly from the impersonality of the system to a characterization of those who claim to know the imperatives of
its development. In the sphere of research this produces a conflict between the requirements of performativity and the energies of what Lyotard
names "paralogy," those moves in the game of inquiry which put estab-

lished ways of doing things in question. The conflict between disruptions of consensus and the dictates of efficient performance produces a version of terror:

Countless scientists have seen their "move" ignored or repressed, sometimes for decades, because it too abruptly destabilised the accepted positions. . . . The stronger the "move," the more likely it is to be denied the minimum precisely because it changes the rules of the game upon which consensus had been based. But when the institution of knowledge functions in this manner, it is acting like an ordinary power centre whose behaviour is governed by the principle of homeostasis.

Such behaviour is terrorist. . . . By terror I mean the efficiency gained by eliminating, or threatening to eliminate, a player from the language game one shares with him. He is silenced or consents, not because he has been refuted, but because his ability to participate has been threatened. (1984: 63–64)

The immediate focus of Lyotard's remarks is on the natural and technological sciences, and, as such, may seem to have little relevance to work in cultural studies. But the process of open inquiry he evokes is not confined to the sciences. Intellectual communities judge statements according to the quality of argumentation which supports them, or according to their generative power (an idea is good because it triggers other ideas). None of these procedures are automatically in line with the demands of performativity.

In *The Postmodern Condition* Lyotard argues that the very sciences which the system requires to improve performance can, in their basic procedures, resist this requirement. The question of a site of resistance or sacrifice or freedom is raised in other forms elsewhere in his work, and in ways which return to the relation of culture to technology. A number of essays in Lyotard's *The Inhuman* take up this theme, but this time under the sign of Kant and Freud rather than Wittgenstein. Two related examples, both concerning the work of memory, are pertinent to any thinking about cultural studies. The first, from the essay "Rewriting Modernity," deepens the idea of imagination presented in *The Postmodern Condition* as the "capacity to articulate what is separate." This is thought again by Lyotard in relation to Freud's stress on "freely floating attention" in the analyst's relation to the utterances of the patient. A link is then made to Kant's *Critique of Judgment* and the account given there of aesthetic imagination as an activity set apart from "any empirical or cognitive interest":[3]

Kant comes round to concluding the imagination gives the mind "a lot to think," a lot more than does the conceptual work of the understanding . . . —the aesthetic grasp of forms is only possible if one gives up all pretension to master time through a conceptual synthesis. For what is in play here is not the "recognition" of the given . . . but the ability to let things come as they present themselves. (Lyotard 1988: 32)

The works of Proust, Benjamin, and Montaigne are offered as instances of this activity of imagination, a kind of thinking and remembering which waits upon what is to come or has past without seeking to subsume it under a concept or assess it according to a goal-oriented research project.

The second example, from Lyotard's essay "*Logos* and *Techne*, or Telegraphy," distinguishes three different relations to the past: habit, remembering, and anamnesis. Each is implicated in technology as a condition of its existence because each requires a mode of inscription. Inscription creates the possibility of a collective understanding. It also permits the conservation and production of "the sign of the past event" (1988: 48).

Habit is the economic repetition of a type of behavior, economic because, once habitual, the behavior can be performed with less expenditure of mental or physical energy. It is a fundamental form of organization which has biological (genetic) as well as cultural instances. It corresponds to an understanding of culture as "nebulae of habits whose continuing action on the individuals who are their elements is looked after by these stable energetic set-ups that contemporary anthropology calls structures" (1988: 49). Habits, in this view, are principles of conservation. Within a culture they take the form of laws governing marriage, barter, and appropriate speech. Habit is the mode of inscribing the past in the present as present. Its unconscious formula is "This is the way it has always been done; there is no other."

Remembering, by contrast, summons the past as past. It brings the past to a reflective awareness and hence to an awareness of its difference to the present. And, according to Lyotard, this presupposes a "language-memory" with "properties unknown to habit": "the denotation of what it retains (thanks to its symbolic transcription), recursivity (the combinations of signs are innumerable, starting from simple generative rules, its 'grammar'), and self-reference (language signs can be denoted by language-signs: metalanguage)" (1988: 52).

The form of inscription which is "language-memory" permits the emergence of a form of critical reflection, based not simply upon an acknowledgment of the difference between the past and the present, but upon the questionable nature of rules. One way of putting things implies another which is excluded. Hence, according to Lyotard, the revelation of "what is finite in every inscription," and hence, too, the study of culture as a history of critical reason, of the emergence of science, of the elaboration and complication of systems (1988: 52).

Lyotard's third term, anamnesis, corresponds to the "freely floating attention" of the psychoanalyst or the free association of the aesthetic imagination. It is not so much a remembering of what has been forgotten as a forgetting of what has been remembered. Lyotard refers to it as a passing beyond or, in Freudian terms, a working through of existing syntheses of knowledge and memory, but not in the name of a new synthesis. It exists at the limit point of technology, "a letting work in a free floating way what passes." Its mode of inscription is writing, in that special French sense explored by Derrida and others.[4] In Lyotard's text the nature of this writing is hinted at in the following way: "The only thing I can see that can bear comparison with this a-technical or a-technological rule is writing, itself an anamnesis of what has not been inscribed. For it offers to inscription the white of the paper, blank like the neutrality of the analytic ear" (1988: 56).

It is, of course, hard to place this practice in terms of a version of the study of culture and its past. It is, if anything, cultural studies as the practice of *memoire involontaire*, a practice not bound by any research protocols or requirements of conceptual synthesis, and, hence, without a place in any academic institution.

Three relations to the past, three implications for what cultural studies might or might not be, but also a continuing tension about technology. Lyotard's arguments in *The Inhuman* accept the centrality of technology as a mode of inscription within what makes human culture human, but then repeatedly return to an anxiety about the effects of the new technologies. In particular, aesthetic imagination seems at risk. According to Lyotard, the new technologies produce a kind of writing or rewriting that erases "all traces left in the text by unexpected and 'fantasy' associations" (1988: 34). Similarly, with anamnesis, there is a risk that its resistance to "clever programmes and fat telegrams" will be overridden by the power of the new technologies to impose new syntheses (1988: 57). Anamnesis is not browsing data-bases.

What I find in both *The Postmodern Condition* and *The Inhuman* is a question about the institutional shape and function of the techno-university. Although the techno-university is assimilated to the requirements of performativity and driven by the latest turn in the relations between the human and the inhuman provoked by the new technologies, the question nonetheless persists of a resistance to these drives that might be located within the techno-university itself. This may take the form of an ethic of intellectual inquiry or of a mode of aesthetic contemplation. What is at stake here is not the preservation of a tradition. It is the defense of a practice which resists the imperatives of speed, of rapid turnover, and of product innovation within the knowledge industries.

I have suggested some of the implications this might have for a working through of what cultural studies is or might be. One final comment needs to be made concerning the historical formation of cultural studies in Britain. It is a commonplace that cultural studies is an interdisciplinary subject drawing variously on the resources of more established academic disciplines. This produces a chronic and, it seems to me, highly productive uncertainty about its identity. But its eccentricity does not stop there. At least in Britain the energy of cultural studies has derived from its place on the boundary between the university as an institution and emergent forms of knowledge and experience that lie beyond it. The early texts of cultural studies—Richard Hoggart's *The Uses of Literacy*, Raymond Williams's *Culture and Society*, E. P. Thompson's *The Making of the English Working Class*—all in their different ways had the effect of bringing the working class as subjects of culture into an institution historically dedicated to either ignoring that subjectivity and that culture or treating it as an object of historical or sociological inquiry. It is no accident that this happened at a moment in British history when the form of the political state was changing in a way that acknowledged the working class as something like a subject with legitimate interests, albeit under the problematic aegis of welfare reform. A similar pattern can be detected in subsequent waves of interest in cultural studies: in feminist critique, for example, or the affirmation of popular tastes and pleasures, or the attention to postcolonial cultures. In each case what was happening in cultural studies within universities corresponded to social or political movements outside them. And those movements were and still are impacting upon universities in other ways, most notably in the changing social composition of those who look upon universities as a resource and not as an exclusion zone.

Perhaps this interpretation does no more than revisit the fact that when cultural studies was first instituted in British universities it was in the form of a center for *contemporary* cultural studies. Initially this dedication to what is called the contemporary set cultural studies apart from the humanist disciplines, whose primary orientation was to the past, just as its research methods set it apart from subjects like sociology or economics, which laid rival claims to a knowledge of what is happening now. But the sensitivity of cultural studies towards whatever was contemporary necessarily called for a rethinking of the past, whether as allegory, genealogy, or materialist critique. The danger in this, it seems to me, is that cultural studies will become just another nostalgic or monumentalizing treatment of the past. As it becomes academically settled, it will lose the energies that come from being on a boundary, which, as Heidegger has reminded us, is not just a place "at which something stops but . . . that from which *something begins its presencing*" (Heidegger 1978: 332).

What I think is coming to presence now in the boundary that is cultural studies is technology as a major form of the contemporary. This does not of course mean that the subject has been ignored until now. There have been detailed historical studies of the different organizations of technological invention in different cultures.[5] In the early work of cultural studies in Britain technological development was depicted in the form of the monstrous (Hoggart) or became the occasion of a critique of "technological determinism" (Williams).[6] Taken together, the two positions constitute a typical antinomy in thinking about technology: either what threatens to enslave or reduce the human, or that which, properly thought, can become an instrument of human will. The work, or working through, I have in mind goes beyond this antinomy but only by rethinking its terms: technology as neither master nor slave, not external to the human but implicated within it. Perhaps the French philosopher Bernard Stiegler provides us with an appropriate closing statement: "The *what* invents the *who* just as much as it is invented by it."[7]

DOUBLE AFTERWORDS

THIS VOLUME has been designed to promote dialogue. Just as the volume opened with a double-voiced, dialogical preface, the ending has to be double-voiced, and in two distinct ways. There are two afterwords, and each of these addresses are voices from "the field," from the academy and the market that sustains its productions. William Germano, the influential publisher at Routledge who, together with other publishers, greatly contributed to the current availability if not the very existence of cultural studies, has some words of caution for all of us engaged in cultural analysis. It is important to keep in mind that his voice here also represents the wish and need of cultural analysis to connect, more consistently than has traditionally been the case, to the "real world out there" in which we do the work that we do.

But on another level, too, Germano and his colleagues have also helped to bridge the gaps. By publishing so actively the kind of work that traditional disciplines were less likely to fathom, they have made this work visible and accessible to others, such as nonacademics working in cultural activities who are interested in an analytical perspective. If the gap between art and art history, literature and literary studies, and so on, has only deepened and widened ever since the inception of the academic study of the art, then a sharp turn is noticeable, as artists become theory-minded and show an interest in the visions developed in cultural studies, which are sometimes acted out in public debates and joint projects. The visibility of books committed to integrative endeavors in the humanities has been a decisive factor in this change.

Jonathan Culler, finally, writes here as "the voice of the profession," again in two distinct ways. As editor of a leading journal in cultural analysis, *Diacritics*, he represents another reality with which cultural analysis has to reckon, another channel in which its ideas and views can be made public. But as one of the "professors of English and comp. lit." who has lived through the developments from disciplinary to interdisciplinary study and followed, and contributed to, cultural studies without renouncing literary studies per se, Culler is in a good position to assess what the relations between this particular tradition and this paticular innovation are. If his position provokes disagreement, he asked for it; if it doesn't, he asked for that as well. Either way, at the end of the volume he opens several doors. Nothing can be more helpful than something that makes you think about what a volume like this one ought to make you think about: where do we take it from here?

—M.B.

Why Interdisciplinarity Isn't Enough

William P. Germano

Something is afoot in the discipline wars. Ever since that moment, sometime after his death, when Dr. Freud became a tenured member of the English Department, the fences between and among disciplines have been unreliable guides to the boundaries of meaning. Academic geographies have become as unstable as political maps. For publishers, this has meant a need simultaneously to watch the decline or alteration of established fields and to observe—with caution, with pleasure—the spontaneous emergence of new subfields, or renegade antifields, or transhistorical concentrations, each laying claim to the attention of readers and markets.

Take these exemplary terms: theory, women's studies, gay studies, cultural studies, interdisciplinary studies. Each has been a figure standing against the ground of traditional organizations of knowledge. In fact, each of these popular moves has been claimed as the ground itself. But if these fields exist, where? and who's in them?

Scholars and scholarly publishers alike are deeply enmeshed in these questions. But for publishers, the issue is not a rarefied one of epistemology: books must be selected, contracts must be offered, investments must pay off. Or else. Publishers and writers alike may be, as Stanley Aronowitz puts it, "cultural workers," but we do our work in different ways.

It is tempting to state flatly that a publisher's job is to move ideas to markets. Even in our post-Gutenbergian era there's still much truth in this. Our task is made more complicated by the Internet's rise to power, but the function we perform may not really have changed. I prefer, however, to suggest that the publisher *mediates*: authors and booksellers and readers and teachers and students are the key terms, but libraries, book wholesalers, and review media are all indispensable. And for any editor, one of the principle mediations is between an author's desires and that author's own best interests (does that history of lampshades really need to be eight hundred pages long? are the color illustrations in that monograph on Nietzsche absolutely necessary?). This mediation, in its various forms, is the cultural work that publishers do. We can help make books better, shaping and directing them, packaging them for audiences that we believe exist (we're not always right about this, of course), and promoting them responsibly and effectively. On one level, our work is nothing more than enlightened interference. But if the publisher is at all motivated to work in "that world of ideas bound to the social," the result can be deeply gratifying. Some publishers want to change the world at least as much as do the authors they present.

Before anything else, however, we must choose the books we wish to publish: fresh, invigorating, hot, useful, compendious, necessary, delicious, succinct, lucid, multilayered, cool books, books that must be brought to light for teaching, for research, for pleasure. And in making the choice of what to publish, we listen carefully to what the author is trying to say, to whom, and in what form. *The discipline within which a scholarly book is written is its principal form.*

Publishers think about markets. And on the rare occasions when they sleep, they even dream about markets. Broadly speaking, *all publishing is market driven*. This accounts for those heady staples of bestseller lists — thrillers, celebrity biographies, and pop psychology. *But scholarly publishing is discipline driven.* The canonical disciplines are still the most important guides to how knowledge is organized, yet new fields do take their place. It took a long time for booksellers in America to identify theory as something worthy of a section in the bookstore, but once a student could get an advanced degree in theory, it seemed that the battle was won. Cultural studies now follows a similar path. Sports and cigarettes, the media and the pulpit, rap and Elvis, fat and hunger, dogs, drag balls, gas stations

—objects and obsessions, unknown archives, the invisible but obvious, a soupçon of politics, a double helping of the everyday. Cultural studies embraces them all and makes possible new inventories, new histories, new sets of relations between areas of experience. Cultural studies mediates.

Yet even in these two famously visible areas, an editor repeatedly gives voice to the explanation "It isn't really about anything. It's theory. And it will sell to the theory crowd" or "I know the historians won't like it, but it isn't really history, it's cultural studies." When a scholarly work is written against the disciplinary grain, booksellers—and publishers—become very nervous.

Publishers think about markets. But how do books get there? The process is not difficult to summarize: After the manuscript has been delivered to and accepted by the publisher, editing and design begin. At the same time, descriptive copy is written for a trade catalogue, the signal purpose of which is to persuade booksellers to order the book in question. Books written within a specific discipline are the easiest to categorize. While the market may be tiny for a study of Rameau, the bookseller knows whether or not the shop has a music section.

When books are written outside a single discipline, they generally fall into three types. The first is the work of theory, in itself often a bookstore category. The second describes certain general trade books. In these first two cases, the bookseller knows whether or not the book fits the store ("I sell theory, and I will buy two copies; I think this general-interest book will appeal broadly, and I will buy twenty"). The third case is the scholarly work that claims membership in more than one discipline, for example, art and literature of the Spanish Baroque, or a transnational study of popular culture among immigrant populations. Here at the interdisciplinary moment, the bookseller must make hard choices: "Where do I put it? Is its audience the sum of the disciplines or only the intersection of them? Why should I risk placing one copy in each section of my store when I could stock other more clearly focused titles?" The problem of promoting interdisciplinary work—what some publishers call crossover titles—is similarly fraught. Can a publisher afford to promote a work partly written for an audience in art history, partly for an audience in Russian politics, and partly for an audience in religion? For many, indeed for most publishers, the answer is a maybe—sliding quickly into a no. Work that ranges across several fields requires considerable resources to see it published well. Bringing disciplines together may be exhilarating for the writer, but it may have its drawbacks.

Why does anyone engage in interdisciplinary work? What after all is interdisciplinarity? And how would we know it if we saw it? It's tempting to place "interdisciplinarity" within that class of concepts, of which pornography is certainly the most familiar, that resists definition but that everyone agrees they will know when they see it.

The vantage of a publisher—particularly a publisher of cultural studies—offers some empirical evidence that not one but a jumble of definitions are in play. Here are a few, drawn from thousands of manuscript proposals I've encountered:

1. An interdisciplinary work links my field with someone else's field.

2. An interdisciplinary work is one in which theory is brought to bear in my resolutely untheoretical discipline.

3. An interdisciplinary work performs simultaneously in more than two fields of knowledge, and is situated comfortably in neither.

4. An interdisciplinary work is radically dislocated from any recognizable academic geography. Its alienation from traditional fields of knowledge is the principal sign of its success.

5. An interdisciplinary work is anything outside art history that requires pictures.

If none of these definitions is adequate, each makes a point. Whatever interdisciplinarity is about, its practice is, to invoke with gentle irony a term so often used in scholarly discourse, "transgressive." But to quote the most urbane of twentieth-century philosophers, Professor Cole Porter, who might have asked of interdisciplinarity (but didn't), "Is it an earthquake, or is it a shock?"

Here I need to raise a key point: the terms "interdisciplinary studies" and "cultural studies" do not necessarily identify the same subject. "Cultural studies" and "interdisciplinarity" are terms whose working definitions embrace many similar elements, but their usages—and I'm speaking here of the Anglo-American context only because that's the one with which I'm familiar—invoke disparate intentions. Publishers engaged in cultural studies would not have any difficulty producing a definition of it. The term "cultural studies" implicates a set of concerns and materials that includes feminism, race, postcoloniality, queer studies, television and media studies, the economies of everyday life, cyberculture, and popular writing, as well as their political and social conditions. And fortunately for author and publisher alike, most American booksellers will recognize cultural studies, even as its definition seems to be expanding, and becoming fuzzier, season after season.

But out in the marketplace, the label "interdisciplinary studies" is another matter. The same bookseller who can welcome a cultural history of kissing, for example, may balk at what is described as an interdisciplinary study of kissing in nineteenth-century European art and literature. And of course, these may both describe the same book. The key difference is, I suspect, the presence of the word "history" in the phrase "cultural history"—it grounds and neutralizes what might otherwise seem facile. (We'll leave aside the problem of facile history, because there's plenty of that as well.)

Is interdisciplinarity getting a bum rap? What's wrong with interdisciplinarity anyway? At present, the interdisciplinary appears to be the high-culture loser in the high-low market wars. Some scholars would like to see cultural studies go away. Others would settle for a new definition of the term. But disciplines (and even antidisciplines) don't reconfigure themselves by fiat. Even publishers would find it difficult to define "cultural studies" so that it might embrace such artifacts as the Isenheim Altarpiece, or the *Tale of Genji*, or Balanchine's *Apollo*. It seems to me that interdisciplinarity takes shape somewhere outside the reach of cultural studies, beyond the arena of the popular and what American scholars refer to as "the political," and often in the aura of Great Works. Rightly or wrongly, the cultural-studies map takes a wide detour around the Great Works program.

The "interdisciplinary" work, on the other hand, isn't canon-shy. It depends upon, and appeals to, the idea of ideas in common.

When I say that interdisciplinarity is not enough, I mean two things: First, the term "interdisciplinary" is an insufficient description of what it is that's being done, and that its use may, at least in the context of

American publishing, have a negative effect on bookselling and thus the market. Second, "being interdisciplinary" is no guarantee of having something to say, or of reaching more readers. The fresh, the unanticipated, the courageous does not de facto have an audience. Creativity is a wonderful thing, but the market economy of ideas resists the interdisciplinary, perhaps more strongly than we realize. This conversation-stopping point ends many publisher-author discussions. "Dear Author: I marvel at the ingenuity of your project, and have seldom encountered so brilliant a mind. Unfortunately we cannot define with confidence a readership for your book." *Interdisciplinarity cannot guarantee that an audience exists.*

Is "*inter*disciplinarity" the wrong term? Others have suggested so. After all, what's *inter* about it? Does "multidisciplinarity," with its implied respect for the integrity of established fields, get us any further to the truth of practice? Does "transdisciplinarity," in which the scholar leaps over tall canons with a single bound, name the act at last? Anyone for "postdisciplinarity"? *Inter, trans, multi, cross, bi, post*: the language of academic writing repeatedly attempts to define a relation to fields of knowledge. Maybe we're between disciplines, like out-of-work musicians between gigs? Are we postdisciplinary? And if so, what do we know? Is our subject now some postdisciplinariness itself?

The problem of post-everythingness looms large for any academic publishing house. And here the problem of theory and its relation to interdisciplinarity comes into the picture. A generation ago, a force we came to call theory passed through the land, leaving in its wake wreckage and opportunity. Theory was a kind of mental urban-renewal project. And build we did.

Most works of theoretical scholarship, however much they have exhilarated us, assume that identity as a result of what are, after all, a rather limited number of explanations of how we know the world. Marx, Freud, Lacan, Derrida, Foucault, Spivak, Bhabha, Butler, Sedgwick—footnote champions all—come immediately to mind. Within this discourse, which I'll call industrial-strength theory, no subject matter is out of bounds. Because theory itself constitutes the bounds, it is the discipline transcendent, or has been for more than a generation. I'd be surprised if a scholar executing a set of Lacanian riffs on film noir, the history of plastic surgery, current ads for impotence treatments, and the plays of Tennessee

Williams would identify her project as interdisciplinary, when its subject would evidently be psychoanalytic criticism grounded in Lacanian theory. Strong theory tends to disguise the multiple locations of work. We fail to see its interdisciplinary scope because we're struggling so hard with the many adventures of the *objet petit a*. *Theory is a dominant genetic trait, interdisciplinarity a recessive one.*

In a widely read essay, Stephen Greenblatt announces that he "begins with a desire to speak with the dead." Does a similar compulsion motivate scholars who engage in interdisciplinary work? And who are the dead? Perhaps members of their own departments? Or of other departments? Or the general educated reader, always about to awake from slumber and storm the bookstores for the important new book? As a publisher, I begin with a desire to speak with the living. (As, of course, does Greenblatt.) But finding the living is not always easy, as marketing departments, or anyone who has ever scheduled a campus speaker, well know. Publishers, who may never before in our lifetimes have been under more pressure to justify intellectual work, take on books only where the living can be found quickly and economically.

What kind of interdisciplinary study would speak with the living? Would have a market? Work that is neither preciously specific nor random, but purposeful. Not defined by a rejection of disciplinary strengths, but building upon those strengths. I imagine an interdisciplinarity in which fields travel in order to reinvent their purpose, so that we might, in T. S. Eliot's phrase, "arrive where we started / And know the place for the first time." Interdisciplinary requires a goal and an audience, and cannot succeed if either is absent.

Working past disciplinary lines is a wonderful idea—a wonderful, dangerous, expensive idea. The fresh combinations of materials is exhilarating, as is the opportunity to speak to audiences who may never have suspected they shared a common interest. Cultural studies has shown that it can be made to work. And who cannot appreciate the not-so-secret triumph in harnessing big theory to interrogate the popular, the everyday, our working life of readymades? Cultural studies delights in restoring to our view materials that we never knew we didn't theorize about. And now we do.

Interdisciplinarity, too, can be restorative, and can produce books readers want. But scholars engaged in interdisciplinary work need to take a serious inventory of their own strengths, their knowledge bases, and the audiences for which they imagine they write. We publishers want you to write about what you know, not about what you don't.

What Is Cultural Studies?

Jonathan Culler

I propose to discuss some problems and issues concerning the nature of cultural studies, as it has emerged in the United States in particular. In the light of some of the papers collected here, I can now do this with a clearer sense of why cultural analysis is not cultural studies. Indeed, I suspect that distinguishing what it does from cultural studies will help ASCA to sustain and continue to develop its distinct identity.

William P. Germano tells us that cultural studies has achieved viability as a market in the United States and thus has come to count as a field—at least in American publishing and intellectual life. It is worth reflecting for a moment on what makes something count as a field, for cultural studies does not yet have much of an existence in institutional structures. So far as I know, there are very few departments of cultural studies and not many institutions where it is possible to take a B.A. or a Ph.D. in cultural studies. I agree with Bill Germano, though, that it is a field. Fields may have an institutional reality, but they have above all an imaginary existence, as fantasmatic objects with which people identify. Bookstores, journals, and especially publishers play a role here. By publishing and displaying exciting books under the rubric of cultural studies, they create the desire and the identifications that make the field a force to be reckoned with, even before it is realized in educational institutions. These same cultural agents helped to make "theory" a significant field, even though there remain to this day very few programs in theory or degrees in theory.

It is understandable that publishers would be attracted to the idea of cultural studies since this category enables them to avoid deciding whether a work should be placed under the heading of sociology or film theory or women's studies or literary criticism or all of the above. But despite the shelves in bookstores and the recent proliferation of introductions and anthologies, it is surprisingly difficult to work out what "cultural studies" means. Routledge's *Cultural Studies*, edited by Larry Grossberg, Cary Nelson, and Paula Treichler, begins by declaring that cultural studies is neither a field nor a method, for culture includes everything and can be studied by a vast range of methods. Cultural studies is "an interdisciplinary, transdisciplinary, and sometimes counter-disciplinary field that operates in the tension between its tendencies to embrace both a broad, anthropological and a more narrowly humanistic conception of culture" (1992: 4). This is a rather strange, grammatically convoluted statement: notice that it declines to say "the tension between the broad conception and the narrow conception," or even "the tension between the tendency to embrace the broad conception and the tendency to embrace the narrow conception," although that is what the sentence must mean. It avoids this, I dare say, because that would seem too much like a binary opposition and a choice, a situation of either/or. Eschewing a structure that would present the possibility of choice, the statement locates the field "in the tension between its tendencies to embrace both."

"Cultural Studies," the introduction continues, "is thus committed to the study of the entire range of a society's arts, beliefs, institutions, and communicative practices" (1992: 4). No question of choosing here. Often the point of cultural studies seems to be to resist any exclusion that definition might involve. Its defining principle is to resist exclusion on principle, as a matter of principle. As a result, it often seems as if the only positive claim is that whatever is studied and by whatever method, cultural studies should aim to make a political difference. Most of those who identify with cultural studies, whatever their approach, "see themselves not simply as scholars providing an account but as politically engaged participants" (1992: 5). "Cultural studies thus believes," Grossberg, Nelson and Treichler write, "that its own intellectual work is supposed to — can — make a difference" (1992: 6). Once again the ways this odd statement trips itself up may be revealing: cultural studies does not believe that its intellectual work *will* make a difference. That would be overweening, not to say naïve. It believes that its work "is supposed to" make a difference. But this is scarcely a credo to energize a field: "I believe that my work is *supposed to* make a difference" is less a rallying cry than an occasion for guilt and self-scrutiny. Perhaps sensing this, the editors insert a parenthetical "can" to supplement "is supposed to," but the distinguishing feature of cultural studies may well be the conviction that its work is supposed to make a political difference. It is as though the redemptive goals that have often animated work in the humanities have been retained by cultural studies, but the idea that such goals are linked either to a particular content (literature will make us whole again) or to a particular method (critique will demystify ideology and make change possible) has been abandoned. But a redemptive scenario that lacks either a distinctive content or a particular method for which claims could be made is scarcely plausible. A strange result indeed!

Culture is, on the one hand, the system of categories and assumptions that makes possible the activities and productions of a society and, on the other hand, the products themselves, so the reach of cultural studies is vast. But since meaning is based on difference, cultural studies in practice has gained its distinctiveness from the interest in popular or mass culture, as opposed to high cultural forms already being studied in universities. In the United States, identifying with cultural studies seems to mean resisting literary studies. Bill Germano notes that to do cultural studies means not to study canonical writers. This is not so true in the Netherlands, where I gather that the teaching of literature in secondary schools has been abandoned for ten years now (teachers are free to use whatever cultural materials they wish), so that literary studies may not be the orthodoxy against which cultural studies defines itself.

Now in Britain, where cultural studies began, the idea of studying popular culture—the habits and pastimes of the working and lower-middle classes, for example—had a political charge. As Jon Cook puts it in this volume, cultural studies was the relay of proletarian experience. In Britain, where the national cultural identity was linked to monuments of high culture—Shakespeare and the tradition of English literature, for example—the very fact of studying popular culture was an act of resistance, in a way that it isn't in the United States, where national identity has often been defined *against* high culture. Griselda Pollock notes in this volume that Jackson Pollock could be hailed as the great American painter because he departed in so many ways from the image of high culture. If we

take Mark Twain's *Huckleberry Finn* as the icon of American literature—
the work which does as much as any other to define Americanness—then
we need only recall the ending, where Huck Finn lights out for the territories because Aunt Sally wants to "sivilize" him. He seeks to escape civilized culture. High culture has not been part of the definition of national
identity in the United States. *Au contraire*, traditionally, the American is
the man on the run from culture. In the United States it is scarcely self-
evident that shunning high culture to study popular culture is a politically
radical or resistant gesture. On the contrary, it may involve the rendering
academic of mass culture more than the radicalizing of academic studies.
If this is so, then it is all the more important for cultural studies, as Jon
Cook suggests, to retain its nonacademic connections and to continue to
move back and forth across the boundaries of the university, if it is not to
make popular culture academic.

The origins of cultural studies in Britain are associated particularly
with the names of Raymond Williams and Richard Hoggart, the latter the
founder of the Birmingham Center for Cultural Studies. In 1980 Stuart
Hall, successor to Hoggart at Birmingham, published an article, "Cultural
Studies: Two Paradigms," contrasting the early model, associated with
Williams and Hoggart, which undertook to study popular culture as a
vital expression of the working class, with a later model—of Marxist structuralism—which studies mass culture as meanings imposed on society,
an oppressive ideological formation. The tension between these two options continues to animate cultural studies today: on the one hand, the
point of studying popular culture is to get in touch with what is important for the lives of ordinary people—their culture—as opposed to that of
aesthetes and professors; on the other, there is a strong impetus to show
how people are being constructed and manipulated by cultural forms.
There is considerable tension here—so much so that I find it tempting to
define the field of cultural studies by this tension (more pertinent than the
tension between the tendencies to embrace both the broad and narrow
conceptions of culture that Grossberg and his colleagues mention). Cultural studies dwells in the tension between, on the one hand, the analyst's
desire to analyze culture as a hegemonic imposition that alienates people
from their interests and creates the desires that they come to have and, on
the other hand, the analyst's wish to find in popular culture an authentic expression of value. If one takes this tension to define cultural studies,

then the central strand of cultural studies would be that which finds a way of negotiating this tension, most often these days by showing that people are able to use the cultural materials foisted upon them by capitalism and its media and entertainment industries in ways that constitute a kind of culture of their own. Popular culture is made from mass culture. Popular culture is made from cultural resources that are opposed to it and thus is a culture of struggle, a culture whose creativity consists in using the products of mass culture. It seems to me that one possibility is to define cultural studies as the negotiation of this tension. This, of course, would be a much narrower and more graspable project—indeed, so much so that it has the air of a project or particular line of argument rather than a field—but it would make it a great deal easier to decide what is cultural studies and what is not—what belongs instead to sociology or film studies or literary criticism—if that seemed important.

In addition to the tension between the critique of mass culture as ideology and the celebration of popular culture as resistance to the hegemony of capitalism, there is the larger uncertainty about whether cultural studies is supposed to study all culture, past as well as present, high as well as low, or whether it focuses on the present and the popular, in contradistinction to traditional forms of study. There is, of course, a great deal of historical writing which investigates the culture, broadly conceived, of past societies, to wit "the entire range of a society's arts, beliefs, institutions, and communicative practices" (Grossberg, Nelson, and Treichler 1992: 4). Indeed, it's hard to imagine any historical study that wouldn't qualify as cultural studies by this definition, but clearly assimilation to the traditional domain of history is not what denizens of cultural studies have in mind, so there must be some crucial distinguishing factor. Cultural *analysis*, it seems, would make the distinguishing factor the reflection on the constitution of the past, the reflection on our own implication in the object of analysis. There is also the key question of whether cultural studies is opposed to contemporary theory or, on the contrary, the concrete expression of contemporary theory. Some students who embrace cultural studies—particularly the study of historically marginalized cultures—see themselves as opposed to theory and as the champions of historical and cultural particularity. I am struck by the fact that Bill Germano accepts theory as one field and cultural studies as another even though his description of the modes of cultural studies—work engaged with race, gender,

postcoloniality, hybridity, feminism, queer theory, film, and cyberspace—
seems to adduce many theory-laden fields. It is clear that, even if the proponents of cultural studies identify against "theory," the majority of work
that presents itself as cultural studies is highly theorized—self-conscious
about and involved with theoretical and methodological questions—and
I suspect that in fact it is in the link with theory that the factor distinguishing cultural studies from historical studies might be found.

When I think about the relation between cultural studies and "high
theory," as it is sometimes called, especially by the partisans of cultural
studies who perhaps are seeking to distinguish themselves from theory in
the hope that this, at least, will give their field an identity, I am struck
by the idea that the difficulty of defining cultural studies is analogous to
the difficulty of defining what we call just "theory" for short. What is
theory? Well, what goes by the nickname "theory" in the United States is
sometimes called "literary theory" because of its links with departments
of literature, but it is certainly not theory of literature in the traditional
sense—accounts of the nature of literature, the distinctiveness of literary
language, and so on. Much of what is central to theory—the historical
and genealogical studies of Michel Foucault, the psychoanalytic theory
of Jacques Lacan, the deconstructive readings of philosophical texts by
Jacques Derrida, and so on—is only marginally concerned with literature.
Like cultural studies, theory is broad, amorphous, interdisciplinary. You
can imagine almost anything fitting in if it is done in an interesting way.
It is difficult to say that any particular discourse is in principle excluded
from theory because what makes something theory, it seems, is that it
is picked up as interesting and suggestive for people working outside the
discipline within which it arises. So discussions of perspective or of madness, of rubbish or tourism or prostitution, can all enter theory if they
seem to have implications, for people in other fields, for their thinking
about signification and the constitution of subjects. Indeed, if we ask what
so-called "theory" is the theory of, the answer can only be something like
signifying practices in general, the constitution of human subjects, and
so on—in short, something like culture, in the sense that it is given in
cultural studies. My second proposal, then, is that cultural studies is—or
should be conceived as—the general name for the activities of which what
we call "theory" for short is the theory. Cultural studies can be the study
of anything whatsoever, when it is made theoretically interesting. There is

therefore a need for a certain surprise, which is hard to theorize and, as the field grows older, hard to achieve.

If cultural studies is the practice of which what we call "theory" is the theory—and I think that it certainly makes sense—then the question becomes not one of the general relationship of cultural studies to theory but, rather, a question of the benefits and virtues of various theoretical discourses for the study of particular cultural practices and artifacts. I think that this would be a beneficial sort of debate, for too often these days in the United States, at least, argument about theoretical discourses or approaches is carried on not in relation to particular sorts of cultural practices but as an abstract evaluation which often appeals to general theoretical and especially political consequences. Approach A, it is claimed, does not grant enough agency to subjects, or approach B makes it difficult for people to convince themselves of the groundedness of their identities, and so on. And because this has been the focus of theoretical debate, there has been too little attention to whether particular theoretical orientations or discourses help to achieve convincing analytical results.

So far I have offered two hypotheses about the nature of cultural studies: the first, the narrow, is that cultural studies investigates how people make popular culture from mass culture; the second is that cultural studies is that practice of which what we call "theory," for short, is the theory. But when I think of my own work, a third hypothesis arises, to set alongside these other two. There are several instances in my book *Framing the Sign* where I am tempted to class what I have written as cultural studies rather than literary criticism or theory. The first is a chapter called "Literary Criticism and the American University," which attempts to analyze the imbrication of developments in criticism with the structures of professional life and to identify models that underlie and make possible this development (1988: 3–40). Then there are essays on junk and rubbish and on tourism, which, though using some discussions of these topics in literature, are not focused on literature but involve identifying structures that underlie the articulation of the social. For instance, in the chapter on rubbish, I am interested in the mechanisms for the establishment of value, in particular the interplay between two incompatible systems, the system of *transience* (things which have value when new and gradually lose it) and the system of *durables* (things presumed to have stable or even increasing value). Junk or rubbish is analyzed as the point of intersection and exchange between these two systems (1988: 168–82). In the discussion of tourism, I focus on the intelligibility of the world that emerges through the agency of the generally denigrated figure of the tourist, who not only seeks in unusually explicit fashion signs of Frenchness and so on, but also, in a dialectic crucial to modern life, tries to see something of the "real Holland," to get off the beaten track, as we say, and experience an authenticity defined in opposition to the explicitly touristic (1988: 153–67).

Now when I think about what it is that makes these essays seem cultural studies rather than something else—philosophy or sociology or history—I conclude that it is the attempt to identify the underlying structures, the powerful mechanisms at work in these cases. I am led to the hypothesis that cultural studies is (or should be) structuralism, that crucial enterprise which has been unfairly, in my view, shunted aside, especially in the United States, in that enthusiasm for the new that generates "post-structuralism." Since what we call "theory" is generally linked with *post*-structuralism, one might imagine that the inclination of people in cultural studies to dissociate themselves from theory might be the displaced form of a return to the analytical projects of structuralism, which sought to help us understand the mechanisms that produce meaning in social and cultural life.

I should add here that if cultural studies is structuralism, it would be a structuralism crucially informed by the work of Michel Foucault. Foucault claimed not to be a structuralist, but this was belied by his work: to study the discourses (such as those of sexuality) that construct the categories which they then treat as natural is a quintessentially structuralist project, constructed on the paradoxes of structuralism. (Language consists of signs but signs are the categories produced by languages, for example.) And the Foucauldian claim that power is not something one possesses but the name of a configuration of relations in a given state of society is a structuralist hypothesis of a classic sort.

I would also note that although post-structuralism caricatures structuralism as blindly scientistic, in fact structuralist works frequently display that move, which ASCA makes part of cultural analysis, of recognizing that your analysis is conditioned by your own place in the present and is thus involved in that which it seeks to analyze. So Lévi-Strauss, the arch-structuralist whom none ere called post-structuralist, concedes that his massive *Mythologiques* is a myth of mythology (1964: 14). Roland Barthes suggests that his breaking up of the text to identify five codes in *S/Z* is, finally, arbitrary (1970b: 20) or declares that "la littérature c'est ce qui s'enseigne. Un point. C'est tout" (1969: 170). Literature is not something existing out there which the critic studies; it is the product of that academic discursive practice in which he is himself engaged.

So this is my third hypothesis: cultural studies is really a disguised return to the uncompleted projects of structuralism, a return which highlights some aspects of structuralism that have been neglected. But I daresay that this hypothesis will be even less popular than the other two.

Why should cultural studies be the new growth area in the humanities? In a sense, its emergence at least in the United States seems a logical result of the extension of literary methods of analysis to a wide range of nonliterary objects and texts. But I want to conclude with a more general question about the emergence of cultural studies, developing some of the ideas of Bill Readings, a brilliant young critic at the University of Montreal, who was tragically killed in a plane crash in the autumn of 1994 and who would have been a most valuable participant in our discussions of cultural analysis. In *The University in Ruins*, a book he was revising at the time of his death, Readings argues that cultural studies is made possible by a recent shift in the governing idea of the university. This connects with Jon Cook's account here of the emergence of the techno-university and the mourning for several figures of thought connected with its predecessor. To put it most simply, Kant based the university on a single regulative principle, the principle of Reason. Humboldt and the German Idealists gave us the modern university by replacing the University of Reason with the University of Culture, an institution whose purpose was jointly teaching and research and which was given its *raison d'être* by the production and inculcation of national self-knowledge, the formation of educated citizens, imbued with a national culture. Here culture is the goal of the university: for instance, the reproduction of the man of culture instantiated in the professor—whence the possibility of such anecdotes as that of a dowager accosting an Oxford don during the first World War: "Young man, why aren't you in France fighting to defend civilization?" "Madam," came the reply, "I *am* the civilization they are fighting to defend."

It was this notion of the university, the University of Culture, that gave literary studies the centrality that philosophy had enjoyed in the University of Reason. Cardinal Newman wrote in *The Idea of a University*, "by great authors the many are drawn up into a unity, national character is fixed, a people speaks, the past and the future, the East and the West are brought into communication with one another" (1926: 193; quoted in Readings 1996: 77). Jon Cook speaks of the goal of the traditional university as that of promulgating the unity of knowledge. I think it was rather to represent it (little promulgation of unity took place): to represent it in its array of departments, in its degree courses, and so on.

With the globalization of capital, the importance of forming national subjects has diminished; the production of the cultured citizen, hitherto the goal of a liberal arts education, has become less central; and the University of Culture has given way, at least in the United States and the United Kingdom, to what Jon Cook calls the techno-university but what I would agree with Bill Readings in calling most simply the University of Excellence. The university has no particular goal, except to have its various parts functioning excellently—where excellence becomes a content-less measure permitting homogenization and bureaucratic control (1996: 21–43). All divisions of the university can be asked to demonstrate their excellence, and since this takes the form of ratings or rankings they are all rendered comparable, even if they engage in radically different sorts of activities—advising students, maintaining buildings, raising funds, teaching history. The techno-university, as described by Jon Cook, appears to have some specific goals, such as processing the largest number of students. The University of Excellence need have no such specific or demeaning goals but is free to strive for excellence without defining it. In practice, excellence is connected with professionalization: you are judged by your peers, which means that excellence is determined by how you are rated by others.

When culture is no longer the goal or purpose of the university, it can become an object of study among others. As Readings writes, "the human sciences can do what they like with culture, can do Cultural Studies, because culture no longer matters as an *idea* for the institution of the university" (1996: 91).

To flesh out this claim, we might say that literature (and to a lesser extent history and art history) was previously the site where culture could be observed, assimilated, studied (and of course there were debates about what precisely in literature was central to the production of cultured citizens). The rise of cultural studies is assisted by arguments that the notion of culture involved in taking literary study as the instrument of culture is elitist, and by recent analyses of the nationalist projects of literary studies. These have helped fuel the move to cultural studies, but cultural studies will not replace literary studies at the center of the university's idea of itself, first, because cultural studies is not based on a project of forming cultured citizens in a nonelitist way. Sometimes in the United States cultural studies is linked to the idea of forming a nonracist, nonhomophobic, multicultural citizenry, but generally this is not the impetus, both because the idea of forming a citizenry seems nationalist and totalizing and because practitioners of cultural studies think that their political intervention will occur at some other level or through some agency other than that of their students (they may believe "that their work is supposed to—can—make a difference" in other ways). The formation of citizens is no longer the project of the university. A few conservatives pretend to argue for the return to the cultivation of traditional subjects, but even they have given up the idea of a national culture as community and are willing to settle for something like what E. D. Hirsch in a best-selling book with this title calls "Cultural Literacy," common information. It is not that people need to have read certain works in order to be educated citizens: they must recognize their titles and other cultural references so that they can be the audience addressed by newspapers and the media. Culture as common information, of course, reinforces administrative authority: the authority of those who select, transmit, and test this information.

Now that the goal of the production of national subjects is no longer central, it is perfectly all right for academics in universities to analyze and to teach all sorts of cultural materials and practices. This is not necessarily subversive. It feeds right into the culture industry and even constitutes something like its exotic arm. The American press is amused by cultural studies and likes to run stories about academics writing about Madonna or cereal boxes. Cultural studies is a continuation of journalism on the one hand and, on the other, a contribution to the general disdain for academics, who are thought to make a complicated fuss about things that really should simply be consumed.

But cultural analysis is not cultural studies—that much I have learned. Cultural analysis is not fighting a battle against literary studies. It is not focused primarily on popular culture or on the present. But cultural analysis therefore needs something else to give it definition, and it finds this in a particular sort of theoretical engagement: its reflection on the way in which its own disciplinary and methodological standpoints shape the objects that it analyzes.

One could say, focusing on this element in particular, that cultural analysis is that kind of analysis of cultural production that constantly risks paralysis by reflecting on itself; it is that mode of analysis and presentation that is compelled to attempt to analyze itself, its own concepts and standpoint. Cultural analysis, thus, would be the site of the anxiety-ridden subject.

In the introduction to this volume, Mieke Bal suggests that the practice of museums might be taken as a general model for cultural analysis. One virtue of this suggestion is that it displaces the potentially paralyzing gesture of self-reflexivity into a feasible research project: the investigation of one's analytic activity as a social, institutional practice and as a form of exposition and presentation. This socializes the act of self-reflection, making some progress possible, though of course it does not avoid the final impossibility of accounting for yourself, of fully analyzing yourself analyzing. But instead of attempting to look inward and anxiously to seize one's assumptions, beliefs, and unspoken commitments as they flit past, one can attempt to examine the social practice in which one is participating.

There seems to me much to recommend the idea of taking the museum as paradigm and analyzing "apo-deictic" discourse, as Bal calls it, but I wonder whether the reflection on the historicity of one's discipline, standpoint, and apo-deictic practice shouldn't be part of *every* discipline, not something particular to or distinctive of cultural analysis. Surely literary studies, art history, sociology, and especially philosophy ought to do this too. But it may well be that at this moment it makes sense to gather the forces of self-reflexivity together in one place, under one capacious tent, or within the covers of one volume.

Cultural analysis—the site where the reflexivity that ought to characterize all disciplines takes place.

This gives cultural analysis a contingent historical identity, related to the particular structures of academic disciplines in a changing university, and allows it to become something else, as it surely will, if it communicates its self-reflexivity to other disciplines. In the meantime, producing a gathering of self-reflexivity certainly creates a lively school of analysis, one that can function, as Jon Cook suggests, as a site for imagination, and perhaps, more specifically, as a rendering permeable of the boundaries of the university—whether it is the University of Culture or the University of Excellence, or something in between, or, preferably, a University not yet imagined.

REFERENCE MATTER

Notes

BAL *Introduction*

1. I found this graffito on a wall in the Biltstraat in Utrecht, the Netherlands, near the beginning of the highway system that provides entrance and exit to the city, in the years that I taught there and passed it every day (1980–87). Just very recently I discovered it has finally and unfortunately been removed.

2. Regarding *apo-deik-numai*, see Nagy (1990: 217–20). Regarding the middle voice, see Barthes's *Le bruissement de la langue* (1984) and White 1992. For a more elaborate version of this argument, see Bal 1996.

3. Apostrophe as the essence of poetry has been masterfully analyzed by Jonathan Culler (1981), and then by Barbara Johnson (1987).

4. In her article "Bodies-Cities," Elizabeth Grosz makes a related point about the relation between cities and bodies. She distinguishes the tropes—she calls them models—of causality, considering that humans make or "cause" cities, and that of the analogy between bodies and cities, both problematic, from a trope of a "fundamentally disunified series of systems and interconnections, a series of disparate flows, energies, events or entities, and spaces, brought together or drawn apart in more or less temporary alignments" (1992: 248). I find her description of the situation too encompassing and, hence, too vague to be helpful in actual analysis, however.

5. This clarifies the theory of color—rather, of black and white or of three-dimensionality in the flat plane—which Louis Marin formulated through an analysis of black in Caravaggio (1995: 169), providing it with a subject-centered "key."

KELLER *The Finishing Touch*

Note: This paper was published earlier in *FutureNatural*, edited by George Robertson, Melinda Mash, Lisa Tickner, Jon Bird, Barry Curtis, and Tim Putnam (London: Routledge, 1996). By publishing it here, the editor hopes to make a contact between these two very different publications, which nevertheless both pursue a similar goal: critical reflection on contemporary culture.

SALOMON *Vermeer's Women*

Note: A shorter version of this paper was initially given at the symposium "New Vermeer Studies," sponsored by the Center for Advanced Study of the Visual Arts, The National Gallery, and the University of Maryland at College Park.

1. This reductive idea has most recently been discussed by Wayne Franits. In his work he cites the relevant previous bibliography on domesticity and Dutch genre painting (1993). For a more sophisticated discussion of the gendered and sexual implications in nineteenth-century images of domestic spaces, see the classic chapter "Modernity and the Spaces of Femininity," in Pollock 1988: 50–90.

2. The art historian who is most fully responsible for this line of thinking is Eddy de Jongh. His articles and exhibition catalogues have spawned a whole generation of iconologists of female morality. His ideas have recently been restated (de Jongh 1995).

3. For the art historian as a special-case spectator, see Holly 1990: esp. 385–88.

4. For a feminist interpretation that brilliantly utilizes and critiques the methods of Lacan and Foucault, see Bal 1991.

5. These images are tangentially related to the discourse of the *omgekeerde wereld*, or "topsy-turvy world," often related to similar images of the period which are sometimes grouped together under the name "power of women topos." See Davis 1975: 124–51, and Dresen-Coenders 1988: 73–84.

6. The most recent reiteration of this strange phenomenon can be found in Westermann 1996: 15, where, at the end of the introduction, she writes, "Many Dutch pictures offered meaningful delight precisely because they oscillate between a faithful reconstruction of reality and a positive or negative articulation of social ideals."

7. This seems more fruitful than postulating some form of collective hypocrisy on the part of the Dutch art consumer, a position first proposed and consistently held by Schama (1979, 1980, and 1987).

8. The complex problem of self-image (as opposed to self-portrait) projected in this painting must be saved for another study. Briefly, these paintings have in common the presentation of a certain persona shared by some Northern Netherlandish artists, which is ultimately unclassical in its orientation and which projected the notion of the creative man as a knave or rogue and as a sexual male. He depicts himself as someone who lives on the periphery of ordered society and therefore can grab life with full gusto. I have elsewhere suggested the progressive identification of not only Northern artists but Netherlandish culture in general with illicit sexuality as a component of their culturally constructed identity presented to the "outside world." This was part of the articulation of what Benedict Anderson has called the "imagined community" (1991).

9. For a fuller discussion of the iconographic and formal conventions and

the possibilities of social meanings developed within this tradition, see my essay "Early Netherlandish *Bordeeltjes* and the Construction of Social 'Realities' " (forthcoming).

10. The description of Vermeer's painting in 1696 which Blankert (Washington 1995–96: 35) calls its "title" is, for him, enough "proof that this beautiful dreamer is a direct descendent of the indecorously sleeping woman in a dingy inn in earlier paintings by Jacob Duck (c. 1600–1667)."

11. This emblem is reproduced in Fuchs 1979 as fig. 7.

12. For examples of the offer of wine as female sexuality in sixteenth-century Netherlandish love songs, see Renger 1985: 40–41.

13. All five versions are reproduced and discussed in Mund 1980. See p. 71 for the proposed dating.

14. For the open tankard as a reference to female sexuality in Netherlandish art and literature, see Renger 1985: 40–41.

15. "Ay laet staen, tis verloren / mijn Borse ghegrepen / Ghy hebtse gheleecht / en mijn pijp al uuyt ghepepe." The Dutch is quoted from Renger 1985: 39; the translation is mine and slightly differs from Renger's German translation.

16. I have made this point in my 1993 paper "Vanishing Acts."

17. For the tradition of low-class figures smiling broadly and showing their teeth in Lombard paintings, see Meijer 1971, especially fig. 3, Lombard School (sixteenth century), *Four Figures and a Cat*, location unknown. For a general discussion see Thomas 1991. See also Hessel Miedema's various responses to Svetlana Alpers, where Miedema talks about laughter as a lower class activity (1977 and 1981: esp. 206–8).

18. Caroto's painting is illustrated in Lavin 1994: 217, as fig. 279.

19. Blankert notes that even in Vermeer's music lesson, where the man was identified in the 1696 auction catalogue as a "Monsieur," it is not clear whether he is meant to be understood as an instructor or as an older suitor (Washington 1995–96: 37).

20. See the illustration in de Lairesse 1740: 55.

ELSAESSER *"Le cinéma d'après Lumière"*

1. In addition to the sources mentioned in my text, I have referred to Elsaesser 1990.

POLLOCK *Killing Men and Dying Women*

1. This argument is based on Laura Mulvey's analysis of the condensation of spectacle and commodity in the cinematic image of women (1995).

2. An article on abstract expressionists featuring Jackson Pollock was entitled "The Wild Ones," in *Time*, Feb. 20, 1956, 75. Pollock was also posthumously linked with James Dean, whose death preceded Pollock's by just one year.

3. The major statement of this genealogy is Courbet's *The Artist's Studio* (1855, Musée d'Orsay, Paris).

4. [Pollock is referring to a section of the paper that had to be sacrificed, in which she develops this theoretical framework. For the extended version of it, the reader is referred to Orton and Pollock 1996. — Ed.]

5. Nemser 1975b: 158.

ZEMEL *Imagining the 'Shtetl'*

1. For an account of Jewish photographers in Poland, see Dobroszycki and Kirshenblatt-Gimblett 1977: 1–38.

2. Chagall's images of Vitebsk in Belarus (c. 1915–25) engage many of the same cultural-national concerns found in these photographs.

3. For an overview of these positions, see Frankel 1992: 81–103.

4. Dubnow 1973: 845–56.

5. Marcus 1983; Pinchuk 1990.

6. Kacyzne wrote the screenplay for the famous 1937 film version of Ansky's play *The Dybbuk.*

7. For HIAS, Kacyzne made a famous series of images detailing the steps to emigration. His pictures are housed in the YIVO archive, New York. After World War II, many of Kacyzne's images were included in a *Forward* publication, *The Vanished World* (1947), which reinforced their status as memorial record.

8. The correspondence between Kacyzne and Abraham Cahan, editor of the *Forward*, is housed in the YIVO archives, New York.

9. In letters to Cahan about his photographs (often complaining about payment and costs), Kacyzne raised the issue of subject matter—the inclusion of orthodox genre figures, and the appeal to workers through worker and "capitalist" imagery. My thanks to Roberta Newman, New York, for sharing her research on Kacyzne's texts with me.

10. For the efforts of progressive authors to introduce sexuality into modern Yiddish literature, see Biale 1992.

11. Vilna's status as a center of Jewish scholarship began in the seventeenth century with the liberal rabbi known as the Vilna Gaon. For the history of Jewish Vilna, see Minczeles 1993.

12. Vorobeichic had also exhibited in Paris. A book on Paris was published the same year, with an introduction by Fernand Leger. Dobroszycki and Kirshenblatt-Gimblett 1977: 33.

13. For this view of the fragment, see Nochlin 1995.

14. Vishniac's account of these images appears fragmentarily in explanatory captions for *A Vanished World*, and in an unpublished manuscript in the archives of the International Center for Photography, New York. Jozef Grosz (1984: 332–34) notes Vishniac's desire "to save Jewish faces" and to represent people who seemed "unmistakably Jewish."

15. Hans Graf von Monts, *De Joden in Nederland* (1942). Thanks to Saskia Klaassen for bringing this text to my attention.

BANN *The Veils of Time*

1. See Barthes 1972. The *Paris-Match* cover in question is no. 326 (June 25–July 2, 1955).
2. See S. Baker 1985.
3. For further discussion of the Stothard print, see Bann 1984: 65–68.
4. See Bann 1984: 14, and also Bann 1995a: 3–16.
5. Meinecke, quoted in Bann 1984: 181 n. 71.
6. See Barthes 1981: 5.
7. There is an interesting discussion of the two works in the Ingres catalog, Petit Palais; see Laclotte et al. 1967: 158–61.
8. See Bann 1995b: 12–13 and 29.
9. See Bann 1994.

GEYER-RYAN *Venice and the Violence of Location*

1. See Geyer-Ryan 1996.

ALPHEN *Affective Reading*

1. Page references are to the 1979 edition published by Faber and Faber. The novel was first published in 1936.
2. See the introduction to this volume.
3. Robin seems to live in a different order precisely because she knows no desire. This suggestion is quite concrete when she is compared to plants or animals. Here is a description of her body: "The perfume that her body exhaled was of the quality of that earth-flesh, fungi, which smells of captured dampness and yet is so dry, overcast with the odour of oil of amber, which is an inner malady of the sea, making her seem as if she had invaded a sleep incautious and entire. Her flesh was the texture of plant life" (55–56). She is referred to as a woman in whom the animal has become human (59). She also exerts a special power for the animals in the circus (59). In the final chapter, Robin, the woman in whom the animal has turned human, seems to become animal again. Barking and yapping, she crawls on all fours in imitation of Nora's dog. For an analysis of this animal/vegetable motif, see Kannenstine 1977: 116–18.
4. For a detailed analysis of the double metaphor in the novel's title, see Zsadányi 1996.
5. Thus, the doctor speaks of "history at night" (126). He refers to moments of degradation, rot, and destruction: the night during which Sodom and Gomorrah were destroyed, and the fire of Rome.

6. For this rhetorical connection between images of parental roles and the major tropes, see Culler 1983 and Bal 1988.

7. For an analysis of androgyny in Plato and *Nightwood*, see Brugman 1982.

8. This view of lesbian love stemming from cultural history is an interpretation of the novel's imagery; it does not entail a position in the debate over psychoanalytic views of female homosexuality.

9. E.g., Pattynama 1983: "*Nightwood* leaves me desperate because I can only describe tiny fragments of what it did to me" (9).

ANKERSMIT   *History and/as Cultural Analysis*

1. An example is Peter Gay's perceptive essay on Gibbon (1974: chap. 1).

2. "The successors of Charles V may disdain their brethren of England [it was widely believed in Gibbon's days that Fielding was a descendant of Charles V]; but the romance of Tom Jones, that exquisite picture of human manners, will outlive the palace of the Escurial, and the imperial eagle of the house of Austria." See Gibbon 1923: 4.

3. In the introduction to the *Metamorphoses*, Ovid informs his readers that he will attempt to "spin an unbroken thread of verse, from the earliest beginnings of the world, down to my own times" ("ab origine mundi ad mea perpetuum deducite tempora carmen"). The juxtaposition of "perpetuum" and "deducite" is interpreted by Myers as a challenge to the generic codes given by Callimachos in his *Aetia*. See Myers 1990: 1.

4. Historians have much discussed the question whether the views Ovid attributed to Pythagoras are actually his own. Most often the question is answered in the affirmative. Thus, Otis writes: "the Pythagorian discourse embraces the entirety of Ovid's carmen perpetuum and represents metamorphosis as the universal key to the secrets of both nature and history" (in Myers 1990: 150).

5. Ovid 1955: 31. Regarding these negative characteristics in Ovid's text, see Gatz 1967: 74.

EXUM   *"Is This Naomi?"*

1. B. Bab. Bathra 91a. As Sasson (1979: 81) points out, "in a polygamous society, however, such a coincidence would not be necessary." It would be odd for the story not to mention it if Boaz had another wife. Most readers assume he did not, and as Landy (1994: 289) observes, this "indeed makes a better story." If we take the woman in the painting as Boaz's wife, living or dead, she is on her way out, so to speak.

2. A classic discussion of gapping in biblical narrative is that of Sternberg (1985: 186–229).

3. In this essay I discuss visual metatexts only; for an expanded discussion of

same-sex and opposite-sex relationships in the book of Ruth as they are commented on or transformed in nonliterary and literary metatexts, see Exum 1996.

4. The film does not emphasize this fact. It is an interesting variation on the rabbinic tradition that Boaz died on their wedding night, immediately after Ruth conceived Obed (*Ruth Zuta* on 4:13). This is in keeping with the notion that virtuous women do not have sex, at least not any more than is necessary; the story of Judith, the heroine who puts aside her widow's garb to "seduce" Holofernes and after assassinating him returns to a life of seclusion, is a variation on this theme.

5. The understanding of the levirate law in the film is not the same as that in the biblical book, nor is the levirate law presumed by the book of Ruth the same as that in the legal material of Deuteronomy 25:5–10.

6. For example, the film gives the name Tov for the unnamed next-of-kin, whom the text calls *peloni 'almoni*, the Hebrew equivalent to "so-and-so"; Naomi's husband, Elimelech, blames himself for the evil that befalls the family in Moab (he and Chilion are about to be killed, and Mahlon will die soon) because he was well off but left his people in Bethlehem in time of trouble; a messenger appears to Naomi to prophesy the birth of a future king from Ruth's line.

7. This is perhaps no more far-fetched than the rabbinic tradition that Ruth was the daughter of the king of Moab, thus providing David with royal ancestry on both paternal and maternal sides (*Ruth Rabbah* 2:9; whereas the midrash emphasizes Ruth's nationalistic change of allegiance, the film foregrounds her religious conversion). In the film, the Moabites are caricatured. The king and his priests are fat and bald; Moabite priestesses live in a kind of convent; the salient feature of Moabite religion is child sacrifice, about which the Moabites are, understandably, "very sensitive." Ruth as a child is *sold* by her needy father to the temple of Chemosh, and would have been sacrificed as a child had a blemish not appeared on her arm just after her selection. No sooner is another child chosen in her place than the blemish vanishes. We know, of course, what caused that blemish. Ruth and Mahlon have a theological discussion about it: Mahlon asks Ruth how Chemosh has been good to her and she tells him this story, concluding, "Chemosh spared me." Mahlon proposes that perhaps it was a higher god, and, anyway, he thought that to be sacrificed to Chemosh was a "coveted honor." Ruth becomes confused, a sign that her theological awakening is beginning.

8. The hidden activity of god is thought by many to be the theme of the book of Ruth; see, *inter alia*, Hals 1969: 11–12 et passim; Campbell 1975: 28–29, 112–13, 138 et passim; Hubbard 1988: 212, 217–18; for a more sanguine evaluation, see Sasson 1979.

9. The Hebrew *'mr*, usually translated "said," can also mean "think."

10. No doubt the film is here offering a nod of recognition to the biblical ambiguity.

11. Another important contribution of this ending is that it makes Ruth, and

not Boaz as in the biblical account, dissemble in a clever way that gets the next-of-kin to renounce his claim. Giving her a voice at the end makes the film Ruth's in a way the book isn't.

12. There is one other time this music is played, after Naomi has told Ruth of Tov's intention to invoke the levirate law in order to marry Ruth. There it signals that Ruth's devotion to Naomi has led to consequences she is willing to accept though it breaks her heart, while also pointing forward to a heterosexual bond, albeit marriage to the wrong man. Though the music is repeated, we hear the lyrics only in the scene where the women cross the wilderness to return to Judah.

13. See, e.g., Gen. 17:17; 21:5; 44:20; 2 Sam. 3:2, 5; 12:14; Jer. 20:15; Isa. 39:7; Job 1:2; 1 Chr. 3:1; 22:9; 2 Chr. 6:9.

14. Cf. Hubbard 1988: 274: "The language ('breast') suggests that Naomi did so as a warm, tender mother." Interestingly, Hubbard also refers to the baby "snuggled peacefully on gray-haired Naomi's bosom," thus reinforcing the assumption that Naomi is an old woman.

15. Campbell (1975: 120) thinks the form is not first person singular but rather an archaic second person feminine ending. Sasson (1979: 68–69) mentions the first person consonantal form and the "allegedly 'archaic' second person feminine singular," but decides that the context "requires us to opt for the 'archaic' sufformative." Pardes (1992: 104–5), in contrast, recognizes the potential that reading with the *kethiv* has for Naomi's "sympathetic identification with her daughter-in-law" (105).

16. The significant role Naomi does not hold is that of husband to Boaz, nor will Ruth hold this symbolic role. Unlike the women, who take a man's symbolic position, the man never symbolically takes a woman's position, though he does take on a woman's point of view (see below). Among the sources I have consulted, Pardes and Fewell and Gunn are most aware of the complex gender symbolism, but they do not develop its implications for gender blurring. Fewell and Gunn speak of Boaz as Naomi's surrogate husband (1990: 82) and of Ruth as "husband" to Naomi (97), and they describe Ruth's mediating role, when after the threshing floor encounter she brings the grain from Boaz to Naomi, in terms of her playing "wife" to Boaz and "husband" to Naomi (103). Pardes (1992: 102–17) offers a particularly perceptive discussion of what she terms "the doubling of the female subject." She concludes, "In a strange way Ruth and Naomi manage to share not only a husband and a son, but also textual subjectivity" (108).

17. Cf. Fewell and Gunn (1990: 97), who observe that "Ruth replaces husband and son as Naomi's caretaker."

18. The most significant difference between the literary and critical metatexts I examine in *Plotted, Shot, and Painted* (Exum 1996) is the willingness of popular (i.e. nonscholarly) works to appropriate in more extreme forms the Ruth-Naomi or Ruth-Boaz relationships for their purposes, and, as a consequence, to ascribe

feelings more freely to the characters. Only in the metatexts can the characters truly fulfill their desire and can they thereby fulfill the reader's desire for mimesis. Whereas traditional biblical commentators, such as Campbell, Sasson, and Hubbard, would prefer to keep modern sentiments out of it, a postmodern reading might question the repression of desire such attempts entail. Hubbard, for example, thinks that Ruth acts solely out of concern for Naomi. In other words, he uses Ruth's loyalty to Naomi as a means of denying any romantic feelings for Boaz on Ruth's part, in effect, denying Ruth's sexual desire altogether (since he does not entertain sexual desire on her part for Naomi). Is this realistic? It seems to me that to answer that question we would need more extensive analysis of ancient views of sexuality, which has not been my subject here, and which has hardly been investigated in the field of biblical studies.

HOVING *Cross-Atlantic Reading*

Note: This essay is based on parts of chapter two, "Tropes of Women's Exile," in Hoving 1995.

1. Ashcroft et al. suggest a dichotomy between time, privileged in European texts, and space, privileged in postcolonial texts. Their observation is based on their reading of the work of, among others, Wilson Harris. See Ashcroft, Griffiths, and Tiffin 1989: 34.

2. Some of the main points of this critique have a bearing on the universalizing tendencies in postcolonial theory, such as its tendency to abstraction and its focus on Western concerns and issues. For an elaboration see Davies 1994 and Hutcheon 1995.

3. Jonathan Culler did not exactly speak of non-Western discourses. He referred to interdisciplinarity. However, I like to extend his stimulating advice to "look at things differently" (1994: 16) to the need to confront the marginalized discourses of the South, that is, the culturally and economically marginalized areas in the Pacific, Latin America, the Caribbean, Africa, Asia, and their diasporas. I use the dichotomy North/South to indicate that places outside Western Europe and the U.S. are (also) different: they know different cultural traditions, conceptualizations of individuality, community, language, theory, history. These discourses can be taught and learned (as C. L. Miller 1990: 4 shows); they are not "pure" but often hybrid and always transforming; they are not necessarily to be found only in isolated places, but also turn up in metropolitan migrant communities, where they take other local forms. My argument is that we need a sense of this difference (and perhaps even a longing for this difference) to counter Western assumptions that the whole world is either postmodern or modern or premodern.

4. See Ward 1990.

5. Elsewhere, I have tried to show the elusiveness of, for example, Antiguan-American writer Jamaica Kincaid's rhetorics of irony, and Tobagon-Canadian

360 Notes to Pages 207–19

Marlene Nourbese Philip's discourse on a nonalienating, noncolonial, maternal language. I have read their writing as a critique of dominant Western discourses.

6. In the main argument of her 1994 study, however, Davies demonstrates convincingly that black women's writing can be studied as an autonomous literary field which, despite its plurality, is structured by continuities. My critique in this essay is directed at the few moments in which she emphasizes the "negative" aspects of black women's writing.

7. In fact, this scholarly attitude will sound as ridiculously self-evident to many of my readers as it sounds to me. However, many cases of postcolonial analysis still prefer to depart from Western concepts exclusively, and to discuss non-Western texts within the framework of Western theories only.

8. For more information about Jamaica Kincaid, see Hoving 1995.

9. The rumor goes that the story is based on an autobiographical event, in which the statement referred to the ruder and more debasing fact of the great man's inability to shit when need made itself felt (Perry 1990: 497). Even so, the published, censored version is more poetic and in a way more significant, since it concerns Columbus's (and the other patriarch's) mobility, which might be seen as the essence of his identity as prototypical traveler—as the traveler.

10. See Lemaire 1986 for a discussion; see too Todorov 1984 and Gikandi 1992.

11. See, for example, Deleuze 1977; Deleuze and Guattari 1980; Clifford 1989, 1992; Said 1983, 1994; and Morris 1992.

12. I would have liked Gikandi to be more precise in his use of the terms "modern," "modernism," "modernity," etc. He relies on Anderson's discussion of these concepts (P. Anderson 1988), but does not state explicitly whether he follows Anderson's descriptions consistently. To me, it seems he implies a problematic continuity between modernism (as the historical epoch heralded by Columbus's journeys, that is, the period following the Middle Ages), the modernism of Enlightenment, modernism as the cultural and literary movement at the beginning of the twentieth century, and maybe even postmodernism.

13. See Baker 1991: 107.

14. One might read this reference to a "deepest self" as a form of essentialism. Instead of criticizing this essentialism, however, I would argue to study its merits. Indeed, essentialism can be indispensable at times, for example in the political struggle.

15. Pratt describes contact zones as the "social spaces where disparate cultures meet, clash, and grapple with each other, often in highly asymmetrical relations of domination and subordination—like colonialism, slavery, or their aftermaths as they are lived out across the globe today" (Pratt 1992: 4).

ZIELINSKI *Variety & Standard*

1. English translation by Gloria Custance, from the French in Baudelaire 1964: 50.

2. This text is an attempt to appraise, both critically and self-critically, the thematic of my own theory and praxis as director and cofounder, as well as theoretician, of a new type of academy in which photographers, cinematographers, engineers, scientists, art historians, philosophers, musicians, and video and performance artists are working together. Further, via this detour, I intend to discuss the subject areas that cultural analysis, theory, and interpretation are currently concerned with, and under which meta-aspects their concepts and methodologies might possibly develop. Or to put it differently, I shall write as someone whose work-focus is technologically cofounded media and arts, the close entwining of traditional audiovisual artifacts and advanced, complex technologies.

3. Quotation and typology taken from Hinderk M. Emrich's stimulating essay "*Vom Nutzen des Vergessens für das Leben—Erinnerung als kulturelle Elementarfunktion und deformierende Belastung*" (Emrich 1994: 16).

4. Translated from Jabès 1989: 69–70.

FABIAN *Culture and Critique*

1. This essay developed from a contribution to a conference entitled "Political Cultures of Criticism," organized by the late Richard Burghart at the Internationales Wissenschaftsforum Heidelberg, October 30–November 2, 1991. I want to dedicate the essay to Richard Burghart's memory.

Though the name of the country has changed recently (to Democratic Republic of Congo), in this essay I have used the name Zaire, which symbolizes the era during which the art discussed here was produced.

2. The exception being a few of the popular painters who also produced (or had ambitions to produce) for academic collectors and a very limited curio market.

3. Inscriptions are written messages that appear on, not under or next to, the paintings. In some cases, placement of inscriptions affects the composition of paintings.

4. On the uses and limits of semiotic decoding of a popular painting from Shaba, see Szombati-Fabian and Fabian 1976. A semiotic approach in a wider sense than the one criticized here is exemplified in Jules-Rosette 1984.

5. Investigation of popular painting in Shaba started in 1973 and was carried out by Ilona Szombati and me. Together with research on popular theater and religion, it was part of a project on "language and work" among Swahili-speaking workers, craftsmen, and artists, and was supported by grants from the National Endowment for the Humanities (RO-6150-72-149) and the Rockefeller Foundation.

6. For my use of popular culture as a conceptual frame capable of development and modification, see Fabian 1978, Fabian and Szombati-Fabian 1980, and my recent attempt to take stock of theoretical issues and empirical studies (Fabian, forthcoming).

7. The topic of narrativity was treated masterfully by Mieke Bal in her work on Rembrandt (1991).

8. See also the remarks, with further references, on performance and survival in Fabian 1990b: 15–18.

9. Tshibumba will have our attention presently (see also Brett 1986 and Jewsiewicki 1986, 1991a, [ed.] 1992). On Lubaki and Djilatendo see references in Jewsiewicki 1991b; on Chéri Samba see Bender 1991, Jewsiewicki 1995.

10. For a full presentation of the images and texts of Tshibumba's *History of Zaire*, as well as its ethnography and critical interpretations, see Fabian 1996.

11. The notion of genre has proven useful in approaching differentiation within the overall process of artistic production in Shaba. As such, it was an extension of the genre concept as applied in the ethnography of communication and in folklore studies (Fabian 1974) rather than what art historians have in mind when they speak of genre painting. Whether there are analogies, perhaps homologies, between Shaba and, say, Dutch genre painting, is another, interesting question that cannot be addressed here.

12. On landscape (painting) and power, as well as resistance, see Mitchell 1994. According to him, landscape painting is "a representation of something that is already a representation in its own right" (14).

13. On the mermaid as a synthetic symbol of the modern, urban condition see Szombati-Fabian and Fabian 1976 and Fabian 1978, and on the wider historical and current performative context of the mermaid motif, see Drewal 1988 and Wendl 1991.

14. This argument was developed in an interpretation of one of the most popular genres of Shaba painting, the *colonie belge*, usually a prison-yard scene in which an African prisoner is caned by a guard while a white officer looks on (see Szombati-Fabian and Fabian 1976).

15. From our first session, recorded in Lubumbashi on October 6, 1974 (a free translation from Shaba Swahili).

16. I have in mind sources such as the *Vocabulary of the Town of Elisabethville*, a colonial history written for the colonized by the colonized (see Fabian 1990a).

17. This is a paraphrase rather than a direct quotation, summarizing statements in the *Vocabulary* (Fabian 1990a: 61–71).

18. Here, my findings contradict a thesis recently formulated by a Zairean observer who writes from a perspective informed by ethnic strife marking the general breakdown of the nation in the late 1980s (Biaya 1988).

DUPRÉ *Cultural Variety and Metaphysical Unity*

1. Ricoeur 1967: 19. Claude Lévi-Strauss, in his beautiful *Tristes Tropiques*, claims that precisely the strangeness of a primitive culture attracts the anthropologist. Once he has become familiar with the totally unfamiliar (in his case,

an undiscovered Amazonian tribe), he feels let down because the strangeness that lured him to it has vanished in the process of pursuing it.

2. I have spelled out its origins in *Passage to Modernity* (1993).

3. I may be allowed to refer to the concluding chapter of my *Passage to Modernity* (1993), in which I have developed this alternative.

DE BOER *Desire, Distance, and Insight*

1. Huizinga 1950: 328, 443, 490, 500, 511.

2. Ibid.: 329, 490, 515, 561ff., 596 (ethics and religion); 490, 568 (the arts).

3. In the case of knowledge which ties in with the model of Aristotelian prudence, see below; there is no gap between theory and practice. One of the reasons we speak of "insight" is that this knowledge can lead to concrete actions. What cultural analysis does is to continue, in a more systematic way, what is already happening outside of science. That is precisely why its results can be integrated into desire.

4. The combination of three-part analysis with the three areas produces the following table. It should be read as an "artige Betrachtung," as Kant used the term.

	desire	*distance*	*insight*
psychoanalysis	drive	analysis	awareness of reality
phenomeno-logical analysis	interest	analysis	tolerance
literary analysis	passion	analysis	catharsis/ anagnorisis

5. Ricoeur appeals to a "phronèsis à plusieurs" (1990: 304).

6. Reinjan Mulder, *NRC/Handelsblad*, Jan. 1, 1995.

7. The Polish writer Czeslaw Milosz, considering the question of whether art compared with action is not betrayal, posits: "Yet to embrace reality in such a manner that it is preserved in all its old tangle of good and evil, of despair and hope, is possible only by soaring above it. . . ." (quoted in Michael Ignatieff, "The Art of Witness," *The New York Review of Books*, 23 March 1995).

8. Applied to Aristotle's sympathy and fear, this means that these emotions, which in daily life are experienced directly, crystallize out by representation (mimesis) in the work of art (in Nijhoff's terms, they become "content of the form"). That is their "purification" by the composition. This presupposes aesthetic anagnorisis in the author and can bring about an aesthetic catharsis for the reader.

NEUBAUER *Cultural Analysis and 'Geistesgeschichte'*

1. My *Symbolismus und symbolische Logik* (Neubauer 1978) is an essay in the history of ideas, which traces the notion "ars combinatoria" from mathematics to philosophy and modern literature. My more recent book on adolescence in fin-de-siècle culture (Neubauer 1992b) tries to link literary themes and forms and various other discourses to social and institutional history.

2. A third example could be Gillispie's reading of Goethe's science as key to a consistent notion of romanticism that has hitherto eluded historians of politics, philosophy, and the arts:

> Romanticism began as a moral revolt against physics, expressed in moving, sad, and sometimes angry attempts to defend a qualitative science, in which nature can be congruent with man, against a measuring, numbering science which alienates the creator of science from his own creation by total objectification of nature. For physics romanticism would substitute biology at the heart of science. For mechanism as the model of order, romanticism would substitute organism, some unitary emanation of intelligence or will, or else identical with intelligence or will. Romanticism might take any form in politics, art, or letters. But in natural philosophy there is an infallible touchstone of romantic tendencies. Its metaphysics treats becoming rather than being. Its ontology lies in metamorphosis rather than atomism. And always it wants more out of nature than science finds there. (Gillispie 1960: 199)

It would require another essay to show how this conflates two overlapping yet distinct discourses.

3. Foucault 1973: 263–64. The term "expressed" is a reductive translation of the French *devait traduire un jour*. The last sentence reads in the original: "C'est ce décalage et cette inversion que Geoffroy Saint-Hilaire devait traduire un jour en disant: 'L'organisation devient un être abstrait . . . susceptible de formes nombreuses'" (Foucault 1966: 276k).

4. Furthermore, it is by no means clear who won the debate and who anticipated the development of biology better, Cuvier, Geoffroy, or, for that matter, Lamarck. Most historians hold that Cuvier scored a decisive victory; Appel argues that Geoffroy's ideas "eventually became an integral part of biological science in both France and Britain," and he observes that the role of morphology and hence of Geoffroy in early nineteenth-century science has become better appreciated in the last few years (Appel 1987: 3).

5. "Tout le Règne animal est équivalent à l'Homme étalé" (Cahn 1962: 138).

COOK *The Techno-University and Knowledge*

1. For Aristotle's account of *technē* and its relation to *ēpistemē* (scientific knowledge) and *phronēsis* (practical wisdom), see his *Nichomachean Ethics*, bk. 6, 1139b25–1143a35.

2. For Foucault on the panopticon, see Foucault 1979: 195–228. For some helpful discussion on the education of Renaissance rulers, see Skinner 1978: 1: 213–44.

3. For Kant's account of imagination see, inter alia, Kant 1952: 175–82.

4. Among Derrida's extensive writings on writing, see Derrida 1978: 3–31.

5. See, for example, Thomas Hughes's study of the organization of electricity in a number of Western cities, in Hughes 1983.

6. See, for example, Hoggart 1973: 246–50. There is of course nothing especially English about this response to technology. See, for example, Adorno's terse comment in *Minima Moralia*: "Technology is making gestures precise and brutal and with them men." For Williams's discussion of "technological determinism," see Williams 1975: 9–32.

7. Stiegler 1994: 185. I am indebted to Richard Beardsworth's translation of Stiegler's text. For an exemplary reading of Stiegler's work, see Beardsworth 1995.

Bibliography

Allison, David, ed. 1977. *The New Nietzsche*. New York: Delta.

Alphen, Ernst van. 1987. "Literal Metaphors: Rereading Post/Modernism." *Style* 21, no. 2: 208–18.

———. 1988. "Reading Visually." *Style* 22, no. 2: 219–29.

———. 1992. *Francis Bacon and the Loss of Self*. London: Reaktion Books; Cambridge, Mass.: Harvard University Press.

Amsterdam Rijksmuseum. 1976. *Rijksmuseum Tot Lering en Vermaak*. By E. de Jongh et al. Amsterdam: Rijksmuseum.

Anderson, Benedict. 1991. *Imagined Communities: Reflections on the Origins and Spread of Nationalism*. London: Verso.

Anderson, Perry. 1988. "Modernity and Revolution." In Nelson and Grossberg 1988: 317–38.

Ankersmit, F. R. 1995. "Historism: An Attempt at Synthesis." *History and Theory* 34, no. 3.

Appel, Toby. 1987. *The Cuvier-Geoffroy Debate: French Biology in the Decades Before Darwin*. New York and Oxford: Oxford University Press.

Aristotle. 1968. *Nichomachean Ethics*. 2d ed. London: Loeb Classical Library.

Arnold, Matthew. 1888. "The Study of Poetry." In his *Essays in Criticism: Second Series*. London: Macmillan.

———. 1993. *Culture and Anarchy* [1869]. Ed. S. Collini. Cambridge, Eng.: Cambridge University Press.

Ashcroft, Bill, Gareth Griffiths, and Helen Tiffin. 1989. *The Empire Writes Back: Theory and Practice in Post-colonial Literatures*. London: Routledge.

Baker, Houston A., Jr. 1991. *Workings of the Spirit: The Poetics of Afro-American Women's Writing*. Chicago: University of Chicago Press.

Baker, Steve. 1985. "The Hell of Connotation." *Word and Image* 1, no. 2: 164–75.

Bal, Mieke. 1987. *Lethal Love: Feminist Literary Readings of Biblical Love Stories*. Bloomington: Indiana University Press.

———. 1988. *Death and Dissymmetry: The Politics of Coherence in the Book of Judges*. Chicago: University of Chicago Press.

————. 1991. *Reading "Rembrandt": Beyond the Word-Image Opposition*. New York: Cambridge University Press.

————. 1995. Introduction and "My Practice of Cultural Analysis." In the program booklet for the conference "The Practice of Cultural Analysis: A Workshop on Interdisciplinarity," 3–5, 10. Amsterdam: Amsterdam School for Cultural Analysis.

————. 1996. *Double Exposures: The Subject of Cultural Analysis*. New York: Routledge.

Bal, Mieke, and Inge E. Boer, eds. 1994. *The Point of Theory: Practices of Cultural Analysis*. Amsterdam: Amsterdam University Press.

Balthasar, Hans Urs von. 1965. *Herrlichkeit*. vol 3. *Im Raum der Metaphysik. Teil 1*. Einsiedeln: Benziger.

Balzac, Honoré. 1976. *La comédie humaine*. Vol 1. Paris: Gallimard.

Bann, Stephen. 1984. *The Clothing of Clio*. Cambridge, Eng.: Cambridge University Press.

————. 1994. "'Wilder Shores of Love': Cy Twombly's Straying Signs." In *Materialities of Communication*, ed. Hans Ulrich Gumbrecht and K. Ludwig Pfeiffer, 198–213. Stanford, Calif.: Stanford University Press.

————. 1995a. *Romanticism and the Rise of History*. New York: Twayne.

————. 1995b. "Les temps voilent l'antiquité." In *Corps de la Mémoire*, catalogue, 12–13. Toulouse: Editions ARPAP, Espace d'Art Moderne et Contemporain de Toulouse.

Barnes, Djuna. 1979. *Nightwood*. With a preface by T. S. Eliot. London: Faber and Faber.

Barthes, Roland. 1969. "Reflexions sur un manuel." In *L'enseignement de la littérature*, ed. Serge Doubrovsky and Tzvetan Todorov, 170–77. Paris: Plon.

————. 1970a. *Mythologies*. 2d edition. Paris: Seuil.

————. 1970b. *S/Z*. Paris: Seuil.

————. 1972. *Mythologies*. Trans. Annette Lavers. St. Albans: Paladin.

————. 1981. "The Discourse of History." Trans. and intro. Stephen Bann. *Comparative Criticism Yearbook* 3: 3–20.

————. 1984. *Le bruissement de la langue*. Paris: Editions du Seuil.

Baudelaire, Charles. 1964. *Les fleurs du mal*. Paris: Editions Gallimard / Livres de poche.

Beardsworth, R. 1995. "From a Genealogy of Matter to a Politics of Memory." *Tekhnema: Journal of Philosophy and Technology* 2: 85–116.

Bell, Daniel. 1978. *The Cultural Contradictions of Capitalism*. New York: Basic Books.

Bender, Wolfgang, ed. 1991. *Chéri Samba*. Munich: Trickster.

Benjamin, Walter. 1973. "The Work of Art in the Age of Mechanical Reproduction" [1936]. In his *Illuminations*, trans. H. Zohn. London: Fontana.

Benveniste, Emile. 1966. *Problèmes de linguistique générale.* Vol. 1. Paris: Gallimard.

———. 1970. "L'appareil formelle de l'énonciation." *Langage* 17: 12–18. (English translation: 1971. *Problems in General Linguistics.* Trans. Mary Elizabeth Meek. Coral Gables: University of Miami Press.)

Bernard, Claude. 1947. *Introduction to the Study of Experimental Medicine.* New York: Schuman.

Bersani, Leo. 1986. *The Freudian Body: Psychoanalysis and Art.* New York: Columbia University Press.

———. 1987. "Is the Rectum a Grave?" *October* 43, special issue, *Aids: Cultural Analysis / Cultural Activism* (winter): 197–223.

Bersani, Leo, and Ulysse Dutoit. 1985. *The Forms of Violence: Narrative in Assyrian Art and Modern Culture.* New York: Schocken Books.

Bhabha, Homi K. 1990. "Introduction: Narrating the Nation" and "DissemiNation: Time, Narrative and the Margins of the Modern Nation." In *Nation and Narration*, ed. Homi K. Bhabha, 1–7, 291–322. London: Routledge.

Biale, David. 1992. *Eros and the Jews.* New York: Basic Books.

Biaya, T. K. 1988. "L'impasse de la crise zaïroise dans la peinture populaire urbaine, 1970–1985." *Canadian Journal of African Studies* 22: 95–120.

Bloom, Harold. 1986. *James Joyce: Modern Critical Views.* New York: Chelsea House.

Bohr, Niels. 1987a. "Light and Life" [1932]. In *The Philosophical Writings of Niels Bohr*, 2: 3–12. Woodbridge, Conn.: Ox Bow Press.

———. 1987b. "Light and Life Revisited" [1962]. In *The Philosophical Writings of Niels Bohr*, 3: 23–29. Woodbridge, Conn.: Ox Bow Press.

Braudy, L. 1970. *Narrative Form in History and Fiction.* Princeton, N.J.: Princeton University Press.

Brett, Guy. 1986. *Through Our Own Eyes: Popular Art and Modern History.* London: GMP.

Brookner, Anita. 1987. *A Friend from England.* London: Selobrook.

Brugman, Margret. 1982. "Androgynie—Loon voor wilskracht versus vrolijke versplintering. Mogelijkheden en beperkingen van een ideaal." *Tijdschrift voor Vrouwenstudies*, no. 10, yr. 3, no. 2, 180–96.

Buffon, G. L. L., Comte De. 1750. *Histoire naturelle.* Vol. 2. Paris: Imprimerie Royale.

Burch, Noel. 1990. *Life to Those Shadows.* Berkeley: University of California Press.

———. 1981. "Charles Baudelaire vs. Dr. Frankenstein." *Afterimage* 8/9 (Spring): 4–21.

Butler, Judith. 1990. *Gender Trouble: Feminism and the Subversion of Identity.* New York: Routledge.

Cahn, Théophile. 1962. *La vie et l'oeuvre d'E. Geoffroy de Saint-Hilaire.* Paris: PUF.

Campbell, Edward F., Jr. 1975. *Ruth.* Anchor Bible, 7. Garden City, N.Y.: Doubleday.

Chapman, H. Perry. 1990. *Rembrandt's Self-Portraits: A Study in Seventeenth-Century Identity*. Princeton, N.J.: Princeton University Press.

Clark, T. J. 1990. "Jackson Pollock's Abstraction." In *Reconstructing Modernism*, ed. Serge Guibaut, 172–243. Cambridge, Mass.: MIT Press.

Clifford, James. 1989. "Notes on Travel and Theory." *Inscriptions* 5: 177–88.

———. 1992. "Traveling Cultures." In Grossberg, Nelson, and Treichler, 96–116.

Cobham, Rhonda, and Merle Collins, eds. *Watchers and Seekers: Creative Writing by Black Women in Britain*. London: The Woman's Press.

Craddock, P. B. 1989. *Edward Gibbon: Luminous Historian, 1772–1794*. Baltimore: Johns Hopkins University Press.

Crary, Jonathan. 1990. *Techniques of the Observer*. Cambridge, Mass.: MIT Press.

Culler, Jonathan. 1981. *The Pursuit of Signs: Semiotics, Literature, Deconstruction*. Ithaca, N.Y.: Cornell University Press.

———. 1983. *On Deconstruction: Theory and Criticism After Structuralism*. London: Routledge and Kegan Paul.

———. 1988. *Framing the Sign: Criticism and Its Institutions*. Oxford: Blackwell.

———. 1994. "What's the Point?" Introduction to *The Point of Theory*, ed. Mieke Bal and Inge E. Boer, 13–17. Amsterdam: Amsterdam University Press; New York: Continuum.

Danto, Arthur C. 1968. *Analytical Philosophy of History*. Cambridge, Eng.: Cambridge University Press.

Davies, Carole Boyce. 1994. *Black Women, Writing and Identity: Migrations of the Subject*. London: Routledge.

Davis, Natalie Zemon. 1975. *Society and Culture in Early Modern France: Eight Essays by Natalie Zemon Davis*. Stanford, Calif.: Stanford University Press.

De Boer, Theo. 1993. *Tamara A., Awater en andere verhalen over subjectiviteit*. Amsterdam and Meppel: Boom.

Debray, Regis. 1995. *Contre Venise*. Paris: Gallimard.

de Jongh, E. 1995. *Kwesties van betekenis: Thema en motief in de Nederlandse schilderkunst van de zeventiende eeuw*. Leiden: Primavera pers.

de Lairesse, Gerard. 1740. *Groot schilderboek*. Haarlem: Marhoorn.

de Lauretis, Teresa. 1984. *Alice Doesn't: Feminism, Semiotics, Cinema*. Bloomington: Indiana University Press.

Deleuze, Gilles. 1977. "Nomad Thought." In Allison 1977: 142–49.

Deleuze, Gilles, and Félix Guattari. 1980. *Mille plateaux: Capitalisme et schizophrénie*. Paris: Editions de Minuit.

Derrida, Jacques. 1962. *Introduction: Edmund Husserl, "L'origine de la géometrie."* Paris: Presses Universitaires de France. (English translation: *Edmund Husserl's "Origin of Geometry": An Introduction*. Trans. John P. Leavy. Pittsburgh: Duquesne University Press, 1978.)

———. 1978. *Writing and Difference*. Trans. Alan Bass. London: Routledge and Kegan Paul.

————. 1984. "Two Words for Joyce." In *Post-Structuralist Joyce: Essays from the French*, ed. Derek Attridge and Daniel Ferrer, 145–59. Cambridge, Eng.: Cambridge University Press; London: Johns Hopkins University Press.

————. 1987. *The Postcard: From Socrates to Freud and Beyond*. Trans. Alan Bass. Chicago: University of Chicago Press.

————. 1988. "Ulysses Gramophone: Hear Say Yes in Joyce." In *James Joyce: The Augmented Ninth*, ed. Bernard Benstock, 27–77. New York: Syracuse University Press.

————. 1994. *Specters of Marx: The State of the Debt, the Work of Mourning, and the New International*. Trans. Peggy Kamuf. New York: Routledge.

Deslandes, Jacques, and Jacques Richard. 1968. *Histoire comparée du cinéma*, vol. 2, *Du cinématographe au cinéma 1896–1906*. Tournai: Casterman.

Deutelbaum, Marshall. 1979. "Structural Patterning in the Lumière Films." *Wide Angle* 3, no. 1: 28–37.

Diamond, Irene, and Lee Quinby. 1988. "On Initiating a Dialogue." In *Feminism and Foucault: Reflections on Resistance*, ed. Irene Diamond and Lee Quinby, 3–60. Boston: Northeastern University Press.

Dibdin, Michael. 1994. *Dead Lagoon*. London: Faber and Faber.

Dobroszycki, Lucjan, and Barbara Kirshenblatt-Gimblett. 1977. *Image Before My Eyes: A Photographic History of Jewish Life in Poland, 1864–1939*. New York: Schocken Books and the YIVO Institute for Jewish Research.

Donaldson, Laura E. 1992. *Decolonizing Feminism: Race, Gender, and Empire-Building*. London: Routledge.

Dresen-Coenders, Lène. 1988. "De omgekeerde wereld: Tot lering en vermaak." In *Helse en hemelse vrouwen: Schrikbeelden en voorbeelden van de vrouw in de christelijke cultuur (1400–1600)*, ed. Marlies Caron, 73–84. Utrecht: Rijksmuseum Het Catharijneconvent.

Drewal, Henry John. 1988. "Performing the Other: Mami Wata Worship in Africa." *The Drama Review*, Summer Issue, 160–85.

Dubnow, Simon. 1958. *Nationalism and History: Essays on Old and New Judaism*. Cleveland: Meridian Books; Philadelphia: Jewish Publication Society of America.

————. 1973. *From the Congress of Vienna to the Emergence of Hitler*. Trans. Moshe Spiegel. Vol. 5 of *History of the Jews*. South Brunswick, N.J.: T. Yoseloff.

Du Maurier, Daphne. 1981. *"Don't Look Now" and Other Stories*. London: Penguin.

Duncan, Carol. 1993. *Aesthetics and Power*, New York: Cambridge University Press.

Dupré, Louis. 1993. *Passage to Modernity*. New Haven, Conn.: Yale University Press.

Dyer, Richard. 1986. *Heavenly Bodies: Film Stars and Society*. New York: St. Martin's Press.

Eco, Umberto. 1976. "A Reading of *Steve Canyon*." Trans. Bruce Merry. *20th Century Studies,* nos. 15/16: 18–33.

Eliot, T. S. 1948. *Notes Towards the Definition of Culture.* London: Faber and Faber.

———. 1974. *"The Four Quartets," "Burnt Norton I," Collected Poems 1909–1962.* London: Faber and Faber.

Eller, K. H. 1982. *Ovid und der Mythos der Verwandlung: Zum mythologischen und poetischen Verständnis des Metamorphosen-Gedichts.* Frankfurt am Main: Suhrkamp.

Elsaesser, Thomas, ed. 1990. *Early Cinema: Space Frame Narrative.* Bloomington: Indiana University Press.

Emrich, Hinderk M. 1994. "Vom Nutzen des Vergessens für das Leben—Erinnerung als kulturelle Elementarfunktion und deformierende Belastung." *Wirtschaft und Wissenschaft* 1.

Exum, J. Cheryl. 1996. *Plotted, Shot, and Painted: Cultural Representations of Biblical Women.* Sheffield: Sheffield Academic Press.

Fabian, Johannes. 1974. "Genres in an Emerging Tradition: An Approach to Religious Communication." In *Changing Perspectives in the Scientific Study of Religion,* ed. A. W. Eister, 249–72. New York: Wiley Interscience.

———. 1978. "Popular Culture in Africa: Findings and Conjectures." *Africa* 48: 315–34.

———. 1990a. *History from Below: The "Vocabulary of Elisabethville" by André Yav. Texts, Translation and Interpretive Essay.* Amsterdam and Philadelphia: John Benjamins.

———. 1990b. *Power and Performance: Ethnographic Explorations Through Proverbial Wisdom and Theater in Shaba (Zaire).* Madison: University of Wisconsin Press.

———. 1996. *Remembering the Present: Painting and Popular History in Zaire.* Berkeley: University of California Press.

———. Forthcoming. *Moments of Freedom: On Popular Culture in Africa.* Charlottesville: University Press of Virginia.

Fell, John L., ed. 1983. *Film Before Griffith.* Berkeley: University of California Press.

Fer, Bryony. 1995. "Poussière/peinture: Bataille on Painting." In *Bataille: Writing the Sacred,* ed. Carolyn Bailey, 154–71. London: Routledge.

Fewell, Danna Nolan, and David Miller Gunn. 1990. *Compromising Redemption: Relating Characters in the Book of Ruth.* Louisville: Westminster/John Knox Press.

Foucault, Michel. 1966. *Les mots et les choses.* Paris: Gallimard.

———. 1972. *The Archeology of Knowledge.* Trans. A. M. Sheridan Smith. New York: Harper.

———. 1973. *The Order of Things.* New York: Vintage.

————. 1979. *Discipline and Punish*. Trans. Alan Sheridan. Harmondsworth, Eng.: Penguin Books.

————. 1980. *The History of Sexuality. Volume I: An Introduction*. Trans. Robert Hurley. New York: Vintage Books.

Franits, Wayne. 1993. *Paragons of Virtue: Women and Domesticity in Seventeenth-Century Dutch Art*. New York: Cambridge University Press.

Frankel, Jonathan. 1992. "Modern Jewish Politics, East and West: Utopia, Myth, Reality." In *The Quest for Utopia: Jewish Political Ideas and Institutions Through the Ages*, ed. Zvi Gitelman, 81–103. Armonk, New York: M. E. Sharpe.

Freud, Sigmund. 1962a. *Civilization and Its Discontents*. Trans. James Strachey. New York: W. W. Norton.

————. 1962b. *Three Essays on the Theory of Sexuality*. Trans. James Strachey. New York: Basic Books.

Friedan, Betty. 1963. *The Feminine Mystique*. New York: Bantam Books.

Fuchs, Edward. 1979. *Die Frau in der Karikatur: Sozialgeschichte der Frau* [1928]. Munich: Verlag Neue Kritik.

Gadamer, H. G. 1965. *Wahrheit und Methode: Grundzüge einer philosophischen Hermeneutik* [1960]. Vol. 2. Tübingen: J. C. B. Mohr.

————. 1971. "Replik." In *Hermeneutik und Ideologiekritik*, ed. Jürgen Habermas, Dieter Henrich, and Jacob Taubes, 283–317. Frankfurt am Main: Suhrkamp Verlag.

Galinsky, G. K. 1975. *Ovid's "Metamorphoses": An Introduction to the Basic Aspects*. Berkeley: University of California Press.

Gates, Henry Louis, Jr., ed. 1990. *Reading Black, Reading Feminist: A Critical Anthology*. New York: Meridian/Penguin.

Gatz, B. 1967. *Weltalter, goldene Zeit und sinnverwante Vorstellungen. Sudasmata Band 16*. Hildesheim: Olms.

Gay, P. 1974. *Style in History*. London: Jonathan Cape.

Geertz, Clifford. 1973. *The Interpretation of Culture*. New York: Basic Books.

Geoffroy Saint-Hilaire, Étienne. 1830. *Principes des philosophie zoologique, discutés en mars 1830, au sein de l'Académie Royale des Sciences*. Paris: Pichon et Didier.

————. 1831. "Sur des écrits de Goethe lui donnant des droits au titre de savant naturaliste." *Annales des sciences naturelles* 22: 188–93.

Geyer-Ryan, Helga. 1996. "Shakespeare After Derrida and Marx: *Death in Venice* and the Utopia of the Open Society." *Arcadia*, no. 1/2: 153–64.

Gibbon, E. 1787–94. *The History of the Decline and Fall of the Roman Empire*. 12 vols. Basel: J. J. Tourneisen.

————. 1923. *Autobiography*. Ed. O. Smeaton. New York: Everyman's Library.

Gikandi, Simon. 1992. *Writing in Limbo: Modernism and Caribbean Literature*. Ithaca, N.Y.: Cornell University Press.

Gilbert, Scott. 1994. "Looking at Embryos: The Visual and Conceptual Aesthetics of Emerging Form." Lecture presented at Boston University, 1994.

Gillispie, Charles Coulston. 1960. *The Edge of Objectivity.* Princeton, N.J.: Princeton University Press.

Glissant, Edouard. 1981. *Le discours antillais.* Paris: Ed. du Seuil.

Goethe, Johann Wolfgang. 1985. *Sämtliche Werke (Münchner Ausgabe).* 22 vols. Munich: Hanser.

Gooneratne, Yasmine. 1986. "Place and Placelessness in the Criticism of the New Literatures in English." In *A Sense of Place in the New Literatures in English,* ed. Peggy Nightingale, 13–21. St. Lucia: University of Queensland Press.

Gossman, L. 1980. *The Empire Unpossess'd.* Cambridge, Eng.: Cambridge University Press.

———. 1990. *Between History and Literature.* Cambridge: Harvard University Press.

———. 1996. "Burckhardts Basel en de kritiek op het modernisme." In *Romantische historische cultuur,* ed. J. Tollebeek, F. R. Ankersmit, and W. Krul, 323–47. Groningen: Historische Uitgeverij.

Gould, Stephen Jay. 1993. "More Light on Leaves." In his *Eight Little Piggies: Reflections on Natural History,* 153–65. New York: Norton.

Greenberg, Clement. 1940. "Towards a Newer Laocoon." *Partisan Review* 7, no. 4 (July–August): 296–310.

Grossberg, Lawrence, Cary Nelson, and Paula Treichler, eds. 1992. *Cultural Studies.* New York: Routledge.

Grosz, Elizabeth. 1992. "Bodies-Cities." In *Sexuality and Space,* ed. Beatriz Colomina, 241–53. New York: Princeton Architectural Press.

Grosz, Jozef. 1984. "Dr. Vishniac's Great Document." *British Journal of Photography* 30 (March): 332–34.

Habermas, Jürgen. 1987. *The Philosophical Discourse of Modernity.* Trans. Frederick Lawrence. Boston: MIT Press.

Hacking, Ian. 1983. *Representing and Intervening.* Cambridge, Eng.: Cambridge University Press.

Hall, Stuart. 1980. "Cultural Studies: Two Paradigms." *Media, Culture, and Society* 2: 57–72.

Hals, Ronald M. 1969. *The Theology of the Book of Ruth.* Philadelphia: Fortress Press.

———. 1942. *Philosophy of Right.* Trans. T. M. Knox. Oxford: Clarendon.

Hegel, G. W. F. 1977. *Phenomenology of Spirit.* Trans. A. V. Miller. Oxford: Oxford University Press.

Heidegger, Martin. 1978. "Building, Dwelling, Thinking" [1954]. In *Martin Heidegger: Basic Writings,* ed. D. F. Kerr. London: Routledge and Kegan Paul.

———. 1985. "The Self-Assertion of the German University" [1933]. Trans. K. Harries. *Review of Metaphysics* 38, no. 3: 470–80.

Hermans, W. F. 1983. *Het sadistische universum 1.* Amsterdam: De Bezige Bij.

Hirsch, E. D. 1987. *Cultural Literacy: What Every American Needs to Know.* Boston: Houghton Mifflin.

Hoberman, J[ames]. 1991. *Bridge of Light: Yiddish Film Between Two Wars.* New York: Museum of Modern Art and Schocken Books.

Hoberman, John. 1994. "Korea and a Career." *Art Forum* 32, no. 5: 11.

Hobsbawm, Eric. 1994. *The Age of Extremes: My Short Twentieth Century.* London: Verso.

Hoggart, R. 1973. *The Uses of Literacy* [1957]. Harmondsworth, Eng.: Penguin Books.

Holly, Michael Ann. 1990. "Past Looking." *Critical Inquiry* 16, no. 2: 371–96.

Horkheimer, Max. 1974. *Eclipse of Reason.* New York: Seabury.

Houdebine, Jean-Louis. 1982. "Joyce Tel Quel." *Tel Quel* 94: 35–44.

Hoving, Isabel. 1995. *The Castration of Livingstone and Other Stories: Reading African and Caribbean Migrant Women's Writing.* Amsterdam: Universiteit van Amsterdam.

Hubbard, Robert L., Jr. 1988. *The Book of Ruth.* Grand Rapids: Eerdmans.

Hughes, T. 1983. *Networks of Power: Electrification in Western Society.* Baltimore: Johns Hopkins University Press.

Huizinga, Johan. 1950. *Verzamelde Werken VII.* Haarlem: Tjeenk Willink.

Hutcheon, Linda. 1995. "Introduction: Colonialism and the Postcolonial Condition: Complexities Abounding." *PMLA* 110, no. 1: 7–16.

Irigaray, Luce. 1985. *This Sex Which Is Not One.* Trans. Catherine Porter. Ithaca, N.Y.: Cornell University Press.

Jabès, Edmond. 1989. *Das Unlesbare.* In *Die Schrift der Wüste*, ed. Felix Philipp Ingold, 61–78. Berlin: Merve.

Jacob, François. 1976. *The Logic of Life.* New York: Vantage Books.

Jaspers, Karl. 1960. *The Idea of the University* [1946]. Trans. H. A. T. Reiche and H. F. Vanderschmidt. London: Peter Owen.

Jewsiewicki, Bogumil. 1986. "Collective Memory and Its Images: Popular Urban Painting in Zaire—A Source of 'Present Past.'" *History and Anthropology* 2: 365–72.

———. 1991a. "Painting in Zaire: From the Invention of the West to the Representation of Social Self." In *Africa Explores: Twentieth-Century African Art*, ed. Susan Vogel and Ima Ebong, 130–51. New York: Center for African Art; Munnich: Prestel.

———. 1991b. "Peintres des cases, imagiers et savants populaires du Congo, 1900–1960." *Cahiers d'Etudes Africaines* 31: 307–26.

———. 1995. *Cheri Samba: The Hybridity of Art.* Westmount, Québec: Galerie Amrad African Art Publications.

———, ed. 1992. *Art pictural zaïrois.* Sillery, Québec: Editions du Septentrion.

Johnson, Barbara. 1982. "The Frame of Reference: Poe, Lacan, Derrida." In *Lit-*

erature and Psychoanalysis: The Question of Reading: Otherwise, ed. Shoshana Felman, 457–506. Baltimore: Johns Hopkins University Press.

———. 1987. *A World of Difference*. Baltimore: Johns Hopkins University Press.

Jules-Rosette, Bennetta. 1984. *The Messages of Tourist Art: An African Semiotic System in Comparative Perspective*. New York: Plenum.

Just, E. E. 1939. *Biology of the Cell Surface*. Philadelphia: Blakiston.

Kannenstine, Louis F. 1977. *The Art of Djuna Barnes: Duality and Damnation*. New York: New York University Press.

Kant, Immanuel. 1952. *Critique of Judgement* [1790]. Trans. J. Meredith. Oxford: Oxford University Press.

———. 1956. *Kritik der reinen Vernunft* [1781]. Hamburg: Felix Meiner.

———. 1963a. *Kritik der Urteilskraft* [1790]. Hamburg: Felix Meiner.

———. 1963b. "Idea for a Universal History." Trans., ed., and intro. Lewis Beck. In *Kant on History*. Indianapolis: Library of Liberal Arts.

Kaplan, Caren. 1987. "Deterritorialization: The Rewriting of Home and Exile in Western Feminist Discourse." *Cultural Critique* 6: 187–98.

Keith, Michael, and Steve Pile, eds. 1993. *Place and the Politics of Identity*. London: Routledge.

Keller, Evelyn Fox. 1992. *Secrets of Life, Secrets of Death: Essays on Language, Gender and Science*. New York: Routledge.

Kennedy, Paul. 1993. *Preparing for the Twenty-First Century*. New York: Harper Collins.

Kincaid, Jamaica. 1985. *Annie John*. London: Picador.

Kristeva, Julia. 1983. "Mémoire." *L'infinie* 1: 39–54.

———. 1986. "A New Type of Intellectual: The Dissident" [1977]. Trans. Séan Hand. In *The Kristeva Reader*, ed. Toril Moi, 292–300. Oxford: Basil Blackwell.

Kummer, E. 1994. "Bagatelles pour un massacre, een biologisch-racistische poëtica." *Bzzlletin* 23, no. 215: 46–61.

Kunze, Reiner. 1994. *Wo Freiheit ist . . . , Gespräche 1977–1993*. Frankfurt am Main: S. Fischer.

Lacan, Jacques. 1971. "Lituraterre." *Littérature* 1, no. 3: 3–10.

———. 1986. *The Four Fundamental Concepts of Psychoanalysis*. Paris: Editions du Seuil, 1973. Reprint, Harmondsworth, Eng.: Penguin Books.

———. 1987. "Joyce: Le symptôme I." In *Joyce avec Lacan*, ed. Jacques Aubert, 19–29. Paris: Navarin/Editions du Seuil.

———. 1992. *The Ethics of Psychoanalysis, 1959–1960*. Vol. 8. Ed. Jacques-Alain Miller. Trans. with notes by Dennis Porter. London: Tavistock/Routledge.

Laclotte, Michel, et al. 1967. *Ingres*. Paris: Le Petit Palais.

Landy, Francis. 1994. "Ruth and the Romance of Realism, or Deconstructing History." *Journal of the American Academy of Religion* 62: 285–317.

Lavin, Irving. 1994. *Past and Present*. Princeton, N.J.: Princeton University Press.

Leavis, F. R. 1979. *Education and the University* [1943]. Cambridge, Eng.: Cambridge University Press.

Lemaire, Ton. 1986. *De Indiaan in ons bewustzijn: De ontmoeting van de Oude met de Nieuwe Wereld.* Baarn: Ambo.

Levinas, Emmanuel. 1986. "Détermination philosophique de l'idée de culture." In *Philosophie et Culture: Actes du XVIIᵉ Congrès Mondial de Philosophie Montréal 1983,* ed. Venant Cauchy, 75. Montreal: Editions du Beffroi.

Levine, Donald N. 1985. *The Flight from Ambiguity.* Chicago: University of Chicago Press.

Lévi-Strauss, Claude. 1955. *Tristes Tropiques.* Paris: Plon.

———. 1964. *Mythologiques,* vol. 1, *Le Crue et le cuit.* Paris: Plon.

Lukács, Georg. 1971. *History and Class Consciousness* [1923]. Trans. Rodney Livingstone. Cambridge, Mass.: MIT Press.

Lurie, A. 1994. *Women and Ghosts.* London: Heinemann.

Luthy, C. H. 1994. "The Expected and the Observed: Microscopy and the Establishment of the Corpuscularian Philosophy." Lecture presented at the History of Science Society Conference, Oct. 15.

Lyotard Jean-François. 1984. *The Postmodern Condition: A Report on Knowledge.* Trans. G. Bennington and B. Massumi. Manchester, Eng.: Manchester University Press.

———. 1988. *The Inhuman: Reflections on Time.* Trans. G. Bennington and R. Bowlby. Stanford, Calif.: Stanford University Press.

Mailer, Norman. 1973. *Marilyn: A Biography.* New York: Grosset and Dunlap.

Mannoni, Laurent. 1994. *Le grand art de la lumière et de l'ombre: Archéologie du cinéma.* Paris: Nathan.

Marcus, Joseph. 1983. *Social and Political in Poland, 1919–1939.* Berlin: Mouton.

Marin, Louis. 1995. *To Destroy Painting.* Trans. Mette Hjort. Chicago: University of Chicago Press. (Originally published as *Détruire la peinture.* Paris: Editions Galilée, 1977.)

McCann, Graham. 1988. *Marilyn Monroe.* Cambridge, Eng.: Polity Press.

McEwan, Ian. 1982. *The Comfort of Strangers.* London: Picador.

McKeon, R., ed. 1941. *The Basic Works of Aristotle.* New York, Random House.

McLuhan, Marshall. 1967. *The Mechanical Bride.* London: Routledge and Kegan Paul.

Meijer, Bert W. 1971. "Esempi del comico figurativo nel rinasciment lombardo." *Arte Lombarda* 16: 259–66.

Metropolitan Museum of Art. 1982. *Art and Autoradiography: Insights into the Genesis of Paintings by Rembrandt, Van Dyck, and Vermeer.* New York: Metropolitan Museum of Art.

Miedema, Hessel. 1977. "Realism and Comic Mode: The Peasant." *Simiolus* 9: 205–19.

———. 1981. "Feestende boeren-lachende dorpers: Bij twee recente aanwinsten van het Rijksprentenkabinet." *Bulletin van het Rijksmuseum* 29, no. 4: 191–213.

Miller, Christopher L. 1990. *Theories of Africans: Francophone Literature and Anthropology in Africa.* Chicago: University of Chicago Press.

———. 1993. "The Postidentitarian Predicament in the Footnotes of *A Thousand Plateaus*: Nomadology, Anthropology, and Authority." *Diacritics* 23, no. 3: 6–35.

Minczeles, Henri. 1993. *Vilna, Wilno, Vilnius: La Jerusalem de Lituanie.* Paris: Editions La Decouverte.

Mitchell, W. J. T., ed. 1994. *Landscape and Power.* Chicago: University of Chicago Press.

Mitry, Jean. 1967–69. *Histoire du cinéma: Art et industrie.* Vol. 1, *1895–1914*, and Vol. 2, *1915–1925*. Paris: Editions Universitaires.

Mooij, A. W. M. 1991. *Psychoanalysis and the Concept of a Rule: An Essay in the Philosophy of Psychoanalysis.* Berlin: Springer Verlag.

Morris, Meaghan. 1992. "Great Moments in Social Climbing: King Kong and the Human Fly." *Colomina*, 1–52.

Muller, John P., and William J. Richardson, eds. 1988. *The Purloined Poe: Lacan, Derrida, and Psychoanalytic Reading.* Baltimore: Johns Hopkins University Press.

Mulvey, Laura. 1989. *Visual and Other Pleasures.* London: Macmillan.

———. 1992. "Pandora's Box: Topographies of the Mask and Curiosity." In *Sexuality and Space*, ed. Beatriz Colomina, 53–72. Princeton, N.J.: Princeton Architectural Press.

———. 1995. "Fetishism and the Cinema." Lecture delivered at the University of Leeds, March 8.

Mund, Hélène. 1980. "La peinture de moeurs chez Pieter Huys." *Revue des archéologues et historiens d'art de Louvain* 13: 64–73.

Munro, Eleanor. 1979. *Originals: American Women Artists.* New York: Simon and Schuster.

Myers, K. S. 1990. *Rerum causae: Ovid's "Metamorphoses" and Aetiological Narrative.* Ann Arbor: University of Michigan Press.

Nagy, Gregory. 1990. *Pindar's Home: The Lyric Possession of an Epic Past.* Baltimore: Johns Hopkins University Press.

Naifeh, Stephen, and Gregory White Smith. 1989. *Jackson Pollock: An American Saga.* New York: Clarkston N. Potter.

Nelson, Cary, and Lawrence Grossberg. 1988. *Marxism and the Interpretation of Culture.* Basingstoke, Eng.: MacMillan Education.

Nemser, Cindy. 1975a. "The Indomitable Lee Krasner." *Feminist Art Journal* 4: 9.

———. 1975b. *Art Talk: Conversations with Twelve Women.* New York: Scribner's.

Neubauer, John. 1978. *Symbolismus und symbolische Logik: Die Idee der ars combinatoria in der Entwicklung der modernen Dichtung.* Munich: Fink.

———. 1988. "Morphological Poetics?" *Style* 22: 263–74.

———. 1992a. "Music and Literature: The Institutional Dimensions." In *Music and Text: Critical Inquiries*, ed. Steven Paul Scher, 3–20. Cambridge, Eng.: Cambridge University Press.

———. 1992b. *The Fin-de-Siècle Culture of Adolescence*. New Haven, Conn.: Yale University Press.

Newcomb, Anthony. 1992. "Narrative archetypes and Mahler's Ninth Symphony." In *Music and Text: Critical Inquiries*, ed. Steven Paul Scher, 118–36. Cambridge, Eng.: Cambridge University Press.

Newman, John Henry, Cardinal. 1926. *The Idea of a University Defined and Illustrated*. London: Longmans, Green.

———. 1957. *Discourses on the Scope and Nature of University Education* [1852]. In *Newman: Prose and Poetry*, ed. G. Tillotson. London: Rupert Hart-Davis.

Nietzsche, Friedrich. 1964. *Der Wille zur Macht: Versuch einer Umwertung aller Werte*. Stuttgart: Alfred Kröner.

———. 1966. *Werke in drei Bänden*. Ed. K. Schlechta. Munich: Carl Hanser.

———. 1990. *Philosophy and Truth: Selections from Nietzsche's Notebooks of the Early 1870s*. Ed. and trans. D. Breazeale. New Jersey: Humanities Press International.

Nightingale, Peggy, ed. 1986. *A Sense of Place in the New Literatures in English*. St. Lucia: University of Queensland Press.

Nijhoff, Martinus. 1982. *Verzameld Werk 2, kritisch en verhalend proza*. Amsterdam: Bert Bakker.

Nochlin, Linda. 1995. *The Body in Pieces: The Fragment as a Metaphor of Modernity*. New York: Thames and Hudson.

O'Hara, Daniel T. 1984. "The Approximations of Romance: Paul Ricoeur and the Ironic Style of Postmodern Criticism." In *Philosophical Approaches to Literature: New Essays on Nineteenth- and Twentieth-Century Texts*, ed. William E. Cain, 183–201. Lewisburg, Pa.: Bucknell University Press.

Organization for Economic Cooperation and Development (OECD). 1983. *Policies for Higher Education in the 1980s*. Paris: OECD.

———. 1987. *Universities Under Scrutiny*. Paris: OECD.

Orton, Fred, and Griselda Pollock. 1996. *Avant-Gardes and Partisans Reviewed*. Manchester: Manchester University Press.

Ovid. 1955. *Metamorphoses*. Trans. and intro. Mary M. Innes. London: Penguin Books.

Pardes, Ilana. 1992. *Countertraditions in the Bible: A Feminist Approach*. Cambridge, Mass.: Harvard University Press.

Parker, Rozsika, and Griselda Pollock. 1995. *Old Mistresses: Women, Art & Ideology* [1981]. London: Pandora Books.

Pattynama, Pamela. 1983. "*Nachtwoud*: Alleen het onmogelijke houdt eeuwig stand." *Lover* 10, no. 1: 6–9.

Perry, Donna. 1990. "An Interview with Jamaica Kincaid." In *Reading Black, Reading Feminist: A Critical Anthology*, ed. Henry L. Gates, 492–509. New York: Meridian.

Peters, M. 1992. "Performance and Accountability in Post-Industrial Societies: The Crisis in British Universities." *Studies in Higher Education* 17, no. 2: 123–39.

Philadelphia Museum of Art. 1984. *Dutch Genre Painting.* Exhibition catalogue. Philadelphia: Philadelphia Museum of Art.

Pinchuk, Ben-Cion. 1990. *Shtetl Jews Under Soviet Rule: Eastern Poland on the Eve of the Holocaust.* London: Basil Blackwell.

Pocock, J. G. A. 1975. *The Machiavellian Moment in the Atlantic Tradition.* Princeton, N.J.: Princeton University Press.

———. 1977. "Between Machiavelli and Hume: Gibbon as Civic Humanist and Philosophical Historian." In *Edward Gibbon and the Decline of the Roman Empire*, ed. G. W. Bowersock, J. Clive, and S. R. Graubard. Cambridge, Eng.: Cambridge University Press.

Podlesney, Teresa. 1991. "Blondes." In *The Hysterical Male: New Feminist Theory*, ed. Arthur and Marilouise Kroker, 69–90. New York: St. Martin's Press.

Pollock, Griselda. 1988. *Vision and Difference: Femininity, Feminism and Histories of Art.* London: Routledge.

———. 1992. *Avant-Garde Gambits: Gender and the Color of Art History.* London: Thames and Hudson.

———. 1993. "Crows, Blossoms and Lust for Death." In *Mythologies of Van Gogh*, ed. T. Kodera, 217–39. Amsterdam: John Benjamins.

———. 1994. *The Point of Theory.* Ed. Mieke Bal and Inge E. Boer. Amsterdam: Amsterdam University Press; New York: Continuum.

Popper, Karl. 1990. *The Open Society and Its Enemies* [1945]. 2 vols. London: Routledge.

Pratt, Mary Louise. 1992. *Imperial Eyes: Travel Writing and Transculturation.* London: Routledge.

Raupp, Hans-Joachim. 1984. *Untersuchungen zu Künstlerbildnis und Künstlerdarstellung in den Niederlanden im 17 Jahrhundert.* Hildesheim: Georg Olms Verlag.

Readings, William. 1996. *The University in Ruins.* Cambridge, Mass.: Harvard University Press.

Renan, Ernest. 1990. "What Is a Nation?" [1882]. In *Nation and Narration*, ed. Homi K. Bhabha, trans. Martin Thom, 8–22. London/New York: Routledge.

Renger, Konrad. 1970. *Lockere Gesellschaft: Zur Ikonographie des Verlorenen Sohnes und von Wirtshausszenen in der niederländischen Malerei.* Berlin: Gebr Mann.

———. 1985. "Alte Liebe, gleich und ungleich: Zu einem satirischen Bildthema bei Jan Massys." In *Netherlandish Mannerism: Papers Given at a Symposium* in *Nationalmuseum Stockholm, September 21–22, 1984*, ed. Görel Cavalli-Björkman, 35–46. Stockholm: Nationalmuseum Stockholm.

Ricoeur, Paul. 1967. *The Symbolism of Evil.* Trans. Emerson Buchanan. Boston: Beacon.

———. 1975. *La métaphore vive.* Paris: Seuil.

———. 1990. *Soi-même comme une autre.* Paris: Seuil.

Ritter, J. 1971–. *Historisches Wörterbuch der Philosophie.* Darmstadt: Wissenschaftliche Buchgesellschaft.

Rorty, Richard. 1979. *Philosophy and the Mirror of Nature.* Princeton, N.J.: Princeton University Press.

Sadoul, Georges. 1973. *Histoire générale du cinéma.* Vols. 1–5. Paris: Denoel.

———. 1986. *Lumière et Méliès.* Paris: Denoel.

Said, Edward W. 1983. *The World, the Text, and the Critic.* Cambridge, Mass.: Harvard University Press.

———. 1994. *Culture and Imperialism.* London: Vintage.

Salomon, Nanette. 1993. "Vanishing Acts: Male Narrativity and the Rhetoric of the Bordello." Paper given at the conference "Questioning the Power of Netherlandish Painting," organized by the Historians of Netherlandish Art and held at Wellesley College, Boston Museum of Fine Arts, and the Worcester Art Museum, Mass.

———. Forthcoming. "Early Netherlandish *Bordeeltjes* and the Construction of Social 'Realities.'" In *The Public and the Private in Dutch Culture of the Golden Age*, ed. Arthur Wheelock and Adele Seef. Newark: University of Delaware Press.

Sartre, Jean Paul. 1964. "Venise, de ma fenêtre." In his *Situations, IV.* Paris: Gallimard.

Sasson, Jack. 1979. *Ruth: A New Translation with a Philological Commentary and a Formalist-Folklorist Interpretation.* Baltimore: Johns Hopkins University Press.

Scarry, Elaine. 1985. *The Body in Pain: The Making and Unmaking of the World.* New York: Oxford University Press.

———. 1992. "The Made-Up and Made-Real." *Yale Journal of Criticism* 5, no. 2: 239–49.

Schama, Simon. 1979. "The Unruly Realm: Appetite and Restraint in Seventeenth-Century Holland." *Daedalus* 108 (Summer): 103–23.

———. 1980. "Wives and Wantons: Versions of Womanhood in Seventeenth-Century Dutch Art." *Oxford Art Journal* 3 (April): 5–13.

———. 1987. *The Embarrassment of Riches: An Interpretation of Dutch Culture in the Golden Age.* New York: Alfred A. Knopf.

Siewerth, Gustav. 1959. *Das Schicksal der Metaphysik von Thomas zu Heidegger.* Einsiedeln: Johannes Verlag.

Silverman, Kaja. 1996. *The Threshold of the Visible World.* New York: Routledge.

Simmel, Georg. 1968. *"The Condition of Modern Culture" and Other Essays.* Trans. K. Peter Etzkorn. New York: Teachers College Press.

Skinner, Q. 1978. *The Foundations of Modern Political Thought.* 2 vols. Cambridge, Eng.: Cambridge University Press.

Spemann, Hans. 1938. *Embryonic Development and Induction.* New York: Hafner Press.

Spengler, Oswald. 1981. *Der Untergang des Abendlandes: Umrisse einer morphologischen Weltgeschichte.* Munich: Beck.

Spivak, Gayatri. 1993. *Outside in the Teaching Machine.* New York: Routledge.

Sternberg, Meir. 1985. *The Poetics of Biblical Narrative: Ideological Literature and the Drama of Reading.* Bloomington: Indiana University Press.

Stiegler, Bernard. 1994. *La technique et le temps: Tome1: La faute de Epimethee.* Paris: Galilee.

Szombati-Fabian, Ilona, and Johannes Fabian. 1976. "Art, History and Society: Popular Painting in Shaba, Zaire." *Studies in the Anthropology of Visual Communication* 3: 1–21.

———. 1980. "Folk Art from an Anthropological Perspective." In *Perspectives on American Folk Art*, ed. Ian M. G. Quimby and Scott T. Swank, 247–92. New York: Norton.

Tagg, John. 1988. *The Burden of Representation: Essays on Photographs and Histories.* Amherst: University of Massachusetts Press.

Thomas, Keith. 1991. Introduction to *A Cultural History of Gesture*, ed. Jan Bremmer and Herman Roodenburg, 1–15. Ithaca, N.Y.: Cornell University Press.

Todorov, Tzvetan. 1984. *The Conquest of America: The Question of the Other.* New York: Harper and Row.

Van Dantzig, A. 1990. *Psychotherapie, Een Vak.* Meppel: Boom.

van de Pol, Lotte C. 1990. "Beeld en werkelijkheid van de prostitutie in de zeventiende eeuw." In *Soete minne en helsche boosheit: Seksuele voorstellingen in Nederland 1300–1850*, ed. Gert Hekma and Herman Roodenburg, 109–44. Nijmegen: SUN.

van der Leeuw, G. 1955. *La religion dans son essence et ses manifestations: Phénoménologie de la religion.* Paris: Payot.

Van Zoest, A. 1994. "Maar ja, ik had erge dorst, de taal van Céline." *Bzzlletin* 23, no. 215: 38–416.

Vaughan, Dai. 1981. "Let There Be Lumière." *Sight and Sound* 50, no. 2 (Spring): 126–27.

Vestdijk, S. 1991. *De glanzende kiemcel.* Amsterdam: Nijgh and Van Ditmar.

Vishniac, Roman. 1983. *A Vanished World.* New York: Farrar, Straus and Giroux.

Vogel, Susan, and Ima Ebong, eds. 1991. *Africa Explores: Twentieth-Century African Art.* New York: Center for African Art; Munich: Prestel.

Vorobeichic, M. 1931. *The Ghetto Lane in Vilna: 65 Pictures.* Zurich: Orell Fussli.

Wagner, Ann. 1989. "Lee Krasner as L. K." *Representations* 25: 42–57.

Wakeman, J., ed. 1987. *World Film Directors.* Vol. 1. New York: Wilson.

Walker, Alice. 1984. *In Search of Our Mothers' Gardens: Womanist Prose.* London: The Woman's Press.

Ward, Cynthia. 1990. "What They Told Buchi Emecheta: Oral Subjectivity and the Joys of 'Otherhood.'" *PMLA* 105, no. 1: 83–97.

Washington, D.C., National Gallery of Art, and The Hague, Royal Cabinet of Paintings Mauritshuis. 1995–96. *Johannes Vermeer.* Exhibition catalogue. Washington and The Hague.

Watson, J. D. 1968. *The Double Helix.* New York: Atheneum.

Weber, Max. 1968. *Methodologische Schriften, Studienausgabe.* Frankfurt am Main: S. Fischer.

Wendl, Tobias. 1991. *Mami Wata oder ein Kult zwischen den Kulturen.* Münster: Lit.

Westermann, Mariët. 1996. *A Worldly Art: The Dutch Republic, 1585–1718.* New York: Harry N. Abrams.

White, Hayden. 1992. "Historical Emplotment and the Problem of Truth." In *Probing the Limits of Representation: Nazism and the "Final Solution",* ed. Saul Friedlander, 37–53. Cambridge, Mass.: Harvard University Press.

Whitehead, Alfred North. 1954. *Adventures of Ideas.* New York: Macmillan.

Williams, Raymond. 1975. *Television, Technology and Cultural Form.* London: Routledge and Kegan Paul.

Windelband, W. 1924. *Präludien: Aufsätze und Reden zur Philosophie und ihrer Geschichte.* Vols. 1–2. Tübingen: J. C. B. Mohr.

Wolff, Janet. 1993. "On the Road Again: Metaphors of Travel in Cultural Criticism." *Cultural Studies* 7, no. 2: 224–39.

Wolff, Katja. 1989. *Der Kabbalistische Baum.* Munich: Knaut.

Womersley, D. 1988. *The Transformation of "The Decline and Fall of the Roman Empire."* Cambridge, Eng.: Cambridge University Press.

Woolf, Virginia. 1967. "On Being Ill." In *Collected Essays,* 4: 193–203. New York: Harcourt, Brace and World.

Zizek, Slavoj. 1992. *Enjoy Your Symptom: Jacques Lacan in Hollywood and Out.* New York: Routledge.

Zsadányi, Edit. 1996. "Reframing the Frame: Analysis of Night-Metaphors in Djuna Barnes's *Nightwood.*" In *Brief: Issues in Cultural Analysis: ASCA Yearbook,* 27–47. Kampen: Kok Pharos.

Index

In this index an "f" after a number indicates a separate reference on the next page, and an "ff" indicates separate references on the next two pages. A continuous discussion over two or more pages is indicated by a span of page numbers, e.g., "21–22." *Passim* is used for a cluster of references in close but not consecutive sequence.

Abramowitz, Sholom, 106
Abrams, M.H., 293, 296
Achterberg, Gerrit, 270, 286
Acres, Birt, 66
Adam (bible), 223, 255
Adorno, Theodor, 365
Aeneas, 134
Alberti, Leon Battista, 63
Aleichem, Sholem, 105ff
Alpers, Svetlana, 353
Alphen, Ernst van, 139
Althusser, Louis, 3
Amsterdam School for Cultural Analysis, *see* ASCA
Anchises, 134
Anderson, Benedict, 107, 352
Anderson, Perry, 360
Ankersmit, Frank, 28, 131, 139f, 186
Ansky, Schlomo, 107f, 354
Antonioni, Michelangelo, 62
Appel, Toby, 299f, 364
Aristophanes, 166
Aristotle, 258, 260, 272, 276, 281–84, 304, 309, 363, 365
Arnold, Matthew, 305–15 *passim*
Aronowitz, Stanley, 327
ASCA (Amsterdam School for Cultural Analysis), 2, 4, 15, 60, 74, 228, 335, 342

Aschenbach, Gustav von, 143–47 *passim*
Ashcroft, Bill, 359
Augustine, St., 131
Augustus, Emperor, 134, 175

Baburen, Dirck van, 48, 50
Bach, Johann Sebastian, 289f
Bachelard, Gaston, 33
Bacon, Francis, 152
Baker, Steve, 125, 131, 355, 360
Bal, Mieke, 191f, 198, 202, 287f, 346, 351f, 356, 362
Balanchine, George, 331
Balzac, Honoré de, 107, 300f
Bambi, 62
Bann, Stephen, 13, 27f, 140, 355
Banza Kongo, 249f
Barbo, Pietro, 153
Barnes, Djuna, 139, 151–70
Barthes, Roland, 5, 28, 48, 103, 122–27 *passim*, 131f, 141, 173, 342, 351, 355
Bataille, Georges, 83, 96, 98
Baudelaire, Charles, 219, 360
Beardsworth, Richard, 365
Beauvoir, Simone de, 84
Beethoven, Ludwig van, 290
Bell, Daniel, 263
Bender, Wolfgang, 362

David (bible), 357
Davies, Carole Boyce, 206f, 211, 359f
Davis, Natalie Z., 352
Dean, James, 66, 353
De Boer, Theo, 231, 233, 284
Debray, Régis, 150
de Jongh, Eddy, 352
de Lairesse, Gerard, 59, 353
de Lauretis, Teresa, 210
Deleuze, Gilles, 205f, 218, 221f, 360
Della Porta, Giambattista, 227
Demeny, Georges, 66
Depardon, Raymond, 16
Derrida, Jacques, 80, 139, 146ff, 149, 322, 332, 340, 365
Deutelbaum, Marshall, 68
d'Hemptinne, Monsignor Jean-Felix, 247
Diamond, Irene, 47
Dibdin, Michael, 144
Dickens, Charles, 107
Dickson, William Kennedy, 66
Dilthey, Wilhelm, 186, 270
DiMaggio, Joe, 84
Diocletian, 179
Djilatendo, 240, 362
Dobroszycki, Lucjan, 354
Donaldson, Laura, 204
Dostoevsky, Fyodor, 283, 285
Dray, William, 278
Dresen-Coenders, L. 352
Drewal, Henry John, 362
Drost, Willem, 195
Dubnow, Simon, 106, 354
Duck, Jacob, 53–57, 353
du Maurier, Daphne, 144
Duncan, Carol, 87
Dupré, Louis, 140, 230f
Duret, F.M., 136
Dutoit, Ulysse, 158
Duyster, Willem, 55
Dyer, Richard, 85

Echo, 173f, 186
Eco, Umberto, 28, 122ff, 126

Eden (bible), 223
Eden, Elana, 194, 196
Edison, Thomas, 66, 69
Eisenhower, Dwight D., 76
Eisenstein, Sergei, 61
Elias, Norbert, 57
Elimelech (bible), 357
Eliot, T.S., 260, 263, 270, 286, 333
Eller, K.H., 180
Elsaesser, Thomas, 25f, 353
Emrich, Hinderk, 361
Erasmus, 57, 265
Esther (*Die zweite Heimat*), 146
Ethelbert of Kent, King, 131
Exum, J. Cheryl, 140f, 357f

Fabian, Johannes, 142, 229ff, 238f, 254, 361f
Falkenberg, Paul, 86
Fer, Bryony, 83
Fewell, Danna, 358
Fielding, Henry, 172
Foucault, Michel, 46ff, 88, 129, 202, 221, 233, 254, 296–302 *passim*, 309, 332, 340, 342, 352, 364f
Frampton, Hollis, 68
Franits, Wayne, 352
Frankel, Jonathan, 354
Frankenthaler, Helen, 81, 89–94 *passim*, 101
Franklin, Rosalind, 29–32, 41
Frederick the Great, 143
Freud, Sigmund, 21, 90, 161ff, 201, 210f, 220, 264, 272f, 320, 322, 327, 332
Friedan, Betty, 81
Fuchs, Rudi, 353
Furhmann, August, 70
Furnese, Sir Robert, 130

Gable, Clark, 62
Gabriel, Ulrike, 227
Gadamer, H.G., 270, 275, 280
Galinsky, G.K., 177–82 *passim*, 186
Garbo, Greta, 66
Gatz, B., 184, 356

Cultural Memory | *in the Present*

Library of Congress Cataloging-in-Publication Data

The practice of cultural analysis : exposing
   interdisciplinary interpretation / edited by Mieke
   Bal with the assistance of Bryan Gonzales.
            p.   cm. — (Cultural memory in the present)
      Includes bibliographical references.
      ISBN 0-8047-3066-0 (cloth). —
      ISBN 0-8047-3067-9 (pbk.)
      1. Culture.   2. History.   3. Memory.   I. Bal,
   Mieke.   II. Gonzales, Bryan.   III. Series.
   HM101.P667   1999
   306—dc21   98-35018

⊗ · This book is printed on acid-free, recycled paper.

Original printing 1999
Last figure below indicates year of this printing:
07   06   05   04   03   02   01   00   99